T3-BHN-676

VISUAL QUICKSTART GUIDE

Unix

Third Edition

Deborah S. Ray and Eric J. Ray

 Peachpit Press

Visual QuickStart Guide
Unix, Third Edition
Deborah S. Ray and Eric J. Ray

Peachpit Press

1249 Eighth Street
Berkeley, CA 94710
510/524-2178
800/283-9444
510/524-2221 (fax)

Find us on the at: www.peachpit.com
To report errors, please send a note to errata@peachpit.com

Peachpit Press is a division of Pearson Education.

Copyright © 2007 by Deborah Ray and Eric Ray

Editor: Marty Cortinas
Technical Editor: Stephen Talley
Production Coordinator: Myrna Vladic
Compositor: Jerry Ballew
Cover Design: Peachpit Press
Indexer: Rebecca Plunkett

Notice of rights

All rights reserved. No part of this book may be reproduced or transmitted in any form by any means, electronic, mechanical, photocopying, recording, or otherwise, without the prior written permission of the publisher. For information on getting permission for reprints and excerpts, contact permissions@peachpit.com.

Notice of liability

The information in this book is distributed on an "As Is" basis, without warranty. While every precaution has been taken in the preparation of the book, neither the authors nor Peachpit Press, shall have any liability to any person or entity with respect to any loss or damage caused or alleged to be caused directly or indirectly by the instructions contained in this book or by the computer software and hardware products described in it.

Trademarks

Visual QuickStart Guide is a registered trademark of Peachpit Press, a division of Pearson Education.

UNIX is a registered trademark of The Open Group. All other trademarks are the property of their respective owners. Many of the designations used by manufacturers and sellers to distinguish their products are claimed as trademarks. Where those designations appear in this book, and Peachpit was aware of a trademark claim, the designations appear as requested by the owner of the trademark. All other product names and services identified throughout this book are used in editorial fashion only and for the benefit of such companies with no intention of infringement of the trademark. No such use, or the use of any trade name, is intended to convey endorsement or other affiliation with this book.

ISBN 0-321-44245-8

9 8 7 6 5 4 3 2 1

Printed and bound in the United States of America

Dedication

To each other, Ashleigh, and Alex.

Acknowledgments

This book came together with the help of many talented and supportive people. A special thanks to Clifford Colby for his confidence and enthusiasm. Marty Cortinas' attention to detail and sharp questions were very valuable. Myrna Vladic did a fantastic job in production.

TABLE OF CONTENTS

Introduction   **xi**

Chapter 1:   **Getting Started with Unix**   **1**
              Getting Unix or Access to a Unix System 3
              Connecting to the Unix System 7
              Logging In 10
              Changing Your Password with passwd 11
              Listing Directories and Files with ls 13
              Changing Directories with cd 15
              Finding Yourself with pwd 17
              Piping Input and Output 18
              Redirecting Output 19
              Using Wildcards 21
              Viewing File Contents with more 22
              Displaying File Contents with cat 23
              Exploring the System 25
              Getting Help with man 26
              Logging Out 28

Chapter 2:   **Using Directories and Files**   **29**
              Creating Directories with mkdir 30
              Creating Files with touch 32
              Copying Directories and Files with cp 34
              Listing Directories and Files with ls
                  (More Goodies) 36
              Moving Files with mv 38
              Removing Files with rm 39
              Removing Directories with rmdir 42
              Finding Forgotten Files with find 44
              Locating Lost Files with locate 46
              Linking with ln (Hard Links) 47
              Linking with ln -s (Soft Links) 49

Chapter 3:   **Working with Your Shell**   **51**
              Discovering What Shell You're Using 52
              Understanding Shells and Options 53
              Changing Your Shell with chsh 55
              Changing Your Shell Temporarily 57
              Using Completion in the bash Shell 59

Viewing Session History in the bash Shell 60
Using Completion in the zsh Shell 62
Viewing Session History in the zsh Shell 63
Using Completion in the ksh Shell 65
Viewing Session History in the ksh Shell 66
Viewing Session History in the csh Shell 68
Changing Your Identity with su 69
Fixing Terminal Settings with stty 71
Exiting the Shell 72

Chapter 4: **Creating and Editing Files** **73**
Choosing an Editor 74
Starting pico and Dabbling with It 77
Saving in pico 78
Cutting and Pasting Text Blocks in pico 79
Checking Spelling in pico 80
Getting Help in pico 81
Exiting pico 82
Starting vi and Dabbling with It 83
Saving in vi 85
Adding and Deleting Text in vi 86
Importing Files into vi 87
Searching and Replacing in vi 88
Exiting vi 90
Starting emacs and Dabbling with It 91
Using emacs Menus to Spell-Check 93
Saving in emacs 94
Exiting emacs 95

Chapter 5: **Controlling Ownership**
& Permissions **97**
Understanding File Ownership
    and Permissions 98
Finding Out Who Owns What 99
Finding Out Which Group You're In 101
Changing the Group Association of Files
    and Directories with chgrp 103
Changing Ownership of Files and
    Directories with chown 105
Changing Permissions with chmod 106
Translating Mnemonic Permissions to
    Numeric Permissions 109
Changing Permission Defaults with umask 110

Chapter 6:   **Manipulating Files**   **113**

Counting Files and Their Contents with wc ... 114
Viewing File Beginnings with head 115
Viewing File Endings with tail 116
Finding Text with grep 117
Using Regular Expressions with grep 118
Using Other Examples of
    Regular Expressions 120
Making Global Changes with sed 121
Changing Files with awk 122
Comparing Files with cmp 124
Finding Differences in Files with diff 125
Finding Differences in Files with sdiff 126
Sorting Files with sort 127
Eliminating Duplicates with uniq 129
Redirecting to Multiple Locations with tee ... 130
Changing with tr 131
Formatting with fmt 133
Preparing to Print with pr 135
Splitting Files with split 137

Chapter 7:   **Getting Information**
       About the System   **139**

Getting System Information with uname 140
Viewing File Systems with df 141
Determining Disk Usage with du 144
Finding Out File Types with file 145
Finding Out About Users with finger 146
Learning Who Else Is Logged in with who 149
Learning Who Else Is Logged in with w 150
Getting Information About
    Your Userid with id 152

Chapter 8:   **Configuring Your Unix Environment**   **153**

Understanding Your Unix Environment 154
Discovering Your Current Environment 156
Adding or Changing Variables 158
Looking at Your zsh Configuration Files 161
Adding to Your zsh Path 165
Changing Your zsh Prompt 167
Looking at Your bash Configuration Files 170
Adding to Your bash Path 173
Changing Your bash Prompt 175
Looking at Your ksh Configuration Files 177
Changing Your ksh Path 180

Changing Your ksh Prompt 182
Looking at Your csh Configuration Files 183
Changing Your csh Path 186
Changing Your csh Prompt 188
Setting Aliases with alias 190

Chapter 9: **Running Scripts and Programs**   **193**
Running a Command 194
Scheduling One-Time Jobs with at 195
Scheduling Regularly Occurring
     Jobs with cron 198
Suspending Jobs 200
Checking Job Status with jobs 201
Running Jobs in the Background with bg 202
Running Jobs in the Foreground with fg 203
Controlling Job Priority with nice 204
Timing Jobs with time 205
Finding Out What Processes
     Are Running with ps 207
Deleting Processes with kill 209

Chapter 10: **Writing Basic Scripts**   **211**
Creating a Shell Script 212
Running a Shell Script 214
Making a Script Executable 215
Getting a Head Start on Scripts
     with history 217
Embedding Commands 218
Looping Your Scripts 220
Creating If-Then Statements 222
Accepting Command-Line Arguments
     in Your Scripts 225
Accepting Input While a Script Is Running ... 226
Debugging Scripts 228

Chapter 11: **Sending and Reading Email**   **229**
Choosing an Email Program
     and Getting Started 230
Reading Email with pine 232
Sending Email with pine 234
Customizing pine 236
Reading Email with mutt 238
Sending Email with mutt 240
Reading Email with mail 242
Sending Email with mail 243

Creating a Signature File 245
Automatically Forwarding
    Incoming Messages 247
Announcing an Absence with vacation 248
Configuring procmail 250
Responding to Email with procmail 252

Chapter 12:   Accessing the Internet   255
Getting Familiar with Unix Internet Lingo 256
Logging in to Remote Systems with ssh 258
Logging in to Remote Systems with telnet ... 259
Communicating with
    Other Users Using write 261
Communicating with
    Other Users Using talk 262
Getting Files from the Internet with ftp 263
Sharing Files on the Internet with ftp 267
Surfing the Web with links 269
Surfing the Web with lynx 270
Downloading Web Sites with wget 272
Checking Connections with ping 273
Tracing Connections with traceroute 274
Matching Domain Names with IP Numbers ... 276
Choosing a News Reader 278
Reading News with pine 279
Reading News with tin 282

Chapter 13:   Working with Encoded
**   & Compressed Files   285**
Encoding Files with uuencode 286
Decoding Files with uudecode 289
Archiving with tar 290
Unarchiving Files with tar 292
Compressing Files with compress 293
Uncompressing Files with uncompress 294
Zipping a File or Directory with gzip 295
Unzipping a gzip File with gunzip 296
Zipping Files and Directories with zip 297
Unzipping Zipped Files with unzip 298
Combining Commands 299

Chapter 14:   Installing Your Own Software   301
Understanding Unix Software Installation 302
Finding Unix Software 303
Downloading, Placing, and
    Uncompressing Software 304

TABLE OF CONTENTS

ix

Configuring Software 306
Compiling and Installing with `make install` ... 311

Chapter 15: **Using Handy Utilities** **315**
Calendaring with `cal` 316
Calculating with `bc` 319
Evaluating Expressions with `expr` 320
Converting with `units` 321
Checking Spelling with `ispell` 322
Looking It up with `look` 323
Printing with `lp` 324
Keeping a Record of Your
    Session with `script` 325

Chapter 16: **Being Root** **327**
Acting Like root with `sudo` 328
Becoming root with `su` 330
Starting, Stopping, and Restarting Daemons ... 332
Changing the System Configuration 334
Monitoring the System 336
Keeping up with `watch` 339
Checking Boot Messages with `dmesg` 340
Setting the Date and Time 342

Chapter 17: **Sensational Unix Tricks** **343**
Cleaning up HTML Documents with `tidy` 344
Searching and Replacing Throughout
    Multiple Documents with `sed` 347
Generating Reports with `awk` 350
Using Input to Customize
    Your Environment 351
Using ROT13 Encoding with `sed` 353
Embedding ROT13 Encoding in a
    Shell Script 355
Making Backups with `rsync` 358
Using Advanced Redirection with `stderr` 360

Appendix A: **Unix Reference** **363**

Appendix B: **What's What and What's Where** **379**

Appendix C: **Commands and Flags** **383**

Index **417**

INTRODUCTION

Greetings, and welcome to Unix! In this book, you'll find the information you need to get started with the Unix operating system, advance your skills, and make Unix do the hard work for you. This book focuses on the most common Unix commands, but it also gives you ideas for working smartly and efficiently.

How Do You Use This Book?

We designed this book to be used as both a tutorial and a reference. If you're a Unix newbie, you should start at the beginning and work forward through the first several chapters. As you progress through the chapters, you'll build on concepts and commands you learned in previous chapters. Then, as you become more proficient, you can start picking and choosing topics, depending on what you want to do. Be sure to reference the table of contents, index, and the appendixes to find information at a glance.

The commands used throughout this book apply to any version of Unix you might be using, including Linux, BSD, Solaris through your local Internet service provider, AIX or HP-UX at work, your Mac OS X or Linux system at home, or any other *flavor* (that's the technical term) you can find. Heck, you can even run Unix from your Windows system with CygWin or VMware. You'll find more about flavors and getting access to Unix in Chapter 1.

Each chapter covers several topics, each of which is presented in its own section. Each section begins with a brief overview of the topic, often including examples or descriptions of how or when you'd use a command.

Next, you'll find a step-by-step list (or a couple of them) to show you how to complete a process. Note that the code you type appears as the numbered step, and a description follows it, like this:

1. The code you type will appear like
  → this in a blocky font.

An explanation will appear like this in a more regular font. Here, we often describe what you're typing, give alternatives, or provide cross-references to related information.

If a line of code in a numbered step is particularly long, the code might wrap to a second line. Just type the characters shown, without pressing `Enter` until the end of the command. Also, in code listings throughout the book, a single line of code on screen might wrap to two lines in the book. If this happens, the continued line will start with a →, so it might look like:

```
The beginning of the code starts here
→ but it continues on this line.
```

Sometimes you'll have to press a special key or key combination—like `Ctrl``C`, which means to hold down the `Ctrl` key and press `C`. We'll use this special keyboard font for these keys, but not for multiple letters, or numbers, or symbols you might type.

Finally, most sections end with a couple of handy tips. Look here for ways to combine Unix commands, suggestions for using commands more efficiently, and ideas for finding out more information.

Who Are You?

We assume that you've picked up this book because you already have a need for or an interest in learning to use Unix, or any Unix-like operating system, like Linux, Mac OS X, BSD, HP UX, AIX, Solaris, or others. We assume that

◆ You want to know how to use Unix to do things at work, school, or home.

◆ You may or may not already have experience with Unix.

◆ You don't necessarily have other geeky—er, um, techie—computer skills or experience.

◆ You want to learn to use Unix, but probably do not want to delve into all of the arcane details about the Unix system.

In short, we assume you want to use Unix to achieve your computing goals. You want to know what you can do, get an idea of the potential that a command offers, and learn how to work smart. Very smart.

You can do all of these things using this book. Basically, all you need is access to a Unix account or system and a goal (or goals) that you want to achieve.

What Do You Need Computer-wise?

Computer-wise, you can learn or experiment with Unix using virtually any computer you might have available. If you're using a Mac with OS X or later, you're all set; it's all Unix under the hood. If you have an extra computer sitting around, even something as old as a Pentium III, you can install several different flavors of Unix on it. Certainly you can install Unix on an extra hard drive (or empty space on your current hard drive) on your regular desktop computer, and generally without affecting your existing Windows configuration.

Alternatively, you can dabble in Unix less invasively by using an account on a system at work, or through an Internet service provider. Probably the easiest option, though, if you have a reasonably new computer and are concerned about not messing up what you have, is to use either CygWin to run Unix as part of your Windows environment, or to use Vmware to run Unix in a "virtual machine" as an application in your Windows environment, or to use a bootable Unix (Linux or Solaris) CD to experiment without having to install anything at all on your computer.

What Do You Need to Know to Get Started?

As you get started learning Unix, keep in mind the following Unix conventions for typing in commands:

◆ Unix terminology and commands are typically arcane, cryptic, and funny-looking. For example, the command to list files or directories is just ls—short and cryptic. We'll walk you through the commands one step at a time, so you know how to read them and apply them to your own uses. Just follow the steps in the order provided.

◆ Unix is case-sensitive, so type commands following the capitalization used in the book.

◆ Whenever you type a command, you also have to press Enter. For example, if we say:

1. `funny-looking command goes here`

   you'll type in the code, then press Enter, which sends the command along to the Unix system.

   Often, we'll tell you to press a combination of keys on the keyboard, as in Ctrl V. Here, all you do is press the Ctrl key plus the (lower-case) V key, both at the same time (sequentially is fine also). Even though the keyboard uses capital letters (and, thus, the little key icons also do in this book), you would *not* take the extra step to capitalize the V (or whatever) in applying key combinations.

INTRODUCTION

◆ Some commands have *flags* associated with them (you might think of flags as options for the command) that give you additional control. For example, you might see the `ls` command used in variations like `ls -la` or `ls -l -a`. In either case, `ls` lists the files in a directory, the optional `-l` flag specifies that you want the long format, and the optional *-a* flag specifies all files, including hidden ones (don't worry, we'll go over this again!). Just keep in mind that flags are essentially options you can use with a given command.

◆ You can also put multiple commands on the same line. All you have to do is separate the commands with a semicolon (;), like this:

```
ls ; pwd
```

which would list the files in the current directory (`ls`) and find out what directory you're in (`pwd`)—all in one step!

So, with these things in mind, see you in Chapter 1!

Anything Else You Should Know?

Yup! Please feel free to send us a message at books@raycomm.com. We welcome your input, suggestions, and questions related to this book. Thanks, and we look forward to hearing from you!

Note to Mac Users

For simplicity, we consistently write Enter (not Return), Ctrl (not Control), Alt (not Option), and we refer (not very often, though) to a Recycle Bin (not a Trash Can). No slight intended to those who do not use PCs or Windows—we just tried to keep the complexity of the instructions to a minimum.

GETTING STARTED WITH UNIX

To start you on your journey through Unix, we'll take a quick look at a few basic concepts and commands. In this chapter, we'll get you started with basic Unix skills, such as accessing a Unix account, logging in, and listing and viewing files and directories, among other things. We'll also show you how to explore Unix, see its capabilities, and discover just what you can do with it.

Chapter Contents

◆ Getting Access to Unix or a Unix system

◆ Connecting to the Unix system

◆ Logging in

◆ Changing your password

◆ Listing directories and files

◆ Changing directories

◆ Finding out where you are in the directory tree

◆ Piping input and output

◆ Redirecting output

◆ Using wildcards

◆ Viewing file contents

◆ Exploring the system

◆ Getting help

◆ Logging out

This chapter is essential for all Unix guru-wannabes. If you're a Unix novice, you should start at the beginning of this chapter and work through each section in sequence. With these basic skills mastered, you can then skip through this book and learn new skills that look useful or interesting to you. If you've used Unix before, you might peruse this chapter to review the basics and dust off any cobwebs you might have.

The skills covered in this chapter apply to any version of Unix you might be using, including Linux, Solaris, or BSD through your local Internet service provider, Solaris, AIX or HP-UX at work, your Mac OS X or Linux system at home, CygWin or Unix through VMware or Unix from a bootable CD on your home system, or any other flavor (that's the technical term) you can find. Keep in mind, though, that the exact output and prompts you see on the screen might differ slightly from what is illustrated in this book. The differences probably won't affect the steps you're completing, although you should be aware that differences could exist. (As much as possible, our examples will give you a sample of the diversity of Unix systems.)

GETTING STARTED WITH UNIX

Getting Unix or Access to a Unix System

People choose to use Unix for a number of reasons, from control (on the legal and licensing side as well as the "getting stuff done" side) to economy (most flavors of Unix offer free or nearly free licensing) to power (experienced Unix geeks can do more with less effort on Unix than Windows—for many things, at least. In the final analysis, though, most Unix people end up sticking with Unix because they tried it, slogged through the initial learning curve, then decided they like it. Using a Unix system is different from working on a PC. Using a PC, the computer's hard drive is your personal space, and—generally—you don't have access to what's on someone else's hard drive. With Unix, you have your own personal space that's located within a much bigger system. You might think of Unix as being an apartment building, with lots of individual apartment spaces, a central office, and perhaps other general spaces, like a maintenance office. With Unix, you have the entire system that houses dozens, hundreds, or even thousands of personal spaces, and private spaces (for, say, the system administrator, bosses, or computer department staff). You can access your apartment only, but the system administrator (or designated people with authorization) can access any apartment.

Different types of Unix access

So, the first question, then, is how you might access a Unix system to get started with all of this. Given that this is Unix, you have exactly 1.2 bazillion options. Let's look at these options:

◆ Connect to a shell account

◆ Access your company's (or school's or organization's) Unix system

◆ Do a Unix-only installation on an old or spare computer

◆ Do a Unix/Windows installation on your everyday computer

Accessing a shell account

The traditional approach (back in the olden days, when we wrote the first version of this book) was to connect to a "shell account" provided by your dialup ISP. That's still an option, if you have certain ISPs (and even with some broadband connections). If your ISP offers a shell account, go ahead and use it; it's still a good option.

Accessing your company's system

If not (that is, if you have a cable modem, DSL connection, or dialup connection through any of the huge companies that provide Internet access, "not" is the case), you still have a ton of options. Check at work; many companies use Unix in a number of ways, and if you can provide the system administrator with appropriate quantities of cookies or other goodies, you may be able to get Unix system access.

Installing Unix on an old or spare computer

Alternatively, if you'd rather keep your Unix explorations closer to home, you can manage that as well. If you have an older computer sitting around (say, anything that's a Pentium III or later), you can just install Unix (Linux, Solaris, or whatever) on that, and likely without hassles or problems. You could make it work on even older computers, but given how cheap new and used computers are, it's likely not worth the trouble. Either way, you'll download a CD or DVD from the Web, burn it onto a disc, and boot your system with the disc in the drive. The installation will start, and a few questions and few minutes later, you'll be all set.

Installing Unix and Windows side by side

You can also download the CD or DVD and install on your everyday desktop computer. Most of the time (actually virtually all the time, but we're making no promises here), you can install Unix onto your desktop right alongside your Windows environment without breaking anything. You'll get it installed, reboot your system, and choose Unix (Linux, Solaris, whatever) or Windows when you boot up. This option isn't bad, but it does require you to stop what you're doing in Windows or Unix to change to the other. If your desktop computer is relatively old, this might be better than the following options, though.

If you have a pretty beefy desktop computer (relatively new with ample memory and disk space), you could try using Vmware, which gives you a *computer emulation* (think "picture in picture" for your computer, but with one operating system within the other operating system).

continues on next page

GETTING UNIX OR ACCESS TO A UNIX SYSTEM

Many of the examples and screenshots for this book were taken from Unix systems running under VMware on one of our desktop systems.

Cygwin provides you with a Unix environment that's actually part of your Windows system. It takes a bit of getting used to, but Cygwin is stable and reliable. The hardest part about using Cygwin is that it can be confusing to know if you're dealing with Unix or Windows at any given moment.

Different Unix flavors

So, given all of those options on how to get access to Unix, the choice of which kind of Unix (which Unix *flavor*) must be clear and straightforward—right? Of course not.

If you're just getting started with Unix, we'd recommend having you choose the flavor that your most techie friends or the folks at work use. This will give you potential built-in tech support options.

If you're starting purely from scratch, look into the most popular and highly-rated Linux distributions. (Currently, the Web site www.distrowatch.com gives a great set of recommendations, but as you know, Web sites change, so you might want to also do some Web searching for recommended Linux distributions.)

A newly popular (or popular again) option is Solaris, from Sun Microsystems. For a while Solaris was a bit tricky (well, a lot tricky) to get installed and functional on a regular desktop system; however, it's now nearly as easy as the easier Linux systems, and it offers a tremendous amount of power and flexibility, in addition to some cutting-edge technologies.

That said, any option you choose will be pretty similar for the purposes of this book. Differences among the options primarily show up in more advanced applications.

✔ Tip

■ If you're using Mac OS X or later, you're already using Unix—you just need to bring up a command window to be able to follow right along with the book.

Connecting to the Unix System

Your first step in using Unix is to connect to the Unix system. Exactly how you connect will vary depending on what kind of Internet connection you use, but the following steps should get you started.

To connect to the Unix system:

1. Connect to the Internet, if necessary.

   If you use a PPP connection to dial into an ISP, launch it now. If you use a full-time Internet connection at home, work, or school, or if you're using your Mac or Linux system at home, just ignore this step.

2. If you're connecting to a remote system, start your SSH program and connect to the Unix system.

   Using SSH you can connect to a remote computer (such as your ISP's computer) and work as if the remote computer were sitting on your desk. Essentially, SSH brings a remote computer's capabilities to your fingertips, regardless of where you're physically located. (See the About Connecting sidebar for more information about connection technologies.)

   Exactly how you connect depends on the particular program you're using. For Windows users, we recommend PuTTY, which is a free SSH client available at www.chiark.greenend.org.uk/~sgtatham/putty/. For Macintosh users (pre-OS X), we recommend the predictably named MacSSH, also free, available at http://pro.wanadoo.fr/chombier/.

   continues on next page

About Connecting

Once upon a time, when dinosaurs roamed the earth, Unix users connected to their systems using telnet. With telnet, your password and everything else you do is sent straight across the wire and can be easily read by anyone on the same part of the network. Yikes is right! That's why, more and more, ISPs and system administrators require something called SSH (Secure SHell) to connect to their systems. With SSH, everything is encrypted, precisely the way your Web connection is encrypted when you use an e-commerce site and see that the little padlock in your Web browser is closed.

Yes, we know, you don't have any secrets, but if a hacker logs into your ISP's system as you, that same hacker has won 50 percent of the battle for taking over that system for any number of illegal activities. Besides which, if your neighbor's 19-year-old son *sniffs* (that's the technical term) your user identification (often called userid or user ID) and password over your cable modem connection (and that's entirely possible), he can probably guess that your eBay password, broker password, or whatever are the same or similar.

Throughout this book, we'll show examples using an SSH connection. If, for whatever reason, your system administrators don't require SSH, we recommend using it anyway; there is absolutely no reason not to, because there are no disadvantages to SSH compared to telnet. If your systems don't support SSH, you can use the telnet or rlogin/rsh programs as alternatives.

And, of course, after you're logged into your Unix-like system, you can use the Unix `ssh` command to access other computers. Each program works a bit differently, and you'll have to refer to the specific documentation for details about using them.

In this example, we're connecting to a Unix system using PuTTY. **Figure 1.1** shows the Connection dialog, in which we've filled in the Host Name (varies), the Port (22), and the Protocol (SSH).

If you're looking for a quick start, just fill in the fields shown in **Figure 1.2** and click Open.

3. Check out the Categories (or the Preferences dialog in many other programs) and become familiar with your options. You will not need to change anything initially, but you might later want to customize colors or other settings. Generally, though, PuTTY provides usable settings.

4. Marvel at the `login:` prompt, which is what you should see if you've connected properly (**Figure 1.3**) and move along to the next section. (PuTTY displays "login as :", while most other programs will just show you "login:". Don't worry about this difference; it's just this program's idiosyncrasy.)

Figure 1.1 Here we're connecting to frazz.raycomm. com using PuTTY. Other SSH programs might look slightly different, but this shows the general idea.

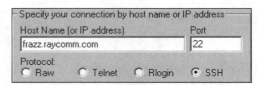

Figure 1.2 For a quick start, fill in these fields, and then click Open.

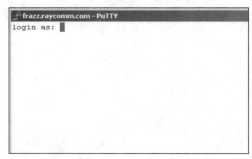

Figure 1.3 PuTTY shows a login as: prompt from frazz. raycomm.com.

Before You Begin

Before you begin, have your connection information, such as your login name and password, handy.

Contact your system administrator if you don't yet have these. Throughout this book, we'll use "system administrator" to refer to your help desk, ISP technical support line, or anyone else you can call on who runs your Unix system and can help you. Sometimes that geeky daughter, brother, or otherwise Unixy-person can help you out with Unix, too; however, in many cases you'll find that you need to troubleshoot a problem with the person who can access *your* account information.

✔ Tips

■ If you modify the connection settings, you may need to disconnect from the session, then reconnect again for the new settings to take effect. See your documentation for specifics about disconnecting from your session.

■ In addition to viewing the buffer to see commands you've used, as mentioned in the *Preferences Dialog* sidebar, you can also use a command to let you review commands that you've issued. For more information, see *Viewing Session History* in Chapter 3.

Write Down Details About Your Specific login Procedure

As you go through your login procedure, take a minute to write down some details for future reference.

Your userid or login name (but not your password):

_____

The name of the program you use (or the icon you click) to connect to your Unix system and the process you use to get connected:

_____

_____

_____

_____

The name of your Unix system (such as `frazz.example.com` or `example.com`):

_____

The IP address of your Unix system (such as `198.168.11.36` or `10.10.22.2`):

_____

CONNECTING TO THE UNIX SYSTEM

Logging In

After you've connected to the Unix system, your next step is to *log in*, or identify yourself to the Unix system. Logging in serves a few purposes, including giving you access to your email, files, and configurations. It also keeps you from inadvertently accessing someone else's files and settings, and it keeps you from making changes to the system itself.

To log in:

1. Have your userid (user identification) and password ready.

   Contact your system administrator if you don't have these yet.

2. Type your userid at the login prompt, then press (Enter).

   Your userid is case-sensitive, so be sure you type it exactly as your system administrator instructed.

3. Type your password at the password prompt, then press (Enter).

   Yup. Your password is case-sensitive, too.

4. Read the information and messages that come up on the screen.

   The information that pops up—the message of the day—might be just a funny, as in **Figure 1.4**, or it might contain information about system policies, warnings about scheduled downtime, or useful tips, as shown in **Figure 1.5**. It may also contain both, or possibly neither, if your system administrators have nothing to say to you.

After you've logged in, you'll see a *shell prompt*, which is where you type in commands. Also, note that you'll be located in your *home directory*, which is where your personal files and settings are stored. Your "location" in the Unix system is a slightly unwieldy concept that we'll help you understand throughout this chapter.

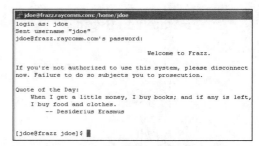

Figure 1.4 Our Unix system (frazz.raycomm.com) greets us with a quote of the day, called a "fortune."

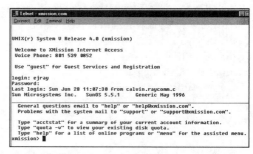

Figure 1.5 Some systems might greet you with system information or helpful tips.

✔ Tips

- If you get an error message after attempting to log in, just try again. You likely just mistyped your userid or password. Whoops!

- When you log in, you might see a message about failed login attempts. If you unsuccessfully tried to log in, then don't worry about it; the message just confirms that you attempted to log in but failed. If, however, all of your login attempts (with you sitting at the keyboard) have been successful or if the number of failed login attempts seems high—say, five or more—then you might also mention the message to your system administrator, who can check security and login attempts. This could be a warning that someone unauthorized is trying to log in as you.

```
$ passwd
Changing password for ejr
(current) Unix password:
New UNIX password:
Retype new UNIX password:
passwd: all authentication tokens updated
 ⟶ successfully
$
```

Code Listing 1.1 Change your password regularly using the passwd command.

The SSH Preferences Dialog

In the Preferences dialog, you can fix some of the idiosyncrasies that are caused by how your SSH program talks to the Unix system. You can't identify these idiosyncrasies until you actually start using your Unix system, but you should remember that you can fix most problems here. For example:

◆ If your (←Backspace) and (Delete) keys don't work, look for an option in your SSH or telnet program that defines these keyboard functions.

◆ If you start typing and nothing shows up onscreen, set local echo to on.

◆ If you start typing and everything shows up twice, set local echo to off.

◆ If you want to be able to scroll up onscreen to see what's happened during your Unix session, change the buffer size to a larger number.

Exactly which options you'll have will vary from program to program, but these are ones that are commonly available. Click OK when you're done playing with the settings.

Changing Your Password with passwd

Virtually all Unix systems require passwords to help ensure that your files and data remain your own and that the system itself is secure from hackers and *crackers* (malicious hackers). **Code Listing 1.1** shows how you change your password.

Throughout your Unix adventure, you'll likely change your password often:

◆ You'll probably want to change the password provided by your system administrator after you log in for the first time. Hint, hint.

◆ You'll probably change your password at regular intervals. Many Unix systems require that you change your password every so often—every 30 or 60 days is common.

◆ You might also change your password voluntarily if you think that someone might have learned it or if you tell anyone your password (although you really shouldn't do that anyway).

To change your password:

1. passwd

   To start, type passwd.

2. youroldpassword

   Enter your old password—the one you're currently using. (Of course, type in your old password, not the sample one we've used here!) Note that the password doesn't show up onscreen when you type it, in case someone is lurking over your shoulder, watching you type, and asking, "whatcha doing?"

   continues on next page

3. yournewpassword

Type in your new password. Check out the Lowdown on Passwords sidebar for specifics about choosing a password.

4. yournewpassword

Here, you're verifying the password by typing it again.

The system will report that your password was successfully changed (specific terminology depends on the system) after the changes take effect. This is also shown in Code Listing 1.1.

✔ Tips

■ Double-check your new password before you log out of the system by typing `su - yourid` at the prompt. Of course, substitute your real username (or login name) for `yourid` here. This command (switch user) lets you log in again without having to log out, so if you made a mistake when changing your password and now get a failed login message, you can find out before you actually disconnect from the system. If you have problems, contact your system administrator before you log out so you can get the problem resolved.

■ In some environments, you will use `yppasswd`, not `passwd`, to change your password, or even use a Web page or other means. When in doubt, defer to what your system administrator told you to do. ("The Rays said to use this other command" is likely to get all of us in trouble.)

CHANGING YOUR PASSWORD WITH passwd

The Lowdown on Passwords

In addition to following any password guidelines your system administrator mandates, you should choose a password that is

◆ At least six characters long

◆ Easy for you to remember

◆ Not a word or name in any dictionary in any language

◆ A combination of capital and lower-case letters, numbers, and symbols

◆ Not similar to your username

◆ Not identical or similar to one you've used recently

◆ Not your telephone number, birth date, kid's birth date, anniversary (even if you can remember it), mother's maiden name, or anything else that anyone might associate with you

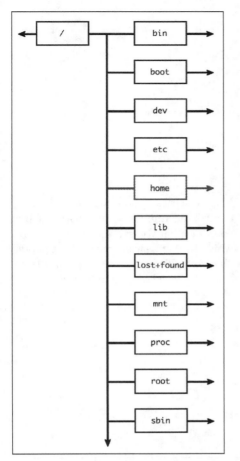

Figure 1.6 All files and directories are nested within the root directory, which serves to contain everything in the system.

Listing Directories and Files with ls

Your Unix system is made up of directories and files that store a variety of information, including setup information, configuration settings, programs, and options, as well as other files and directories. You might think of your Unix system as being a tree (tree roots, actually), with subdirectories stemming from higher-level directories. As shown in **Figure 1.6**, all of these files and directories reside within the root directory, which contains everything in the system.

Using the ls command, you can find out exactly what's in your Unix system and thereby find out what's available to you. You can list the files and directories of a directory that you're currently in or a directory that you specify.

To list the files and directories of the directory you're in:

◆ ls

At the shell prompt, type ls to list the files and directories in the current directory, which in this case is our home directory (**Code Listing 1.2**).

```
[jdoe@frazz jdoe]$ ls
limerick  mail/  Project/  public_html/
 → testfile  testlink@  tmp/
[jdoe@frazz jdoe]$
```

Code Listing 1.2 Use ls by itself to list the files and directories of the directory you're in.

To list the files and directories of a specified directory:

◆ ls /bin

Here, you type the ls command plus the name of a directory. As shown in **Code Listing 1.3**, this command lists the files and directories in the /bin directory, in which you'll find system commands and programs.

✔ Tips

■ You can list the files and directories of the *root directory* at any time and in any place by typing ls /. The root directory is the highest-level directory in a Unix system; all other directories are below the root directory.

■ Can't remember that pesky filename? Just use ls to help jog your memory. Or, refer to *Finding Forgotten Files with find* in Chapter 2, which can also help you remember filenames.

■ Many other ls options are available to control the amount of information about your files that you see and the format in which they appear onscreen. See Chapter 2's *Listing Files and Directories with ls (More Goodies)* section for details.

```
[jdoe@frazz jdoe]$ ls /bin
arch*            domainname@      ipcalc*          open*            tar*
awk@             echo*            ipv6c            eys*             red@             unlink*
chmod*           fbresolution*    login*           rm*              usleep*
chown*           fgrep@           ls*              rmdir*           vi@
consolechars*    find*            lsb_release*     rpm*             view@
cp*              gawk*            mail*            rvi@             vim@
cpio*            gawk-3.1.1@      mkdir*           rview@
date*            gtar@            more*            sleep*           zcat*
dd*              gunzip*          mount*           sort*            zsh*
df*              gzip*            mv*              stat*
dmesg*           hostname*        netstat*         stty*
dnsdomainname@   id*              nice*            su*
doexec*          igawk*           nisdomainname@   sync*
[jdoe@frazz jdoe]$
```

Code Listing 1.3 Use ls with the name of a directory to list the contents of that directory (/bin, in this case).

```
[jdoe@frazz jdoe]$ cd /
[jdoe@frazz /]$ cd
[jdoe@frazz jdoe]$ cd /home/jdoe/Project/
[jdoe@frazz Project]$ cd /etc
[jdoe@frazz etc]$ cd /home/jdoe/
[jdoe@frazz etc]$ cd /home/jdoe/mail/
[jdoe@frazz mail]$ cd ..
[jdoe@frazz jdoe]$
```

Code Listing 1.4 Using cd, you can change directories and move around in the system. Note that the prompt in this code listing shows the name of the current directory, which can be handy.

Changing Directories with cd

To explore Unix and its capabilities, you'll need to move around among the directories. You do so using the cd command, which takes you from the directory you're currently in to one that you specify. **Code Listing 1.4** illustrates how you use cd to change directories.

To change directories:

1. cd Projects

   To move to a specific directory, type cd plus the name of the directory. In this example, we move down in the directory tree to a subdirectory called Projects. (See the *Moving Up and Down* sidebar for an explanation of what "up" and "down" mean in Unix terms.)

2. cd ..

   Type cd .. to move up one level in the directory tree.

3. cd /etc

   Here, /etc tells the system to look for the etc directory located at the system root.

   continues on next page

continues on next page

Moving Up and Down

Throughout this book, we'll talk about moving "up" and "down" through the Unix file system. Moving "up" means moving into the directory that contains the current directory—that is, closer to the root directory. Moving "down" means moving into subdirectories that are contained by the current directory—that is, farther from the root directory.

CHANGING DIRECTORIES WITH cd

✔ Tips

■ If you don't remember the name of the directory you want to change to, you can use `ls` to list the directories and files in your current directory, then use `cd` as shown above. See the previous section, *Listing Directories and Files with ls*, for more information.

■ You can return to your home directory from anywhere in the Unix system by entering `cd` without specifying a directory.

■ You can often use a tilde (~) as a handy shortcut to your home directory. For example, if you want to change to the `Urgent` directory within the `Projects` directory in your home directory, you could use something like `cd /home/users/y/yourid/Projects/Urgent` or just use the shortcut `cd ~/Projects/Urgent`

■ Keep in mind that your home directory isn't the same as the system root directory. You might think of your home directory as "the very small section of the Unix system that I can call my own." Every person using the Unix system has his or her own little personal section.

The current directory is always indicated with a `.`, while the next higher directory (the one that contains the current directory) is indicated with `..` That is why you use `cd ..` to move up a directory. In Chapter 10, you will see a specific use for `.` to specify the current directory when running scripts or programs.

■ Visit Chapter 2 for much more about directories and files.

```
[jdoe@frazz jdoe]$ pwd
/home/jdoe
[jdoe@frazz jdoe]$ ls ; pwd
codelisting1.2  codelisting1.4  mail/
 → public_html/  testlink@
codelisting1.3  limerick  Project/  testfile
 → tmp/
/home/jdoe
[jdoe@frazz jdoe]$ cd
[jdoe@frazz jdoe]$ cd /
[jdoe@frazz /]$ pwd
/
[jdoe@frazz /]$
```

Code Listing 1.5 pwd displays the name of the current directory, which is particularly handy if you've been exploring the system. By combining commands, you can request the directory's name and contents at one time.

Finding Yourself with pwd

As you begin using Unix and start moving around in directories and files, you're likely to get a bit lost—that is, forget which directory or subdirectory you're in. You can use the pwd command to get a reminder of where you are, as shown in **Code Listing 1.5**.

You can request just the directory name, or you can get fancy and request the directory's name and its contents, courtesy of ls.

To find out the name of the current directory:

◆ pwd

This command displays the path and name of the directory you are currently in. The path names each of the directories "above" the current directory, giving you the full picture of where you are in relationship to the system root.

To find out the name of the current directory and its contents:

◆ ls ; pwd

By combining the ls and pwd commands, you can request the directory's contents and name, as shown in Code Listing 1.5.

✔ Tips

■ Type in pwd immediately after you log in. You'll see where your home directory is in the overall system (aka the full path name for your home directory).

■ On some Unix systems, you won't need to use pwd to find out where you are. Some systems display the current directory at the shell prompt by default—something like /home/ejr>. If you'd like to add or get rid of this, or if you want more information about shells and customizing your shell, see Chapter 8, *Configuring Your Unix Environment.*

FINDING YOURSELF WITH pwd

Piping Input and Output

In general, you can think of each Unix command (ls, cd, and so on) as an individual program that Unix executes. For example, if you type cat /etc/mold at the prompt, Unix will display the contents of mold in the /etc directory. Each program requires input (in this example, cat, the program, takes the contents of /etc/mold as input) and produces output (i.e., the displayed results).

Frequently, you'll want to run programs in sequence. For example, you could tell Unix to read your resume and then spell-check it. In doing this, you connect two commands together and have them run in sequence. This process, in which you connect the output of one program to the input of another, is called piping. Depending on what you want to do, you can pipe together as many commands as you want—with the output of each command acting as the input of the next.

As **Figure 1.7** shows, you pipe commands together using the pipe symbol, which is the | character. In the following example, we'll pipe the output of the ls command (which lists the contents of a directory) to the more command (which lets you read results one screen at a time). For details about more, see *Viewing File Contents* with more, later in this chapter.

To pipe commands:

◆ ls | more

Here, all you do is include a pipe symbol between the two commands, with a space on both sides of the pipe. This code produces a list of the files in the current directory, then pipes the results to more, which then lists the results one screen at a time (see Figure 1.7).

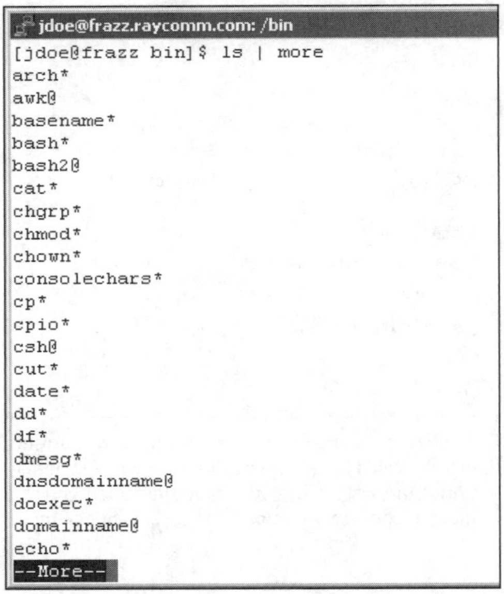

```
jdoe@frazz.raycomm.com: /bin
[jdoe@frazz bin]$ ls | more
arch*
awk@
basename*
bash*
bash2@
cat*
chgrp*
chmod*
chown*
consolechars*
cp*
cpio*
csh@
cut*
date*
dd*
df*
dmesg*
dnsdomainname@
doexec*
domainname@
echo*
--More--
```

Figure 1.7 To execute multiple commands in sequence, pipe them together using the pipe symbol (|).

✔ Tips

■ If you want to pipe more than two commands, you can. Just keep adding the commands (with a pipe symbol in between each, like | this) in the order you want them executed.

■ Remember that the output of each command is piped to the next command. So a piped command, such as ls | spell | sort, could list files within a directory, then spell-check the list, then sort the misspelled words and display them onscreen. The filenames that are found in the system dictionary would not appear.

■ Venture to Chapter 15 to find out more about running a spell-checker and Chapter 6 to find out more about sorting.

Redirecting Output

Suppose you've developed your resume and spell-checked it. As you learned in the previous section, the results you see onscreen will be the output of the last command—in this case, a list of misspelled words. A lot of times, you'll want to redirect the final output to another location, such as to a file or a printer (if a printer is an option for you), rather than view it onscreen. You can do this using *redirection*, which sends the final output to somewhere other than your screen.

As shown in **Code Listing 1.6**, you will often redirect output results to a file. Notice the greater-than symbol (>), which indicates that the output of the program is to be redirected to the location (or filename) you specify after the symbol.

In the following examples, we'll show you how to redirect output to a new file and how to redirect output to append it to an existing file.

```
[jdoe@frazz jdoe]$ ls /usr/local/bin > local.programs.txt
[jdoe@frazz jdoe]$ ls local*
localize  localono  local.programs.txt  localyokel
[jdoe@frazz jdoe]$ ls /usr/bin >> other.programs.txt
[jdoe@frazz jdoe]$
```

Code Listing 1.6 In this case, the output of ls gets redirected to local.programs.txt, as indicated by the greater-than (>) symbol. The asterisk wildcard (*) acts as a placeholder for letters or numbers. Finally, the listing of /usr/bin gets appended to the other.programs.txt file.

To redirect output to a new file:

1. `ls /usr/local/bin > local.programs.txt`

In this case, we start with the `ls` command and a specific directory, add a greater-than symbol (>), and then specify a file-name. This will redirect the output of `ls` to a file named `local.programs.txt`.

Be careful with this! If the file already exists, it could be replaced with the output of the `ls` program here.

2. `ls local*`

Here, we're just checking to see that the new `local.programs.txt` file has successfully been created. The asterisk wildcard (*) specifies that we want a list of all files that begin with the word `local`, such as `localize`, `localyokel`, or `localuno` (see Code Listing 1.6). See the next section, *Using Wildcards*, for handy wildcard information.

To append output to an existing file:

◆ `ls /usr/bin >> all.programs.txt`

Appending output to an existing file is similar to redirecting it to a new file; however, instead of creating a new file to hold the output (or replacing the contents of an existing file), you add content to the end of an existing file. Notice that you use two greater-than symbols here, rather than one.

✔ Tip

■ You can pipe and redirect at the same time. For example, you might list a directory, pipe it to `wc` to count the entries, then append the results to a `directoryinfo` file, like this: `ls | wc -l >> directoryinfo`. You can learn more about counting files and their contents with `wc` in Chapter 6.

```
[jdoe@frazz Project]$ ls
keep  keeper.jpg  keptkidder.txt
 → kiddo  kidnews  kidneypie
 → kids  kidupdate
[jdoe@frazz Project]$ ls ki
kidder.txt     kiddo     kidnews kidneypie
 → kids  kidupdate
[jdoe@frazz Project]$ ls kid*
kidder.txt     kiddo     kidnews kidneypie
 → kids  kidupdate
[jdoe@frazz Project]$ ls k???
keep  keptkids
[jdoe@frazz Project]$ ls *date
kidupdate
[jdoe@frazz Project]$ ls *up*
kidupdate
[jdoe@frazz Project]$ ls k?d*
kidder.txt     kiddo     kidnews kidneypie
 → kids  kidupdate
[jdoe@frazz Project]$
```

Code Listing 1.7 You use wildcards (? or *) to act as placeholders for missing characters.

Using Wildcards

You might think of wildcards as being place-holders for omitted letters or numbers. For example, if you're looking for a file but aren't sure whether you named it kidnews or kidupdate, you can include a wildcard to stand for the part you're uncertain of. That is, you could list the files of a directory with ls kid* (**Code Listing 1.7**), which would list all files starting with the characters "kid". In the resulting list, you'd find a file named kid if there were one, as well as files that begin with kid but have varying endings, such as kidnews (aha, the lost file!), kiddo, or kidneypie.

You can use wildcards for just about any purpose in Unix, although listing files and directories will likely be the most common use. Just follow these guidelines:

◆ You use ? as a placeholder for one character or number.

◆ You use * as a placeholder for zero or more characters or numbers. Zero characters, in case you're curious, specifies that the search results include all variants of kid, including the word itself with no suffix.

◆ You can include a wildcard at any place in a name: at the beginning (*kid), somewhere in the middle (k*d), at the end (ki*), or even in multiple places (*kid*).

Viewing File Contents with more

As you become more familiar with Unix, you'll want to start exploring the contents of files, including some program files and scripts as well as files you (eventually) create. One of the easiest ways to view file contents is to use the more command, which tells Unix to display files onscreen, a page at a time. As shown in **Figure 1.8**, long files are displayed with "More" at the bottom of each screen so that you can move through the file one screen at a time using the z.

To view a file with more:

1. `more fortunes`

   At the prompt, type more plus the name of the file you want to view. You'll see the contents of the file you requested, starting at the top (Figure 1.8).

2. Spacebar

   Press the Spacebar to see the next screen of information. As you move through the file, you can press B to move back through previous screens.

3. Q

   When you're done, press Q to go back to the shell prompt.

✔ Tips

- If you want to view just an additional line (rather than an entire screen) when using more, press Enter instead of the Spacebar.

  You can also use less to view files. less is very similar to more, but more powerful and flexible. How can less be more and more be less? As you'll see in Appendix C: *Commands and Flags*, the more command has 10 options or so; the less command has about 40.

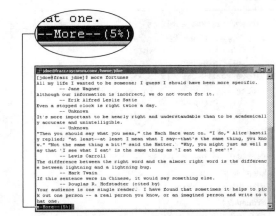

Figure 1.8 The more command lets you move through a file one screen at a time, providing a "More" indicator at the bottom of each screen.

- You can also view files using the cat command. See the next section for the full scoop.

```
[jdoe@frazz jdoe]$ cat newest.programs.txt
...
xpmtoppm*
xpp*
xpstat*
xrfbviewer*
xscreensaver.kss*
xvminitoppm*
xwdtopnm*
xxd*
yaf-cdda*
yaf-mpgplay*
yaf-splay*
yaf-tplay*
yaf-vorbis*
yaf-yuv*
ybmtopbm*
yelp*
yes*
ypcat*
ypchfn*
ypchsh*
ypmatch*
yppasswd*
ypwhich*
yuvsplittoppm*
yuvtoppm*
z42_cmyk*
z42tool*
zcmp*
zdiff*
zeisstopnm*
zforce*
zgrep*
zipgrep*
zipinfo*
zless*
zmore*
znew*
[jdoe@frazz jdoe]$ cat newer.programs.txt
 → newest.programs.txt > all.programs
[jdoe@frazz jdoe]$
```

Code Listing 1.8 With cat, long files whirl by, and all you'll see is the bottom of the file. You can also redirect cat output to a file, as shown at the end of the listing.

Displaying File Contents with cat

Instead of using more to display files, you can use cat (as in "concatenate"), which displays files but does not pause so you can read the information. Instead, it displays the file or files—which whiz by onscreen—and leaves you looking at the last several lines of the file (**Code Listing 1.8**).

The cat command also lets you redirect one or more files, offering a function that some versions of more do not.

To display file contents with cat:

◆ cat newest.programs

To begin, type cat plus the filename (probably not newest.programs unless you're naming your files just like we are).

The file contents will appear onscreen; however, if the file is longer than a single screen, the contents will whirl by, and all you'll see is the bottom lines of the file—the 24 or so that fit on a single screen.

Or

◆ cat newer.programs newest.programs

You can also specify multiple files for cat, with each file being displayed in the order specified. In this example the contents of newer.programs will zip by, then the contents of newest.programs will zip by.

continues on next page

DISPLAYING FILE CONTENTS WITH cat

Or

◆ `cat newer.programs newest.programs >`
  `→ all.programs`

In this example, we've added a redirection symbol (>) plus a new filename. This tells Unix to print out both files; however, instead of displaying the files onscreen, it redirects them to the file called `all.programs`. Aha! Here's where `cat` does something better than `more`. See *Redirecting Output*, earlier, for more information about redirecting commands.

✔ Tips

■ If you inadvertently use `cat` with a *binary file* (a non-text file), you might end up with a whole screen of garbage. On some systems, you might try `stty sane` to fix it—more on this in *Fixing Terminal Settings with `stty`* in Chapter 3. You could also just close your terminal window and log in again to fix it.

■ The `tac` command is just like `cat`, but backward. Try it! Oddly handy, eh?

■ You can also view file contents using the `more` command. See the previous section for details.

Table 1.1

Common Unix Directories and Their Contents	
DIRECTORY	CONTENTS
/bin	Essential programs and commands for use by all users
/etc	System configuration files and global settings
/home	Home directories for users
/sbin	Programs and commands needed for system boot
/tmp	Temporary files
/usr/bin	Commands and programs that are less central to basic Unix system functionality than those in /bin but were installed with the system
/usr/local	Most files and data that were developed or customized on the system
/usr/local/bin	Locally-developed or installed programs
/usr/local/man	Manual (help) pages for local programs
/usr/share/man	Manual (help) pages
/var	Changeable data, including system logs, temporary data from programs, and user mail storage

Exploring the System

With these few key skills in hand, you're ready to start exploring your Unix system. In doing so, you can quickly get an idea of what's available and gain some useful experience in entering commands.

Think of your Unix system as being a thoroughly kid-proofed house: You can look around and touch some stuff, but you can't do anything to hurt yourself or the system. So, don't worry! You can't hurt anything by looking around, and even if you tried to break something, most Unix systems are configured well enough that you couldn't.

Table 1.1 shows some of the directories you're likely to find most interesting or useful (Appendix B of this book provides a more comprehensive list of directories). You can use the following steps to get started exploring.

To explore locally installed programs:

1. cd /usr/bin

   Change to /usr/bin, which is where most installed programs are.

2. ls | more

   List the files (which will be programs, in this example) and pipe the output to more so you can read the names one screen at a time.

3. ssh

   Type the name of any program you want to run; ssh, in this case, allows you to connect to another system and use it just as you're using your Unix system now.

✔ Tip

■ You can type man followed by a command name to learn more about Unix programs. See the next section for information about Unix help.

Getting Help with man

Occasionally, you may need a bit of help remembering what a particular command does. Using man (which is short for "manual"), you can look up information about commands and get pointers for using them efficiently. **Figure 1.9** shows a Unix help page (also called a man page, for obvious reasons) for passwords. In the following steps, we'll show you how to look up specific Unix commands and find related topics.

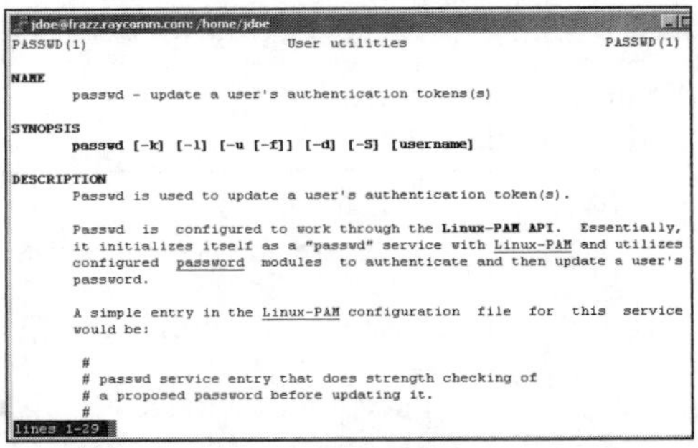

Figure 1.9 Using man passwd, you can access the standard man file about the passwd program.

To access a man page:

◆ man passwd

At the prompt, type man plus the name of the command you want help with (in this case, passwd). You'll get the man page for that command. Use the [Spacebar] and [B] (for Back) to navigate through the file, just as you do with more.

To find a specific man page:

1. man -k passwd

Type man -k plus the name of the command or the topic you want help with (in this case, passwd). As **Code Listing 1.9** shows, you'll see a list of possible man pages, command names, man page names, and a description. Note the man page name (and number if more than one page with the same name exists) so you can reference it in the next step.

```
$ man -k passwd
chpasswd (8)   - update password file in batch
gpasswd (1)    - administer the /etc/group file
mkpasswd (1)   - generate new password, optionally apply it to a user
mkpasswd (8)   - Update passwd and group database files
passwd (1)     - update a user's authentication tokens(s)
passwd (5)     - password file
userpasswd (1)   - A graphical tool to allow users to change their passwords
$
```

Code Listing 1.9 man -k passwd gives you these results, showing specific password-related man pages.

2. man 5 passwd

Here, you type man, the man page you want to view (indicated by 5 in this case to specify section 5—this is necessary because more than one man page with the name passwd was listed in the last step), and the command name (passwd). Figure 1.9 shows the resulting man page.

✔ Tips

■ You can make a copy of a man page so you can edit it or comment on it, adding additional notes for your information or deleting irrelevant (to you) stuff. Just type in man command name | col –b -x > somefilename. For example, use man passwd | col –b –x > ~/my.password .command.notes to make a copy of the passwd man page, sans formatting, in your home directory, under the name my.password.command.notes. Then you'll use an editor (from Chapter 4) to edit, add to, and tweak the important points. (The col –b -x command fixes some formatting oddities; without it, all of the underlined words show up as _u_n_d_e_r_l_i_n_e.)

■ You can use apropos instead of the man –k flag. For example, you might use this: apropos passwd

■ Some Unix systems might require a -s before the section number, as in man -s 5 passwd

GETTING HELP WITH man

Logging Out

When you finish your session, you need to log out of the system to ensure that nobody else accesses your files while masquerading as you.

To log out:

◆ logout

That's it! Just type logout, and the system will clean up everything and break the connection, and the SSH program might very well just vanish completely.

✔ Tip

■ On some Unix systems, you can type exit or quit instead of logout, or press Ctrl D on your keyboard.

USING DIRECTORIES AND FILES

2

As you learned in Chapter 1, directories and files are the heart of Unix; they contain things like setup information, configuration settings, programs, and options, as well as anything that you create. You access directories and files every time you type in a Unix command, and for this reason, you need to become familiar with the various things you can do with them.

Again in this chapter, the skills and commands we'll cover apply to any Unix flavor. What you see onscreen (particularly system prompts and responses) may differ slightly from what's illustrated in this book. The general ideas and specific commands, however, will be the same on all Unix systems.

Chapter Contents

◆ Creating directories

◆ Creating files

◆ Copying directories and files

◆ Listing directories and files

◆ Moving directories and files

◆ Removing files

◆ Removing directories

◆ Finding files

◆ Locating program files

◆ Linking with hard links

◆ Linking with soft links

Creating Directories
with mkdir

You might think of directories as being drawers in a file cabinet; each drawer contains a bunch of files that are somehow related. For example, you might have a couple of file drawers for your unread magazines, one for your to-do lists, and maybe a drawer for your work projects.

Similarly, directories in your Unix system act as containers for other directories and files; each subdirectory contains yet more related directories or files, and so on. You'll probably create a new directory each time you start a project or have related files you want to store at a single location. You create new directories using the mkdir command, as shown in **Code Listing 2.1**.

```
$ ls
Projects  all.programs.txt   local.programs.txt         schedule
Xrootenv.0   files   newer.programs short.fortunes
all.programs fortunes    newest.programs     temp
$ mkdir Newdirectory
$ ls -l
total 159
drwxrwxr-x    2 ejr     users     1024 Jun 29 11:40 Newdirectory
drwxrwxr-x    2 ejr     users     1024 Jun 28 12:48 Projects
-rw-rw-r–     1 ejr     users     7976 Jun 28 14:15 all.programs
-rw-rw-r–     1 ejr     users     7479 Jun 28 14:05 all.programs.txt
-rw-rw-r–     1 ejr     users     858 Jun 28 12:45 files
-rw-rw-r–     1 ejr     ejr     128886 Jun 27 09:05 fortunes
-rw-rw-r–     1 ejr     users     0 Jun 28 14:05 local.programs.txt
-rw-rw-r–     1 ejr     users     497 Jun 28 14:13 newer.programs
-rw-rw-r–     1 ejr     users     7479 Jun 28 14:13 newest.programs
lrwxrwxrwx    1 ejr     users     27 Jun 26 11:03 schedule -> /home/deb/Pre
-rw-rw-r–     1 ejr     ejr     1475 Jun 27 09:31 short.fortunes
drwxrwxr-x    2 ejr     users     1024 Jun 26 06:39 temp
$
```

Code Listing 2.1 Typing mkdir plus a directory name creates a new directory. Listing the files, in long format, shows the new directory. The "d" at the beginning of the line shows that it's a directory.

Naming Directories (and Files)

As you start creating directories (and files), keep in mind the following guidelines:

◆ Directories and files must have unique names. For example, you cannot name a directory Golf and a file Golf. You can, however, have a directory called Golf and a file called golf. The difference in capitalization makes each name unique. By the way, directories are often named with an initial cap, and filenames are often all lowercase.

◆ Directory and filenames should not include the following characters: angle brackets (< >), braces ({ }), brackets ([ ]), parentheses (( )), double quotes (" "), single quotes (' '), asterisks (*), question marks (?), pipe symbols (|), slashes (/ \), carets (^), exclamation points (!), pound signs (#), dollar signs ($), ampersands (&), and tildes (~).

  Different shells handle special characters differently, and some will have no problems at all with these characters. Generally, though, special characters are more trouble than they're worth.

◆ Generally, avoid names that include spaces and hyphens (-). Some programs don't deal with them correctly, so to use spaces and hyphens you have to use odd workarounds. Instead, stick to periods (.) and underscores (_) to separate words, characters, or numbers.

◆ Use names that describe the directory's or file's contents so you easily remember them.

To create a directory:

1. ls

   Start by listing existing directories to make sure that the planned name doesn't conflict with an existing directory or filename.

2. mkdir Newdirectory

   Type the mkdir command to make a new directory; in this case, it's called Newdirectory. Refer to the sidebar *Naming Directories (and Files)* for guidelines.

3. ls -l

   Now you can use ls -l (the -l flag specifies a long format) to look at the listing for your new directory (**Code Listing 2.1**). The d at the far left of the listing for Newdirectory indicates that it's a directory and not a file. Of course, after you trust Unix to do as you say, you can skip this verification step.

✔ Tips

■ If you attempt to create a directory with a file or directory name that already exists, Unix will not overwrite the existing directory. Instead, you'll be told that a file by that name already exists. Try again with a different name.

■ You can create several directories and subdirectories at once with the –p flag. For example, if you want to create a new subdirectory called Projects with a subdirectory called Cooking in that and a subdirectory called Desserts in that, you can use mkdir –p Projects/Cooking/Desserts and get it all done at once. Without the –p flag, you have to create Projects, Cooking, then Desserts in order, which is a longer recipe to make the same tree structure.

CREATING DIRECTORIES WITH mkdir

Creating Files with touch

Another skill you'll use frequently is creating files. You might think of creating files as getting an empty bucket that you can later fill with water...or sand...or rocks...or whatever. When you create a file, you designate an empty space that you can fill with programs, activity logs, your resume, or configurations—practically anything you want, or nothing at all.

Of course, you can always create a file by writing something in an editor and saving it, as described in Chapter 4, but you will sometimes encounter situations where you just need an empty file as a placeholder for later use. You create empty files using the touch command, as shown in **Code Listing 2.2**.

To create a file:

1. touch file.to.create

   To create a file, type touch followed by the name of the file. This creates an empty file.

```
$ ls
$ touch file.to.create
$ ls -l file*
-rw-rw-r–      1 ejr      users      0 Jun 29 11:53 file.to.create
$ touch -t 12312359 oldfile
$ ls -l
total 0
-rw-rw-r–      1 ejr      users      0 Jun 29 11:53 file.to.create
-rw-rw-r–      1 ejr      users      0 Dec 31  1998 oldfile
$ touch -t 200312312359 new.years.eve
$ ls -l
total 0
-rw-rw-r–      1 ejr      users      0 Jun 29 11:53 file.to.create
-rw-rw-r–      1 ejr      users      0 Dec 31  2003 new.years.eve
-rw-rw-r–      1 ejr      users      0 Dec 31  1998 oldfile
$
```

Code Listing 2.2 Use the touch command to create files, update their modification times, or both.

2. `ls -l file*`

Optionally, verify that the file was created by typing `ls -l file*`. As shown in **Code Listing 2.2**, you'll see the name of the new file as well as its length (0) and the date and time of its creation (likely seconds before the current time, if you're following along).

✔ Tips

■ You can also use touch to update a file's date and time. For example, typing touch -t 12312359 oldfile at the prompt would update oldfile with a date of December 31, 23 hours, and 59 minutes in the current year. Or, typing touch -t 200612312359 new.years.eve would update the file called new.years.eve to the same time in the year 2006.

■ Each time you save changes in a file, the system automatically updates the date and time. See Chapter 4 for details about editing and saving files.

■ Refer to the sidebar *Naming Directories (and Files)* in this chapter for file-naming guidelines.

CREATING FILES WITH touch

Copying Directories and Files with cp

When working in Unix, you'll frequently want to make copies of directories and files. For example, you may want to copy a file you're working on to keep an original, unscathed version handy. Or, you might want to maintain duplicate copies of important directories and files in case you inadvertently delete them or save something over them. Accidents do happen, according to Murphy.

Whatever your reason, you copy directories and files using the cp command, as shown in **Code Listing 2.3**. When you copy directories and files, all you're doing is putting a duplicate in another location; you leave the original untouched.

To copy a directory:

1. cp -r /home/ejr/Projects
   → /home/shared/deb/Projects

   At the shell prompt, type cp -r, followed by the old and new (to be created) directory names, to copy a complete directory. The r stands for "recursive," if that'll help you remember it.

2. ls /home/shared/deb/Projects

   You can use ls plus the new directory name to verify that the duplicate directory and its contents are in the intended location (**Code Listing 2.3**).

```
$ cp -r /home/ejr/Projects
→ /home/shared/deb/Projects
$ ls /home/shared/deb/Projects
current   new.ideas   schedule
$
```

Code Listing 2.3 Use cp -r to copy directories.

```
$ cp existingfile newfile
$ ls -l
total 7
-rw-rw-r–   1 ejr   users   1475 Jun 29
→ 12:18 existingfile
-rw-rw-r–   1 ejr   users   1475 Jun 29
→ 12:37 newfile
-rw-rw-r–   1 ejr   users   2876 Jun 29
→ 12:17 oldfile
$ cp -i existingfile oldfile
cp: overwrite 'oldfile'? n
$
```

Code Listing 2.4 Just use cp to copy files and add -i to insist that the system prompt you before you overwrite an existing file.

- You can copy directories and files to or from someone else's directory. Skip to Chapter 5 to find out how to get access, then use the copying procedure described here.

- Use cp with a -i flag to force the system to ask you before overwriting files. Then, if you like that, visit Chapter 8 to find out about using aliases with cp so that the system always prompts you before over-writing files.

To copy a file:

1. cp existingfile newfile

At the prompt, type cp, followed by the old and new (to be created) filename.

2. ls -l

Optionally, check out the results with ls -l. The -l (for long format) flag displays the file sizes and dates so you can see that the copied file is exactly the same as the new one (**Code Listing 2.4**).

3. cp -i existingfile oldfile

If you use cp with the -i flag, it prompts you before overwriting an existing file, also shown in Code Listing 2.4.

✔ Tips

- When copying directories and files, you can use either *absolute* (complete) names, which are measured from the root directory (/home/ejr/Projects), or *relative* (partial) names, which specify files or directories in relationship to the current directory (ejr/Projects) and aren't necessarily valid from elsewhere in the Unix file system. Using absolute names, you can manipulate directories and files anywhere in the Unix system. Using relative names, you can manipulate files only with reference to your current location.

- You can compare the contents of two files or two directories using cmp and dircmp, respectively. For example, typing cmp filename1 filename2 would compare the contents of the specified files. Use diff or sdiff to see the differences between files. See Chapter 6 for more information.

COPYING DIRECTORIES AND FILES WITH cp

Listing Directories and Files with ls (More Goodies)

If you've been following along, you're probably an expert at using ls to list directory contents and to verify that files and directories were copied as you intended. ls, though, has a couple more handy uses. In particular, you can also use it to

◆ List filenames and information, which is handy for differentiating similar files (**Figure 2.1**).

◆ List all files in a directory, including hidden ones, such as .profile and .login configuration files (**Code Listing 2.5**). See Chapter 8 for more about configuration files.

To list filenames and information:

◆ ls -l

At the shell prompt, type ls -l (that's a lowercase "L," not a one). You'll see the list of files in your directory fly by with the following information about each file (**Code Listing 2.6**):

▲ Filename

▲ File size

▲ Date of last modification

▲ Permissions information (find out more about permissions in Chapter 5)

▲ Ownership and group membership (also covered in Chapter 5)

Ownership and group membership   *Date of last modification*   *Filename*

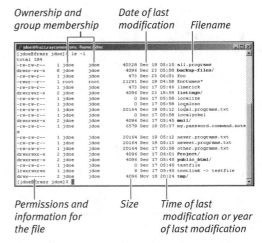

Permissions and information for the file   *Size*   *Time of last modification or year of last modification*

Figure 2.1 Use ls -l to get extra information about the directories and files in a specific directory.

```
$ ls -a
.       .stats  deb.schedule    other
..      current new.ideas schedule
```

Code Listing 2.5 If you want to see hidden files, use ls -a.

```
$ ls -l
total 13
-rw-rw-r-- 1 ejr   users 2151 Jun 29 12:26 current
-rw-rw-r-- 2 ejr   users 1475 Jun 29 12:35 deb.schedule
-rw-rw-r-- 1 ejr   users 4567 Jun 29 12:26 new.ideas
drwxrwxr-x 2 ejr   users 1024 Jun 29 13:06 other
-rw-rw-r-- 1 ejr   users 1475 Jun 29 12:22 schedule
```

Code Listing 2.6 Use ls -l to see a listing of the contents of a directory in long format.

LISTING DIRECTORIES AND FILES WITH ls

▲ Time of last modification (if the file's been modified recently) or year of last modification (if the file was last modified more than six months previously). Check out **touch** earlier in this chapter to see how files might have modification dates in the future.

To list all files in a directory:

◆ `ls -la`

Enter `ls -a` at the shell prompt to list all the files in the directory, including hidden files, with full information, as shown in **Code Listing 2.7**.

✔ Tips

■ You can hide files by giving them a name that starts with a dot (.). That is, `profile` would not be hidden, but `.profile` would be.

■ Remember, you can combine any flags to specify multiple options. For example, if you want to list all files (`-a`) in the long format (`-l`) you would use `ls -la`.

■ Try `ls -ltR` to get the complete listing of your current directory, the directories it contains, and so forth until you run out of subdirectories to descend into.

```
$ ls -la
total 22
drwxrwxr-x  3 ejr    users   1024 Jun 29 13:07 .
drwxrwx--   7 ejr    users   1024 Jun 29 12:16 ..
-rw-rw-r-   1 ejr    users   6718 Jun 29 13:00 .stats
-rw-rw-r-   1 ejr    users   2151 Jun 29 12:26 current
-rw-rw-r-   2 ejr    users   1475 Jun 29 12:35 deb.schedule
-rw-rw-r-   1 ejr    users   4567 Jun 29 12:26 new.ideas
drwxrwxr-x  2 ejr    users   1024 Jun 29 13:06 other
-rw-rw-r-   1 ejr    users   1475 Jun 29 12:22 schedule
$
```

Code Listing 2.7 If you want to see everything, use `ls -la`.

Moving Files with mv

Moving directories and files means moving them from one location (think of location as an absolute file path, like /home/ejr/aFile) in your system to another location (say, /temp/File or /home/ejr/AnotherFile). Essentially, you have only one version of a file, and you change the location of that version. For example, you might move a directory when you're reorganizing your directories and files. Or, you might move a file to rename it—that is, move a file from one name to another name.

You move directories and files using mv, as shown in **Code Listing 2.8**.

To move a file or directory:

1. ls

To begin, use ls to verify the name of the file you want to move. If you're changing the name of the file, you'll want to ensure that the new filename isn't yet in use. If you move a file to an existing filename, the contents of the old file will be replaced with the contents of the new file.

2. mv existingfile newfile

Type mv plus the existing filename and the new filename. Say goodbye to the old file and hello to the new one (**Code Listing 2.8**).

You use the same process—exactly—to move directories; just specify the directory names, as in mv ExistingDirectory NewDirectory.

3. ls

Verify that the file is now located in the location you intended.

```
$ ls
Complete      existingfile    oldfile
$ mv existingfile newfile
$ ls
Completed     newfile         oldfile
$
```

Code Listing 2.8 List files to see the current files, then use mv to rename one of the files.

✔ Tips

- You can also use mv to move files into or out of directories. For example, mv Projects/temp/testfile /home/deb/ testfile moves testfile from the Projects and temp subdirectories of the current directory to Deb's home directory, also using the name testfile.

- Use mv -i oldfilename newfilename to require the system to prompt you before overwriting (destroying) existing files. The -i is for "interactive," and it also works with the cp command.

- Visit Chapter 8 to find out about using aliases with mv so that the system always prompts you before overwriting files and you don't have to remember the -i flag.

- If you use mv and specify an existing directory as the target (as in, mv something ExistingDirectory), "something," in this case, will be placed into ExistingDirectory. "Something" can be either a file or a directory.

```
$ ls
Completed            oldfile
Newfile              soon.to.be.gone.file
$ rm -i soon.to.be.gone.file
rm: remove  'soon.to.be.gone.file'? y
$ ls
Completed    newfile  oldfile
$
```

Code Listing 2.9 Use rm -i to safely and carefully remove directories and files.

Removing Files with rm

You can easily—perhaps too easily—remove (delete) files from your Unix system. As Murphy will tell you, it's a good idea to think twice before doing this; once you remove a file, it's gone (unless, of course, you plead with your system administrator to restore it from a backup tape—but that's another story). At any rate, it's permanent, unlike deletions in Windows or the Macintosh OS, where the Recycle Bin or Trash give you a second chance.

You remove files using rm, as shown in **Code Listing 2.9**. And, as you'll see in the following steps, you can remove files one at a time or several at a time.

To remove a file:

1. ls -l

   List the files in the current folder to verify the name of the file you want to remove.

2. rm -i soon.to.be.gone.file

   At your shell prompt, type rm -i followed by the name of the file you want to remove. The -i tells the system to prompt you before removing the files (Code Listing 2.9).

3. ls

   It is gone, isn't it?

To remove multiple files:

1. `ls -l *.html`

List the files to make sure you know which files you want to remove (and not remove).

2. `rm -i *.html`

Using the asterisk wildcard (*), you can remove multiple files at one time. In this example, we remove all files in the current directory that end with `.html`. (Refer to Chapter 1, specifically the section called *Using Wildcards*, for details about using wildcards.)

Or

1. `rm -i dangerous`

Here, `-i` specifies that you'll be prompted to verify the removal of a directory or file named `dangerous` before it's removed.

2. `rm -ir dan*`

This risky command removes all of the directories or files that start with `dan` in the current directory and all of the files and subdirectories in the subdirectories starting with `dan`. If you're sure you're sure, don't use the `-i` flag to just have the files removed without prompting you for confirmation. (Remember that the flags `-ir` could also be written as `-i -r` or `-ri` or `-r -i`. Unix is rather flexible.)

✔ Tips

■ If you have system administrator rights (and are logged in as `root`, rather than with your userid), be extremely careful when using `rm`. Rather than remove merely your personal directories or files, you could potentially remove system directories and files. Scope out the sidebar called *Can You Really Screw Up the System?*

Can You Really Screw Up the System?

In general, no. When you log in to a Unix system and use your personal userid, the worst you can do is remove your own directories and files. As long as you're logged in as yourself, commands you type won't affect anything critical to the Unix system, only your own personal directories and files. Score one for Unix—as an average user, you cannot really break the system. With Windows or Macintosh, though, it can be different story.

If you have system administrator rights, meaning that you can log in as `root` (giving you access to all the system directories and files), you can do a lot of damage if you're not extremely careful. For this reason, don't log in as `root` unless you absolutely have to.

See Chapter 3 for information about `su`, which can help reduce the risk of being logged in as `root`.

■ This is a good time to remind you to use the handy cp command to make backup copies of anything you value—before you experiment too much with rm. Even if the system administrator keeps good backups, it's ever so much easier if you keep an extra copy of your goodies sitting around. Try cp -r . backup-files for a space-hogging—but effective—means of making a quick backup of everything in the current directory into the backup-files directory. (Just ignore the error message about not copying a directory into itself—the system will do the right thing for you, and you don't have to worry about it.)

■ We suggest using rm -i, at least until you're sure you're comfortable with irrevocable deletions. The -i flag prompts you to verify your command before it's executed.

■ Visit Chapter 8 to find out about using aliases with rm so that the system always prompts you before removing the directories or files even if you forget the -i flag.

■ If you accidentally end up with a file that has a problematic filename (like one that starts with -, which looks to Unix like a command flag, not a filename), you can delete it (with a trick). Use rm -i - -badfilename to get rid of it.

REMOVING FILES WITH rm

Removing Directories with `rmdir`

Another handy thing you can do is to remove directories using `rmdir`. Think of removing directories as trimming branches on a tree. That is, you can't be sitting on the branch you want to trim off. You have to sit on the next closest branch; otherwise, you'll fall to the ground along with the branch you trim off. Ouch! Similarly, when you remove a directory, you must not be located in the directory you want to remove.

You must remove a directory's contents (all subdirectories and files) before you remove the directory itself. In doing so, you can verify what you're removing and avoid accidentally removing important stuff. In the following steps (illustrated in **Code Listing 2.10**), we'll show you how to remove a directory's contents, then remove the directory itself.

```
$ cd /home/ejr/Yourdirectory
$ ls -la
total 7
drwxrwxr-x     2 ejr     users        1024 Jun 29 20:59 .
drwxrwx--     8 ejr     users        1024 Jun 29 20:59 ..
-rw-rw-r-     1 ejr     users        1475 Jun 29 20:59 cancelled.project.notes
-rw-rw-r-     1 ejr     users        2876 Jun 29 20:59 outdated.contact.info
$ rm *
$ cd ..
$ rmdir Yourdirectory
$ ls
Newdirectory      all.programs.txt      newer.programs        short.fortunes
Projects          files                 newest.programs       temp
Xrootenv.0        fortunes              newstuff              touching
all.programs local.programs.txt schedule
$
```

Code Listing 2.10 Removing directories with `rmdir` can be a little tedious — but better safe than sorry.

To remove a directory:

1. `cd /home/ejr/Yourdirectory`

   To begin, change to that directory by typing **cd** plus the name of the directory you want to remove.

2. `ls -a`

   List all (**-a**) of the files, including any hidden files that might be present, in the directory, and make sure you don't need any of them. If you see only . and .. (which indicate the current directory and its parent directory), you can skip ahead to step 4.

3. Do one or both of these:

   ▲ If you have hidden files in the directory, type **rm .* *** to delete those files plus all of the rest of the files.

   ▲ If you have subdirectories in the directory, type **cd** and the subdirectory name, essentially repeating the process starting with step 1. Repeat this process until you remove all subdirectories.

   When you finish this step, you should have a completely empty directory, ready to be removed.

4. `cd ..`

   Use the change directory command again to move up one level, to the parent of the directory that you want to remove.

5. `rmdir Yourdirectory`

   There it goes—wave goodbye to the directory! See Code Listing 2.10 for the whole sequence.

✔ Tips

- You can remove multiple directories at one time. Assuming you're starting with empty directories, just list them like this:
  `rmdir Yourdirectory Yourotherdirectory OtherDirectory`

- As an alternative to `rmdir`, you can remove a directory and all of its contents at once using `rm` with the `-r` flag; for example, `rm -r Directoryname`. Be careful, though! This method automatically removes the directory and everything in it, so you won't have the opportunity to examine everything you remove beforehand. If you're getting asked for confirmation before deleting each file and you're really, absolutely, positively, completely sure that you're doing the right thing, use `rm -rf Directoryname` to force immediate deletion.

- If you're getting comfortable with long command strings, you can specify commands with a complete directory path as in `ls /home/ejr/DirectorytoGo` or `rm /home/ejr/DirectorytoGo/*`. This technique is particularly good if you want to be absolutely sure that you're deleting the right directory, and not a directory with the same name in a different place on the system.

Finding Forgotten Files with `find`

Where, oh where, did that file go? Sometimes finding a file requires more than cursing at your computer or listing directory contents with `ls`. Instead, you can use the `find` command, which lets you search in dozens of ways, including through the entire directory tree (**Code Listing 2.11**) or through directories you specify (**Code Listing 2.12**).

To find a file:

◆ `find . -name lostfile -print`

Along with the `find` command, this specifies to start in the current directory with a dot (.), provide the filename (`-name lostfile`), and specify that the results be printed onscreen (`-print`). See Code Listing 2.11.

To find files starting in a specific directory:

◆ `find /home/deb -name 'pending*'`
  `→ -print`

This command finds all of the files with names starting with `pending` under Deb's home directory. You must use single quotes if you include a wildcard to search for.

Or, you can find files under multiple directories at one time, like this:

◆ `find /home/deb /home/ejr -name`
  `→ 'pending*' -print`

This command finds files with names starting with `pending` in Deb's and Eric's home directories or any subdirectories under them (Code Listing 2.12).

```
$ find . -name lostfile -print
./Projects/schedule/lostfile
$
```

Code Listing 2.11 Use `find` to locate a missing file.

```
$ find /home/deb -name 'pending*' -print
/home/deb/Projects/schedule/pending.tasks
$ find /home/deb /home/ejr -name
→ 'pending*' -print
/home/deb/Projects/schedule/pending.tasks
/home/ejr/pending.jobs.to.do.today.to.do
$
```

Code Listing 2.12 By using wildcards and specifying multiple directories, you can make `find` yet more powerful.

To find and act on files:

◆ find ~/ -name '*.backup' -ok rm {} \;
Type find with a wildcard expression,
followed by -ok (to execute the following
command, with confirmation), rm (the
command to issue), and {} \; to fill
in each file found as an *argument* (an
additional piece of information) for the
command. If you want to, say, compress
matching files without confirmation,
you might use find ~/ -name '*.backup'
-exec compress {} \; to do the work
for you.

✔ Tips

■ On some Unix systems, you may not need
the -print flag. Try entering find without the -print flag. If you see the results
onscreen, then you don't need to add the
-print flag.

■ Avoid starting the find command with
the root directory, as in find / -name
the.missing.file -print. In starting
with the root directory (indicated by the
/), you'll likely encounter a pesky error
message for each directory you don't
have access to, and there will be a lot of
those. Of course, if you're logged in as
root, this doesn't apply.

■ If you know only part of the filename,
you can use quoted wildcards with find,
as in find . -name 'info*' -print.

■ find offers many chapters worth of
options. If you're looking for a specific file
or files based on any characteristics, you
can find them with find. For example,
you can use find /home/shared -mtime
-3 to find all files under the shared directory that were modified within the last
three days. See Appendix C for a substan-
tial (but not comprehensive) listing
of options.

FINDING FORGOTTEN FILES WITH find

Locating Lost Files with locate

If you're looking for a system file—that is, a program or file that is part of the Unix system itself, rather than one of your personal files in your home directory—try locate to find it. You'll get more results than you can handle, but it's a quick and easy way to locate system files.

The locate command isn't available on all Unix systems, but it is worth a try at any rate. See **Code Listing 2.13** for locate in action.

To locate a file:

◆ locate fortune

If you try to locate fortune, you'll get a listing of all of the system files that contain "fortune" in them. This listing includes the fortune program, fortune data files for the fortune program to use, and related stuff. It's a huge list in most cases (Code Listing 2.13).

✔ Tips

■ Use locate in combination with grep (see *Using Regular Expressions with grep* in Chapter 6) to narrow down your list, if possible.

■ Many people use locate to get a quick look at the directories that contain relevant files (/usr/share/games/fortunes contains a lot of files related to the fortune program), then other tools to take a closer look.

■ Not all systems include fortune—it's certainly just a fun thing and not essential by any means. If you don't "locate" it, try bash or csh to see how locate works. (See Chapter 8 for more information about different shells and their benefits and drawbacks.)

```
[jdoe@frazz jdoe]$ locate fortune
/usr/share/man/man6/fortune.6.bz2
/usr/share/doc/fortune-mod-1.0
/usr/share/doc/fortune-mod-1.0/cs
/usr/share/doc/fortune-mod-1.0/cs/
→ HISTORIE
/usr/share/doc/fortune-mod-1.0/cs/LICENSE
/usr/share/doc/fortune-mod-1.0/cs/README
/usr/share/doc/fortune-mod-1.0/fr
/usr/share/doc/fortune-mod-1.0/fr/
→ COPYING.linuxfr
/usr/share/doc/fortune-mod-1.0/fr/
→ COPYING.glp
/usr/share/doc/fortune-mod-1.0/fr/ffr

...

/usr/share/games/fortunes/songs-poems
/usr/share/games/fortunes/sports.dat
/usr/share/games/fortunes/sports
/usr/share/games/fortunes/startrek.dat
/usr/share/games/fortunes/startrek
/usr/share/games/fortunes/translate-me.dat
/usr/share/games/fortunes/translate-me
/usr/share/games/fortunes/wisdom.dat
/usr/share/games/fortunes/wisdom
/usr/share/games/fortunes/work.dat
/usr/share/games/fortunes/work
/usr/share/games/fortunes/zippy.dat
/usr/share/games/fortunes/zippy
/usr/share/sol-games/fortunes.scm
/usr/games/fortune
[jdoe@frazz jdoe]$
```

Code Listing 2.13 Use locate to find everything— *everything*—related to most system files.

Linking with `ln` (Hard Links)

Suppose your boss just hired an assistant for you ('bout time, right?). You'll need to make sure your new helper can access your files so you can pawn off your work on him. And, you'll need to access the revised files just so you can keep up with what your helper's been doing—and perhaps take credit for his work at the next staff meeting.

A great way to give your helper easy access to your files is to create a *hard link* from your home directory. In making a hard link, all you're doing is starting with an existing file and creating a link, which (sort of) places the existing file in your helper's home directory. The link does not create a copy of the file; instead, you're creating a second pointer to the same physical file on the disk. Rather than the additional pointer being secondary (like an alias or shortcut in Macintosh or Windows computers), both of the pointers reference the same actual file, so from the perspective of the Unix system, the file actually resides in two locations (**Code Listing 2.14**).

Because using hard links often requires that you have access to another user's home directory, you might venture to Chapter 5 for details about using chmod, chgrp, and chown to access another user's directories and files.

```
$ ls /home/deb/Projects/schedule/our* /home/helper/our*
ls: /home/helper/our*: No such file or directory
/home/deb/Projects/schedule/our.projects.latest
/home/deb/Projects/schedule/our.projects.other
$ ln /home/deb/Projects/schedule/our.projects.latest /home/helper/our.projects
$ ls -l /home/helper/o*
-rw-r--r--   3 ejr      users       1055 Jun 26 11:00 /home/helper/our.projects
$
```

Code Listing 2.14 Hard links let two users easily share files.

To make a hard link:

1. `ls -l /home/deb/Projects/schedule/`
   `→ our* /home/helper/our*`

   To begin, list the files in both directories to make sure that the file to link exists and that there's no other file with the intended name in the target directory. Here, we list the files that start with `our` in both `/home/deb/Projects/schedule` and in `/home/helper`. In this example, we're verifying that the file does exist in Deb's directory and that no matching files were found in the helper's directory (**Code Listing 2.14**).

2. `ln /home/deb/Projects/schedule/`
   `→ our.projects.latest`
   `→ /home/helper/our.projects`

   Here, `ln` creates a new file with a similar name in the helper's home directory and links the two files together, essentially making the same file exist in two home directories.

3. `ls -l /home/helper/o*`

   With this code, your helper can verify that the file exists by listing files that begin with `o*`.

   Now the file exists in two places with exactly the same content. Either user can modify the file, and the content in both locations will change.

✔ Tips

■ You can remove hard links just like you remove regular files, by using `rm` plus the filename. See the section called *Removing Files with rm* in this chapter.

■ If one user removes the file, the other user can still access the file from his or her directory.

■ Hard links work from file to file only within the same file system. To link directories or to link across file systems, you'll have to use soft links, which are covered in the next section.

■ If you're sneaky, you can use hard links to link directories, not just files. Make a new directory where you want the linked directory to be, and then use `ln /home/whoever/existingdirectory/* /home/you/newdirectory/` to hard link all of the files in the old directory to the new directory. New files won't be linked automatically, but you could use a `cron` job to refresh the links periodically—say, daily. See Chapter 9 for `cron` details.

Linking with `ln -s` (Soft Links)

Now suppose you want to pawn off your entire workload on your new helper. Rather than just give him access to a single file, you'll want to make it easy for him to access your entire project directory. You can do this using soft links (created with `ln -s`), which essentially provide other users with a shortcut to the file or directory you specify.

Like hard links, *soft links* allow a file to be in more than one place at a time; however, with soft links, there's only one copy of it and, with soft links, you can link directories as well. The linked file or directory is dependent on the original one—that is, if the original file or directory is deleted, the linked file or directory will no longer be available.

Soft links are particularly handy because they work for directories as well as individual files, and they work across different file systems (that is, not just within /home, but anywhere on the Unix system).

Like hard links, soft links sometimes require that you have access to another user's directory and files. See Chapter 5 for more on file permissions and ownership and Chapter 7 for the lowdown on file systems.

To make a soft link:

1. `ls -l /home/deb /home/helper`

To begin, list the contents of both users' home directories. Here, we're verifying that the directory we want to link does exist in Deb's directory and that no matching directories or files exist in the helper's directory. See **Code Listing 2.15**.

2. `ln -s /home/deb/Projects/`
`→ /home/helper/Project`

This command creates a soft link so the contents of Deb's home directory can also be easily accessed from the helper's home directory.

3. `ls -la /home/helper`

Listing the contents of `/home/helper` shows the existence of the soft link to the directory. Notice the arrow showing the link in Code Listing 2.15.

✔ Tip

- If you only need to create a link between two files within the same file system, consider using hard links, as discussed in the previous section, *Linking with ln (Hard Links)*.

```
$ ls /home/deb /home/helper
/home/deb:
Projects

/home/helper:
our.projects
$ ln -s /home/deb/Projects /home/helper/Projects
$ ls -la /home/helper/
total 11
d-wxrwx--    2 helper    users    1024 Jun 29 21:18 .
drwxr-xr-x  11 root      root     1024 Jun 29 21:03 ..
-rw-rwxr-    1 helper    users    3768 Jun 29 21:03 .Xdefaults
-rw-rwxr-    1 helper    users      24 Jun 29 21:03 .bash_logout
-rw-rwxr-    1 helper    users     220 Jun 29 21:03 .bash_profile
-rw-rwxr-    1 helper    users     124 Jun 29 21:03 .bashrc
lrwxrwxrwx   1 ejr       users      18 Jun 29 21:18 Projects -> /home/deb/Projects
-rw-rwxr-    3 ejr       users    1055 Jun 26 11:00 our.projects
$
```

Code Listing 2.15 Use `ln -s` to make soft links and connect directories.

WORKING WITH YOUR SHELL

3

When you access a Unix system, the first thing you see is the prompt, called the *shell prompt*, which is where you interact with Unix. The shell determines how easily you can enter and reenter commands and how you can control your environment. What's cool about Unix is that you're not stuck with one shell—that is, on most systems you can choose to use shells that have different features and capabilities.

In this chapter, we'll look at your shell, show you how to change your shell, and get you started using a few of the more common shells.

Chapter Contents

- Discovering which shell you're using
- Understanding shells and options
- Changing your shell
- Changing your shell temporarily
- Using completion in the bash shell
- Viewing session history in the bash shell
- Using completion in the zsh shell
- Viewing session history in the zsh shell
- Using completion in the ksh shell
- Viewing session history in the ksh shell
- Viewing session history in the csh shell
- Changing your identity
- Fixing terminal settings
- Exiting the shell

Discovering What Shell You're Using

When you first log in to your Unix account, you'll be using the default shell on your system. The default shell, its features, and its options depend completely on what your system administrator specifies. **Code Listings 3.1** and **3.2** show examples of how default shell prompts differ on two different systems.

To discover what shell you're using:

◆ echo $SHELL

At your shell prompt, type echo $SHELL (capitalization counts!). This command tells Unix to display (echo) information about shell settings. This information, by the way, is contained in one of the environment variables, so the technical phrasing (which you might hear in Unix circles) is to "echo your shell environment variable."

The system's response will be the full path to your shell—something like /bin/csh, /bin/bash, or /bin/ksh.

✔ Tips

■ You can also use finger userid, substituting your login name for userid, to find out more about your shell settings. You can substitute any other userid and see comparable information about the other account holders. See Chapter 7 for more about finger. (Some systems do not support finger, because finger can be a bit of a security hole.)

■ You'll find more information about different shells and their capabilities throughout this chapter.

```
xmission> echo $SHELL
/bin/csh
xmission> finger ejray
Login name: ejray      In real life:
"RayComm
Directory: /home/users/e/ejray      Shell:
 → /bin/csh
On since Jul 23 06:58:48 on pts/16 from
 → calvin.raycomm.com
1 minute 28 seconds Idle Time
No unread mail
No Plan.
xmission>
```

Code Listing 3.1 This ISP account uses the /bin/csh shell by default.

```
[ejr@hobbes ejr]$ echo $SHELL
/bin/bash
[ejr@hobbes ejr]$ finger ejr
Login: ejr        Name: Eric J. Ray
Directory: /home/ejr      Shell: /bin/bash
On since Wed Jul 22 07:42 (MDT) on tty1
 → 3 hours 15 minutes idle
On since Thu Jul 23 08:17 (MDT) on ttyp0
 → from calvin
No mail.
Project:
Working on UNIX VQS.
Plan:
This is my plan—work all day, sleep all
 → night.
[ejr@hobbes ejr]$
```

Code Listing 3.2 On hobbes, a Linux system, the default shell is /bin/bash.

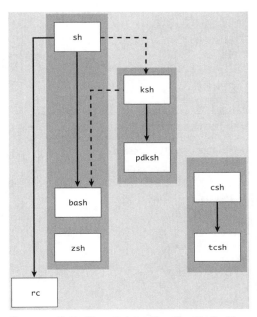

Figure 3.1 Shells fit neatly into a few "families" with the exception of a few stragglers. Each shell in a family shares many characteristics with the others in the same family.

Understanding Shells and Options

Depending on the particular Unix system you're using, you may have several shells available to you. **Table 3.1** describes a few of the more common ones. Each of these shells has slightly different capabilities and features. Keep in mind that the differences in shells do not affect what you can do in Unix; rather, they affect how easily and flexibly you can interact with the system.

You'll likely have bash, ksh, or tcsh (csh) as your shell, but you can change to one of many other shells fairly easily. As **Code Listings 3.3** and **3.4** show, you can start by finding out which shells are available to you. **Figure 3.1** shows some shells and how they relate to each other.

Table 3.1

Common Unix Shells	
SHELL NAME	FEATURES
sh	This shell, which is the original Unix shell (often called the Bourne shell), is fine for scripting but lacks a lot of the flexibility and power for interactive use. For example, it doesn't have features like command completion, email checking, history, or aliasing.
csh and tcsh	This family of shells adds great interactive uses but discards the popular scripting support that sh-related shells offer in favor of a C programming-like syntax. Because of the C syntax, this shell is often just called the C shell. Unless you're a C programmer, these are not likely to be your best choices.
ksh, bash, and zsh	These provide a good blend of scripting and interactive capabilities, but they stem from different sources (bash is most similar to sh, hence the Bourne Again SHell name).

To see which shells are available to you:

◆ `cat /etc/shells`

At the shell prompt, type `cat /etc/shells` to find out which shells are available to you. **Code Listings 3.4** and **3.5** show the results of this command on two different systems.

✔ Tips

- Before you go leaping forward through the next sections and changing your shell, you might check with your system administrator or help desk to find out which shells they support and sanction.

- If all else is equal in terms of support from your system administrator or help desk, and you have no clear preference, we'd suggest **zsh** as a first choice, with **bash** as a close second. For most purposes, either will be fine. Power users will like **zsh** better in the long run.

- Not all systems use /etc/shells to list acceptable shells--you may have to just look for specific shells, as shown later in this chapter.

```
[ejr@hobbes]$ more /etc/shells
/bin/bash
/bin/sh
/bin/tcsh
/bin/csh
[ejr@hobbes]$
```

Code Listing 3.3 A minimal listing of available shells on a Unix system, including the basics but not too much in the way of choices.

```
xmission> cat /etc/shells
/usr/local/bin/tcsh
/bin/csh
/usr/bin/csh
/bin/ksh
/usr/bin/ksh
/sbin/sh
/usr/bin/sh
/usr/local/bin/zsh
/usr/local/bin/bash
/usr/local/bin/nologin
/usr/local/bin/terminated
/usr/local/bin/xmmenu.email
/usr/local/bin/xmmenu.noshell
/usr/lib/uucp/uucico
xmission>
```

Code Listing 3.4 These shells are available through an ISP. Notice the additional, custom shells that this ISP uses, including shells that provide special features such as not allowing logins.

```
[ejr@hobbes ejr]$ cat /etc/shells
/bin/bash
/bin/sh
/bin/tcsh
/bin/csh
/bin/zsh
[ejr@hobbes ejr]$ chsh
Changing shell for ejr.
Password:
New shell [/bin/bash]: /bin/zsh
Shell changed.
ejr@hobbes ~ $
ejr@hobbes ~ $ su - ejr
Password:
ejr@hobbes ~ $
```

Code Listing 3.5 You must remember the path to the shell to change shells on this system. Additionally, the password check helps ensure that only the account owner changes the shell.

Changing Your Shell with chsh

If you decide that you want to change your shell, you probably can, depending on how your system administrator has set things up. As Code Listing 3.5 shows, you would do so using chsh. We usually change to bash.

To change your shell with chsh:

1. `cat /etc/shells`

    At the shell prompt, list the available shells on your system with `cat /etc/shells`.

2. `chsh`

    Enter chsh (for "change shell"). Code Listing 3.5 shows the system response. Some systems prompt for a password, and some don't.

3. `/bin/zsh`

    Type in the path and name of your new shell.

4. `su - yourid`

    Type in su - and your userid to relog in to verify that everything works correctly. If it doesn't, use chsh again and change back to the original shell or to a different one. If you can't change back, email your system administrator for help.

continues on next page

CHANGING YOUR SHELL WITH chsh

✔ Tips

- After changing shells, you might have problems running some commands or have a prompt or display that's not as good as the original. That's likely a result of your default shell being carefully customized by your system administrator. You're probably on your own to set up and configure your new shell, and Chapter 8 can help you do this.

- Some systems don't let users use chsh to change shells. If this is the case, you'll need to email your system administrator and ask for a change, or see if there are alternative methods, as shown in **Figure 3.2**. You could also change your shell temporarily, as described in the next section.

- See *Changing Your Identity with su* later in this chapter for more about the su command.

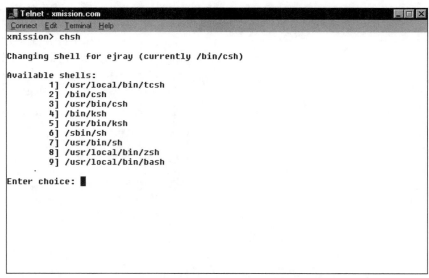

Figure 3.2 Some ISPs provide a handy interface for changing shells that lets users pick their new shells from a menu, like this one.

```
[ejr@hobbes]$ cat /etc/shells
/bin/bash
/bin/sh
/bin/tcsh
/bin/csh
[ejr@hobbes]$ ls /usr/local/bin/*sh
/usr/local/bin/pdksh
[ejr@hobbes]$
```

Code Listing 3.6 Checking the list of shells from /etc/shells and looking for other programs that end with "sh" is a good way to find all of the shells on the system.

```
[ejr@hobbes]$ /usr/bin/csh
ejr>
```

Code Listing 3.7 Type in the shell name (which is really just another Unix command) to change shells.

Changing Your Shell Temporarily

You can change your shell temporarily by creating a subshell and using that instead of the original shell. You can create a subshell using any shell available on your Unix system. This means that you can look in the /etc/shells file and use a shell listed there, or you can use a shell installed elsewhere on the system (**Code Listing 3.6**).

To find out which temporary shells you can use:

1. `cat /etc/shells`

   At the shell prompt, type `cat /etc/shells` to find out which shells are listed in the shells file.

   If you don't find a shell you want to use in the shells file, look for other shells installed elsewhere on the system.

2. `ls /usr/local/bin/*sh`

   At the shell prompt, type `ls /usr/local/bin/*sh` to find additional shells in the /usr/local/bin directory. Note that not all programs that end with sh are shells, but most shells end with sh (Code Listing 3.6).

To create a temporary shell (subshell):

◆ `/usr/bin/csh`

   At the shell prompt, type the path and name of the temporary shell you want to use. In this case, we're using the csh shell, located at /usr/bin/csh. You might see a new prompt, perhaps something like the one shown in **Code Listing 3.7**.

To exit a temporary shell (subshell):

◆ `exit`

At the shell prompt, type `exit`. You'll be returned to the shell from which you started the subshell. If you created more than one subshell, you'll have to exit all of them.

✔ Tips

■ Using temporary shells is a great way to experiment with other shells and their options. We'd recommend using a temporary shell to experiment with the shells covered in this chapter.

■ You can also often use Ctrl D to exit from a subshell, but this depends on the system configuration. Try it out and see.

■ See Chapter 1, specifically the listings of directories containing programs, for other places to look for shells.

```
bash-2.00$ ls
Complete NewProject bogus2
 → ftp   puppy
Completed   News   dead.letter
 → mail temp
Mail access files
 → public_html  testme
bash-2.00$ cd public_html/
bash-2.00$
```

Code Listing 3.8 In this example, we typed only the ls command followed by "cd pub" and pressed the Tab key; bash completed the command for us.

Using Completion in the bash **Shell**

One of the cool features of the bash shell is *command argument completion*, with which you can type just part of a command, press Tab, and have bash complete the command for you (**Code Listing 3.8**).

To use completion in the bash shell:

1. ls -l

   Use ls -l to list the files in your current directory.

2. cd pub Tab

   Type in a partial command, then press Tab to complete the command. In this example, we typed the cd command and part of the public_html directory (truncated to pub in the example), then pressed Tab to complete it (see Code Listing 3.8).

✔ Tips

- Completion works only if there's just one possible match to the letters you type before you hit Tab. For example, if you type cd pu (for public_html) and there's another subdirectory called puppy, the shell will beep and wait for you to type in enough letters to distinguish the two subdirectories.

- You can use completion to complete commands, directory names within commands, and nearly anything else you might enter that's sufficiently unambiguous.

Viewing Session History in the bash Shell

Another cool feature of the bash shell is that it lets you easily reuse commands from your session history, which shows you the list of commands you've used during a session or in previous sessions (**Code Listing 3.9**). Viewing history is handy for reviewing your Unix session, using previous commands again (rather than retyping them), and modifying (rather than completely retyping) complex commands.

To view session history in the bash shell:

1. Use the shell for a little while, changing directories, redirecting output, or doing other tasks.

   Take your time. We'll wait.

2. Press ⬆ one time.

   Note that the last (previous) command you used appears on the command line, as shown in Code Listing 3.9. To reissue the command, just press Enter.

3. Continue to press ⬆ or ⬇ to scroll back or forward through your history. When you reach a command you want to use, press Enter.

   If you see a command that's close, but not exactly what you want to use, you can edit it. Just use the ⬅ and ➡ keys to move across the line, insert text by typing it in, and use Backspace or Delete to delete text. When you've fixed the command, press Enter (you don't have to be at the end of the line to do so).

4. history

   Type history at the shell prompt to see a numbered list of previous commands you've entered.

```
[ejr@hobbes clean]$ ls
background.htm  info.htm      logo.gif
[ejr@hobbes clean]$ ls
background.htm  info.htm       logo.gif
[ejr@hobbes clean]$ history
    1  free
    2  id deb
    3  id ejr
    4  uname -a
    5  ls

...

   40  cd
   41  cp .bash_history oldhistory
   42  vi .bash_history
   43  elm
   44  ls -la
   45  ls -la .e*
   46  elm
   47  lynx
   48  history
   49  vi .bash*his*
   50  history
   51  cd clean
   52  ls
   53  ls
   54  history
[ejr@hobbes clean]$ !40
cd
[ejr@hobbes ejr]$
```

Code Listing 3.9 In this example, we typed the first command, then pressed ⬆ to reuse the previous ls command. !40 recycled the 40th command from the listing.

VIEWING SESSION HISTORY IN THE bash SHELL

✔ Tips

■ Commands from the current session are kept in memory to scroll through, while commands from previous sessions are kept in the ~/.bash_history file. You can edit .bash_history with any editor to delete unneeded commands or simply delete the file to get rid of the whole history file, which will then be re-created with the next command you issue. (A history of commands is a great jumping-off point to write a script to do the commands automatically. Chapter 10 gives you the specifics.)

■ When you're viewing the history, you can recycle commands by typing an exclamation point (!) and the line number of the command you want to run again. You'd type !40, for example, to rerun command 40.

■ Use history followed by a number to specify the number of items to list. For example, history 10 shows the last 10 commands.

VIEWING SESSION HISTORY IN THE bash SHELL

Using Completion in the zsh Shell

The zsh shell also offers completion but with added twists over the bash shell for the power user. Basically, though, you can type just part of a command, press Tab, and have the Z-shell complete the command for you (**Code Listing 3.10**).

To use completion in the zsh shell:

1. ls -l

   Use ls -l to list the files in your current directory.

2. cd pub Tab

   Type in a partial command, and then press Tab to complete the command. In this example, we typed the cd command and part of the public_html directory (truncated to pub in the example), and then pressed the Tab key to complete it (see Code Listing 3.10).

✔ Tips

- In the Z-shell, command completion works even if multiple files might match the partial command that you type. For example, if you type cd pu (for public_html) and there's another subdirectory called puppy, then use Tab to complete the name, the shell will show you the options (public_html and puppy), then cycle through the options as you continue hitting Tab.

- You can use command completion to complete commands, directory names within commands, and nearly anything else you might enter.

- The Z-shell is smart enough to show you only the subdirectories you could change to. bash, on the other hand, would show you files and directories, and beep at you— not as helpful, for sure.

```
$ ls
Complete NewProject bogus2
 → ftp    puppy
Completed   News    dead.letter
 → mail  temp
Mail access files
 → public_html  testme
$ cd public_html/
$
```

Code Listing 3.10 In this example, we typed only the ls command followed by cd pub and pressed the Tab key; zsh completed the command for us.

```
[ejr@hobbes clean]$ ls
background.htm  info.htm      logo.gif
[ejr@hobbes clean]$ ls
background.htm  info.htm      logo.gif
[ejr@hobbes clean]$ history
    1  free
    2  id deb
    3  id ejr
    4  uname -a
    5  ls

...

   40  cd
   41  cp .bash_history oldhistory
   42  vi .bash_history
   43  elm
   44  ls -la
   45  ls -la .e*
   46  elm
   47  lynx
   48  history
   49  vi .bash*his*
   50  history
   51  cd clean
   52  ls
   53  ls
   54  history
[ejr@hobbes clean]$ !40
cd
[ejr@hobbes ejr]$
```

Code Listing 3.11 In this example, we typed the first command, and then pressed the ↑ to reuse the previous command. !40 recycled the 40th command from the listing.

Viewing Session History in the zsh Shell

The Z-shell also lets you easily reuse commands from your session history, which is the list of commands you've used during a session or in previous sessions (**Code Listing 3.11**). The history functions are handy for reviewing your Unix session, reusing previous commands (instead of retyping), and modifying (rather than completely redoing) long or complex commands.

To view session history in the zsh shell:

1. Use zsh as you usually would, changing directories, redirecting output, or doing other tasks. For example, review the previous chapter and practice the commands you've learned so far.

2. Press ↑ one time.
   Note that the last (previous) command you used appears on the command line, as shown in Code Listing 3.11. To reissue the command, just press Enter.

3. Continue to press ↑ or ↓ to scroll back or forward through your history. When you reach a command you want to use, press Enter.
   If you see a command that's close, but not exactly what you want to use, you can edit it. Just use ← and → to move across the line. Then, insert text by typing it in or using Backspace or Delete to delete text. When you've modified the command, press Enter (you don't have to be at the end of the line to do so).

4. Type history at the shell prompt to see a numbered list of previous commands you've entered.

continues on next page

✔ Tips

- If you have just a minor change to a command, you can edit it quickly and easily. For example, if you just used `ls /home/users/e/eric` and wanted to issue `cd /home/users/e/eric` next, you could just type `^cd^ls` to tell the system to replace `cd` from the previous command with `ls` and then reissue the command.

- You can use Ctrl A and Ctrl E while editing a command line to move to the beginning and end of the line, respectively.

- Commands from the current session are kept in memory to scroll through, while commands from previous sessions are kept in the `~/.zsh_history` file. You can edit `.zsh_history` with any editor to delete unneeded commands or simply delete the file to get rid of the whole history file, which will then be re-created with the next command you issue.

- Reviewing session history is a great way to identify your work patterns and needs. If you find yourself repeatedly using the same series of commands, consider writing a script to do the commands automatically, as Chapter 10 describes.

- Most of the command completion options from **bash** also work in **zsh**. Give it a try!

```
$ ls
Complete NewProject bogus2 files
 → public_html  testme
Completed   News   chat.conf
 → ftp   puppy
Mail access dead.letter
 → mail  temp
$ cd pub^[^[
ksh: pub: not found
$ set -o emacs
$ cd public_html/
$
```

Code Listing 3.12 After listing the files and directories, we set our options, then successfully completed a command. The ^[^[is how (Esc) appears on the screen when the shell doesn't know to use it to complete commands.

✔ Tips

- If you don't have ksh installed on your system, you might also look for pdksh, which is a freely distributable and nearly identical version of ksh.

- You can also type in set -o vi to use vi commands (instead of the command given in step 1). We've found, though, that this isn't as intuitive or effective, so we recommend the emacs mode.

- See Chapter 4 for more information about editors.

- If you use ksh, you'll probably want to add the set -o emacs command to your personal configuration files so you don't have to manually enter the command in each session. See Chapter 8 for the specifics of editing configuration files.

Using Completion in the ksh Shell

ksh is another shell that offers command completion. You type part of a command, press (Esc) twice, and ksh completes the command for you (see **Code Listing 3.12**). Using command completion in ksh isn't as easy as it is in zsh or bash, but the results are the same.

To use completion in the ksh shell:

1. set -o emacs

   To begin, you must enable command completion by entering set -o emacs. This command enables command completion and sets it to use emacs commands. (Emacs is an editor, but you do not need to use or be familiar with it to recycle ksh commands.)

2. ls -l

   Use ls -l to list the files in your current directory. You do this so you know which directory (public_html) you can change to in step 3.

3. cd pub (Esc)(Esc)

   Type in a partial command.

   In this example, we typed the cd command and part of the public_html command (truncated to pub).

   Press (Esc) two times to complete the command. (Depending on your terminal emulation, you might need to use (Ctrl)([) twice instead of (Esc) twice.)

Viewing Session History in the ksh Shell

Using ksh, you can also view session history. In doing so, you can get a quick reminder of what you've been doing (**Code Listing 3.13**), reuse commands, and modify commands you've already used.

```
$ ls
Complete        NewProject          bogus2          files       public_html     testme
Completed       News                chat.conf       ftp         puppy
Mail            access              dead.letter     mail        temp
$ ls
Complete        NewProject          bogus2          files       public_html     testme
Completed       News                chat.conf       ftp         puppy
Mail            access              dead.letter     mail        temp
$
$ history
56              cd ..
57              ls
58              lynx
59              ls temp
60              more Complete
61              ls
62              more testme
63              ls
64              ls
65              history
66              lynx
67              ftp ftp.raycomm.com
68              ls
69              ls
70              ls
71              history
$ r 64
ls
Complete        NewProject          bogus2          files       public_html     testme
Completed       News                chat.conf       ftp         puppy
Mail            access              dead.letter     mail        temp
$
```

Code Listing 3.13 Although it looks like we typed ls for both the first and second commands, we really just pressed Ctrl P to get the second ls command. The r 64 command recycles the command numbered 64 in the list.

Table 3.2

ksh **History Navigation Commands**

COMMAND	FUNCTION
Ctrl P	Recalls the previous command
Ctrl N	Recalls the next command (works only after you've moved to a previous command)
Ctrl R *something*	Gets the previous command containing "something"
Ctrl B	Moves back one character within a command
Ctrl F	Moves forward one character within a command
Ctrl A	Goes to the beginning of the line within a command
Ctrl E	Goes to the end of the line within a command
Ctrl D	Deletes the current character

To view session history in the ksh shell:

1. `set -o emacs`

   To begin, you must enter `set -o emacs`. This command enables history reuse and command completion, and sets the shell to use `emacs` commands. (Emacs is an editor, but you do not need to use or be familiar with it for now.) If you've already done this during your current session, you don't need to do it again.

2. Use the shell for a little while, changing directories, redirecting output, or doing other tasks.

3. Ctrl P

   Recall the previous command with Ctrl P. **Table 3.2** shows you other keyboard combinations that you can use to navigate through the session history.

   After you've finished recalling and, optionally, editing the command, press Enter (you don't have to be at the end of the line to do so).

4. `history`

   Type `history` at the shell prompt to see the list of the most recent commands you've entered (Code Listing 3.13).

   Notice the command number by each command. You can type R Spacebar and the command's number to rerun it.

✔ Tip

- If you use ksh, you'll probably want to add the `set -o emacs` command to your personal configuration files so you don't have to manually enter the command in each session. See Chapter 8 for the specifics of editing configuration files.

Viewing Session History in the csh Shell

If you're a C programmer (or have C programmers to turn to for help), csh might be a good shell for you because the syntax is quite similar to the C programming language. csh doesn't offer command completion, but the history capabilities are fairly similar to those of bash or zsh (see **Code Listing 3.14**). In general, csh is a powerful scripting shell (and acceptable interactive shell) for those who take the time and effort to become familiar with it.

To view session history in the csh shell:

1. If you haven't already, use the shell for a little while, changing directories, redirecting output, or doing other tasks.

2. history

   Type history at the shell prompt to see the list of the most recent commands you've entered. Note the number of each command line (Code Listing 3.14).

3. !10

   Type ! followed by the command number (no space in between) to rerun one of the commands. In this example, we're rerunning command 10.

✔ Tips

- See Chapter 8 for how to make csh easier and more productive, particularly if you don't have any other shell options available to you.

- You can edit commands in the session history. With csh, however, it's far easier to retype the commands than to edit them.

```
xmission> history
     1  ls
     2  vi temp.info
     3  ls
     4  cd pub*
     5  ls
     6  cp *.pdf ..
     7  cd ..
     8  rm *.pdf
     9  history
    10  lynx
    11  ftp ftp.wustl.edu
    12  ls
    13  vi .plan
    14  finger ejr@raycomm.com
    15  history
    16  finger ejr@hobbes.raycomm.com
    17  ls
    18  pine
    19  history
    20  lynx
    21  history
xmission> !12
ls
Desktop  files  tmp  bin  a.out
xmission>
```

Code Listing 3.14 csh also lets you recycle commands by number, although other history functions are not available.

- If you like csh, check for the availability of tcsh on your system. It's like csh but adds command completion and other similar capabilities that are comparable to bash.

- Sometimes, the length of the history is set to 0 (keeping no history lines) by default. If your history doesn't seem to work, try set history=100 to save 100 lines of history. Add this to your startup files (next chapter) if you want it to be available every time.

Changing Your Identity with su

Occasionally, you may need to log in with a userid other than your own or need to relog in with your own userid. For example, you might want to check configuration settings that you've changed before logging out to make sure that they work. Or, if you change your shell, you might want to check it before you log out (and you should do that, by the way).

You can use the su (substitute user) command to either log in as another user (**Code Listing 3.15**) or to start a new login shell.

```
[ejr@hobbes asr]$ ls
Projects  testing
[ejr@hobbes asr]$ su asr
Password:
[asr@hobbes asr]$ ls
Projects  testing
[asr@hobbes asr]$ su - ejr
Password:
[ejr@hobbes ejr]$ ls
Mail                editme              script2.sed
Projects            fortunes.copy       scriptextra.sed
Xrootenv.0          fortunes1.txt       sedtest
above.htm           fortunes2.txt       sorted.address.temp
address.book        groups              temp.htm
address.temp        history.txt         tempsort
axhome              html.htm            test
bogus               html.html           test2
chmod.txt           mail                testing.gif
clean               manipulate          testing.wp
compression         nsmail              typescript
[ejr@hobbes ejr]$ exit
[asr@hobbes asr]$ exit
[ejr@hobbes ejr]$ exit
```

Code Listing 3.15 Changing back and forth from one user to another (and exiting from multiple shells) can get a little confusing, but the prompt often tells you who you are and what directory you're in.

To log in as a different user with su:

◆ `su asr`

At the shell prompt, type su plus the userid of the user you're logging in as. You'll be prompted for a password just as though you were logging in to the system for the first time (Code Listing 3.15).

If you do not specify a username, the system will assume you mean the root user.

If you're logged in as root to begin with, you won't be prompted to give a password.

You will now be logged in as the new user and be able to work just as if you were that user, though you'll be in the same directory with the same settings that you had before you issued the su command.

To start a new login shell with su:

◆ `su - yourid`

At the shell prompt, type su - yourid (of course, use your own userid or that of the user you want to change to). The addition of the hyphen (-) will force a new login shell and set all of the environment variables and defaults according to the settings for the user.

To return to the previous shell:

◆ `exit`

Type exit at the shell prompt to leave the current shell and return to the previous one. If you use exit from the original login shell, you'll log completely out of the Unix system.

✔ Tips

■ If you have root access and you ssh to the system to administer it, you should use su to provide a little extra security. Rather than log in directly as root and leave the remote possibility of having your password stolen (or sniffed) off your local system, log in as yourself, then use su (with no other information) to change to root.

■ If you su to another user with su user (no hyphen) and the new user doesn't have read and execute permissions for the current directory, you will see shell error messages. You can disregard these. See Chapter 5 for more about read and execute permissions.

CHANGING YOUR IDENTITY WITH SU

```
xmission> ls ^?^?^?^?
 : No such file or directory
xmission> stty erase '^?'
xmission> ls
```

Code Listing 3.16 You can often straighten out a confused telnet program or Unix system by using a stty command. This one fixes the errant Backspace key.

```
xmission> jf^H^H
jf^H^H: Command not found
xmission> ls ^H^H
 : No such file or directory
xmission> stty erase '^H'
xmission>
```

Code Listing 3.17 The stty command here fixes the Delete key to work like Backspace.

✔ Tips

- If stty sane doesn't fix a messed-up display, try logging out and logging back in or restarting your terminal program.

- You can fix Backspace oddities permanently by adding the appropriate stty command to your configuration files or by making changes in your terminal client. See Chapter 8 for details about your configuration files. Refer to Chapter 1 for more helpful details about terminal programs like SSH and telnet.

Fixing Terminal Settings with stty

Another handy thing you can do with your shell is use it to fix those annoying problems that occur with terminal programs. Back in Chapter 1, we mentioned that you might encounter oddities such as your Backspace and Delete keys not working properly. You can fix these problems using stty (see **Code Listing 3.16**).

To fix Backspace and Delete key oddities with stty:

- stty erase '^?'

   If you're used to Backspace erasing characters to the left of the cursor and you just get a bunch of ^? symbols on the screen when you try it, you need to educate the terminal about your preferences. Type stty erase Backspace to fix it (Code Listing 3.16).

   In some cases, depending on your terminal program, you might need to set stty erase '^H' and then use Ctrl H to backspace. To enter this command, type stty erase '^V' Ctrl H (**Code Listing 3.17**).

To fix general terminal weirdness with stty:

- stty sane

   Typing stty sane at the shell prompt will fix a lot of oddities. For example, if you accidentally issue a bad command and all of a sudden nothing shows up on the screen or if you have general gibberish showing up on the screen, stty sane may return your terminal session to sanity.

   The reset command is also often effective at fixing a messed up terminal.

Exiting the Shell

When you're finished with your Unix session, you need to exit the Unix shell. If you've been playing with the su and shell commands, you might actually have shells within shells and need to exit from all of them. All you have to do is type exit once for each shell.

To exit from the shell:

◆ exit

At the shell prompt, type exit. Ta-da!

✔ Tips

■ If you're located at the login shell prompt, you could also type logout rather than exit. At all other shells, though, you need to type exit. In some cases, you could also press Ctrl D, but that depends on your local system configuration.

■ Be sure to log off rather than simply close your window or break your connection. It's possible, if the settings at your Unix host are seriously incorrect, that your session could remain open and someone else could pick up right where you left off with your session under your userid.

CREATING
AND EDITING FILES

4

Creating and editing files are likely the most common tasks you'll perform in Unix. If you're programming, developing Web pages, sending email (uh-huh, really), or just writing a letter, you'll spend a lot of time in an editor.

In this chapter, we'll introduce you to three of the most common editors: `pico`, `vi`, and `emacs`. We'll launch this chapter with a general overview of each, and then discuss some how-tos of using each one. With the information presented here, you'll be able to choose an editor based on your needs and get started using it (or using all of them).

Chapter Contents

- Choosing an editor
- Starting `pico` and dabbling with it
- Saving in `pico`
- Cutting and pasting text blocks in `pico`
- Checking spelling in `pico`
- Getting help in `pico`
- Exiting `pico`
- Starting `vi` and dabbling with it
- Saving in `vi`
- Adding and deleting text in `vi`
- Importing files into `vi`
- Searching for and replacing text in `vi`
- Exiting `vi`
- Starting `emacs` and dabbling with it
- Using `emacs` menus to spell-check
- Saving in `emacs`
- Exiting `emacs`

Choosing an Editor

Basically, all editors are designed to do the same things: enable you to create, modify, and save text files. These files could include configuration files, email messages, or shell scripts—essentially any text file you can create. Exactly which editor you choose is up to you, depending on your specific needs and how much you're willing to learn.

In this book, we'll stick to three biggies—pico, vi, and emacs—which will likely give you all the capabilities you'll need. We chose these because pico is (arguably) the easiest Unix editor to use, vi is one of the most powerful and is available on almost every Unix system, and emacs provides an unbelievable number of options and is a handy tool for the up-and-coming Unix pro to have.

About pico

pico is one of the more straightforward Unix editors and has become quite popular because it's extremely easy to use. In particular, as shown in **Figure 4.1**, it's menu-driven and intuitive. All of the commands are visible, and you can open, modify, and close files with little effort. pico is a great choice if you're just getting started with Unix or if you won't be needing an editor able to leap tall files in a single bound.

pico is distributed with the pine email program, so if you have pine available to you, you likely also have pico. (See Chapter 1 for a reminder on how to find out if pine and pico are available to you.) If pico is not available to you, ask your system administrator to install it.

Figure 4.1 pico offers onscreen command reminders to make it easier to use.

Editors Abound

By the way, dozens of other editors exist, such as

◆ ed, ex, and red, which are simple (in functionality, but not necessarily usage) line-by-line editors

◆ joe and jed, which are fairly simple editors and comparable to pico in many ways

Figure 4.2 vi gives you a clean screen and makes you remember all of its cryptic commands.

Figure 4.3 emacs provides both menus and power, all at once.

About vi

Although vi is likely responsible for much of Unix's reputation for being complicated and confusing, it offers enormous power and flexibility—it will leap tall files in a single bound and do much, much more. Plus, vi is universally available (unlike pico), so for these two reasons, you should consider taking the time to learn it. You might find vi cryptic, counterintuitive, and nitpicky, and for this reason, you might want to choose a different editor if you won't require vi's capabilities. As **Figure 4.2** shows, if you use vi, you won't have menus at your disposal—you'll have to get used to using commands like Esc:q or Esc:%s/vi is arcane/vi is powerful/.

About emacs

With emacs, you start to understand how incredibly customizable Unix can be. It can be "just" an editor—although a very powerful one with all kinds of helpful features—or it can be an email program, file manager, or darn near anything else. We're going to stick to just the editorial functions, but if you find that you like emacs, don't hesitate to explore the Web for other options and features of this editor. **Figure 4.3** shows you what to expect from emacs, including the handy (and fairly familiar) menus.

✔ Tips

- You're not bound to one editor or another. You can use any editor at any time. We often use `pico` for email or plain writing because we can type without thinking. We switch to `vi` when we really need power or just want to make a quick edit without `pico`'s menus, which often seem cumbersome to us.

- You can specify a default editor that will start automatically in programs that start up an editor for you. Chapter 8 provides details about setting your editor environment variable.

- See Chapter 8 for more information about configuration files, Chapter 10 for more information about shell scripts, and Chapter 11 for more information about email.

- If you type `pico` and get an error message telling you that the command is not found, use `find`, `whereis`, or `ls` to search through the likely directories (`/usr/bin` or `/usr/local/bin`) to see whether the program is available but not located where your shell can find it. See Chapter 1 for a quick review.

- After you establish a file and start adding content, save your changes using the instructions in the next section.

- You can get helpful information about `pico`'s features by accessing `pico` help. See the section called *Getting Help in pico* later in this chapter.

CHOOSING AN EDITOR

Figure 4.4 pico offers an intuitive interface for editing text.

Starting pico and Dabbling with It

You can start and dabble with pico using the following steps. Notice that the pico interface is intuitive and easy to navigate in, as shown in **Figure 4.4**.

To start pico and dabble with it:

1. pico

   To begin, type pico at the shell prompt. The program starts up and you'll see something like Figure 4.4, with the text area up at the top of the window and the command hints down at the bottom.

   If you know the name of the file you want to edit, type pico at the shell prompt followed by the path and name of the file you want to edit (hairyspiders, for example).

2. hairyspiders

   Go ahead. Type in something—anything—just to try it out.

   ▲ Use [Del] and [Backspace] to help edit text.

   ▲ Use the arrow keys to move up, down, right, or left.

✔ Tips

- Start pico with the -w option (e.g., pico -w filename) to disable word wrapping. You'll find this particularly useful when editing configuration files, as covered in Chapter 8.

- Throughout pico, you'll see ^C, ^J, and dozens of other ^something characters hanging out in the menu at the bottom. The ^ stands for Ctrl, so ^C is [Ctrl][C], ^J is [Ctrl][J], and so on.

Saving in pico

You'll generally save your files frequently whenever you're editing them—and you should. Remember, Murphy is watching you....

To save in pico:

1. Ctrl O

Use Ctrl O periodically to save (write "out") the text you're editing.

2. hairyspiders

Specify the filename for your file (**Figure 4.5**).

✔ Tips

■ After you save a file for the first time and want to save new changes, just press Ctrl O then press Enter to confirm the current filename and save it.

■ When you exit pico, you'll get a last chance to save your changes. See *Exiting pico* in this chapter for the specifics.

■ If you try to save a new file over an existing one—which would obliterate the original—pico carefully asks you if you want to overwrite the file. Yes, and you'll no longer have the original. No, and you'll get to choose a new filename.

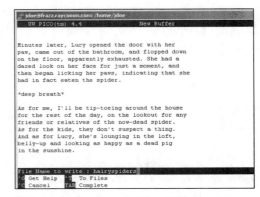

Figure 4.5 In pico lingo, "writing out" just means "saving."

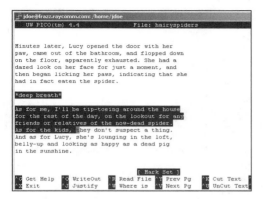

Figure 4.6 Marking, cutting, and pasting text in pico can be very handy.

Cutting and Pasting Text Blocks in pico

As you're typing along in pico, you'll probably need to cut and paste blocks of text, as shown in **Figure 4.6**.

To cut and paste text in pico:

1. pico hairyspiders

   At the shell prompt, type pico followed by the name of the file to edit.

2. Move the cursor to the first line of the text you want to cut.

3. Ctrl ^

   Press Ctrl ^ to mark the beginning of the text you want to cut. (Note that Ctrl ^ is really Ctrl Shift 6—it might work without Shift, but it might not, depending on your terminal program. Try it out and see what happens.)

4. Use the arrow keys to move the cursor to the end of the text you want to cut.

   Note that the text gets highlighted as you select it (Figure 4.6).

5. Ctrl K

   This "kuts" the text.

6. Using the arrow keys, move the cursor to where you want to insert the cut text.

7. Ctrl U

   Use this key combination to paste the cut text into the file at the new location.

✔ Tips

- You can select and cut blocks of text without also pasting them back into a file. Just skip steps 6 and 7.

- You can paste text blocks as many times as you want. After you select and cut text, just press Ctrl U at each place where you want to insert the cut text.

- If you don't select text, Ctrl K just cuts a single line.

Checking Spelling in pico

Another handy thing you can do in pico is chek yoor speling, as shown in **Figures 4.7** and **4.8**.

To spell-check in pico:

1. pico hairyspiders

   At the shell prompt, type pico and the filename of the file to edit.

2. Ctrl T

   Pressing this command starts spell-checking the file. pico will stop at each misspelled word (**Figure 4.7**).

3. correctspelling

   Type in the correct spelling for any words flagged as misspelled, or press Enter to accept the current spelling and move along to the next word.

✔ Tips

- You can press Ctrl C to cancel spell-checking at any time.

- Because the spell-checker in pico isn't full-featured, consider using an alternate spell-check program by specifying it on the command line, like pico -s ispell hairyspiders, so you can get a little more assistance. See Chapter 15 for more information.

- When the entire document has been spell-checked, pico will tell you that it's done checking spelling, and you can continue editing the file (**Figure 4.8**).

Figure 4.7 pico prompts you to correct the spelling of misspelled words.

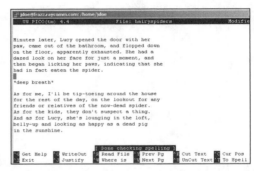

Figure 4.8 pico informs you when the procedure is complete.

Figure 4.9 pico gives you all the information you need.

Getting Help in pico

A great way to find out more about pico is to access pico help. In addition to finding answers to your questions, you can also find out about pico features and capabilities of which you may not be aware (**Figure 4.9**).

To get help in pico:

1. ⌈Ctrl⌉⌈G⌉

In pico, press ⌈Ctrl⌉⌈G⌉ to access help.

2. Move through the help pages:

▲ ⌈Ctrl⌉⌈V⌉ moves you down through the help page.

▲ ⌈Ctrl⌉⌈Y⌉ moves you up through the help page.

3. ⌈Ctrl⌉⌈X⌉

Use this combination to exit help.

To get help with pico startup options:

◆ man pico

At the shell prompt, type man pico to learn more about startup options, including a variety of options that control how pico works.

✔ Tips

■ Keep your eyes on the pico status line for current information, error messages, and occasional hints about using pico. The status line is the third line from the bottom of the screen, just above the menu, as shown in Figure 4.9.

■ Keep in mind that pico really is a very basic program. If you're looking for a command or function that isn't readily available, it's probably not there. You might check out vi or emacs instead.

Exiting pico

When you're done editing in pico, you'll exit it using the following steps.

To exit pico:

1. Ctrl X

   Within pico, press Ctrl X. If you haven't made any changes to the text since you last saved the file, you'll find yourself immediately back at the shell prompt. If you have made changes, you'll be prompted to "Save modified buffer" (**Figure 4.10**).

2. At the "Save modified buffer" prompt:

   ▲ Press Y if you want to save your changes. Proceed to step 3.

   ▲ Press N if you don't want to save your changes. You'll end up back at the shell prompt.

3. bighairyspiders

   Specify the filename for your file if it's the first time you've saved it. If you've saved it before, press Enter to confirm the current filename or change the name to save a copy and not change the original file.

✔ Tip

■ A *buffer* is what the computer uses to temporarily store information, and if it's modified, that means that it's temporarily storing something that you haven't saved to disk.

Figure 4.10 pico gives you the opportunity to "Save modified buffer." Without the techno-babble, this means to save the text you just wrote or edited before you exit.

EXITING pico

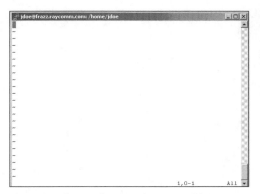

Figure 4.11 The vi editor inundates you with tons of onscreen help and advice, as shown here. Well, documentation is available, but the vi interface itself isn't really helpful at all!

Starting vi and Dabbling with It

Before you go running off to use vi, understand that it has two modes (both of which look pretty much like **Figure 4.11**):

◆ *Input mode* (sometimes called insert mode), in which the keys you press actually show up in the file that you're editing. You use this mode to add or change text.

◆ *Command mode*, in which every keystroke is interpreted as a command. You use this mode to do everything except enter text.

What's confusing for many people about vi is that it starts you in command mode, meaning that if you just start typing, you may see some blank spaces, characters, and bits of words that you type—essentially, a bunch of garbage that does not exactly represent what you're typing—and you'll hear a lot of beeping. So, as we'll show you in the following steps, you'll need to access the input mode as soon as you start vi.

To start vi:

1. vi

At the shell prompt, type vi. The program starts up and you'll see something like Figure 4.11. The ~ symbols show blank lines below the end of the file.

2. i

Type i to get into input mode. This itself is a command issued in command mode, so it won't show up on the screen.

continues on next page

3. `hairy spiders lurk`

In input mode, type anything you want.

Everything you type will show up on the screen until you return to command mode by pressing Esc. When you are in command mode, you can use the arrow keys to navigate up and down in the file line by line and Ctrl F and Ctrl B to scroll one screen forward and backward, respectively.

✔ Tips

■ To get help for vi, type `man vi`. See Chapter 1 for more about `man` pages.

■ If you're not sure what mode you're in, press Esc to go into command mode. If you're already in command mode, you'll hear a beep. If you're in input mode, you'll change to command mode.

■ Many Unix-like systems, including Linux and Mac OS, actually provide a program called `vim` in the place of `vi`. `vim` (VI iMproved) is like `vi` but feature-rich and more flexible, and you still start it with the command `vi`.

■ You can open specific files or even multiple files when you access `vi`. At the shell prompt, type `vi filetoedit` (or whatever) to open a specific file. Or, for example, type `vi *.html` to open all of the HTML documents in a directory, then use Esc`:n` Enter (for "next") to move to each subsequent file.

■ See *Adding and Deleting Text in vi* later in this chapter for more details about editing in `vi`.

Figure 4.12 Save early, save often. That's the safe rule for vi.

Saving in vi

You'll want to save changes to your documents frequently, especially as you're learning to use vi (**Figure 4.12**). Until you're accustomed to switching between command and input mode, you may accidentally type in commands when you think you're typing text, with unpredictable results. To save files, just follow these steps.

To save text in vi:

◆ (Esc):w limerick

Press (Esc) to get out of input mode and into command mode, then type :w (for "write," as in write to the disk) followed by a space and then the filename (limerick, in this example) you want to use for the file, then press (Enter). If you've already saved the file once, just press (Esc) and type :w then press (Enter).

✔ Tips

■ If you've already saved your file at least once, you can save changes and exit vi in one fell swoop. In command mode, type :wq (for "write quit"). For more information about quitting vi, see the section called *Exiting vi* later in this chapter.

■ If you want to save a file over an existing file (obliterating the original as you do), use :w! existingfilename in command mode. The ! forces vi to overwrite the original.

Adding and Deleting Text in vi

Adding and deleting text in vi is a bit more complicated than doing the same in pico. Whereas in pico, you basically just place your cursor where you want to make changes, vi has a whole slew of commands that you use to specify where the changes should occur. (**Tables 4.1**, **4.2**, and **4.3** list only a very few of your options.) Plus, to issue the commands, you have to switch to command mode.

To add or delete text in vi:

1. vi

To begin, type vi at the shell prompt.

2. i

Change into input mode.

3. There once was a man from Nantucket

Type in some text that you'll want to add to.

4. (Esc)

Press (Esc) to enter command mode before you issue the commands.

5. Choose a command, based on what you want to do to the text.

Table 4.1 lists commands to add text.

Table 4.2 lists commands to delete text.

Table 4.3 lists miscellaneous editing commands.

6. dd

Type the command. Here, we're deleting the current line of text.

Table 4.1

vi **Commands to Add Text**	
COMMAND	FUNCTION
a	Adds text after the cursor
A	Adds text at the end of the current line
i	Inserts text before the cursor
I	Inserts text at the beginning of the current line
o	Inserts a blank line after the current line
O	Inserts a blank line before the current line

Table 4.2

vi **Commands to Delete Text**	
COMMAND	FUNCTION
x	Deletes one character (under the cursor)
X	Deletes one character (behind the cursor)
dd	Deletes the current line
5dd	Deletes five lines starting with the current line (any number would work here)
dw	Deletes the current word
cw	Changes the current word (deletes it and replaces it with the next word you type)
r	Replaces the character under the cursor with the next character you type
R	Replaces the existing text with the text you type (like overtype mode in most word processors)

Table 4.3

Other Handy vi **Editing Commands**	
COMMAND	FUNCTION
yy	Copies the current line
p	Pastes the copied line after the cursor or line
J	Joins the current and following lines
u	Undoes the last change
U	Undoes all changes on the current line
.	Repeats the last command

Figure 4.13 Reading an additional file into the current one can make your editing tasks much easier.

Importing Files into vi

You can also merge multiple files in vi by reading additional files into the current one, as shown in **Figure 4.13**. Basically, all this means is that you insert one file into the file you're currently editing.

To import files in vi:

1. vi hairyspider

   At the shell prompt, type vi followed by the filename to start vi with, in this case, the hairyspider file.

2. Esc :r filename

   At the point in the file where you want to import text, press Esc, then type :r and the filename you want to read into the file.

✔ Tip

- vi also lets you read the output of commands into the file. For example, if you want to read the list of files in a specific directory into the file, use Esc :r !ls in command mode.

Searching and Replacing in vi

One of vi's better features (and advantages over pico) is that it allows you to search and replace throughout entire files. As shown in the next sections, you can just find a specific string of text (a *regular expression*, in Unix lingo; see **Figure 4.14**), or you can find the text and replace it with other text, as in **Figure 4.15**.

To find a string of text in vi:

1. vi hairyspider

For starters, access vi and a specific file.

2. (Esc)/spider

Enter command mode, then type / followed by the text you're looking for. Here, we're looking for "spider," but you may be looking for "the fly" or "wiggled and jiggled and tickled inside her." Or whatever.

3. (Enter)

Press this to find the first occurrence of the term. Press (n) to find the next one.

To search and replace in vi:

1. vi hairyspider

For starters, access vi and a specific file.

2. (Esc):%s/swallowed the fly/swallowed a spider to catch the fly/

Enter (Esc):%s/ plus the text to find, followed by the replacement text, as in Figure 4.15. Here, we replace "swallowed a fly" with "swallowed a spider to catch the fly," but perhaps you might forego the spider and simply go for some antacid.

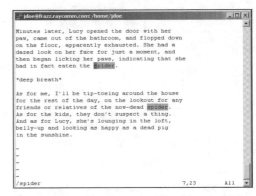

Figure 4.14 Searching for text in vi is quick and reliable.

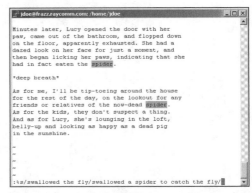

Figure 4.15 Replacing text in vi requires a bit of arcane syntax, but you get used to it quickly.

✔ Tips

- A great use for the search-and-replace feature is if you end up with DOS text files in your Unix account (through uploading a text file from a DOS or Windows machine as a binary file, most likely). If you view DOS files through a Unix shell, all the lines within the file will end with ^M. But if you try to type ^M when you're doing a search and replace, the ^M won't show up. What to do? Press Ctrl V, then Ctrl M. Just search and replace with :%s/Ctrl V Ctrl M//g. The Ctrl V command "escapes" the following character, so you can type it without actually doing what the command would otherwise do. If you don't escape the Ctrl M, vi thinks you just pressed Enter and tries to execute the unfinished command.

- See the section on grep in Chapter 6 for information about searching with regular expressions.

- Add a g at the end of the command to make it apply to all occurrences in the file. Otherwise, it applies only to the first occurrence on each line.

SEARCHING AND REPLACING IN vi

Exiting vi

Whew! Time to exit vi (**Figure 4.16**).

To exit vi:

◆ [Esc] :q

Enter command mode with *q*, then type
:q to quit vi. If you haven't saved your
latest changes, vi will not quit and will
tell you to use ! to override. To quit without saving your changes, use :q!, as
shown in Figure 4.16.

✔ Tips

■ If you don't really want to quit but want
to edit a different file instead, type
:e filename to open a new file to edit.

■ We recommend that you take a few minutes and try out some of the commands
that you'll use throughout your vi experience. If you don't think you'll be needing
this range of commands, consider using
pico rather than vi.

■ It takes some practice to get accustomed
to vi, but the time spent is well worth it.
With patience and practice, you'll quickly
become proficient in using vi. Take your
time, take deep breaths, and plow ahead.

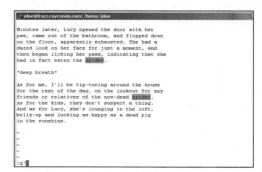

Figure 4.16 Use [Esc] :q! to quit vi without saving
changes.

EXITING VI

Figure 4.17 emacs starts out with some basic information, but you can just start typing if you want.

Figure 4.18 emacs might helpfully start out in a spiffier interface if you're sitting at the keyboard of a Linux system. You can get the plain variety, though.

Starting emacs and Dabbling with It

For the novice, emacs offers a reasonable middle ground between the user-friendliness of pico and the power of vi (or vim). It's not available on all systems, though, so you'll just have to type in the command to see if you have access to it. (Refer back to Chapter 1 if you don't.)

Using emacs, you can just type, as you'd expect, then use command sequences, which are basically Ctrl keys, to make emacs do useful things like save, quit, and the like. When you start emacs, it'll probably look very much like **Figure 4.17**. If you're on a Linux system, which "helpfully" opens a new window and gives you the graphical version, you'll see something like **Figure 4.18**.

To start emacs:

1. emacs

    At the shell prompt, type emacs. The program starts up and you'll see something like Figure 4.17. The helpful information may or may not be present, but you can ignore it for now at any rate.

2. This morning I got up, went downstairs, and found a humongous spider in the bathroom. After I quietly composed myself, I looked around the house for something to put him in...the kids' bug catcher thing (nowhere to be found)...a jar... tupperware...a lidded cup...the salad spinner (BwaaaaHaaaHaaa!)....

    Type anything you want.

    You can use the arrow keys to navigate up and down in the file line by line.

    continues on next page

✔ Tips

- To get help in emacs, type man emacs. See Chapter 1 for more about man pages.

- If emacs helped you out by starting in the graphical mode, but you want to play along with us in the text mode, use emacs –nw to start the program. (The –nw flag means "no windows.")

- emacs uses both Ctrl keys and the "meta" key to issue commands. PC users should use Alt in place of the meta key (but you should remember that you'll see *M+* or *Meta+* in most emacs documentation). For those of you using keyboards that actually have a key labeled "Meta," by all means, you should use it when you see Alt . Mac users should use Option .

- As useful as emacs is, it does have a few quirks. For example, if you want to access help, you press the Backspace key, which issues the Ctrl H command. To fix this idiosyncrasy, enter Alt X then normal-erase-is-backspace.

Table 4.4

Handy emacs Commands	
COMMAND	FUNCTION
Ctrl X Ctrl F	Opens a new file (existing or new)
Ctrl U	Undoes the last change
Ctrl G	Cancels the current operation
Esc Esc Esc	Bails out of menu selections (and other things)
Ctrl V	Moves down one page (screen)
Alt V	Moves up one page (screen)
Alt <	Moves to the beginning of the file
Alt >	Moves to the end of the file

Figure 4.19 Navigating emacs menus isn't exactly intuitive, but it's straightforward after you get started.

Using emacs **Menus to Spell-Check**

Spell-checking is good. Learning to use emacs menus is good. And in emacs, learning to spell-check also allows you to familiarize yourself with emacs menus. Use F10, then a key letter of each menu, menu item, and submenu as needed to navigate through the menus. (You'll see hints and prompts at the bottom of the screen, as shown in **Figure 4.19**.) Follow along to use the menus to spell-check your file.

To use emacs **menus to spell-check:**

1. `emacs hairyspiders`

   For starters, fire up emacs and a specific file.

2. Press F10 to access the menus.

3. `t`

   Next, type the first letter of the menu you want—this example uses **t** for Tools for now.

4. `0`

   Try **0** (zero) for spell-checking.

5. Press Enter and enjoy your spell-check.

✔ Tips

■ Use Esc Esc Esc to back out of places (like menu selection choices) you do not want to be.

■ Reading and following along with the tips onscreen is essential to having a happy life (or a tolerable coexistence) with emacs.

Saving in emacs

Save yourself potential headaches by saving frequently. To save files in emacs (**Figure 4.20**), follow these steps.

To save text in emacs:

◆ Ctrl X Ctrl S hairyspiders

Press Ctrl X to let emacs know that another command is coming, and then Ctrl S to save. Finally, type the filename (hairyspiders, in this example) you want to use for the file, then press Enter. If you've already saved the file once, just press Ctrl X Ctrl S.

✔ Tips

■ If you look around in your home directory (or whatever directory you're working in) after experimenting with emacs, you'll probably notice a slew of files with names ending in ~. Those are emacs backup files, created for your convenience and sanity. If you don't need them, just delete them with rm -i *~. If you do need them, just use mv oopsie~ oopsie and you're back in business.

■ If you want to save a file over an existing file, use Ctrl X Ctrl W, and then enter the existing filename to overwrite the original.

Figure 4.20 Saving is very important—at least if you want to keep the results of your efforts.

Figure 4.21 Use Ctrl X Ctrl C to quit emacs.

Exiting emacs

Wow! It's already time to exit emacs (**Figure 4.21**).

To exit emacs:

◆ Ctrl X Ctrl C

Press Ctrl X to let emacs know that another command is coming, then Ctrl C to close. If you haven't saved your latest changes, emacs expects you to decide if you want to save or discard unsaved changes, as shown in Figure 4.20.

✔ Tip

■ If you end up down at the command line but don't want to save or anything—you just want to return to your file—use Ctrl G to cancel.

EXITING emacs

CONTROLLING OWNERSHIP & PERMISSIONS

Unix and Unix-like operating systems are multiuser systems in which your files are separate from Jane's files, which are separate from Joe's files, and so on. Any file you create is separate from other users' files and usually cannot be directly accessed by Jane, Joe, or any other user.

Occasionally, though, you will need to share files. For example, you might be collaborating on a project with Jane where sharing files (rather than creating and maintaining separate ones) is essential.

This chapter provides an overview of Unix file permissions and ownership. For many systems, though, only the root user can make ownership changes, so you may have to ask for help from your system administrator to actually do this.

Chapter Contents

- Understanding file ownership and permissions
- Finding out who owns what
- Finding out which group you're in
- Changing the group association of files and directories
- Changing ownership of files and directories
- Changing permissions
- Translating mnemonic permissions to numeric permissions
- Changing permission defaults

Understanding File Ownership and Permissions

Unix provides three levels of file ownership:

◆ **User.** Refers to the single userid that's primarily in charge of the file. You have this level of ownership for the files you create.

◆ **Group.** Refers to the group (of users) associated with a specific file. All users within a group have the same permissions for interacting with a file.

◆ **Other.** Refers to any users not identified with either the group or user for a file.

Within these groups, you can specify permissions for file access and rights in three categories:

◆ **Read.** Users with read permission can only view a file; they cannot make changes to it.

◆ **Write.** Users with write permission can make changes to or delete a file.

◆ **Execute.** Users with execute permission can run files (programs or scripts) and view directories.

In this chapter, we'll show you some of the commands that can be used (sometimes by you, usually by the root user) to set ownership and permissions. Keep in mind that you can set or change any permissions for files you create and possibly for files created by others; however, exactly which permissions and ownerships you can change depends on the system. Even if you don't currently need to change file ownerships or permissions, you should take a quick read through this chapter to see what options might be available to you.

✔ Tips

■ An interesting twist on this whole ownership issue is that not all "owners" are people. Programs or processes (discussed in Chapter 9) run as a specific user, and if they create files, those files have permissions reflecting the individual and group membership of the program. See Chapter 9 for more information.

■ Some Unix-like operating systems have additional or supplementary means of controlling access to specific files. Usually, though, you'll know if such a system is in use. For now, just know that such things exist; the procedures in this chapter will handle 95 percent of your needs.

Finding Out Who Owns What

Your first step in changing ownership and permissions is to find out who owns which files. You'll need this information to find out if you can make changes to the permissions.

To find out who owns what:

1. cd

   At the shell prompt, type cd to return to your home directory.

2. ls -l

   Enter ls -l to see the long listing of the files in the current directory. (See **Code Listing 5.1**.)

   The left column contains ten characters, the last nine of which specify permissions for each file:

continues on next page

```
xmission> cd
/home/users/e/ejray
xmission> ls -l
total 60          OWNER    GROUP
drwx-x-x    2 ejray    users       512 Jul 21 13:32 Complete/
drwx-x-x    2 ejray    users       512 Jun 24 09:23 Completed/
drwx-x-x    2 ejray    users       512 Sep 15  1997 Mail/
drwx-x-x    2 ejray    users       512 Jun 24 09:35 NewProject/
drwx-x-x    2 ejray    users       512 Sep 15  1997 News/
drwx-x-x    2 ejray    users       512 Sep 15  1997 access/
-rw----    1 ejray    users       163 Jul 22 07:28 bogus2
drwxrwx-x   2 ejray    www         512 Jul 24 04:44 chat.conf/
-rw----    1 ejray    users       853 Sep 13  1997 dead.letter
-rw----    1 ejray    users     14286 Jun 28 12:40 files
lrwxrwxrwx  1 ejray    users        27 Sep 15  1997 ftp -> /home/ftp/pub/users
-rw----    1 ejray    users        36 Jul 24 12:09 limerick
drwx-x-x    2 ejray    users       512 Jun  8 13:32 mail/
drwxr-s-x  15 ejray    www        2560 Jul 10 10:30 public_html/
drwx-x-x    2 ejray    users       512 Jul 22 08:23 puppy/
drwx-x-x    2 ejray    users       512 Jul 24 04:44 temp/
-rw----    1 ejray    users         0 Jul 19 13:24 testme
```

Code Listing 5.1 Many systems use only a few group names to allow easy file sharing and collaboration.

▲ r means read permission, w means write permission, and x means execute permission.

▲ The first set of rwx is for the user, the second set is for the group, and the last set is for other.

▲ A dash (-) instead of a letter indicates that the user/group/other does not have that level of permission. For example, rwx--- would mean that the user has read, write, and execute permission, while group and other have no permissions at all.

The two columns in the middle indicate the file's owner (in all likelihood your userid, for this example) and the group membership for the file. In Code Listing 5.1, ejray is the owner of all the files. Most of the files are associated with the users group, while just a few directories are associated with the www group.

On this system, files that individual users create are associated with the user's group, while files destined for the Web have www group associations. On other systems, the default group for files might be a group with the same name as the userid, as shown in **Code Listing 5.2**.

3. ls -l /etc

You can also use the ls -l command on a system directory, such as /etc. Here, you'll see that most of the files are owned by root, possibly with a variety of different group memberships (see **Figure 5.1**).

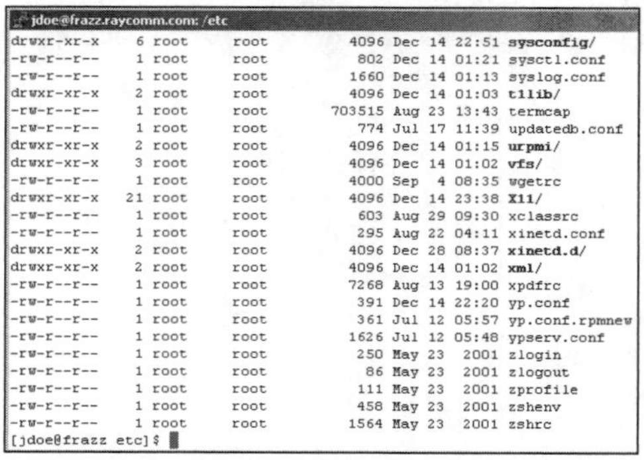

Figure 5.1 Most of the files in /etc are owned by root.

✔ Tips

■ Sometimes you'll see references to world-readable or world permissions. This is the same as other. "Other" just refers to anyone who is not you or not in the group.

■ You might also hear of s or SetUID permissions, which indicate that the program or file can run with the effective userid of the file's owner (usually root). For example, /usr/bin/passwd has s permissions because you can run passwd to change your password, but the command needs to run as root to actually modify the password database.

■ You might also see a t at the end of the list of permissions, which indicates that the sticky bit is set. Setting the "sticky bit" means primarily that, in a shared directory, you can delete only your own files (and not accidentally delete files belonging to others).

```
[ejr@hobbes permissions]$ ls -l
total 152
-rw-rw-r-    1 ejr   ejr      128889 Jul 24 14:33 sage.sayings
-rw-rw-r-    1 ejr   ejr      23890 Jul 24 14:33 sayings
[ejr@hobbes permissions]$
```

Code Listing 5.2 Sometimes the group name and user name are the same, depending on how the system was set up.

```
[ejr@hobbes permissions]$ grep ejr
→ /etc/passwd
ejr:aag2.UyC7yJKJWE:500:500:Eric J.
Ray:/home/ejr:/bin/bash
[ejr@hobbes permissions]$
```

Code Listing 5.3 You'll find tons of information in /etc/passwd, including your default group number.

```
[ejr@hobbes permissions]$ cat /etc/group
kmem::9:
wheel::10:root,ejr
mail::12:mail
news::13:news
uucp::14:uucp
man::15:
games::20:
gopher::30:
dip::40:
ftp::50:
nobody::99:
users::100:ejr,deb,asr,awr
floppy:x:19:
pppusers:x:230:
popusers:x:231:
slipusers:x:232:
postgres:x:233:
ejr:x:500:
bash:x:501:
csh:x:502:
asr:x:503:
awr:x:504:
deb:x:505:
[ejr@hobbes permissions]$
```

Code Listing 5.4 The group file lists groups and additional members (as shown in the users group).

Finding Out Which Group You're In

If you want to collaborate on a project and share files, for example, you'll need to be in the same group with the other people on the team. Your first step is to find out which group you're in, as shown in **Code Listing 5.3**.

To find out which group you're in:

1. `grep yourid /etc/passwd`

   Here, `grep yourid` pulls your userid out of the `/etc/passwd` file (which is where user information is stored) and displays it as shown in Code Listing 5.3. From left to right, you see

   ▲ Your username

   ▲ The encoded password (or nothing, or an x if the system is configured for "shadow" passwords)

   ▲ Your userid (each user has a unique number in the system)

2. Note the number of the group.

   You'll need the number to match it up with a group name in step 3. In this case, our group id is 500.

3. `more /etc/group`

   Here, we're exploring the contents of the `/etc/group` file using `more` to see which groups are currently defined on the system. As shown in **Code Listing 5.4**, the first column contains the name of the group, the third contains the group number, and the last column contains extra names the system administrator added to the group. Users can belong to multiple additional groups, and this is how the additional group membership is indicated.

4. Match up the group number for your ID with the group name.

   Our number was 500, which corresponds to the `ejr` group name here.

✔ Tips

- If you're collaborating on a project, ask your system administrator to create a special group just for the project. That way, you and your teammates can easily share files.

- You can also use the `groups` or `id` commands, which offer a quicker way of finding out about group membership. These give you essential details about group membership (and userids, too), but they don't flood you with these other most interesting and potentially useful details about the system. Wander to Chapter 7 for more information.

- Check out Chapter 1 for more on `more`.

- See Chapter 6 for the full scoop on `grep`.

Changing the Group Association of Files and Directories with chgrp

Suppose you have a file called black that is currently being used by the pot group and you want to change the file's permissions so that it can be accessed by the kettle group. To do this, you'll need to change which group the file is associated with—in this case, change the association from the pot group to the kettle group. You can change which group a file or directory is associated with using chgrp, as shown in **Code Listing 5.5**.

To change group association with chgrp:

1. ls -l

   Type ls -l at the shell prompt to verify the file's name and the group it's associated with. Remember that the second column in the middle of the listing, just before the file sizes, lists the group membership.

2. chgrp kettle black

   Type chgrp followed by the name of the new group you want the file to be associated with and the filename. Here, the chgrp command changes the group association for the file called black to the kettle group.

```
[ejr@hobbes permissions]$ ls -l
total 178
-rw-rw-r-- 1 ejr  pot     24850 Jul 24 14:59 black
-rw-rw-r-- 1 ejr  ejr    128889 Jul 24 14:33 sage.sayings
-rw-rw-r-- 1 ejr  ejr     23890 Jul 24 14:33 sayings
[ejr@hobbes permissions]$ chgrp kettle black
[ejr@hobbes permissions]$ ls -l
total 178
-rw-rw-r-- 1 ejr  kettle  24850 Jul 24 14:59 black
-rw-rw-r-- 1 ejr  ejr    128889 Jul 24 14:33 sage.sayings
-rw-rw-r-- 1 ejr  ejr     23890 Jul 24 14:33 sayings
```

Code Listing 5.5 Pots and kettles can both be black, but only one at a time.

✔ Tips

- If you try to change group ownership and get an error message like "Not owner" or something similarly obscure, your userid doesn't have the necessary authority to make the change. You'll have to ask your system administrator for help.

- Change group association only if you have a specific need to do so; you don't want to make your files available to other people unnecessarily. Unless you are the system administrator, you won't be able to control exactly who belongs to the group to which you've given access to your files.

- If you change the group association of a specific directory, you also need to check permissions for the directory containing it. Users will not be able to change into the specific directory (regardless of their group membership) unless they also have read and execute permission for the directory containing it.

- Just as with the cp and mv commands, covered in Chapter 2, you can use a -R flag with chgrp to recursively apply changes to a directory and all of the subdirectories and files in it. For example, to change the group association of the LatestProject directory and all its contents to the project group, use chgrp -R project LatestProject from the directory above LatestProject.

CHANGING GROUP ASSOCIATIONS WITH chgrp

✔ Tips

- After you change a file's ownership, what you can do with the file depends on the group and other permissions and memberships. The new owner, however, will be able to do anything with the file.

- When changing the ownership of a directory, you can add the -R flag to chown to make it apply recursively to all files and directories below it.

- If the system does not allow you to use chown to give files away, consider using cp to make a copy of a file to accomplish the same thing. If you copy someone else's file (that you have permission to read) to another name or location, the copy is fully yours. (In this giving-the-file-away example, the recipient should use cp.)

- Even if you can't use chown, you could still be able to request that the system administrator change file ownership for you: "Could you please change the ownership of my rowyourboat file to Merrilee, with chown merrilee /home/shared/me/rowyourboat. Thanks!" (This could happen because many versions of Unix don't allow non-root users to change file ownership.)

Changing Ownership of Files and Directories with chown

Suppose you've been working on a file called rowyourboat, and your boss decides to let a coworker, Merrilee, take over the project. In this case, to fully pawn off the project to your coworker, you need to change ownership of the file from you to her. Depending on how your system administrator set up the system, you can usually change ownership of files using chown (**Code Listing 5.6**).

To change ownership with chown:

1. ls -l

   For starters, type ls -l at the shell prompt to verify the file's name and ownership, as in Code Listing 5.6. Remember that the ownership information is located after the permissions and linking information.

2. chown merrilee rowyourboat

   Type chown followed by the userid of the person you want to transfer ownership to and the filename. In this case, the chown command changes the ownership for rowyourboat to merrilee. rowyourboat and its associated problems will now be hers, and life will be but a dream.

```
[ejr@hobbes merrilee]$ ls -l
total 26
-rw-rw-r--     1 ejr        users        24850 Jul 24 15:17 rowyourboat
[ejr@hobbes merrilee]$ chown merrilee rowyourboat
[ejr@hobbes merrilee]$ ls -l
total 26
-rw-rw-r--     1 merrilee   users        24850 Jul 24 15:17 rowyourboat
[ejr@hobbes merrilee]$
```

Code Listing 5.6 Changing ownership of files transfers complete control.

Changing Permissions with chmod

Suppose you've been working on a file called rowyourboat and you want to have your coworkers down the stream review it. To do so, you'll need to give other people permission to access the document. You can either give people in specific groups access or give everybody on the Unix system access. In particular, you can specify permissions for u(ser—that's you), g(roup), o(thers), and a(ll).

In addition to specifying permissions, you can also specify how much access a person or group can have to your file. For example, you can specify r(ead), w(rite), and (e)x(ecute) access, depending on how much you trust them not to ruin your rowyourboat masterpiece.

As shown in **Code Listing 5.7**, your first step is to check out what the current permissions are. Then, you can set permissions, add to them, or remove them as necessary.

To check current permissions:

◆ ls -l r*

To begin, type ls -l r* to get a long listing of rowyourboat in the current directory. Code Listing 5.7 shows that the permissions are -rwxr-x–. This is actually three sets of permissions:

▲ For the user (rwx, in this example)

▲ For the group (r-x, here)

▲ For the world (---, here)

In this example, the user has read, write, and execute permissions; the group has only read and execute permissions; and all other users have no permissions.

```
[ejr@hobbes permissions]$ ls -l r*
-rwxr-x--- 1 ejrusers   152779 Jul 24 15:10
  → rowyourboat
[ejr@hobbes permissions]$
```

Code Listing 5.7 Use ls -l to see the permissions on files.

To set permissions:

◆ `chmod u=rwx,g=rx,o=r row*`

Type `chmod` and specify who has access. In this case users have read, write, and execute permissions; the group has read and execute permissions; and others have read permission for all files in the directory that start with `row` (**Code Listing 5.8**).

The equals sign (=) specifies that the permissions granted in the command are the only permissions that apply. Any previous permissions will be removed.

The wildcard expression here (`row*`) specifies that the command applies to all files and directories that start with "row" in the current directory.

✔ Tips

■ There are about a million and one ways to express permissions. For example, you could use `chmod ugo= *` (note the space before the *) or `chmod u-rwx,g-rwx, o-rwx *` to revoke all permissions from all files in the directory. (Note that you'll have to add your own permissions back to the files before you can do anything with them, if you try this out.)

■ If you want to change permissions for multiple files, either use a wildcard expression or separate the filenames with commas (but no spaces).

■ You can also use the -R flag with `chmod` to recursively apply the changes you make to permissions to all files and subdirectories in a directory. For example, `chmod -R go-rwx *` revokes all permissions from everyone except the user for all files in the current directory, all subdirectories in the current directory, and all files in all subdirectories.

CHANGING PERMISSIONS WITH chmod

```
[ejr@hobbes permissions]$ ls -l
total 332
-rw-rw-r--    1 ejr    users    24850 Jul 24 14:59 black
-rwxr-x---    1 ejr    users   152779 Jul 24 15:10 rowyourboat
-rw-rw-r--    1 ejr    users   128889 Jul 24 14:33 sage.sayings
-rw-rw-r--    1 ejr    users    23890 Jul 24 14:33 sayings
[ejr@hobbes permissions]$ chmod u=rwx,g=rx,o=r row*
[ejr@hobbes permissions]$ ls -l
total 329
-rwxr-xr--    1 ejr    users    24850 Jul 24 14:59 black
-rwxr-xr--    1 ejr    users   152779 Jul 24 15:10 rowyourboat
-rwxr-xr--    1 ejr    users   128889 Jul 24 14:33 sage.sayings
-rwxr-xr--    1 ejr    users    23890 Jul 24 14:33 sayings
[ejr@hobbes permissions]$
```

Code Listing 5.8 You can set permissions to ensure that all files have equivalent permissions.

To add permissions:

◆ chmod g+w rowyourboat

At the shell prompt, enter chmod, followed by

▲ The category. In this case, we've used
g, for group, but you could also use o
for others, ...or, of course, u for user,
but you already have that access. You
could also use a for all users (which
includes u, g, and o).

▲ A plus sign indicates that you're adding the permission to the existing permissions, rather than setting absolute
permissions.

▲ The permissions to grant. Here, we've
used w, for write permission, but you
could also use r for read or x for execute permissions, as your needs dictate.

▲ The filename (rowyourboat)

To remove permissions:

◆ chmod go-w rowyourboat

At the shell prompt, use chmod go-w plus
the filename to remove write permissions
for everyone except you, the file's owner.
Note that we handled both group and
other in a single command this time,
although we could have used chmod g-w
rowyourboat and chmod o-w rowyourboat
to accomplish the same thing.

Table 5.1

Numeric Equivalents for Mnemonic Permissions		
MNEMONIC (RWX) PERMISSIONS	BINARY EQUIVALENT	NUMERIC EQUIVALENT
---	000	0
--x	001	1
-w-	010	2
-wx	011	3
r-	100	4
r-x	101	5
rw-	110	6
rwx	111	7

Translating Mnemonic Permissions to Numeric Permissions

The permissions of a file, as you've seen throughout this chapter, come in sets of three—rwx, for read, write, and execute permissions. And, as we showed you, you set these permissions by specifying that each one is either "on" or "off." For example, ugo+rwx sets read, write, and execute permissions to "on" for user, group, and other, while a+rw sets read and write to "on" for everyone, and a-x sets execute to "off" (indicated in directory listings with the -).

Rather than set permissions with letters and hyphens, however, you can translate them into numeric values, using 1 for "on" and 0 for "off." So, rw-, with read and write "on" and execute off, would translate into the numbers 110. You could think of this as counting in binary—000, 001, 010, 011, 100, 101, 110, 111, with a 1 in each place that the permission is set to "on."

Each of these combinations of on/off permissions (or binary numbers) can be expressed as a unique decimal digit between 0 and 7, as shown in **Table 5.1**. It is these decimal digits that you use to set permissions.

To set permissions using numeric equivalents:

◆ chmod 777 rowyourboat

Type chmod followed by the desired permissions for user, group, and other using the numeric equivalents listed in Table 5.1, followed by the filename. In this example, we've used 777 to set read, write, and execute permissions to "on" for the user, group, and other.

Or, for example, 724 would give the user full read, write, and execute permissions, the group only write permissions, and other only read permissions.

✔ Tips

■ Setting permissions with numeric equivalents sets permissions absolutely, rather than adding to or subtracting from existing permissions.

■ Numeric equivalents don't give you any more control than you have with ugo+rwx; however, you will need to use the numeric system to set default permissions that apply when you create new files. See the next section, *Changing Permission Defaults with umask*, for the full scoop.

Changing Permission Defaults with umask

Every time you create a file, the Unix system applies default permissions for you. This is great because, for many uses, the default permissions will be just what you want. In other cases, though, you'll want to specify different default permissions.

You can change the default permissions using umask. The umask command uses a numeric representation for permissions (as discussed in the previous section), but the numeric value you specify here is not the same as the one you'd use with chmod. (Don't ask why. We assume that Batman and Robin got together and made this command usable only by the Wonder Twins when their powers were activated.) So you have to figure out the umask value for the permissions you want, then use that value to set the new default permissions.

Note that you cannot set execute permissions by default, so you're really only figuring out the read and write permissions for u, g, and o categories.

To figure the umask value:

1. 666

    Start with 666. Again, don't ask why; it's just what you're supposed to start with.

2. Figure out which numeric values you'd use to set your desired permissions with the chmod command.

    You might review the previous section, Translating Mnemonic Permissions to Numeric Permissions, and peek at Table 5.1 in that section.

3. Subtract that numeric value from 666.

    For example, if the numeric value you'd use with chmod is 644, subtract that value from 666: 666–644=022. 022 is the number you'll use with umask.

```
[ejr@hobbes permissions]$ umask 022
[ejr@hobbes permissions]$ touch tryit
[ejr@hobbes permissions]$ ls -l try*
-rw-r–r– 1 ejr  users  0 Jul 26 16:35 tryit
```

Code Listing 5.9 Use umask to set default permissions for future files.

To set default file-creation permissions with umask:

◆ umask 022

Enter umask plus the number you calculated in the previous steps in this section (**Code Listing 5.9**).

✔ Tips

■ Any changes made with umask apply only to the current shell session. If you want to revert to the default permissions but don't remember what they were, just log out and log back in and you'll be back to normal.

■ If you want to change permission defaults permanently—or at least beyond the current shell session—change them in the configuration files as discussed in Chapter 8.

■ You cannot set the default permissions to include execute permission; it's a security feature, not an omission in Unix's capabilities. For example, suppose you make a new file and copy your favorite commands (or the ones you often forget) into it. If you accidentally type the filename, and the file is executable, you'll run that list of commands and the consequences could be unfortunate. Therefore, you have to explicitly grant execute permission for all files.

■ Yes, 666 is considered the Number of the Beast. We think that it's just a coincidence, but given the potential for confusion in this section, we're not sure.

■ Use umask or umask -s (depending on your specific shell and environment settings) to display your current umask settings.

MANIPULATING FILES

As you learned back in Chapter 4, you can fairly easily work with text by opening up an editor and making the changes you want. But you can do more than just copy, paste, cut, or move text in files. As we'll discuss in this chapter, you can manipulate entire files and look at specific parts of them, get information about the files, find text in files, compare files, and sort files. All kinds of neat stuff!

In this chapter, we'll use a lot of flags to augment commands. You'll find a full list of the most common commands and their flags in Appendix C if you need further explanation or a quick reminder later.

Chapter Contents

- Counting files and file contents
- Viewing file beginnings
- Viewing file endings
- Finding text
- Using regular expressions
- Making global changes
- Changing files
- Comparing files
- Finding differences in files
- Sorting files
- Formatting files
- Redirecting files to two locations
- Splitting

Counting Files and Their Contents with wc

One of Unix's handiest capabilities lets you count files and their contents. For example, you can count the number of files in a directory, or you can count the number of words or lines in a file. You do this counting with the wc command, as shown in **Code Listing 6.1**.

To count words using wc:

◆ wc -w honeydo

At the shell prompt, type wc -w (for words) and the name of the file in which you want to count the words. wc will oblige, as shown in Code Listing 6.1.

To count lines with wc:

◆ wc -l honeydo

Use wc -l followed by the filename to count the lines in the file (**Code Listing 6.2**). This is useful for poetry or for things like lists (e.g., our "honey-do" list always has a minimum of 73 items on it).

✔ Tips

■ You can find out how many files you have in a directory by using ls | wc -l to count the regular files and directories, or ls -A | wc -l to count all files and directories (except for the . and .. directories).

■ You can also find out how many bytes a specific file takes up using wc -c. Or, you can use wc with no flags at all to get the lines, words, and bytes.

```
[ejr@hobbes manipulate]$ wc -w honeydo
    235 honeydo
```

Code Listing 6.1 Use wc -w to count the words in a file. The "honey-do" list in this example is quite a way from being the length of a novel.

```
[ejr@hobbes manipulate]$ wc -l honeydo
    85 honeydo
```

Code Listing 6.2 With 85 separate items in the list, however, it's plenty long enough.

```
[ejr@hobbes manipulate]$ head honeydo
Take garbage out
Clean litter box
Clean diaper pails
Clean litter box
Mow lawn
Edge lawn
Clean litter box
Polish swamp cooler
Buff garage floor
Clean litter box
[ejr@hobbes manipulate]$
```

Code Listing 6.3 Use head to look at just the top of a file, which gives you a manageable view of the file.

```
[ejr@hobbes manipulate]$ head honey* | more
==> honeyconsider <==
Mother-in-law visits next week
Cat mess in hall to clean up
Cat mess in entry to clean up
Cat mess in living room to clean up
Toddler mess in family room to clean up
Cat and toddler mess in den to clean up
IRS called again today
Neighbors on both sides looking for
donations
        for the annual fund drive
Boss called last Friday and said it's urgent
==> honeydo <==
Take garbage out
Clean litter box
Clean diaper pails
Clean litter box
Mow lawn
Edge lawn
Clean litter box
Polish swamp cooler
Buff garage floor
```

Code Listing 6.4 head, with the help of more, lets you see the beginnings of several files in sequence.

Viewing File Beginnings with head

Using head, as shown in **Code Listing 6.3**, you can find out in a jiffy what's in a file by viewing the top few lines. This is particularly handy when you're browsing file listings or trying to find a specific file among several others with similar content.

To view file beginnings with head:

◆ head honeydo

At the shell prompt, type head followed by the filename. As Code Listing 6.3 shows, you'll see the first ten lines on the screen. Notice that "lines" are defined by hard returns, so a line could, in some cases, wrap to many screen lines.

To view a specified number of lines:

◆ head -20 honeydo

Add -20 (or whatever number of lines you want to view) to view a specific number of lines.

To view the beginnings of multiple files:

◆ head honey* | more

You can view the tops of multiple files by piping head (plus the filenames) to more. Note that head conveniently tells you the filename of each file, as shown in **Code Listing 6.4**.

Viewing File Endings with `tail`

Occasionally, you might also need to use `tail`, which displays the last lines of a file. `tail` is particularly handy for checking footers or for updating information in a footer (see **Code Listing 6.5**). Just as with `head` (described in the previous pages), `tail` offers several options for viewing files.

To view file endings with `tail`:

◆ `tail honeydo`

At the shell prompt, type `tail` followed by the filename. As Code Listing 6.5 shows, you'll see the last ten lines on the screen.

To view a specified number of lines:

◆ `tail -15 honeydo`

Here, all you do is add a specific number of lines you want to view (-15).

To view the endings of multiple files:

◆ `tail honey* | more`

Pipe the `tail` command and the files (multiple files indicated with *) to `more` (**Code Listing 6.6**).

✔ Tip

■ `head` and its counterpart, `tail`, are great for splitting long files. Use `wc -l` to count the lines. If the file has 500 lines, but you care about only the beginning and ending lines, then type `head -25 filename > newfilename` to put the first 25 lines of the file into a new file. Then do the same with `tail` to put the last 25 lines of the file into another new file.

```
[ejr@hobbes manipulate]$ tail honeydo
Empty diaper pails
Take garbage out.
-End of today's list-

Buy more garbage bags
Get cleaning supplies at store
Take cat to vet
Fix lawnmower

[ejr@hobbes manipulate]$
```

Code Listing 6.5 `tail` lets you check out just the end of files.

```
[ejr@hobbes manipulate]$ tail honey* | more
==> honeyconsider <==
Cat mess in entry to clean up
Cat mess in living room to clean up
Toddler mess in family room to clean up
Cat and toddler mess in den to clean up
IRS called again today
Neighbors on both sides looking for donations
          for the annual fund drive
Boss called last Friday and said it's urgent
-End of today's list-

==> honeydo <==
Empty diaper pails
Take garbage out
-End of today's list-

Buy more garbage bags
Get cleaning supplies at store
Take cat to vet
Fix lawnmower

-More-
```

Code Listing 6.6 Use `tail` with `more` to see the ends of multiple files.

```
[ejr@hobbes manipulate]$ grep bucket
→ limericks
Who carried his lunch in a bucket,
[ejr@hobbes manipulate]$
```

Code Listing 6.7 Use grep to see all occurrences of a specific string in a file.

```
[ejr@hobbes manipulate]$ grep -5 bucket
→ limerick
he strummed and he hummed,
and sang dumdeedum,
But him a musician...whoda thunk it?

There once was a man from Nantucket,
Who carried his lunch in a bucket,
Said he with a sigh,
As he ate a whole pie,
If I just had a donut I'd dunk it.

A nice young lady named Debbie,
[ejr@hobbes manipulate]$
```

Code Listing 6.8 grep can show the context around instances of the string as well.\

✔ Tips

- Use the -n flag (for example, grep -n string file) to print each found line with a line number.

- You can use grep with multiple filenames, such as in grep Nantucket lim* or grep Nantucket lim* poetry humor.

- If you want to get creative, you can look for spaces as well, but you need to use quotes, like grep "from Nantucket" limerick*.

- Win nerdy bar bets by knowing the heritage of grep.

Finding Text with grep

You can search through multiple files for specific strings of characters and then view the list of matching files onscreen. You do this using the grep command (which stands for "global regular expression print," a once useful and now rather arcane ed or vi command), as shown in **Code Listing 6.7**. As we'll show you, you can add several flags to grep to get slightly different results.

To find text strings with grep:

- grep bucket limericks

  At the shell prompt, type grep, the text you're trying to locate (in this case, bucket), and the file you're searching in (here, limericks). grep will return all lines in the file that contain the specified string, as shown in Code Listing 6.7.

- grep -5 bucket limericks

  You can specify that a number of lines (say 5) on either side of the found text string should also be displayed. Sometimes you can't tell what you need to know with just the line that contains your search string, and adding lines around it can help give you a context (see **Code Listing 6.8**). Note that this option isn't available on all versions of grep, but it'll work for most.

- grep -c Nantucket limericks

  By adding the -c flag, you can find out how many times a text string appears in a file.

- grep -v Nantucket limericks

  Or, with the -v flag, you can find all of the lines that do not contain the specified string.

- grep -i nantucket limericks

  With the -i flag, you can search without case-sensitivity. Here any line with nantucket or Nantucket or nAntuCKet would be found.

Using Regular Expressions with grep

In addition to using grep to search for simple text strings, you can also use grep to search for regular expressions. Regular expressions are kind of like fancy wildcards, where you use a symbol to represent a character, number, or other symbol. With regular expressions, you can search for different parts of files, such as the end of a line or a text string next to another specified text string. **Table 6.1** lists some of the more common regular expressions.

To use regular expressions with grep:

◆ `grep .logan limerick`

Type grep followed by the regular expression and the filename. Here, we've used the regular expression `.logan` to find all instances of "logan" that are preceded by a single character (**Code Listing 6.9**). Note that this usage of a . to match a single character closely resembles the ? wildcard used with ls.

You could also use multiple periods for specific numbers of characters. For example, to find "Dogbert" and "Dilbert," you might use `grep D..bert plagiarized.sayings`.

In some cases, you may need to structure the search string slightly differently, depending on the expression you're using and the information you're looking for. Check out the additional examples in Table 6.1 for more information.

```
[ejr@hobbes manipulate]$ grep .logan
→ limerick
Worked hard all day on a slogan,
You see, the slogan's still brogan.
[ejr@hobbes manipulate]$
```

Code Listing 6.9 Use grep with regular expressions to create fancy wildcard commands.

✔ Tips

- "Regular expression" is often abbreviated as "regexp" in Unix documentation and Internet discussions.

- The command `egrep` is closely related to `grep`, adding a little more flexibility for extended regular expressions, but it fundamentally works the same. On many systems the `grep` command is really `egrep`—when you type in either one, you're really running `egrep`.

- If you're searching for whole words through large files, use `fgrep` for faster searching. It uses the same general syntax as `grep`, but searches only for whole words (not regular expressions) so goes much faster.

- See Chapter 1 for details about wildcards.

USING REGULAR EXPRESSIONS WITH grep

Table 6.1

Regular Expressions, Examples, and Explanations

REGULAR EXPRESSION	FUNCTION	EXAMPLE	EXPLANATION
.	Matches any character	grep b.rry	This finds all instances of "berry" or "barry."
*	Matches zero or more instances of the preceding item, so a*b would find "b" as well as "ab" and "aaab," but not "acb"	grep 's*day' /home/ejr/schedule	Here, the * matches zero or more of the items that immediately precede the *, in this case the letter 's'.
^	Matches only instances of the string at the beginning of a line	grep '^Some' sayings	With the ^, you specify that the search string must appear at the beginning of a line. The example would find a line beginning with "Some" but not one beginning with "Read Some."
$	Matches only instances of the string at the end of a line	grep 'ach$' sayings	This example finds all lines in the file sayings that end with "ach".
\	Escapes (quotes) the following character—so you can search for literal characters like * or $ that are also operators	grep '*' sayings	grep * saying searches for all instances of "*" in the sayings file. The \ tells grep to interpret the * literally, as an asterisk character, rather than as a wildcard.
[ ]	Matches any member of the set, like [a-z], [0-6], or [321] (three or two or one)	grep 'number[0-9]' specifications	Use square brackets ([ ]) to enclose a set of options. Here, number[0-9] would match all instances of number1, number2, number3, and so forth in the file called specifications.

Using Other Examples of Regular Expressions

In the previous section, we showed you how to use the grep command to search with regular expressions. You can, though, do other neat finding tasks, as we'll discuss in this section.

To find lines with specific characteristics:

◆ grep '^Nantucket' limerick*

Here, we use grep to find all of the lines in the limericks that start with Nantucket, if there are any.

◆ grep 'Nantucket$' limerick*

Similarly, you can find the lines that end with Nantucket.

◆ grep '^[A-Z]' limerick

Or, you can find the lines that start with a capital letter by including the [A-Z] regular expression.

◆ grep '^[A-Z a-z]' limerick

Here, you can find all the lines that start with any letter, but not a number or symbol. Fancy, huh?

✔ Tip

■ You can also use regular expressions with awk and sed. See *Making Global Changes with sed* and *Changing Files with awk* in this chapter for details.

```
[ejr@hobbes manipulate]$ sed
 → 's/oldaddr@raycomm.com/newaddr@
 → raycomm.com /g'
 → address.htm > address-new.htm
[ejr@hobbes manipulate]$ head
 → address-new.htm
<BODY BACKGROUND="/images/background.gif"
BGCOLOR="#FFFFFF" TEXT="#000000" LINK=
"#009900" VLINK="#000000"
ALINK="#ff0000">
<P>
Please send all comments to
 → <A HREF="mailto:newaddr@raycomm.com">
 → newaddr@raycomm.com</A>.
</P>

<TABLE BORDER=0>
<TR>
<TD WIDTH="150" VALIGN=TOP>
[ejr@hobbes manipulate]$
```

Code Listing 6.10 You can use sed to make changes throughout files, such as the address change here.

✔ Tips

- You can have sed zip through multiple documents. See Chapter 10 for information on how to make a shell script with a loop.

- Because sed commands can be long and unwieldy, it might be helpful to save the commands in a separate text file (so you don't have to retype them). For example, if you saved the command s/oldaddr@raycomm.com/newaddr@raycomm.com/g in a file called script.sed, you could issue sed -f script.sed address.htm > address-new.htm to run the sed commands from the script.sed file. You can have as many commands as you want in your script.sed file.

Making Global Changes with sed

Another handy command you can use is sed, which lets you make multiple changes to files, without ever opening an editor. For example, as a new Webmaster, you might use sed to change all occurrences of the previous Webmaster's email address to your own. As we'll show in this section, you can use sed to make global changes within documents.

To make global changes with sed:

- sed 's/oldaddr@raycomm.com
  → /newaddr@raycomm.com /g' address.htm
  → > address-new.htm
  Type sed, followed by
  - ▲ A single quote (')
  - ▲ A leading "s"
  - ▲ A slash (/)
  - ▲ The text you want to replace (oldaddr@raycomm.com)
  - ▲ Another slash (/)
  - ▲ The replacement text (newaddr@raycomm.com/g)
  - ▲ Another single quote (')
  - ▲ Yet another /
  - ▲ g, which tells sed to apply the change globally. (If you omit the g, only the first occurrence on each line will be changed.)
  - ▲ The name of the file in which the changes should be made (address.htm)

You can redirect the output to a new filename (see **Code Listing 6.10**) or pipe it to another command entirely. You cannot redirect to the same filename or you'll end up with no content in your file.

Changing Files with awk

While sed is line-oriented and lets you fiddle and diddle to your heart's content, awk is field-oriented and is ideal for manipulating database or comma-delimited files. For example, if you have an address book file, you can use awk to find and change information in fields you specify, as in **Code Listing 6.11**. In the following steps, we'll show you a sampling of the things you can do using awk to modify, in this example, an address book file.

To change files with awk:

1. `awk '{ print $1 }' address.book`

    At the shell prompt, use `awk '{ print $1 }' address.book` to look at the `address.book` file and select (and send to standard output) the first field in each record (line). More specifically, starting from the inside out

    ▲ `$1` references the first field in each line. Unless you specify otherwise, awk assumes that a space separates the fields, so the first field starts at the beginning of the line and continues to the first space.

    ▲ `{}` contain the awk command, and the quotes are necessary to tie the awk command together (so the first space within the command isn't interpreted by the shell as the end of the command). See Code Listing 6.11.

2. `awk -F, '{ print $1 }' address.book`

    The `-F` flag tells awk to use the character following it—in this case, a comma (`,`)—as the field separator. This change makes the output of the command a little cleaner and more accurate. If you were working with `/etc/passwd`, you'd use `-F:` to specify that the `:` is the field separator.

```
[ejr@hobbes manipulate]$ awk '{ print $1 }'
→ address.book
Schmidt,
Feldman,
Brown,
Smith,
Jones,
[ejr@hobbes manipulate]$
```

Code Listing 6.11 awk lets you access individual fields in a file.

De-what?

A *delimited file* uses a specific character to show where one bit of information ends and another begins. Each piece of information is a separate field. For example, a file that contains "John, Doe, Thornton, Colorado" is comma-delimited, sporting a comma between fields. Other files, such as the `/etc/passwd` file, use a colon (`:`) to separate the fields. Just about any symbol that's not used in the content could be used as a delimiter.

```
[ejr@hobbes manipulate]$ awk -F, '{print
→ $2 "" $1 " " $7 }' address.book
→ > phone.list
[ejr@hobbes manipulate]$ more phone.list
        Sven Schmidt  555-555-8382
        Fester Feldman
        John Brown  918-555-1234
        Sally Smith  801-555-8982
        Kelly Jones  408-555-7253
[ejr@hobbes manipulate]$
```

Code Listing 6.12 With a little more tweaking, awk lets you do a lot of processing on the files to get just the information you need.

3. awk -F, '{ print $2 " " $1 " " $7 }'
   → address.book > phone.list

With this code, you can pull specific fields, in an arbitrary order, from your database. Although it looks complex, it's just one additional step from the previous example. Rather than printing a single field from the address book, we're printing field 2, then a space, then field 1, then a space, then field 7. The final bit just redirects the output into a new file. This example would produce a list of names and phone numbers, as shown in **Code Listing 6.12**.

4. awk -F, '/CA/{ print $2 $1 $7 }'
   → address.book > phone.list

You can also specify a matching pattern. Here, we added /CA/ to search and act on only the lines that contain CA, so only those lines will be in the phone.list file.

✔ Tips

- You can load awk scripts from a file with awk -f script.awk filename. Just as with sed, this keeps the retyping to a minimum, which is helpful with these long and convoluted commands. Refer to Chapter 10 for more details about scripting.

- Take a glance at *Sorting Files* with sort later in this chapter and consider piping your awk output to sort. Let Unix do the tedious work for you!

CHANGING FILES WITH awk

Comparing Files with cmp

Suppose you've been working on the dearliza file and you want to know how it differs from the dearhenry file. Using cmp, you can compare the two files as shown in **Code Listing 6.13**.

To compare files with cmp:

◆ cmp dearliza dearhenry

At the shell prompt, type cmp followed by both filenames. As Code Listing 6.13 shows, these two files are not the same.

If the files are identical, you'll find yourself back at the shell prompt with no comment from cmp. If both files are identical until one of them ends—that is, say, the first 100 lines are the same, but one continues and the other ends—then you'll see an EOF (end of file) message, as in **Code Listing 6.14**.

✔ Tips

■ You can find out other ways that files differ using diff, as described in the next section, *Finding Differences in Files with diff*.

■ Unix provides an exit status message that you can use to get more information about how the program stopped and why. See *Using Advanced Redirection* in Chapter 17 for more information.

■ You can also use diff to find out which files are in one directory but not another. Just type diff followed by the names of the two directories; for example, diff /home/ejr/Directory/home/ejr/ Newdirectory

■ You might also check out the section, *Finding Differences in Files with sdiff*, for yet another way to compare files.

```
[ejr@hobbes manipulate]$ cmp dearliza
 → dearhenry
dearliza dearhenry differ: char 20, line 2
[ejr@hobbes manipulate]$
```

Code Listing 6.13 cmp gives just the facts about the first difference between two files.

```
[ejr@hobbes manipulate]$ cmp limerick
 → limericks
cmp: EOF on limerick
[ejr@hobbes manipulate]$
```

Code Listing 6.14 cmp also tells you if the files matched until one ended (EOF stands for "end of file").

COMPARING FILES WITH CMP

```
[ejr@hobbes manipulate]$ diff dearliza
  → dearhenry
2,3c2,3
< Dear Liza,
< There's a hole in my bucket, dear Liza,
  → dear Liza, dear Liza.
> Dear Henry,
> Please fix it dear Henry, dear Henry,
  → dear 'Henry.
5,6c5,6
< Henry
<
> Liza
> PS, you forgot your toolbox last time.
[ejr@hobbes manipulate]$
```

Code Listing 6.15 diff tells you all you ever wanted to know about the differences between two files but not in an easily readable manner.

Finding Differences in Files with diff

In addition to using cmp to find out how files differ, you can also use diff. This command tells you specifically where two files differ, not just that they differ and at which point the differences start (see **Code Listing 6.15**).

To find differences with diff:

◆ diff dearliza dearhenry

Type diff, followed by both filenames. The diff output, as in Code Listing 6.15, shows lines that appear only in one file or the other. The lines from file 1 are indicated with <, while the lines from file 2 are indicated with >.

Above each line are the affected line numbers in the first file, then d, a, or c, then the corresponding line numbers from the second file:

▲ d means that the line would have to be deleted from file 1 to make it match file 2.

▲ a means that text would have to be added to file 1 to match file 2.

▲ c means that changes would have to be made to the line for the two files to match.

✔ Tip

■ If you're comparing email messages or other less-structured documents, you might consider adding the flags -i (case insensitive), -b (ignore blank lines), or even -w (ignore spaces and tabs) to avoid cluttering your results with unimportant differences. For example, you could use diff -ibw file1 file2 to find all differences between two files except those involving blank lines, spaces, tabs, or lowercase/uppercase letters.

Finding Differences in Files with sdiff

Yet another way to compare files is to use sdiff, which presents the two files onscreen so that you can visually compare them (see **Code Listing 6.16**).

To compare files with sdiff:

◆ sdiff dearliza dearhenry

At the shell prompt, type sdiff and the filenames to compare the two files. The output, as shown in Code Listing 6.16, presents each line of the two files side by side, separating them with

▲ (Nothing) if the lines are identical

▲ < if the line exists only in the first file

▲ > if the line exists only in the second file

▲ | if they are different

✔ Tips

■ If most of the lines are the same, consider using the -s flag so the identical lines are not shown. For example, type sdiff -s dearliza dearhenry

■ If the output scoots by too fast to read, remember that you can pipe the entire command to more, as in sdiff dearliza dearhenry | more

```
[ejr@hobbes manipulate]$ sdiff dearliza
 → dearhenry
July 25, 1998    July 25, 1998
Dear Liza,       | Dear Henry,
There's a hole in my bucket, dear Liza,
dear Liza.    | Please fix it dear Henry,
                 dear Henry.
Yours,           Yours,
Henry            | Liza
       | PS, you forgot your toolbox last time.
[ejr@hobbes manipulate]$
```

Code Listing 6.16 sdiff puts the files side by side, so you can easily see the differences.

Sorting Files with sort

If you want to be really lazy—er, um, smart—let Unix sort files for you. You can use sort to, for example, sort your address book alphabetically—as opposed to the random order in which you might have entered addresses (see **Code Listing 6.17**).

To sort files with sort:

◆ sort address.book >
  ›sorted.address.book

To begin, type sort, followed by the name of the file you want to sort. Unix will sort the lines in the file alphabetically and present the sorted results in the file you specify (here, sorted.address.book), as shown in Code Listing 6.17.

continues on next page

```
[ejr@hobbes manipulate]$ more address.book
Schmidt, Sven, 1 Circle Drive, Denver, CO, 80221, 555-555-8382
Feldman, Fester, RR1, Billings, MT 62832, 285-555-0281
Brown, John, 1453 South Street, Tulsa, OK, 74114, 918-555-1234
Smith, Sally, 452 Center Ave., Salt Lake City, UT, 84000, 801-555-8982
Jones, Kelly, 14 Main Street, Santa Clara, CA, 95051, 408-555-7253
[ejr@hobbes manipulate]$ sort address.book
Brown, John, 1453 South Street, Tulsa, OK, 74114, 918-555-1234
Feldman, Fester, RR1, Billings, MT 62832, 285-555-0281
Jones, Kelly, 14 Main Street, Santa Clara, CA, 95051, 408-555-7253
Schmidt, Sven, 1 Circle Drive, Denver, CO, 80221, 555-555-8382
Smith, Sally, 452 Center Ave., Salt Lake City, UT, 84000, 801-555-8982
[ejr@hobbes manipulate]$ sort address.book > sorted.address.book
[ejr@hobbes manipulate]$ cat sorted.address.book
Brown, John, 1453 South Street, Tulsa, OK, 74114, 918-555-1234
Feldman, Fester, RR1, Billings, MT 62832, 285-555-0281
Jones, Kelly, 14 Main Street, Santa Clara, CA, 95051, 408-555-7253
Schmidt, Sven, 1 Circle Drive, Denver, CO, 80221, 555-555-8382
Smith, Sally, 452 Center Ave., Salt Lake City, UT, 84000, 801-555-8982
[ejr@hobbes manipulate]$
```

Code Listing 6.17 An unsorted address book springs to order with the help of sort.

✔ Tips

■ If you have multiple files to sort, you can use `sort file1 file2 file3 > complete. sorted.file`, and the output will contain the contents of all three files—sorted, of course.

■ You can sort fields in comma-delimited files by adding -t to the command. For example, `sort -t, +1 address.book` tells Unix to sort by the second field. The -t and following character (,) indicate what character separates the fields—the comma in this case. If a character isn't given, `sort` thinks that white space marks the boundaries between fields. The +1 says to skip the first field and sort on the second one.

■ You can sort numerically, too, with `sort -n filename`. If you don't use the -n flag, the output will be ordered based on the leftmost digits in the numbers—for example "1, 203, 50"—because the alphabetic sort starts at the left of the field.

Eliminating Duplicates
with `uniq`

If you've sorted files using the handy-dandy `sort` command, you might end up with results that have duplicates in them. Heck, you might have files with duplicates. At any rate, here's how to find and work with them. As **Code Listing 6.18** shows, you can get rid of duplicate lines by using the `uniq` command (short for "unique") in conjunction with `sort`.

To eliminate duplicates with `uniq`:

◆ `sort address.book | uniq`

At the shell prompt, type `sort` and the filename, then type `| uniq` to pipe the output to `uniq`. The output of `uniq` will not contain any duplicated entries (Code Listing 6.18).

✔ Tips

■ `uniq` finds only identical, adjacent (sorted) lines. For example, if you have both `Jones` and `jones` in your address book, `uniq` won't identify either entry because they differ in capitalization.

■ You can also use the `-d` flag to specify that you want to see only the duplicate lines. For example, say you want to see all of the people who are in both your `carpool` file and your `nightout` file. You'd just use `sort carpool nightout | uniq -d`

■ You can sort and eliminate duplicates in one step with `sort -u address.book`.

```
[ejr@hobbes manipulate]$ more long.address.book
Schmidt, Sven, 1 Circle Drive, Denver, CO, 80221, 555-555-8382
Feldman, Fester, RR1, Billings, MT 62832, 285-555-0281
Brown, John, 1453 South Street, Tulsa, OK, 74114, 918-555-1234
Smith, Sally, 452 Center Ave., Salt Lake City, UT, 84000, 801-555-8982
Jones, Kelly, 14 Main Street, Santa Clara, CA, 95051, 408-555-7253
Schmidt, Swen, 1 Circle Drive, Denver, CO, 80221, 555-555-8382
Feldman, Fester, RR1, Billings, MT 62832, 285-555-0281
Brown, Jonathon, 1453 South Street, Tulsa, OK, 74114, 918-555-1234
Smith, Sally, 452 Center Ave., Salt Lake City, UT, 84000, 801-555-8982
Jones, Kelly, 14 Main Street, Santa Clara, CA, 95051, 408-555-7253
[ejr@hobbes manipulate]$ sort long.address.book | uniq
Brown, John, 1453 South Street, Tulsa, OK, 74114, 918-555-1234
Brown, Jonathon, 1453 South Street, Tulsa, OK, 74114, 918-555-1234
Feldman, Fester, RR1, Billings, MT 62832, 285-555-0281
Jones, Kelly, 14 Main Street, Santa Clara, CA, 95051, 408-555-7253
Schmidt, Sven, 1 Circle Drive, Denver, CO, 80221, 555-555-8382
Smith, Sally, 452 Center Ave., Salt Lake City, UT, 84000, 801-555-8982
[ejr@hobbes manipulate]$
```

Code Listing 6.18 Use sort with uniq to eliminate duplicates.

129

Redirecting to Multiple Locations with tee

Suppose you just updated your address book file and want to send it to your boss in addition to putting it in your own files. You can, using tee, which redirects output to two different places (see **Code Listing 6.19**).

To redirect output to two locations with tee:

◆ sort address.book new.addresses
  → | tee sorted.all | mail
  → boss@raycomm.com -s "Here's the
  → address book, boss" -

At the shell prompt, use the tee command plus a filename in the middle of the pipe line to send the sorted information to that filename as well as to the standard output (which could, of course, be redirected to another filename). Here, we send the results of the sort to the sorted.all file and to standard output, where mail will take over and send the file to the boss. See Chapter 11 for more on fancy mail tricks.

Tee Time?

You might think of the tee command as being similar to a plumber's pipe joint—that is, it takes stuff from one location and sends it out to two different places.

```
[ejr@hobbes manipulate]$ sort address.book new.addresses | tee sorted.all | mail
 → boss@raycomm.com -s  "Here's the address book, boss" -
[ejr@hobbes manipulate]$
```

Code Listing 6.19 Use tee to send output to two different places at once.

```
[jdoe@frazz jdoe]$ cat limerick
There once was a man from Nantucket,
Who carried his lunch in a bucket,
Said he with a sigh,
As he ate a whole pie,
If I just had a donut I'd dunk it.

[jdoe@frazz jdoe]$ cat limerick | tr
→ a-zA-Z A-Za-z
tHERE ONCE WAS A MAN FROM nANTUCKET,
wHO CARRIED HIS LUNCH IN A BUCKET,
sAID HE WITH A SIGH,
aS HE ATE A WHOLE PIE,
iF i JUST HAD A DONUT i'D DUNK IT.

[jdoe@frazz jdoe]$ cat limerick | tr -c
→ a-zA-Z "\n"
There
once
was
a
man
from
Nantucket

Who
carried
his
lunch
in
a
bucket

Said
he
with
a
sigh

As
he
ate
a
whole
pie
```

Code Listing 6.20 Use tr to translate characters in files.

Changing with tr

Sometimes you just have to make changes to a file to change all occurrences of one term or character to another. For example, you might have reversed the case in a file (by accidentally typing with Caps Lock on...argh!) and need to change it back. Or you might want to turn a document into a list of words (one per line) that you can sort or count. The tr utility is just what you need (see **Code Listing 6.20**).

To translate case with tr:

◆ cat limerick | tr a-zA-Z A-Za-z

At the shell prompt, use the **cat** command and the pipe to send a file to **tr**, which will then translate lowercase to uppercase, and vice versa.

To break lines with tr:

◆ cat limerick | tr -c a-zA-Z "\n"

Change anything that's not a letter (upper or lowercase) to a new line, thus breaking the limerick into a list of words. The –c indicates that anything that does not match the first set of characters (the complement of those characters) should be changed to the new character.

continues on next page

```
(continued)
If
I
just
had
a
donut
I
d
dunk
it
```

✔ Tips

■ Rather than use cat to send the file to tr, you can use spiffy Unix redirection tools (< in this case) to do it. An equivalent command to translate case would be tr a-zA-Z A-Za-z < limerick

■ With tr, you can accomplish all kinds of translations. For example, you could set up a bit of a code to keep secret information somewhat secret, by translating letters to garble your text, then retranslating when you want them. For example, use cat limerick | tr a-mA-Mn-zN-Z n-zN-Za-mA-M > limerick.rot13 to encode and cat limerick.rot13 | tr n-zN-Za-mA-M a-mA-Mn-zN-Z to decode. This is the same as ROT13, discussed in Chapter 17, but far more flexible and spiffy if you use tr to do it.

■ Check out the man page for tr (man tr) for details on the other cool translations and conversions it can do.

Formatting with fmt

After you've been typing away—writing the Great American Novel, perhaps—you might notice that you're suffering from creeping margin uglies, like those shown in **Code Listing 6.21**. Never fear, fmt can help. Just run your text through fmt, and all will be well.

To format with fmt:

◆ `fmt spiderstory.unformatted`

   At the shell prompt, just tell fmt to do its thing, and you'll be in business.

✔ Tip

■ You can supplement fmt with handy flags to help make lines more readable. For example, you can often use fmt –u to make spacing uniform: one space between words, and two spaces between sentences. Or, try fmt –w to specify the width of the formatted text; for example, –w 60 would specify a 60-character-wide line.

continues on next page

FORMATTING WITH fmt

```
[jdoe@frazz jdoe]$ cat spiderstory.unformatted
This morning I
got up, went
downstairs, and found a HUMONGOUS spider
in the bathroom where the little potty is.
After I
quietly composed myself
from the shock (I didn't want
to alert the kids),

I looked around the
house for
something to put him in...the
kids' bug catcher thing
(nowhere to be found)...a jar...tupperware...a lidded
cup...the
salad spinner (BwaaaaHaaaHaaa!)....

I went back and checked on the spider and decided that I just couldn't face putting him in
something.
I mean, what if he got close to me...or TOUCHED
me?!?!
And, since I hate the crunching sound and feel of
squashing bugs,
I knew I couldn't just kill him.
This    spider had *bones*, I'm tellin' ya'. So, I
hunted for bug spray.
And hunted. But
nothing.

[jdoe@frazz jdoe]$ fmt spiderstory.unformatted
This morning I got up, went downstairs, and found a HUMONGOUS spider in
the bathroom where the little potty is.  After I quietly composed myself
from the shock (I didn't want to alert the kids),

I looked around the house for something to put him in...the kids' bug
catcher thing (nowhere to be found)...a jar...tupperware...a lidded
cup...the salad spinner (BwaaaaHaaaHaaa!)....

I went back and checked on the spider and decided that I just couldn't
face putting him in something.  I mean, what if he got close to me...or
TOUCHED me?!?!  And, since I hate the crunching sound and feel of
squashing bugs, I knew I couldn't just kill him.  This spider had
*bones*, I'm tellin' ya'. So, I hunted for bug spray.  And hunted.
But nothing.
```

Code Listing 6.21 With fmt you can clean up all kinds of idiosyncrasies in the format of your documents.

Preparing to Print with pr

Although old-fashioned line printers—those obnoxiously loud ones that clatter out character by character, or the dot-matrix printers that zing out line after line—aren't terribly easy to find anymore, the pr command is finding new life in the age of the Internet.

Why? Well, nothing says email as quickly, easily, effectively, and safely as plain text. Plain text attaches no viruses. Plain text works in every email system, including handheld computers, and the like. Plain text works great—often better than a word processor—for one-off messages, pages, and short documents that just don't merit firing up a full-blown word processor. **Code Listing 6.22** shows an example of text processed with pr.

To process with pr:

◆ `pr spiderstory.formatted`

Turn pr loose, and you'll be the talk of the town.

✔ Tips

■ Two utilities that work great together are fmt and pr. See Code Listing 6.22 to see what `fmt -w 30 spiderstory.unformatted | pr -2` will do for you.

■ Use the –n and –d flags if you're printing something that will be reviewed by others. Using these flags, you get line numbers and double-spacing, which will make the review process easier.

■ Add in a –T flag so the output doesn't even pretend to be appropriate for a printer—there are no headers or footers or other pagination for actual printed output.

continues on next page

```
[jdoe@frazz jdoe]$ pr spiderstory.formatted
2003-01-01 12:   spiderstory.formatted Page 1

This morning I got up, went downstairs, and found a HUMONGOUS spider in
the bathroom where the little potty is.  After I quietly composed myself
from the shock (I didn't want to alert the kids),
I looked around the house for something to put him in...the kids' bug catcher thing
(nowhere to be found)...a jar...tupperware...a lidded cup...the salad spinner
(BwaaaaHaaaHaaa!)....
I went back and checked on the spider and decided that I just couldn't face putting
him in something.  I mean, what if he got close to me...or TOUCHED me?!?!  And, since
I hate the crunching sound and feel of squashing bugs, I knew I couldn't just kill
him.  This   spider had *bones*, I'm tellin' ya'.  So, I hunted for bug spray.  And
hunted. But nothing.
[jdoe@frazz jdoe]$ fmt -u -w 30 spiderstory.unformatted | pr —columns=2
2003-01-01 12:59 Page 1


This morning I got up,                (BwaaaaHaaaHaaa!)....
went downstairs, and found            I went back and checked on
a HUMONGOUS spider in the             the spider and decided that
bathroom where the little             I just couldn't face putting
potty is.  After I quietly            him in something.  I mean,
composed myself from the              what if he got close to
shock (I didn't want to alert         me...or TOUCHED me?!?!  And,
the kids),                            since I hate the crunching
                                      sound and feel of squashing
I looked around the house for         bugs, I knew I couldn't just
something to put him in...the         kill him.  This spider had
kids' bug catcher thing               *bones*, I'm tellin' ya'.  So,
(nowhere to be found)...a             I hunted for bug spray.
jar...tupperware...a lidded           And hunted. But nothing.
cup...the salad spinner
```

Code Listing 6.22 The pr utility can help you get your output spiffed up, even if you aren't printing it.

Splitting Files with split

Suppose you're futzing with your new digital camera and want to share a photo of your new computer (what else is cool enough to take pictures of?!) via email with your friends and family. You access the file, attach it to an email message, and then—argh!—your ISP fails to send the file because it's too big. While you could modify the file itself—reduce the physical size, reduce the number of colors used, or crop out nonessential parts, for example—you can also just split the file with split. For example, if the ISP tells you that no files larger than 0.51 MB will be accepted, you can use split to send the file in chunks—all using one easy command (**Code Listing 6.23**).

```
[jdoe@frazz split]$ ls -lh
total 1.1M
-rwxrwxr-x   1 jdoe  jdoe     1.0M Jan  1 12:42 mongopicture.jpg*
[jdoe@frazz split]$ ls -l
total 1060
-rwxrwxr-x   1 jdoe  jdoe     1079300 Jan  1 12:42 mongopicture.jpg*
[jdoe@frazz split]$ split -b 500k mongopicture.jpg
[jdoe@frazz split]$ ls -lh
total 2.1M
-rwxrwxr-x   1 jdoe  jdoe     1.0M Jan  1 12:42 mongopicture.jpg*
-rw-rw-r-   1 jdoe  jdoe     500K Jan  1 13:03 xaa
-rw-rw-r-   1 jdoe  jdoe     500K Jan  1 13:03 xab
-rw-rw-r-   1 jdoe  jdoe     54K Jan  1 13:03 xac
[jdoe@frazz split]$ split -b 500k mongopicture.jpg chunk
[jdoe@frazz split]$ ls -lh
total 3.2M
-rw-rw-r-   1 jdoe  jdoe     500K Jan  1 13:03 chunkaa
-rw-rw-r-   1 jdoe  jdoe     500K Jan  1 13:03 chunkab
-rw-rw-r-   1 jdoe  jdoe     54K Jan  1 13:03 chunkac
-rwxrwxr-x   1 jdoe  jdoe     1.0M Jan  1 12:42 mongopicture.jpg*
-rw-rw-r-   1 jdoe  jdoe     500K Jan  1 13:03 xaa
-rw-rw-r-   1 jdoe  jdoe     500K Jan  1 13:03 xab
-rw-rw-r-   1 jdoe  jdoe     54K Jan  1 13:03 xac
 [jdoe@frazz split]$ cat chunkaa chunkab chunkac > reconstitutedpicture.jpg
[jdoe@frazz split]$ cmp mongopicture.jpg reconstitutedpicture.jpg
[jdoe@frazz split]$
```

Code Listing 6.23 Use split to break files into smaller chunks.

To split files with `split`**:**

◆ `split -b 500k mongopicture.jpg`

With that, split gives you three files (xaa, xab, xac) that are each 500 KB (the first two) or less (the last one, containing the leftovers). Mail each of those, and you've squeaked under the ISP's size limit.

✔ Tips

■ Control the names of the files by adding a prefix at the end. For example, try `split -b 500k mongopicture.jpg chunk` to get three pieces called chunkaa, chunkab, and chunkac.

■ Use cat to restore the original. For example, `cat xaa xab xac > reconstituted-picture.jpg`

■ If you're following the photo file example used here, note that the recipient of the emailed file pieces will have to assemble the pieces in order to view the photo. Even if the recipient isn't a Unix user, all systems have utilities to accomplish this task. Now, whether your recipient would want to take the time or would have the skill to do this is another question. You might check with him or her first.

GETTING INFORMATION ABOUT THE SYSTEM

7

Now is your chance to nose around in everyone else's business! In this chapter, we'll show you how to get information about the system, about other users, and about your own userid.

Chapter Contents

- Finding out system information
- Viewing file systems
- Determining disk usage
- Finding out file types
- Finding out about other users
- Learning who else is logged in
- Getting information about your userid

Getting System Information with uname

Information about your Unix system might come in handy if you're planning to try some new software or need to figure out system idiosyncrasies. Some systems tell you this information when you log in. Sometimes, however, especially if you're using an ISP, you may not have been told any particulars about the Unix system. You can easily find out what kind of Unix system you're using with uname, as shown in **Code Listings 7.1** and **7.2**.

To find out about the system using uname:

1. uname

To begin, type uname to find out what kind of a system you're on. The Unix system in Code Listings 7.1 and 7.2 is Solaris (aka, SunOS). Other common systems (not an exhaustive list, by any means) are Linux, AIX, BSD, and HP/UX.

2. uname -sr

Add the -sr flags to the command, yielding uname -sr, to find out both the operating system type and the release level. This is useful to find out whether specific software is compatible with the operating system.

3. uname -a

For the whole nine yards, use uname -a to print all information, including the operating system type, host name, version, and hardware. The specifics you get here will vary a bit from system to system.

```
ejray@home $ ssh frizz
Last login: Wed Oct 10 09:59:09 from frazz
Sun Microsystems Inc.  SunOS 5.9  Generic
  → May 2002
ejray@frizz $ uname
SunOS
ejray@frizz $ uname -sr
SunOS 5.9
ejray@frizz $ uname -a
SunOS frizz 5.9 Generic_112233-01 sun4u
  → sparc SUNW,Ultra-5_10
```

Code Listing 7.1 Variants on the uname command provide all kinds of interesting or useful information about the system.

```
ejray@frazz $ uname
Linux
ejray@frazz $ uname -sr
Linux 2.4.19-16mdk
ejray@frazz $ uname -a
Linux frazz.raycomm.com 2.4.19-16mdk #1 Fri
  → Sep 20 18:15:05 CEST 2002 i686 unknown
  → unknown GNU/Linux
ejray@frazz $
```

Code Listing 7.2 On a different system, the same commands provide slightly different details, although the basic information remains the same.

Viewing File Systems with df

If you're used to Windows or Macintosh (prior to OS X) operating systems, you're probably accustomed to having separate hard drives (C:, D:, E: for Windows users, or real names for Macs), which are just different storage spaces. In Unix systems, different storage spaces are grafted onto the overall tree structure—tacked onto what already exists without any clear distinction indicating where actual disk drives are located. For example, if you have a folder on a Windows computer, you know that all of the subfolders and files within it are located on the same hard drive. In Unix, everything resides within the root directory, but any different directory could be located on a different physical hard drive. You might think of it as tacking a new branch onto your artificial Christmas tree.

These tacked-on storage spaces are called *file systems*. Particularly if you're running a Unix system (as opposed to just using one), you might need to find out what file systems are in use (or *mounted* in the system, in technical terms), how much space they have, and where they attach to the Unix system (or where their mountpoints are). You can find out this information using df, as shown in **Code Listings 7.3** and **7.4.**

```
[ejr@hobbes ejr]$ df
Filesystem      1024-blocks  Used Available Capacity Mounted on
/dev/hda1       515161       316297  172255    65%      /
/dev/hdb4       66365        4916    58022     8%       /home
/dev/hdb1       416656       324633  70504     82%      /usr/local
/dev/sbpcd      596704       596704  0         100%     /mnt/cdrom
[ejr@hobbes ejr]$
```

Code Listing 7.3 This small Linux system has relatively simple file systems.

To find out about file systems with df:

◆ df

At the shell prompt, type df. You'll usually get output showing you

▲ The name of the device, which refers to the physical part that stores the data, such as a hard drive, CD-ROM, or whatever. In Code Listing 7.3 the first one is /dev/hda1, indicating the first hard drive in the system.

▲ The number of blocks, which are 1 Kbyte-sized storage units. (1 Kbyte-sized in this case, although some systems report them as 512 bytes.)

▲ The number of used and available blocks on the device.

▲ The percentage of the space on the device that is being used.

▲ The name of the file system, which is the full path name from the Unix system. This is also known as the mountpoint.

```
xmission> df
/                    (/dev/dsk/c0t3d0s0 ):  154632 blocks     71721 files
/usr                 (/dev/dsk/c0t3d0s6 ):  225886 blocks     144820 files
/proc                (/proc            ):  0 blocks          7830 files
/dev/fd              (fd               ):  0 blocks          0 files
/var                 (/dev/dsk/c0t1d0s0 ):  1001142 blocks    962598 files
/tmp                 (swap             ):  1236032 blocks    95277 files
/usr/local           (/dev/dsk/c0t1d0s5 ):  630636 blocks     457211 files
/archive             (/dev/dsk/c0t1d0s3 ):  1180362 blocks    1789487 files
/var/mail            (mail.xmission.com:/var/mail):          2776576 blocks  1438385 files
/home                (krunk1.xmission.com:/home):            20091072 blocks 13066932 files
/var/spool/newslib   (news.xmission.com:/var/spool/newslib):  19327664 blocks 1248s
/.web                (krunk1.xmission.com:/.web):            1019408 blocks   470095 files
/var/maillists       (lists.xmission.com:/var/maillists):    293744 blocks    89732s
xmission>
```

Code Listing 7.4 This large ISP's file systems are considerably more complex.

Code Listings 7.3 and 7.4 show the output of df on two different systems.

If you're a system administrator, you can use this information to help diagnose problems occurring in the system. If you're an average user (of above-average curiosity), you can use this information to satisfy your inquisitive inclinations or to tip off a system administrator to problems. For example, if you're getting odd errors or unpredictable results with a specific program, using df might reveal that the /home file system is full or maybe that you don't have the /dev/cdrom file system that you thought was installed and mounted. Hmmm!

✔ Tips

- You can use df with a specific directory to get a report on the status of the file system containing that directory. For example, you might use df /usr/local/src to find out where that directory is mounted and how much space is available on it.

- Use df -k to make sure that the usage is reported in 1 Kbyte blocks, not in 512 byte blocks. Adding the -k flag will also ensure that you get output like that shown in Code Listing 7.3.

- Use df -h to get "human readable" output. This works with most commands (like ls, for example) that output marginally comprehensible file information.

VIEWING FILE SYSTEMS WITH df

Determining Disk Usage with du

Another piece of information that you can access is how much disk space within the Unix system is in use. You can do so using du, as shown in **Code Listing 7.5**.

To determine disk usage with du:

◆ du

At the shell prompt, enter du. As Code Listing 7.5 shows, you'll get information about disk usage in the current directory as well as in all subdirectories. The numbers are usually measured in 1 Kbyte blocks (as with df). You can actually read the output by using du -h.

✔ Tips

■ If you're on a system that enforces disk-space quotas (as most ISPs do), you can find out what your quota is and how close you are to reaching it. Just type quota -v at the shell prompt.

■ You can use du with a path name to check the disk usage in just a single directory or subdirectory (see **Code Listing 7.6**). du summarizes the usage by subdirectory as it prints the results.

■ Use du -s, optionally with a specific directory, to just print a summary of the amount of space used.

```
[ejr@hobbes ejr]$ du
2     ./Mail
1     ./nsmail
1     ./.netscape/cache/0F
3     ./.netscape/cache/1A
22    ./.netscape/cache
1     ./.netscape/archive
172   ./.netscape
1     ./Projects
28    ./.wprc
3     ./axhome
5     ./groups
1     ./manipulate/empty
154   ./manipulate
1     ./mail
1     ./unixvqs/ch6
2     ./unixvqs
6     ./dupgroups
255   ./compression/Folder
670   ./compression/temp/BackupFolder
1921  ./compression/temp
670   ./compression/BackupFolder
4657  ./compression
5     ./clean
1     ./.elm
15    ./editors
5619  .
[ejr@hobbes ejr]$
```

Code Listing 7.5 The du command reports—exhaustively—about the disk usage in the current directory and in its subdirectories.

```
[ejr@hobbes ejr]$ du
/home/ejr/compression
255   /home/ejr/compression/Folder
670   /home/ejr/compression/temp/
        → BackupFolder
1921  /home/ejr/compression/temp
670   /home/ejr/compression/BackupFolder
4657  /home/ejr/compression
[ejr@hobbes ejr]$
```

Code Listing 7.6 Using du with a specific directory name gives you focused results.

```
[ejr@hobbes ejr]$ file /usr/bin/pico
/usr/bin/pico: ELF 32-bit LSB executable,
  → Intel 80386, version 1, dynamically ld
[ejr@hobbes ejr]$ file temp.htm
temp.htm: ASCII text
[ejr@hobbes ejr]$
```

Code Listing 7.7 The `file` command provides useful information about what kind of data is in specific files.

Finding Out File Types with `file`

If you come from a Windows or Macintosh background, you're probably used to accessing files and being able to see what type of files they are—HTML files, GIFs, documents, or whatever. In Unix, though, you often can't tell the file type just by listing files or displaying directory contents. That's where `file` comes in handy, as shown in **Code Listing 7.7**.

To identify file types with `file`:

◆ `file /usr/bin/pico`

At the shell prompt, type `file`, followed by the path (if necessary) and filename. You'll see output similar to that in Code Listing 7.7.

✔ Tip

■ Not all files have the "magic" information associated with them that makes `file` work, but most do. Where they don't, you get a best-guess response, like the second response in Code Listing 7.7. Unfortunately, you can't tell by looking if it's definitive information or a guess, but if it's terse (as in the second response), take it with a grain of salt.

Finding Out About Users with `finger`

Using the `finger` command, you can find out who is currently logged into the Unix system as well as what they're doing, how long they've been logged in, and other snoopy, not-necessarily-your-business information (**Code Listing 7.8**).

To find out who is logged in using `finger`:

1. `finger`

   At the shell prompt, type `finger` to see who else is logged into the system and to get a little information about them (Code Listing 7.8).

2. `finger @example.com`

   Type `finger`, `@`, and a host name (in this case `example.com`) to find out who is logged into another host.

   Fingering a different host doesn't always work, depending on security settings on the other host computer(s). If the host doesn't allow it, you'll get a message like the one in Code Listing 7.8.

FINDING OUT ABOUT USERS WITH finger

```
[ejr@hobbes ejr]$ finger
Login       Name              Tty      Idle     Login Time      Office     Office Phone
asr                           *4       1        Jul 24 13:32
deb                           5        1        Jul 24 13:32
ejr         Eric J. Ray       1        3:20     Jul 22 07:42
ejr         Eric J. Ray       p1       1:12     Jul 24 12:14 (calvin)
ejr         Eric J. Ray       p0                Jul 24 13:02 (calvin)
root        root              *2       1d       Jul 22 15:13
[ejr@hobbes ejr]$ finger @example.com
[example.com]
No one logged on
 [ejr@hobbes ejr]$ finger @osuunx.ucc.okstate.edu
[osuunx.ucc.okstate.edu]
finger: connect: Connection refused
[ejr@hobbes ejr]$
```

Code Listing 7.8 The `finger` command often provides interesting information about who is logged onto different systems.

To find out about users using `finger`:

1. `finger ejr`

   At the shell prompt, type `finger` followed by the userid of the person you want to know about. You'll get a ton of information, including some or all of the following: the user's name, home directory, and default shell; when, from where, and for how long they've been logged on; and whatever other information they choose to provide. **Code Listing 7.9** shows two users with varying activity. `deb` has apparently been loafing, and `ejr` has been working his buns off.

2. `finger ejray@xmission.com`

   Using `finger` plus a specific user address, you can find out about users on other systems. As with generic `finger` requests, sometimes they're blocked for security reasons.

   continues on next page

```
[ejr@hobbes ejr]$ finger deb
Login: deb                      Name:
Directory: /home/deb            Shell: /bin/bash
Never logged in.
No mail.
No Plan.
[ejr@hobbes ejr]$ finger ejr
Login: ejr                      Name:
Directory: /home/ejr            Shell: /bin/bash
On since Wed Jul 22 07:42 (MDT) on tty1        2 hours 32 minutes idle
On since Wed Jul 22 06:58 (MDT) on ttyp1 from calvin
No mail.
Project:
Working on  VQS.
Plan:
This is my plan—work all day, sleep all night.
[ejr@hobbes ejr]$
[ejr@hobbes ejr]$ finger ejray@xmission.com
[xmission.com]
Login       Name        TTY        Idle       When        Where
ejray       "RayComm    pts/57     <Jul 22 09:39> calvin.raycomm.c
  [ejr@hobbes ejr]$
```

Code Listing 7.9 The `finger` command can also provide in-depth information about specific users.

✔ Tips

■ You can also sniff out user information using who (see the next section).

■ You can provide extra information to anyone who gets your user information with finger by creating files that describe your "plan" and "project" (as ejr has done in Code Listing 7.9). Use your favorite editor to create .plan and .project files in your home directory. Then, change the protection so that the files are both world readable (chmod go+r .plan ; chmod go+r .project) and so the directory is accessible (chmod go+x .). See Chapter 5 for specifics about chmod.

■ Information you obtain through finger can be handy when diagnosing connection difficulties. In particular, system administrators or help desk personnel are likely to ask where you're connected (pts57, for ejray@xmission.com) and what kind of software you're using.

```
[ejr@hobbes ejr]$ who
ejr    tty1    Jul 22 07:42
root   tty2    Jul 22 15:13
asr    tty4    Jul 24 13:32
deb    tty5    Jul 24 13:32
ejr    ttyp1   Jul 24 12:14
  → (calvin.raycomm.com)
ejr    ttyp0   Jul 24 13:02
  → (calvin.raycomm.com)
[ejr@hobbes ejr]$
```

Code Listing 7.10 Use who to find out who else is currently logged into the system.

Learning Who Else Is Logged in with who

If you're not interested in all the gory details you get about users when you finger them, you can instead use who to get just the basics. With who you get just the users' names, connection information, login times, and host names, as shown in **Code Listing 7.10**.

To snoop with who:

◆ who

At the shell prompt, type who. You'll get user information like that shown in Code Listing 7.10. Optionally, you could pipe the output of who to more, as in who | more, which would give you a long list of results one screen at a time.

✔ Tips

■ If you're a system administrator or use several different userids, you might occasionally need to use a special case of who, called whoami. Just type whoami at the shell prompt, and it'll tell you which userid you're currently logged in as.

■ See Chapter 1 for more on more and on piping commands.

Learning Who Else Is Logged in with w

Another way to find out about other people logged into the Unix system is to use w, which tells you who is logged in, what they're doing, and a few other details (**Code Listing 7.11**).

To find out who is logged in with w:

◆ w

At the shell prompt, type w. You'll usually see output much like that in Code Listing 7.11. The top line shows

▲ The time

▲ System uptime in days, hours, and minutes (uptime is how long it's been since the system was restarted and is usually measured in weeks or months for Unix systems, as opposed to hours or days for personal computers).

▲ The number of users

▲ System load averages (the numbers indicate jobs—programs or scripts to execute—lined up to run in the past 1, 5, and 15 minutes)

```
[ejr@hobbes ejr]$ w
  1:49pm up 6 days,        4:21,      6 users, load average: 0.08, 0.02, 0.01
USER     TTY      FROM      LOGIN@    IDLE    JCPU     PCPU     WHAT
ejr      tty1               Wed 7am   3:36m   7.07s    6.01s    -bash
root     tty2               Wed 3pm   28:46m  1.22s    0.32s    -bash
asr      tty4               1:32pm    17:22   1.04s    0.30s    pine
deb      tty5               1:32pm    3.00s   1.22s    0.42s    lynx
ejr      ttyp1    calvin    12:14pm   1:28m   1.33s    0.57s    vi hairyspiders
ejr      ttyp0    calvin    1:02pm    1.00s   1.70s    0.24s    w
[ejr@hobbes ejr]$
```

Code Listing 7.11 The w command provides tons of information about the system and its users

The following lines, one per logged-in user, show

▲ The login name

▲ The `tty` name (the connection to the host)

▲ The remote host name

▲ The login time

▲ Current idle time (that is, the time since a key on the keyboard was touched)

▲ JCPU (job CPU time, or the total processing time for jobs on the current connection, which is the `tty`, for those into the jargon)

▲ PCPU (process CPU time, or the processing time for the current process)

▲ The command line of the current process

Whew! As you can see from Code Listing 7.11 and **Code Listing 7.12**, different systems' w commands produce slightly different (but similar) output.

✔ Tip

■ Use w with `grep` to find information (slightly more abbreviated) about a specific user. For example, `w | grep ejr` gives limited information, but just about a specific user. See Chapter 1 for more information about piping commands.

```
xmission> w
  1:47pm     up 38 day(s), 23:35, 36 users, load average: 1.58, 1.78, 1.75
...
ejraypts/16 Thu 6am 1:14    -csh
...
```

Code Listing 7.12 w yields different information on different systems.

Getting Information About Your Userid with `id`

Occasionally, you may need to find out information about your userid, such as your userid's numeric value and to what groups you belong. This information is essential when you're sharing files (as discussed in Chapter 5) because you'll need it to let people access your files and to access theirs. You can easily get information about your userid with `id`, as shown in **Code Listing 7.13**.

To check userid information using `id`:

◆ `id`

At the shell prompt, type `id` to find the numeric value of your userid and to what groups (by name and numeric userid value) you belong (see Code Listing 7.13). See *Finding Out Which Group You're In*, in Chapter 5, for more about the `/etc/ group` file.

✔ Tips

■ You can also check someone else's status with `id` to find out what groups they're in. Just use `id userid` (substituting the other person's userid for `userid`, of course).

■ Use `groups` to find out which groups— in human-readable terms—a specific userid is in. For example, `ejr` is in the `ejr`, `wheel`, and `users` groups, as shown in Code Listing 7.13.

```
[ejr@hobbes ejr]$ id
uid=500(ejr) gid=500(ejr)
groups=500(ejr),10(wheel),100(users)
[ejr@hobbes ejr]$ id deb
uid=505(deb) gid=505(deb) groups=100(users)
[ejr@hobbes ejr]$ groups ejr
ejr : ejr wheel users
```

Code Listing 7.13 Use `id` to get information about userids and group memberships.

CONFIGURING YOUR UNIX ENVIRONMENT

8

Chapter Contents

◆ Understanding your Unix environment

◆ Discovering your current environment

◆ Adding or changing variables

◆ Looking at your zsh configuration files

◆ Changing your zsh path

◆ Changing your zsh prompt

◆ Looking at your bash configuration files

◆ Changing your bash path

◆ Changing your bash prompt

◆ Looking at your ksh configuration files

◆ Changing your ksh path

◆ Changing your ksh prompt

◆ Looking at your csh configuration files

◆ Changing your csh path

◆ Changing your csh prompt

◆ Setting aliases

Back in Chapter 3, we introduced you to Unix shells—what they are and what you can do with them. In this chapter, we'll take you a bit further and look at configuring your environment using the zsh, bash, csh, and ksh shells. By configuring your environment, you can make the Unix system adapt to your needs, rather than adapting to an existing environment that may not work for you. These configuration tips differ (slightly) for different shells, so make sure you're following along with the instructions appropriate for the shell you use.

Understanding Your Unix Environment

Environment variables are settings in the Unix system that specify how you, your shell, and the Unix system interact. When you log in to the Unix system, it sets up your standard environment variables—the shell prompt you want to use, the default search path, and other information to help programs run, among other things. You might think of your environment variables as being similar to having a standing order with a deli to deliver the same thing to you every day. You set up your "standing environment variables" and the Unix system delivers them to you session after session unless you specify otherwise.

Technically, there is a distinction between "shell" variables, which exist in the particular shell you're using, and "environment" variables, which are in your environment and independent of your particular shell. For most purposes, though, including this book, you can do as we're doing and conveniently blur the distinction. As long as you know that they're not precisely synonymous, you'll be fine.

Basically, just like with the lunch deli, you can configure your environment in one of two ways:

◆ Changing the variables for the current session—kind of like calling in a special order for the day (as in ordering onion and extra cheese on the day's sandwich). You do this from the shell prompt, as discussed in the *Adding or Changing Variables* section in this chapter.

♦ Changing the variables for all subsequent sessions—kind of like changing your standard order (say, when the doctor tells you to cut back on mayonnaise and suggests mustard for your long-term deli order). You do this within the configuration files, as discussed in sections following *Adding or Changing Variables*.

If you want to change your environment variables, you should first try changing them from the shell prompt for the current session. This way, you can try out the changes before you make them permanent in your configuration files.

When you do change your environment in the configuration files, keep in mind that configuration files are generally run in a specific order:

♦ Systemwide configuration files (such as /etc/profile) run first upon log in. These systemwide configuration files in /etc (if they exist) help set up your environment, but you cannot change them.

♦ Configuration files specific to your Unix account (such as ~/.profile and ~/.kshrc) run next if they're available. If you want to change environment variables originally set in the systemwide files, you can reset the values in your own personal files.

What this order means to you is that your own personal configurations override system ones. So, in making changes to your configuration files, make sure that you make changes to the configuration file that runs last. We'll tell you which specific files to look for in the relevant sections of this chapter.

Find out about discovering your current environment variables and adding or changing environment variables manually in the next two sections in this chapter.

✔ Tips

■ You can use echo $SHELL to remind yourself of what shell you're using. Visit Chapter 3 for more details.

■ Find out about changing environment variables in your system configuration files in other sections of this chapter, according to which shell you're using.

UNDERSTANDING YOUR UNIX ENVIRONMENT

Discovering Your Current Environment

A good first step in changing your environment is determining what environment you have. Using the steps in this section, you can discover which environment and shell variables are currently set—including ones set in the configuration files as well as ones you've set for the current session (**Code Listings 8.1** and **8.2**).

As you're going through these steps, you might check out the sidebar *Variables in Your Environment You Shouldn't Touch* in this section for a list of variables you should leave alone. Then, in the next section, check out *Variables You Can Mess With* to find ones you can change.

To show your current environment in zsh, bash, or ksh:

◆ set

   At the shell prompt, type set. You'll see a list of the current environment and shell variables, as shown in Code Listing 8.1.

   Some of the variables may look familiar to you (such as the ones showing your shell or user name), while others are likely to be more cryptic (such as the line showing the last command you ran, in this case, _=cd).

To show your current environment in csh:

◆ setenv

   At the shell prompt, type setenv. As Code Listing 8.2 shows, the preconfigured variables will closely resemble the environment variables that bash or ksh offer.

```
[ejr@hobbes ejr]$ set
BASH=/bin/bash
BASH_VERSION=1.14.7(1)
COLUMNS=80
ENV=/home/ejr/.bashrc
EUID=500
HISTFILE=/home/ejr/.bash_history
HISTFILESIZE=1000
HISTSIZE=1000
HOME=/home/ejr
HOSTNAME=hobbes.raycomm.com
HOSTTYPE=i386
IFS=
LINES=24
LOGNAME=ejr
MAIL=/var/spool/mail/ejr
MAILCHECK=60
OLDPWD=/home/ejr/src/rpm-2.5.1
OPTERR=1
OPTIND=1
OSTYPE=Linux
PATH=/usr/local/bin:/bin:/usr/bin:/usr/
→ X11R6/bin:/home/ejr/bin
PPID=1943
PS1=[\u@\h \W]\$
PS2=>
PS4=+
PWD=/home/ejr
SHELL=/bin/bash
SHLVL=3
TERM=vt220
UID=500
USER=ejr
USERNAME=
_=cd
[ejr@hobbes ejr]$
```

Code Listing 8.1 You can find out which variables exist in the zsh, bash, or ksh shells with set.

```
xmission> setenv
HOME=/home/users/e/ejray
PATH=/usr/local/bin:/usr/local/bin/X11:/
→ usr/openwin/bin:/usr/bin:/usr/ucb:/usr/.
LOGNAME=ejray
HZ=100
TERM=vt100
TZ=MST7MDT
SHELL=/usr/bin/csh
MAIL=/var/mail/ejray
PWD=/home/users/e/ejray
USER=ejray
EDITOR=pico -t
OPENWINHOME=/usr/openwin
MANPATH=/usr/man:/usr/local/man:/usr/
→ openwin/man
LD_LIBRARY_PATH=/usr/local/lib:/usr/
→ openwin/lib
PAGER=more
xmission>
```

Code Listing 8.2 Or, use setenv to find out which variables exist in the csh shell at the c-shore.

✔ Tips

■ If you do as we often do and try to use show to show the environment variables ("showing" the variables seems logical, right?), you might get a weird question about the standard mail directories and the MH mailer. Just press Ctrl C to return to your shell prompt.

■ If the list of environment variables is long, you can pipe set or setenv to more so that you can read the variables one screen at a time. Try set | sort | more or setenv | sort | more. See Chapter 1 for a reminder about piping commands.

Variables in Your Environment You Shouldn't Touch

Before you go running off and changing your environment, note that there are some things you should really leave alone. These variables that the shell automatically sets affect how your Unix system works (or doesn't work, if you try to change some of these variables!). Some of these cannot be changed, but some can, with unpredictable results. When in doubt, don't. See the sidebar *Variables You Can Mess With* in the following section for a list of variables you can change.

ZSH, BASH, AND KSH	CSH	DESCRIPTION
HISTCMD		Keeps track of the number of the current command from the history.
HOSTTYPE		Holds a string describing the type of hardware on which the shell is running.
IFS		Specifies the characters that indicate the beginning or end of words.
LINENO		Contains the number of the current line within the shell or a shell script.
OLDPWD		Contains the previous working directory.
OSTYPE		Holds a string describing the operating system on which the shell is running.
PPID		Contains the process ID of the shell's parent.
PWD	cwd	Contains the current working directory.
RANDOM		Contains a special value to generate random numbers.
SECONDS		Contains the number of seconds since the shell was started.
SHELL	shell	Contains the name of the current shell.
SHLVL		Contains a number indicating the sub-shell level (if SHLVL is 3, two parent shells exist and you'll have to exit from three total shells to completely log out).
UID		Contains the userid of the current user.

DISCOVERING YOUR CURRENT ENVIRONMENT

Adding or Changing Variables

After you've poked around in your environment, you might determine that you want to set a variable that's currently not available or change one to make it better meet your needs. In general, you won't randomly specify variables; you'll do it because a certain program requires a specific variable in order to run.

Variables You Can Mess With

The following table includes some of the variables you can safely change. Keep in mind that the shell itself might not use a specific variable, like NNTPSERVER, while programs running under the shell might. Sometimes shells assign default variables, while in other cases you'll have to manually set the value.

ZSH, BASH, AND KSH	CSH	DESCRIPTION
CDPATH	cdpath	Specifies the search path for directories specified by cd. This is similar to PATH.
COLUMNS		Specifies width of the edit window in characters.
EDITOR		Specifies the default editor.
ENV		Specifies where to look for configuration files.
HISTFILE		Specifies the name of the file containing the command history.
HISTFILESIZE	savehist	Specifies the maximum number of lines to keep in the history file.
HISTSIZE	history	Specifies the number of commands to keep in the command history.
HOSTFILE		Specifies the name of the file containing host name aliases for expansion.
IGNOREEOF	ignoreeof	Specifies that Ctrl D should not log out of the shell. Use IGNOREEOF=.
LINES		Specifies the number of lines on the screen.
MAIL	mail	Specifies the location of incoming mail so bash can notify you of mail arrival.
MAILCHECK	mail	Specifies how often (in seconds) bash checks for mail.
MAIL_WARNING		Specifies the message to be displayed if you have read mail but not unread mail.
noclobber	noclobber	Specifies that the shell should not overwrite an existing file when redirecting output.
PATH	path	Specifies the search path for commands, including multiple paths separated by colons.
PROMPT_COMMAND		Specifies the command to be run before displaying each primary prompt (does not apply to ksh).
PS1	prompt	Specifies the primary prompt.
PS2		Specifies the default second-level prompt.
PS3		Specifies the prompt for the select command in scripts.
PS4		Specifies the prompt used when tracing execution of a script.
TMOUT		Specifies time in seconds to wait for input before closing the shell.
VISUAL		Specifies the default visual editor—usually the same as EDITOR, but referenced by different programs.

```
[ejr@hobbes ejr]$
→ NNTPSERVER=news.xmission.com
[ejr@hobbes ejr]$ export NNTPSERVER
[ejr@hobbes ejr]$ echo $NNTPSERVER
news.xmission.com
[ejr@hobbes ejr]$
```

Code Listing 8.3 In the zsh, bash, and ksh shells, you can add a new environment variable by specifying the variable and its value, then exporting the variable to the system.

Fill in Your bash **System Configuration Files**

_____

_____

_____

_____

_____

_____

Fill in Your zsh **System Configuration Files**

_____

_____

_____

_____

_____

_____

_____

_____

By following the steps in this section, you can add or change environment variables for the current session. As **Code Listing 8.3** shows, for example, you can specify a news server environment variable (called NNTPSERVER) that some Usenet news readers require to access the news (nntp) server.

To add or change a variable in zsh, bash, or ksh:

1. `NNTPSERVER=news.xmission.com`

   At the shell prompt, type the name of the variable (in this case, NNTPSERVER), followed by = and the value you want for the variable (here, news.xmission.com), as shown in Code Listing 8.3. In this step, you're setting up the variable and its value and making it available to all programs and scripts that run in the current shell session.

   If the value contains spaces or special characters, put the value in quotes.

2. `export NNTPSERVER`

   Type export followed by the name of the variable. By exporting the variable, you make it available to all programs and scripts that run in the current shell session (again, Code Listing 8.3).

   Until it is exported, it is a shell variable, which will not be available to other processes that this shell starts.

3. `echo $NNTPSERVER`

   Optionally, type echo followed by a $ and the name of the variable to have the shell tell you what the variable is set to.

✔ Tip

■ In bash, ksh, or zsh, save a step by typing export NNTPSERVER=news.xmission.com.

ADDING OR CHANGING VARIABLES

To add or change a variable in csh:

1. `setenv NNTPSERVER news.xmission.com`

   Type `setenv` followed by the name of the variable, a space, and the value of the variable. In this step, you're setting up the variable and its value and making the environment variable available to all programs and scripts that run in the current shell session (**Code Listing 8.4**).

   If the value contains spaces or special characters, put the value in quotes.

2. `echo $NNTPSERVER`

   Optionally, type `echo` followed by a $ and the name of the variable to have the shell tell you what the variable is set to.

✔ Tips

■ If you want to change or add to your variables so that the new settings exist from session to session, use the instructions for changing the environment variables in your configuration files, as described throughout the rest of this chapter.

■ Find out more about news readers in Chapter 12.

```
xmission> setenv NNTPSERVER
→ news.xmission.com
xmission> echo $NNTPSERVER
news.xmission.com
```

Code Listing 8.4 The process for the csh shell is similar to the process for the *bash* and *ksh* shells.

Looking at Your zsh Configuration Files

Your first step in modifying or adding zsh environment variables in your configuration files is to look at the configuration files, which show you the variables that are explicitly defined. As **Code Listing 8.5** shows, you do this using more or the editor of your choice.

Remember that zsh configuration files exist in two places:

◆ Systemwide configuration files (such as /etc/zprofile or /etc/zshenv)

◆ Configuration files specific to your Unix account (such as ~/.zprofile or ~/.zshrc)

```
jdoe@sulley ~ $ more ~/.z* /etc/zl* /etc/zprofile /etc/zsh*
::::::::::::::
/home/jdoe/.zprofile
::::::::::::::
# /etc/zprofile and ~/.zprofile are run for login shells
#
::::::::::::::
/home/jdoe/.zshenv
::::::::::::::
export X11HOME=/usr/X11R6

if (( EUID == 0 )); then
    path=(/sbin /usr/sbin)
fi

typeset -U path
path=($path $X11HOME/bin /bin /usr/bin /usr/local/bin)
PATH=$PATH:/home/jdoe/scripts
::::::::::::::
/home/jdoe/.zshrc
::::::::::::::                                    continues on next page
```

Code Listing 8.5 Your zsh configuration files set up your environment variables and other features of your Unix experience.

```
# Reset prompts
PROMPT="%n@%m %3~ %(!.#.$) "    # default prompt
#RPROMPT=' %~'   # prompt for right side of screen

# bindkey -v # vi key bindings
bindkey -e   # emacs key bindings

if [[ ! -r ${ZDOTDIR:-$HOME}/.zshrc ]];then
    if  [[ -f /usr/share/zsh/$ZSH_VERSION/zshrc_default ]];then
    source /usr/share/zsh/$ZSH_VERSION/zshrc_default
    fi
fi
::::::::::::::
/etc/zlogin
::::::::::::::
# /etc/zlogin and .zlogin are sourced in login shells.

::::::::::::::
/etc/zlogout
::::::::::::::
# /etc/zlogout and ~/.zlogout are run when an interactive session ends
# clear
::::::::::::::
/etc/zprofile
::::::::::::::
#
::::::::::::::
/etc/zshenv
::::::::::::::
export X11HOME=/usr/X11R6

if (( EUID == 0 )); then
    path=(/sbin /usr/sbin)
fi

typeset -U path
path=($path $X11HOME/bin /bin /usr/bin /usr/local/bin)
::::::::::::::
/etc/zshrc
::::::::::::::

if [[ $(id -gn) = $USERNAME && $EUID -gt 14 ]]; then
    umask 002
else
    umask 022
```

Code listing 8.5 *continued*

```
fi
# Get keys working
if [[ $TERM = "linux" ]];then
    bindkey "^[[2~" yank
    bindkey "^[[3~" delete-char
    bindkey "^[[5~" up-line-or-history
    bindkey "^[[6~" down-line-or-history
    bindkey "^[[1~" beginning-of-line
    bindkey "^[[4~" end-of-line
elif [[ $TERM = "xterm" || $TERM = "rxvt"  ]];then
    bindkey "^[[2~" yank
    bindkey "^[[3~" delete-char
    bindkey "^[[5~" up-line-or-history
    bindkey "^[[6~" down-line-or-history
    bindkey "" beginning-of-line
      bindkey "" end-of-line
fi


# Set prompts
PROMPT="%n@%m %3~ %(!.#.$) "    # default prompt
#RPROMPT=' %~'   # prompt for right side of screen


# Some environment variables
path=($path $HOME/bin)
export HISTFILE=${HOME}/.bash_history
export HISTSIZE=1000
export SAVEHIST=1000
export USER=$USERNAME
export HOSTNAME=$HOST


# bindkey -v # vi key bindings
bindkey -e   # emacs key bindings


for profile_func ( /etc/profile.d/*.sh ) source $profile_func


unset profile_func


# See comment at top.
if [[ ! -r ${ZDOTDIR:-$HOME}/.zshrc ]];then
    if  [[ -f /usr/share/zsh/$ZSH_VERSION/zshrc_default ]];then
    source /usr/share/zsh/$ZSH_VERSION/zshrc_default
    fi
fi
jdoe@sulley ~ $
```

Code listing 8.5 *continued*

To look at your zsh configuration files:

1. `more ~/.z* /etc/zl* /etc/zprofile`
`→ /etc/zsh*`

At the shell prompt, type `more` followed by each of the possible system configuration filenames to view your configuration files. If you don't have all (or any) of the files mentioned here, don't worry. Just make note of the ones you do have. Code Listing 8.5 shows an example of what you might see.

2. Write down, for your reference, the system configuration files and the order in which they're run. (Remember, settings in the last file run override all previous ones.) Our system configuration files, all automatically called by the system, include

- ▲ `/etc/zshenv` then `~/.zshenv`

- ▲ `/etc/zprofile` then `~/.zprofile`

- ▲ `/etc/zshrc` then `~/.zshrc`

- ▲ `/etc/zlogin` then `~/.zlogin`

Keep in mind that the files you have may differ from the files that we have.

✔ Tips

- Take special note of any lines in any of the files that end with a path and filename, or that reference other files directly, with something like `/etc/profile` on a line by itself. Each of those lines references another file that plays a role in getting you set up. Notice that some of the lines will reference others that don't directly configure your environment.

  Some files include oddities like `export HISTFILE=${HOME}/.bash_history` line that reference the `.bash_history` file, containing the list of commands you've run. (Looks like a goof by the Linux distributor. Good thing you're checking up on them, huh?)

- You can use `grep` to make it easier to find the configuration files that set your path. `grep -i path ~/.z*` is a good way to start.

- If you see something like `path=($path $HOME/bin)` in your configuration files, that's okay. Just go ahead and use the syntax shown in this section on the following line anyway. It's a feature of `zsh` that it understands about a bazillion different ways to express any single command.

```
jdoe@sulley ~ $ tail .zshrc

# See comment at top.
if [[ ! -r ${ZDOTDIR:-$HOME}/
↝ .zshrc ]];then
     if [[ -f
/usr/share/zsh/$ZSH_VERSION/
↝ zshrc_default ]];then
         source /usr/share/zsh/$ZSH_VERSION/
↝ zshrc_default
         fi
fi

PATH=/bin:/usr/bin:/opt/bin

jdoe@sulley ~ $
```

Code Listing 8.6 You should find your path statement in your configuration files.

Adding to Your zsh Path

One of the most useful changes you can make to your environment is adding to the default path, which is determined by the *path statement*. The path statement tells the shell where to look for commands, scripts, and programs. That is, if you issue a command, the path statement tells the system to look for that command in each of the named directories in a specific order.

Be sure not to remove anything from your path unless you really know what you're doing, but feel free to add as many additional directories to it as you want. For example, if you get started writing scripts (as described in Chapter 10), you might put them in a scripts subdirectory and want to add that directory to your path.

As the following steps show, you change your zsh path by first identifying where your path statement is located, then editing the file that contains it (**Code Listing 8.6**).

To change your zsh path:

1. more ~/.zshenv ~/.zprofile ~/.zshrc

   To begin, view your configuration files (just the ones you can edit) in the order they're executed.

   Look through your system configuration files for a path statement. As Code Listing 8.6 shows, it will look something like PATH=/bin:/usr/bin:/opt/bin. If you have more than one path statement, find the last one executed.

   Remember that different systems will have different configurations, so you might need to do a little digging to find your personal path statement(s).

   continues on next page

2. `cp .zshrc .zshrc_backup`

Make a backup of the file containing the path statement so that you can recover the file when problems or errors occur. See Chapter 2 if you need more information on copying files.

3. `vi .zshrc`

Use your favorite editor to open up the file whose path you want to change.

4. `PATH=$PATH:$HOME/scripts`

Add a new path statement immediately below the last path statement. In this example, PATH is set to its current value ($PATH) plus the directory ($HOME/scripts) you wish to append to your path. (**Figure 8.1**).

5. Save the file and exit from your editor. Refer to Chapter 4 for help if you need it.

6. `su - yourid`

As you learned back in Chapter 3, this command starts a new login shell so you can test your changes before logging out.

7. `echo $PATH`

Display the current path environment variable. This should include the addition you just made. It's there, right? (See **Code Listing 8.7**.)

✔ Tip

- If you look through the path statements in your various configuration files, you might find a path statement that includes just a . (dot). For example, you might see something like `PATH=/usr/bin:/usr/local/bin:.:`. The . adds your current directory, whatever it might be, to your path. Keep in mind, though, that it's often safer not to have the current directory in the path so you don't unintentionally run a different program from the one you expect.

```
jdoe@sulley ~ $ su - jdoe
Password:
jdoe@sulley ~ $ echo $PATH /bin:
→ /usr/bin:/opt/bin:/home/jdoe/scripts/
jdoe@sulley ~ $
```

Code Listing 8.7 Test out your edits to the configuration files.

```
jdoe@frazz.raycomm.com: /home/jdoe
export HISTFILE=${HOME}/.bash_history
export HISTSIZE=1000
export SAVEHIST=1500
export USER=$USERNAME
export HOSTNAME=$HOST

# bindkey -v          # vi key bindings
bindkey -e            # emacs key bindings

for profile_func ( /etc/profile.d/*.sh ) source $profile_func

unset profile_func

# See comment at top.
if [[ ! -r $(ZDOTDIR:-$HOME)/.zshrc ]];then
    if [[ -f /usr/share/zsh/$ZSH_VERSION/zshrc_default ]];then
        source /usr/share/zsh/$ZSH_VERSION/zshrc_default
    fi
fi

PATH=/bin:/usr/bin:/opt/bin
PATH=$PATH:$HOME/scripts/
                                                          64
```

Figure 8.1 You add or modify a zsh path statement in your editor.

ADDING TO YOUR zsh PATH

```
jdoe@frazz.raycomm.com: /home/jdoe
elif [[ $TERM = "xterm" || $TERM = "rxvt"  ]];then
        bindkey "^[[2~" yank
        bindkey "^[[3~" delete-char
        bindkey "^[[5~" up-line-or-history
        bindkey "^[[6~" down-line-or-history
        bindkey "^[[7~" beginning-of-line
        bindkey "^[[8~" end-of-line
fi


# Set prompts
#PROMPT="%n@%m %3~ %(!.#.$) "    # default prompt
#RPROMPT=' %~'     # prompt for right side of screen
PROMPT="%n %d $ "
█
# Some environment variables
path=($path $HOME/bin)
export HISTFILE=$(HOME)/.bash_history
export HISTSIZE=1000
export SAVEHIST=1500
export USER=$USERNAME
export HOSTNAME=$HOST

                                                    40
```

Figure 8.2 Edit your zsh prompt statement in the editor of your choice.

Changing Your zsh Prompt

Your default prompt (the text on the screen in front of the place you type commands) may vary a bit, depending on your Unix system; you might see just a dollar sign ($), a dollar sign and date, or other information as outlined in the *Setting Your zsh Prompt Promptly* sidebar. You can set your prompt to include information that's handy for you.

You actually have multiple prompts:

◆ The main prompt that you usually think of as the shell prompt. This prompt is called PS1 or just PROMPT.

◆ A secondary prompt that you see when the system requires additional information to complete a command. Logically, this prompt is called PS2.

You can change either of these prompts using the following steps. You start by finding your prompt statement (**Code Listing 8.8**), then modifying it in your editor (**Figure 8.2**).

CHANGING YOUR zsh PROMPT

```
jdoe@sulley ~ $ grep -i PROMPT ~/.z*; grep -i PS1 ~/.z*
/home/jdoe/.zshrc:# configuration for keys umask PROMPT and variable
/home/jdoe/.zshrc:# Set prompts
/home/jdoe/.zshrc:PROMPT="%n@%m %3~ %(!.#.$) "          # default prompt
jdoe@sulley ~ $
```

Code Listing 8.8 Use grep to search your configuration files for a zsh prompt statement.

To change your zsh prompt:

1. `grep -i PROMPT ~/.z*; grep -i PS1`
→ `~/.z*`

To begin, search through the configuration files located in your home directory and, if necessary, in the `/etc` directory, to find your prompt statement. It will look something like `PROMPT="%n@%m %3~ %(!.#.$) " # default prompt`, as shown in Code Listing 8.8.

The *Setting Your zsh Prompt Promptly* sidebar will help translate these symbols.

2. `cp ~/.zshrc ~/.zshrc-backup; vi`
→ `~/.zshrc`

Make a backup copy. The `~/.zshrc` file is a likely place for your prompt to be set, as it is only read when your shell is interactive.

Setting Your zsh Prompt Promptly

You can set your prompt to contain all sorts of information. The following list shows you what code to use to add certain kinds of information to your prompt (as well as help you translate the code in your existing prompt):

◆ %n shows the userid of the current user—that's you.

◆ %~ shows the current working directory with a path, using a ~ notation within your home directory.

◆ %c shows the current directory without the path.

◆ %t shows the time.

◆ %w shows the date without the year.

◆ %W shows the date with the year.

◆ \n forces a new line, making the prompt appear split on two lines (you need single quotes around the prompt).

◆ %m shows the host name of the computer (like the frazz and hobbes examples in this book).

◆ %M shows the complete host name of the computer, including the domain name.

```
jdoe@sulley ~ $ vi .zshrc
jdoe@sulley ~ $ su - jdoe
Password:
jdoe /home/jdoe $ PROMPT=$'Top line
→ \nNext line $'
Top line
Next line $pwd
/home/jdoe
Top line
Next line $
```

Code Listing 8.9 Testing after you update your prompt is always a good idea.

3. PROMPT="%n %d $ "

   For example, we often set our prompt to include two tidbits of information: the userid (as we have many different accounts, we can always use a reminder!) and the date (time flies when you're having fun, right?!). We're adding these bits of information instead of the existing default prompt, but saving the default with a # sign at the beginning, just in case (Figure 8.2).

4. Save the file and exit from the editor.

5. su - ejr

   Log in again with your changed prompt to try it out.

✔ Tips

■ Note the trailing space in the prompt code: PROMPT="%n %d $ ". This space can help make it easier to use the prompt because it keeps your commands from bumping into your prompt.

■ You can also set your prompt so that the information you set appears on one line and your actual prompt appears on the next (**Code Listing 8.9**). To do so, use single quotes (' ') and a $ in the environment variable setting then a \n for the new line, as in PROMPT=$'%n %W\n $'. This forces the shell to treat the \n as a new line, not just as random characters in the prompt string.

Looking at Your *bash* Configuration Files

Your first step in modifying or adding bash environment variables in your configuration files is to look at the configuration files, which show you the variables that have been defined. As **Code Listing 8.10** shows, you do this using more or the editor of your choice.

Remember that configuration files run in a specific order:

◆ Systemwide configuration files (such as /etc/profile) run first upon log in.

◆ Configuration files specific to your Unix account (such as ~/.bash_profile or ~/.profile) run next if they're available.

To look at your bash configuration files:

1. more ~/.bash* ~/.profile
   → /etc/bash* /etc/profile

   At the shell prompt, type more followed by each of the possible system configuration filenames to view your configuration files. If you don't have all of the files mentioned here, don't worry. Just make note of the ones you do have. Code Listing 8.10 shows an example of what you might see. Notice that some of the lines will reference other files, like the ENV=$HOME/.bashrc line that references the .bashrc file, containing other configuration settings.

   continues on next page

```
[ejr@hobbes ejr]$ more ~/.bash* ~/.profile /etc/bash* /etc/profile
::::::::::::::
/home/ejr/.bash_profile
::::::::::::::
# .bash_profile
# Get the aliases and functionsif [ -f ~/.bashrc ]; then
```

Code Listing 8.10 Your configuration files set up your environment variables and other features of your Unix experience.

```
        . ~/.bashrc
fi
# User-specific environment and startup programs
PATH=$PATH:$HOME/bin
ENV=$HOME/.bashrc
USERNAME=""
export USERNAME ENV PATH
/home/ejr/.profile: No such file or directory
::::::::::::::
/etc/bashrc
::::::::::::::
# /etc/bashrc
# System-wide functions and aliases
# Environment stuff goes in /etc/profile
# Putting PS1 here ensures that it gets loaded every time.
PS1="[\u@\h \W]\\$ "
alias which="type -path"
::::::::::::::
/etc/profile
::::::::::::::
# /etc/profile
# System-wide environment and startup programs
# Functions and aliases go in /etc/bashrc
PATH="$PATH:/usr/X11R6/bin"
PS1="[\u@\h \W]\\$ "
ulimit -c 1000000
if [ 'id -gn' = 'id -un' -a 'id -u' -gt 14 ]; then
     umask 002
else
     umask 022
fi
USER='id -un'
LOGNAME=$USER
MAIL="/var/spool/mail/$USER"
HOSTNAME='/bin/hostname'
HISTSIZE=1000
HISTFILESIZE=1000
export PATH PS1 HOSTNAME HISTSIZE HISTFILESIZE USER LOGNAME MAIL
for i in /etc/profile.d/*.sh ; do
     if [ -x $i ]; then
     . $i
     fi
done
unset i
[ejr@hobbes ejr]$
```

Code Listing 8.10 *continued*

2. Write down, for your reference, the system configuration files and the order in which they're run. (Remember, settings in the last file run override all previous ones.) Our system configuration files include

- ▲ /etc/profile (automatically called by the system if it exists)

- ▲ ~/.bash_profile (automatically called by the system if it exists)

- ▲ ~/.bashrc (automatically called by the system if it exists)

- ▲ /etc/bashrc (often called by ~/.bashrc)

- ▲ ~/.bashrc (automatically called by the system if it exists)

Keep in mind that the files you have may differ from the files that we have.

✔ Tips

- The bash shell sometimes *daisychains* configuration files together, referencing one from the previous one. Be careful to preserve the references and sequence as you edit your configuration files, or you might end up with unexpected results.

- All lines that start with # are comments, which contain notes to help you better understand the files. Comments don't actually do anything, but they help you see what each section in the file does.

- The techie term (that you'll likely see in these files) for executing a configuration file or a script is to *source* it. That is, when you log in, your .profile may source .kshrc.

```
[ejr@hobbes ejr]$ more ~/.bash_profile
→ ~/.bashrc
::::::::::::::
/home/ejr/.bash_profile
::::::::::::::
# .bash_profile

# Get the aliases and functions
if [ -f ~/.bashrc ]; then
      . ~/.bashrc
fi

PATH=/bin:/usr/bin:/usr/local/bin

# User-specific environment and startup
programs

PATH=$PATH:/usr/local/games
ENV=$HOME/.bashrc
USERNAME=""

export USERNAME ENV PATH

—More—(Next file: /home/ejr/.bashrc)
```

Code Listing 8.11 Your first step is finding out the location of your path statement(s).

Adding to Your bash Path

One of the most useful changes you can make to your environment is adding to the default path, which is determined by the *path statement*. The path statement tells the shell where to look for commands, scripts, and programs. That is, if you issue a command, the path statement tells the system to look for that command in each of the named directories in a specific order.

Be sure not to remove anything from your path unless you really know what you're doing, but feel free to add as many additional directories as you want to it.

As the following steps show, you change your bash path by first identifying where your path statement is located, then editing the file that contains it (**Code Listing 8.11**).

To change your bash path:

1. `more ~/.bash_profile ~/.bashrc`

   To begin, view your configuration files (just the ones you can edit) in the order they're executed.

   Look through your system configuration files for a path statement. As Code Listing 8.11 shows, it'll look something like PATH=/bin:/usr/bin:/usr/local/bin. If you have more than one path statement, find the last one executed.

   Remember that different systems will have different configurations, so you might need to do a little digging to find your personal path statement(s).

2. `cp .bash_profile .bash_profile_backup`

   Make a backup of the file containing the path statement so that you can recover if you make mistakes. See Chapter 2 if you need more information on copying files.

continues on next page

3. `vi .bash_profile`

Use your favorite editor to open up the file in which you'll be changing the path.

4. `PATH=$PATH:$HOME/scripts`

Add a new path statement immediately below the last path statement. In this example, PATH is set to its current value ($PATH) plus the directory ($HOME/scripts) you wish to append to your path." (**Figure 8.3**).

5. Save the file and exit from your editor.

Refer to Chapter 4 for help if you need it.

6. `su - yourid`

As you learned back in Chapter 3, this command starts a new login shell so you can test your changes before logging out.

7. `echo $PATH`

Display the current path environment variable. This should include the addition you just made. It's there, right? (See **Code Listing 8.12**.)

✔ Tips

- If you look through the path statements in your various configuration files, you might find a path statement that includes just a . (dot). For example, you might see something like `PATH=/usr/bin:/usr/local/bin:.:`. The . adds your current directory, whatever it might be, to your path. Keep in mind, though, that it's often safer not to have the current directory in the path so you don't unintentionally run a program that isn't the one you expect to run (because there's an executable file by the same name in your current directory).

- You can use `grep` to make it easier to find the configuration files that set your path. `grep PATH ~/.bash* ~/.profile` is a good way to start, and `grep PATH /etc/*` is another goodie.

```
 jdoe@frazz.raycomm.com: /home/jdoe
#
#ejray test
echo "~/.bash_profile"
# .bash_profile

# Get the aliases and functions
if [ -f ~/.bashrc ]; then
        . ~/.bashrc
fi

# User specific environment and startup programs

PATH=$PATH:/usr/local/bin
PATH=$PATH:$HOME/bi█

export PATH
unset USERNAME
~
~
~
~
~
~
".bash_profile" 17L, 254C
```

Figure 8.3 You add or modify a bash path statement in your editor.

```
[ejr@hobbes ejr]$ echo $PATH
/bin:/usr/bin:/usr/local/bin:/usr/bin/X11
:/
usr/X11R6/bin:/usr/local/games:/home/ejr/
bin
[ejr@hobbes ejr]$
```

Code Listing 8.12 Using echo, you can verify that your new path statement exists.

- Your system configuration files will be much less confusing later on if you keep all related changes together. Therefore, you should keep the path statements together, rather than just plug an entirely random PATH statement into your configuration files.

```
[ejr@hobbes ejr]$ grep PS1 ~/.bash*
↦ ~/.bashrc /etc/bashrc
/home/ejr/.bashrc:PS1="\u \d $ "
/etc/bashrc:PS1="[\u@\h \W]$ "
[ejr@hobbes ejr]$
```

Code Listing 8.13 Use grep to search your configuration files for a prompt statement.

```
 jdoe@frazz.raycomm.com: /home/jdoe
# .bashrc

# User specific aliases and functions

# Source global definitions
if [ -f /etc/bashrc ]; then
        . /etc/bashrc
fi

PS1="\u \d $ "█
~
~
~
~
~
~
~
~
~
~
~
~
-- INSERT --
```

Figure 8.4 Edit your bash prompt statement in the editor of your choice.

Changing Your bash Prompt

Depending on your Unix system, by default you might see as your prompt just a dollar sign (**$**), or perhaps a dollar sign and date, or other information as outlined in the *Setting Your bash Prompt Promptly* sidebar. You can set your prompt to include information that's handy for you.

You actually have multiple prompts in bash:

◆ The main prompt that you usually think of as the shell prompt. This prompt is called PS1.

◆ A secondary prompt that you see when the system requires additional information to complete a command. Logically, this prompt is called PS2.

You can change either of these prompts using the following steps. You start by finding your prompt statement (**Code Listing 8.13**), then modifying it in your editor (**Figure 8.4**).

To change your bash prompt:

1. grep PS1 ~/.bash* '~/.bashrc
   ↦ /etc/bashrc

   To begin, search through the configuration files located in your home directory and in the /etc directory to find your prompt statement. It'll look something like PS1="$ " or PS1="[\u@\h \W]$ ", as shown in Code Listing 8.13.

   The *Setting Your bash Prompt Promptly* sidebar will help translate these symbols.

   continues on next page

CHANGING YOUR bash PROMPT

175

2. `vi ~/.bashrc`

Because the files with the prompt setting are in the systemwide `/etc` directory, we cannot change them directly, so we have to make the changes to `.bashrc` or a different configuration file in our home directory.

3. `PS1="\u \d $ "`

For example, we often set our prompt to include the userid (because we have enough different accounts on different systems that we need a reminder) and the date (because we're scattered). We're adding this at the end of the file so it will take precedence over the PS1 setting in the `/etc/bashrc` file that is referenced from the `~/.bashrc` file (Figure 8.4).

4. Save the file and exit from the editor.

5. `su - ejr`

Log in again with your changed prompt to try it out.

✔ Tips

■ Note the trailing space in the prompt code: `PS1="\u \d $ "`. This space can help make it easier to use the prompt because it keeps your commands from bumping into your prompt.

■ Consider changing your PS1 environment variable at the shell prompt, as discussed in Chapter 3, before you make changes in your configuration files. This way, you can try out a modified shell prompt before you change it in your configuration files.

Setting Your bash Prompt Promptly

You can set your prompt to contain all sorts of information. The following list shows you what code to use to add certain kinds of information to your prompt (as well as help you translate the code in your existing prompt):

◆ `\u` shows the userid of the current user—that's you.

◆ `\w` shows the current working directory with a path, using a ~ notation within your home directory.

◆ `\W` shows the current directory without the path.

◆ `\t` shows the time.

◆ `\d` shows the date.

◆ `\n` forces a new line, making the prompt appear split on two lines.

◆ `\h` shows the host name of the computer.

CHANGING YOUR bash PROMPT

Looking at Your ksh Configuration Files

As **Code Listing 8.14** (on the next page) shows, you look at your ksh configuration files using more or the editor of your choice. Keep in mind that configuration files are run in a specific order:

◆ System-wide configuration files (such as /etc/profile) run first upon log in.

◆ Configuration files specific to your Unix account (such as ~/.profile) run next if they're available.

To look at your ksh configuration files:

1. more /etc/profile ~/.profile

   Type more followed by the names of traditional Korn shell configuration files. You'll see something similar to Code Listing 8.14. As before, look for any other filenames or ENV statements in the listings that would indicate other files that play a role in getting your ksh environment configured.

2. For your own information, list the system configuration files that your system uses and the order in which they're called. For our system, we have

   ▲ /etc/profile (automatically called by the system)

   ▲ ~/.profile (automatically called by the system)

✔ Tip

■ The .profile file is executed when you start a new login shell (by logging in or with su - yourid). The .kshrc file is read each time you start any ksh subshell.

Fill in Your ksh System Configuration Files

_____

_____

_____

_____

_____

_____

_____

```
$ more /etc/profile ~/.profile
::::::::::::::
/etc/profile
::::::::::::::
#ident    "@(#)profile1.17    95/03/28 SMI"   /* SVr4.0 1.3   */
# The profile that all logins get before using their own .profile.
trap ""   2 3
export LOGNAME PATH
if [ "$TERM" = "" ]
then
     if /bin/i386
     then
     TERM=AT386
     else
     TERM=sun
     fi
     export TERM
fi
#     Login and -su shells get /etc/profile services.
#     -rsh is given its environment in its .profile.
case "$0" in
-sh | -ksh | -jsh)
     if [ ! -f .hushlogin ]
     then
     /usr/sbin/quota
     #   Allow the user to break the Message-Of-The-Day only.
     trap "trap '' 2"  2
     /bin/cat -s /etc/motd
     trap "" 2
     /bin/mail -E
     case $? in
     0)
     echo "You have new mail."
     ;;
     2)
     echo "You have mail."
     ;;
     esac
     fi
esac
umask 022
trap  2 3
```

Code Listing 8.14 Look for file and path names or ENV statements in the configuration file listings (for the files you have) to identify all of the files that help set up your environment.

```
: : : : : : : : : : : : : :
/home/users/e/ejray/.profile
: : : : : : : : : : : : : :
#
PATH=$PATH:$HOME/bin:.  # set command search path
export PATH
if [ -z "$LOGNAME" ]; then
      LOGNAME='logname'  # name of user who logged in
      export LOGNAME
fi
MAIL=/usr/spool/mail/$LOGNAME   # mailbox location
export MAIL
if [ -z "$PWD" ]; then
      PWD=$HOME   # assumes initial cwd is HOME
      export PWD
fi
if [ -f $HOME/.kshrc -a -r $HOME/.kshrc ]; then
      ENV=$HOME/.kshrc   # set ENV if there is an rc file
      export ENV
fi
# If job control is enabled, set the suspend character to ^Z (control-z):
case $- in
*m*) stty susp '^z'
      ;;
esac
set -o ignoreeof # don't let control-d logout
PS1="$ "
export PS1
export ENV=$HOME/.kshrc
: : : : : : : : : : : : : :
/home/users/e/ejray/.kshrc
: : : : : : : : : : : : : :
#
# If there is no VISUAL or EDITOR to deduce the desired edit
#  mode from, assume vi(C)-style command line editing.
if [ -z "$VISUAL" -a -z "$EDITOR" ]; then
      set -o vi
fi
/etc/ksh.kshrc: No such file or directory
$
```

Code Listing 8.14 *continued*

Changing Your ksh Path

The path statement tells the shell where to look for commands, scripts, and programs. For example, if you issue a command, the path statement tells the system to look in the named directories in a specific order.

As the following steps show, you change your ksh path by first identifying where your path statement is located, then editing the file that contains it (**Code Listing 8.15**).

To change your ksh path:

1. `grep PATH ~/.profile ~/.kshrc`

   To begin, check for path statements in the configuration files located in your home directory. If you wanted, you could also review the /etc/profile file, but you cannot edit that one.

2. Look through your system configuration files for a path statement. As Code Listing 8.15 shows, it'll look something like PATH=/usr/bin:/usr/local/bin:/usr/sbin. Remember, if you have more than one path statement, find the last one executed. If you don't have a path statement in your personal configuration files at all, then add one.

3. `cp ~/.profile ~/.profile.backup`

   Make a copy of the file containing the path statement so that you can recover if you make mistakes. See Chapter 2 if you need more information on copying files.

4. `vi ~/.profile`

   Use the editor of your choice to edit the configuration file with the path statement.

```
$ grep PATH ~/.profile ~/.kshrc
/home/users/e/ejray/.profile:PATH=/usr/
→ bin:/usr/local/bin:/usr/sbin:
/home/users/e/ejray/.profile:export PATH
$
```

Code Listing 8.15 First, find out the location of your path statement(s).

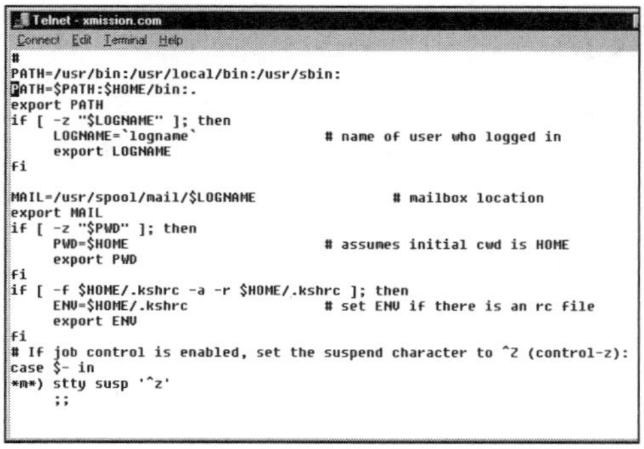

Figure 8.5 Add or modify a ksh path statement in your editor.

```
$ echo $PATH
/usr/bin:/usr/local/bin:/usr/sbin:/home/
→ users/e/ejray/bin:.
$
```

Code Listing 8.16 Verify that your new path statement exists.

5. `PATH=$PATH:$HOME/scripts`

Add a new path statement immediately below the last path statement. In this example, PATH is set to its current value ($PATH) plus the directory ($HOME/scripts) you wish to append to your path. (**Figure 8.5**).

6. Save the file and exit from your editor. Refer to Chapter 4 for help if you need it.

7. `su - yourid`

As you learned back in Chapter 3, this command starts a new login shell so you can test your changes before logging out.

8. `echo $PATH`

Display the current path environment variable. This should include the addition you just made (see **Code Listing 8.16**).

CHANGING YOUR ksh PATH

181

Changing Your ksh Prompt

Like bash, ksh has two prompts you can edit:

- The main prompt that you usually think of as the shell prompt, called PS1.

- A secondary prompt that you see when the system requires additional information to complete a command. Logically, this prompt is called PS2.

You can change either of these prompts using the following steps (we'll modify PS1 in the example). You start by finding your prompt statement (**Code Listing 8.17**), then modifying it in your editor.

To change your ksh prompt:

1. `grep PS1 /etc/profile ~/.profile`
   `→ ~/.kshrc`

   To begin, search through the configuration files located in your home directory and in the /etc directory for your prompt statement. It'll look something like `PS1="$ "` or `PS1='$PWD $ '`, as shown in Code Listing 8.17. Keep in mind that you can edit the files in your home directory only, not those in the /etc directory.

   The *Setting Your ksh Prompt Promptly* sidebar will help translate these symbols.

2. `vi .profile`

   Use your favorite editor to edit the configuration file with the PS1 setting in it or to add a PS1 setting to a configuration file in your home directory.

3. `PS1='$LOGNAME in $PWD $ '`

   Change the prompt to display the information you want—in this case, the user name and the current working directory.

✔ Tip

- Note the trailing space in the prompt code: `PS1="$ "`. This space keeps your commands from bumping into your prompt.

```
$ grep PS1 /etc/profile ~/.profile ~/
→ .kshrc
/home/users/e/ejray/.profile:PS1="$ "
/home/users/e/ejray/.profile:export PS1
$
```

Code Listing 8.17 List your zsh configuration files and look for a prompt statement.

Setting Your ksh Prompt Promptly

You can set your ksh prompt to contain some different kinds of information—but not as much as with zsh or bash shells. The following list shows you what code to use to add certain kinds of information to your prompt (as well as help you translate the code in your existing prompt):

- `$LOGNAME` shows the userid of the current user—that's you.

- `${PWD##*/}` shows the current working directory without the path.

- `$PWD` shows the current working directory with the path.

- `$HOST` shows the host name of the computer

Looking at Your csh Configuration Files

As **Code Listing 8.18** (on the next page) shows, you can use more or the editor of your choice to peek at your csh configuration files. As with other shells, the csh configuration files run in a specific order:

◆ System-wide configuration files (such as /etc/csh.cshrc) are read first upon log in.

◆ The main configuration files specific to your Unix account (~/.cshrc) are read next if they're available.

◆ The ~/.login configuration file is read last.

To look at your csh configuration files:

◆ more ~/.cshrc ~/.login

Type more followed by .cshrc and .login, which are the only possible names for csh configuration files. You'll see something similar to Code Listing 8.18. For our system, we have

▲ ~/.cshrc (automatically called by the system)

▲ ~/.login (automatically called by the system) if the shell is a login shell

✔ Tip

■ The .cshrc file is executed when you start a new csh shell of any kind. The .login file is executed when you start a new login shell (by logging in or with su - yourid).

Fill in Your csh System Configuration Files

```
xmission> more ~/.cshrc ~/.login
::::::::::::::
.cshrc
::::::::::::::
# <@>(#)Cshrc 1.6 91/09/05 SMI
set path = (/usr/local/bin /usr/local/bin/X11 /usr/openwin/bin /usr/bin
     /usr/ucb /usr/etc /usr/local/games .)
alias pwd    'echo $cwd'
umask 066
if ($?USER == 0 || $?prompt == 0) exit
set filec
set history=40
set prompt="'hostname'> "
# Edit the following lines as you wish
setenv EDITOR "pico -t"
setenv OPENWINHOME /usr/openwin
setenv MANPATH /usr/man:/usr/local/man:/usr/openwin/man
setenv LD_LIBRARY_PATH /usr/local/lib:/usr/openwin/lib
setenv PAGER more
limit coredumpsize 0
#     commands for interactive shells
alias ls 'ls -F'
alias cd 'cd \!*;echo $cwd'
alias home   'cd ~'
# MS-DOS aliases
alias dir    'ls -alg'
alias del    'rm -i'
alias delete 'rm -i'
alias copy   'cp -i'
alias md 'mkdir'
alias move   'mv -i'
alias cls    'clear'
alias clr    'clear'
alias type   'more'
# Terminal settings
setenv TERM vt100
/usr/bin/stty rows 24
/usr/bin/stty cols 80
/usr/bin/stty erase '^?'
```

Code Listing 8.18 Look for references to other paths or files in the listings, which might indicate other files used to set up your environment.

```
:::::::::::::::
.login
:::::::::::::::
# <@>(#)Login 1.14 90/11/01 SMI
#     general terminal characteristics
#/usr/bin/stty -crterase
#/usr/bin/stty -tabs
#/usr/bin/stty crt
#/usr/bin/stty erase '^h'
#/usr/bin/stty werase '^?'
#/usr/bin/stty kill '^['
#/usr/bin/stty new
#     environment variables
#setenv EXINIT 'set sh=/bin/csh sw=4 ai report=2'
#setenv MORE '-c'
#setenv PRINTER lw
#     commands to perform at login
#w    # see who is logged in
notice   # system information that must be read
#
# If possible, start the windows system.  Give user a chance to bail out
#
if ( 'tty' != "/dev/console" || $TERM != "sun" ) then
     exit    # leave user at regular C shell prompt
endif
xmission>
```

Code Listing 8.18 *continued*

Changing Your csh Path

The path statement tells the shell where to look for commands, scripts, and programs. So if you issue a command, the path statement tells the system to look for the command in the named directories in a specific order. As the following steps show, you change your csh path by first identifying where your path statement is located, then editing the file that contains it (**Code Listing 8.19**).

To change your csh path:

1. `grep -i path ~/.cshrc ~/.login`

   To begin, list the configuration files located in your home directory and in the /etc directory. Look through your system configuration files for a path statement. As Code Listing 8.19 shows, it'll look something like `set path = (/usr/local/bin /usr/local/bin/X11 /usr/openwin/bin /usr/bin)`. If you have more than one path statement, find the last one executed.

2. `cp ~/.cshrc ~/.cshrc.backup`

   Make a copy of the file containing the path statement so that you can recover if you make mistakes. See Chapter 2 if you need more information on copying files.

3. `vi .cshrc`

   Use the editor of your choice to edit the file with the path statement in it.

4. `set path = (/usr/local/bin /usr/bin`
   `→ /usr/ucb /usr/etc /home/users/e/`
   `→ ejray/bin)`

   Edit the path statement to add the full path to the bin subdirectory in your home directory, as shown in **Figure 8.6**.

```
xmission> grep -i path ~/.cshrc ~/.login
.cshrc:set path = (/usr/local/bin /usr/
→ local/bin/X11 /usr/openwin/bin
→ /usr/bin)
xmission>
```

Code Listing 8.19 Use grep to find the path statement in your configuration files.

Figure 8.6 Edit your path statement to add your home directory.

```
xmission> echo $path
/usr/local/bin:/usr/bin:>/usr/ucb:
→ /usr/etc:/home/users/e/ejray/in
xmission>
```

Code Listing 8.20 Here's your new path statement!

5. Save the file and exit from your editor. Refer to Chapter 4 for help if you need it.

6. `su - yourid`

As you learned back in Chapter 3, this command starts a new login shell so you can test your changes before logging out.

7. `echo $path`

Display the current path environment variable. This should include the addition you just made. Lo and behold! There it is! (See **Code Listing 8.20**.)

Changing Your csh Prompt

Your system's default prompt might be just a dollar sign ($) or perhaps a dollar sign and date, or other information as outlined in the *Setting Your csh Prompt Promptly* sidebar. You can change this prompt using the following steps. You start by finding your prompt statement (**Code Listing 8.21**), then modifying it in your editor (**Figure 8.7**).

To change your csh prompt:

1. `grep prompt ~/.cshrc ~/.login`

   To begin, list the configuration files located in your home directory and in the /etc directory. Look through your system configuration files for your prompt statement. It'll look something like `set prompt="> "` or `set prompt="'hostname'> "`. It's likely in your .cshrc file, as shown in Code Listing 8.21.

   The *Setting Your csh Prompt Promptly* sidebar will help you translate this code.

2. `vi .cshrc`

   Use the editor of your choice to edit the configuration file with the prompt setting in it.

3. `set prompt="$LOGNAME > "`

   Set your prompt to something more suitable, as shown in Figure 8.7.

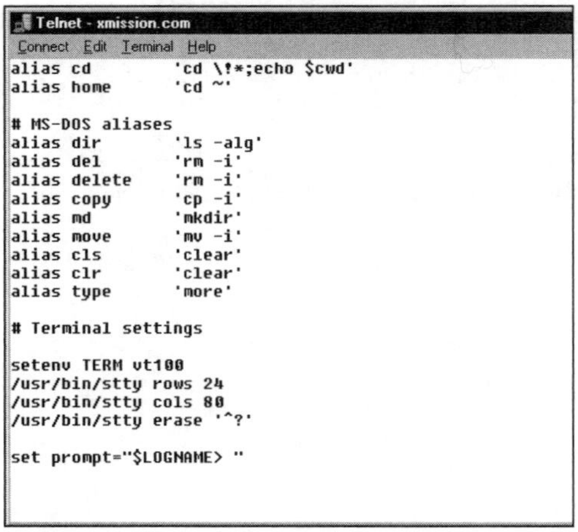

Figure 8.7 Edit your prompt to include the details you want.

```
xmission> grep prompt ~/.cshrc ~/.login
/home/users/e/ejray/.cshrc:if ($?USER == 0 || $?prompt == 0) exit
/home/users/e/ejray/.cshrc:set prompt="'hostname'> "
/home/users/e/ejray/.login: exit    # leave user at regular C shell prompt
xmission>
```

Code Listing 8.21 The prompt statement will likely be in your .cshrc file.

4. Save the file and exit from the editor.

5. `su - yourid`

Log in again to try it out (**Code Listing 8.22**).

✔ Tip

■ Note the trailing space in the prompt code: `set prompt="$LOGNAME > "`. This extra space makes the prompt easier to use.

Setting Your csh Prompt Promptly

You can set your csh prompt to contain some types of information, but not as many as the bash or zsh prompts. The following list shows you what code to use to add certain kinds of information to your prompt (as well as help you translate the code in your existing prompt):

◆ `$LOGNAME` shows the userid of the current user—that's you.

◆ `'uname -n'%` shows the host name of the computer

```
xmission> su - ejray
Password:
Sun Microsystems Inc.   SunOS 5.5.1Generic May 1996
You have mail.
NOTE! As of 7/15/98, "tin" has been backed out its prior version.   NNTP
      support was compiled in directly as well.  We hope that this will
      stabilize its problems.


-----------------------------------------------------------------
  General questions email to "help" or "help@xmission.com".
  Problems with the system mail to "support" or "support@xmission.com".

  Type "acctstat" for a summary of your current account information.
  Type "quota -v" to view your existing disk quota.
  Type "help" for a list of online programs or "menu" for the assisted menu.
ejray>
```

Code Listing 8.22 Test out your new prompt to see if you like it.

Setting Aliases with alias

Aliases are nicknames of sorts that you use to enter commands more easily. For example, if you frequently use the command mail -s "Lunch today?" deb < .signature, you could set an alias for this command and call it lunch. Then, in the future, all you have to do is type in lunch, and the result is the same as if you typed in the longer command.

To set an alias with alias:

1. Choose the appropriate file to edit, depending on which shell you're using.

   ▲ zsh users should use ~/.zshrc

   ▲ bash users should use ~/.bashrc

   ▲ ksh users should use ~/.profile

   ▲ csh users should use ~/.cshrc

   If you don't have the appropriate file, you're welcome to use a different configuration file. Many people store all their aliases in a separate .alias file and update their standard configurations with a line that references their new .alias file.

2. vi .bashrc

   Edit the configuration file you've selected.

3. alias quit = "logout"

   Type alias followed by the term you want to use as the alias, =, and the command for which you're making an alias (in quotes). Here, we're setting the word quit as an alias for the system command logout, so we can type quit instead of logout (**Figure 8.8**).

4. Add as many other aliases as you want.

   See the sidebar called *Good Aliases to Set* for more ideas.

5. Save the file and exit from the editor.

   See Chapter 4 for details about saving and exiting in vi and pico.

```
 jdoe@frazz.raycomm.com: /home/jdoe
# .bashrc

# User specific aliases and functions

# Source global definitions
if [ -f /etc/bashrc ]; then
        . /etc/bashrc
fi

PS1="\u \d $ "

alias quit="logout"

~
~
~
~
~
~
~
~
-- INSERT --
```

Figure 8.8 Setting aliases can keep you from typing long names and code.

```
xmission> alias
cd      cd !*;echo $cwd
clr     clear
cls     clear
copy    cp -i
del     rm -i
delete    rm -i
dir     ls -alg
home    cd ~
ls      ls -F
md      mkdir
move    mv -i
pwd     echo $cwd
type    more
xmission>
```

Code Listing 8.23 Type alias at the shell prompt to see a list of aliases you've set.

6. su - yourid

   Start a new login shell to test out the alias.

7. alias

   Type alias at the shell prompt for a listing of all the aliases you have defined (**Code Listing 8.23**).

   continues on next page

Good Aliases to Set

Here are a few aliases you might find worthwhile to set on your system:

- alias rm="rm -i" causes the system to prompt you about all deletions.

- alias quit="logout" lets you use quit as a synonym for logout.

- alias homepage="lynx http://www.raycomm.com/" lets you use homepage to start the lynx browser and connect to the Raycomm home page (substitute your home page as necessary).

Or, if you're coming from a DOS background, you might find the following aliases handy:

- alias dir="ls -l" lets you use dir to list files.

- alias copy="cp" lets you use copy to copy files.

- alias rename="mv" lets you use rename to move or rename files.

- alias md="mkdir" lets you use md to make a directory.

- alias rd="rmdir" lets you use rd to remove a directory.

SETTING ALIASES WITH alias

191

✔ Tips

- You can put aliases in other files, but it's customary to put them in the `.bashrc` file (or other appropriate rc file, such as `.cshrc`), so they'll be set automatically when you log in, rather than having to be manually set.

- You can also issue `alias` commands from the shell prompt to set aliases for the current session.

- Be sure to make a backup copy of any configuration files you plan to change before you change them. That way, if you mess up, you still have the original file to work with.

- For you csh users, you'll need to set aliases without using the = sign—just use "alias quit logout" and you'll be set to use quit to mean logout.

SETTING ALIASES WITH alias

RUNNING SCRIPTS AND PROGRAMS

9

Throughout this book, you've been running scripts and programs by typing in commands and pressing (Enter). The commands zoom along to the Unix system, which responds by obediently doing whatever the command or script dictates. In doing this, you run the commands and scripts—called *jobs* in this context—right then and there.

You can also run jobs at specified times; run them on a schedule you set up; or start, stop, or delete them as you choose. Plus, you can find out when they are scheduled to run, time how long they take, or monitor them as they run. Sound cool? Great! Let's take a look.

Chapter Contents

◆ Running commands

◆ Scheduling one-time jobs

◆ Scheduling regularly occurring jobs

◆ Suspending jobs

◆ Checking job status

◆ Running jobs in the background

◆ Running jobs in the foreground

◆ Controlling job priority

◆ Timing jobs

◆ Finding running processes

◆ Deleting processes

Running a Command

Throughout this book, you've been practicing running a single command. Unix doesn't really care if you're running a built-in command that came with the system, a program you installed later, or a script your best friend wrote—it's all the same to Unix. **Code Listing 9.1** shows some options on running a command.

To run a command:

◆ `ls`

At the shell prompt, type the command and press Enter.

To run a specific command:

◆ `/home/jdoe/scripts/ls`

It's certainly possible that you would want to write a script that would list the files in your directory in a special way—for example, a script to list the files and to save the listing into a new file for later reference. (You might name it something else but could certainly call it `ls` if you want to.) To run the specific script, enter the whole path to the script (so Unix doesn't just run the first one it finds in your path). See Chapter 8 for more about path statements.

✔ Tips

■ You can combine commands on the same line, as you've seen earlier in this book. Just use a ; to separate the commands, and you're set. For example, you could do `ls; pwd` to list files and show the current directory.

```
[jdoe@frazz Project]$ ls
keep  keeper.jpg  kept  kidder.txt  kiddo
→ kidnews  kidneypie  kids  kidupdate
[jdoe@frazz Project]$ /bin/ls
keep  keeper.jpg  kept  kidder.txt  kiddo
→ kidnews  kidneypie  kids  kidupdate
[jdoe@frazz Project]$ /home/jdoe/
→ scripts/ls
keep  keeper.jpg  kept  kidder.txt  kiddo
→ kidnews  kidneypie  kids  kidupdate
You listed these files.
[jdoe@frazz Project]$ ls ; pwd
keep  keeper.jpg  kept  kidder.txt  kiddo
→ kidnews  kidneypie  kids  kidupdate
/home/jdoe/Project
[jdoe@frazz Project]$
```

Code Listing 9.1 To run a script, command, or program, just enter the name or the path and the name at the shell prompt.

■ If you use a && to combine commands, the system will run both in sequence but run the second only if the first succeeds. For example, you could use `mv todolist todolist.done && touch todolist` to move your to-do list to a different file and create a new to-do list. If the first command fails (for example, because you don't have permission to create a new file), the second command won't run.

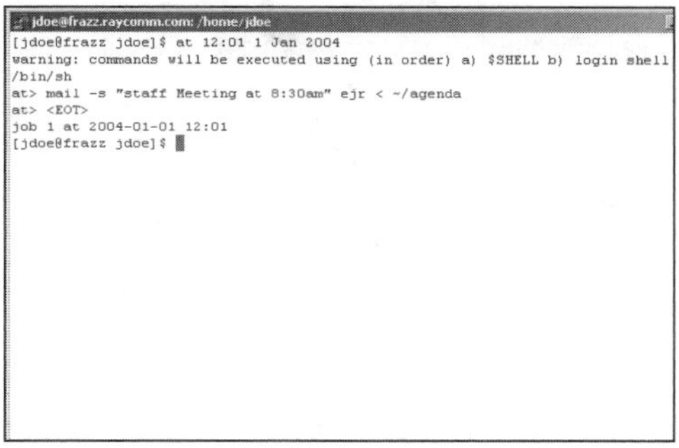

```
jdoe@frazz.raycomm.com: /home/jdoe
[jdoe@frazz jdoe]$ at 12:01 1 Jan 2004
warning: commands will be executed using (in order) a) $SHELL b) login shell
/bin/sh
at> mail -s "staff Meeting at 8:30am" ejr < ~/agenda
at> <EOT>
job 1 at 2004-01-01 12:01
[jdoe@frazz jdoe]$ ▋
```

Figure 9.1 To schedules a one-time job, all you have to do is specify the time and the job to run.

Scheduling One-Time Jobs with at

Occasionally, you may need to schedule jobs to run one time, at a time you designate. For example, you could schedule an email message to yourself, reminding you to attend a staff meeting. Or, you could schedule a meeting reminder for your co-workers that includes a meeting agenda. You can schedule these and other one-time jobs using at, which lets you designate a time at which a job (or jobs) should run. **Figure 9.1** demonstrates scheduling an email about that all-important staff meeting.

To schedule a one-time job with at:

1. at 12:01 1 Jan 2007

   To begin, specify when you want the job to run, using at plus a time statement (Figure 9.1). In this example, we specify a time, month, date, and year, although you can create a variety of other time statements, like these

   ▲ at noon tomorrow

   ▲ at 01/01/07

   ▲ at 3:42am

   ▲ at now + 3 weeks

   ▲ at teatime

   Yes, teatime is a valid option. It's at 4 p.m., by the way.

2. mail -s "Staff Meeting at 8:30am"
   → ejr < ~/agenda

   Specify the job. In this case, it sends email to the user (ejr), specifies the subject "Staff Meeting at 8:30am" and sends the contents of the file called agenda. See Chapter 11 for the full scoop on using mail.

3. Ctrl D

   Indicate that you've finished issuing commands.

To schedule sequential one-time jobs with at:

1. `at midnight`

   Specify when you want the sequential jobs to run, using `at` plus a time statement (**Code Listing 9.2**). You can use a variety of time statements, as shown in the previous example.

2. `tar -icf ~/bigdog.tar ~/HereKittyKitty`

   Enter the first job you want to run. This job collects all of the files from the directory called ~/HereKittyKitty into a single file called ~/bigdog.tar. Chapter 13 will tell you more about archiving with `tar`.

3. `gzip ~/bigdog.tar`

   Enter the next job to run. This compresses the ~/bigdog.tar file, making it easier to store and email.

4. `mutt -a bigdog.tar.gz -s "Read this`
   `→ by lunch time!" deb < /dev/null`

   Specify the next job in the sequence. Here, we're using `mutt`'s command-line mail options to attach a file, specify a subject, and mail the whole shebang to Deb. See Chapter 11 for more on emailing with `mutt`.

5. Ctrl D

   Ta-daaaa! Use this key combination to finish the sequence.

```
[ejr@hobbes ejr]$ at midnight
at> tar -icf ~/bigdog.tar
~/HereKittyKitty
at> gzip ~/bigdog.tar
at>mutt -a bigdog.tar.gz -s "Read this
 → by lunch time" deb < /dev/null
at>
at> <EOT>
warning: commands will be executed using
 → /bin/sh
job 12 at 2003-08-28 00:00
[ejr@hobbes ejr]$
```

Code Listing 9.2 To schedule sequential one-time jobs, just specify the time and the jobs in the order you want them to run.

```
[ejr@hobbes ejr]$ atq
4      2003-08-28 12:01 a
9      2004-01-01 12:01 a
13     2003-08-27 16:00 a
12     2003-08-28 00:00 a
[ejr@hobbes ejr]$ atrm 12
[ejr@hobbes ejr]$ atq
4      2003-08-28 12:01 a
9      2004-01-01 12:01 a
13     2003-08-27 16:00 a
[ejr@hobbes ejr]$
```

Code Listing 9.3 Delete scheduled jobs by specifying the job number.

To delete a scheduled job:

1. atq

   For starters, show the list of jobs waiting in the at queue with atq (**Code Listing 9.3**). The second column, which shows the scheduled time, should jog your memory about which job is which. The first column, which specifies the job number for each job, lets you identify which job to delete in the next step.

2. atrm 12

   Remove the queued job by typing atrm and the job number—in this case, job number 12.

✔ Tips

- atq is also handy for reviewing jobs that you've scheduled.

- Use at to send yourself reminders.

- If you have a long list of commands that you want to run periodically, consider making them into a brief shell script, then using at to run the shell script. It's less work in the long run, and you don't have to concentrate on getting the commands just right as you do when telling at what to do. See Chapter 10 for the full scoop on shell scripts.

- Different flavors of Unix sometimes present the information from at differently. You get all the information you need, but it may be arranged somewhat differently.

SCHEDULING ONE-TIME JOBS WITH at

Scheduling Regularly Occurring Jobs with cron

Suppose you want to send yourself a reminder message just before you go home at the end of each day—say, a reminder to turn off the coffeepot. Or, suppose you want to make a backup copy of specific files each week. You can do this by using the `crontab` command to schedule commands or scripts to run regularly at times you specify. In doing so, you can schedule tasks to occur on specific days at specific times and know that the jobs will happen unattended (**Figure 9.2**).

Figure 9.2 The cron file, which is where you specify the cron job, opens in your default editor. If you've previously specified cron jobs, they'll show up in the editor.

To schedule a regularly occurring job with cron:

1. `crontab -e`

   At the shell prompt, type `crontab`, followed by the `-e` flag, which lets you edit your cron file. As shown in Figure 9.2, your cron file will appear in your default editor. It's likely to be empty (if you haven't set up cron jobs before), but you might have some content in there.

2. `55 16 * * 1-5 mail -s "Go home now!"`
   → `ejray@raycomm.com`

   On the first line of the cron file, enter values for minutes, hours, day of the month, month, and day of the week, then the command you want to run. See the *What Are Those Funky Numbers?* sidebar for more details about specifying times and days. In this example, we're sending an email to `ejray` every weekday at 4:55 p.m. reminding him to go home.

```
55 16 * * * mail -s "Go Home Now!"
ejray@raycomm.com  < /dev/null
~
~
~
~
~
~
~
~
~
~
~
~
~
~
~
~
~
"/tmp/crontab.16206" 3 lines,
 → 192 characters written
crontab: installing new crontab
[ejr@hobbes ejr]$
```

Code Listing 9.4 This job reminds ejray to go home every day. The message toward the end indicates that the cron job has been successfully entered.

3. Save and close the file.

Chapter 4 will give you a quick reminder about saving and closing with pico and vi.

If you set the times and dates correctly (that is, if you didn't accidentally set them to happen in the 59th hour of the day or whatever), you'll see a message like the one near the end of **Code Listing 9.4**, confirming that you're all set. (You'll get an appropriate error message if you scheduled something to happen at 55 hours, 12 minutes, on the ninth day of the week.)

✔ Tips

■ When scheduling cron jobs, you need to specify full and absolute paths to the files—that is, specify /home/ejray/file rather than file. Also, if you write a shell script and reference it in a cron job, you'll need to specify paths in the shell script as well. cron doesn't check out your personal environment variable settings when it runs, so the full path name is essential.

■ Use crontab -l to display a listing of your cron jobs.

What Are Those Funky Numbers?

When entering a cron job, you specify

◆ Minutes (0–59)

◆ Hours (0–23)

◆ Day of the month (1–31)

◆ Month (1–12)

◆ Days of the week (0–6, with Sunday as 0)

If you replace the number with a *, cron will match all possible values, so, if a job is scheduled for

◆ 1 * * * *, it will happen at one minute after every hour

◆ 15 3 * * *, it will happen at 3:15 a.m. every day

◆ 59 23 31 * *, it will happen at 11:59 p.m., seven times a year (once in each of the months with a 31st)

◆ 0 12 * * 0, it will happen at noon on Sundays

You can use a comma to separate multiple values. For example, if you want something to happen on the hour and half-hour during December, you might use 0,30 * * 12 *.

Use a hyphen (-) to indicate a range. For example, to schedule something for every hour from 9 a.m. to 5 p.m. every day, use 0 9-17 * * *.

Suspending Jobs

Suppose you've just started a job that requires no input from you—say, downloading multiple files with ftp—and you suddenly realize that you've got to finish something else right now. Instead of waiting for the files to download or stopping the job completely, you can instead just suspend the job and resume it later (**Code Listing 9.5**). In doing so, you can make the Unix system work your way—that is, you don't lose the progress you've made toward getting the job done, and you can do the other stuff you need to do as well.

To suspend a job:

◆ ⌈Ctrl⌉⌈Z⌉

While the job is running, press these keys to suspend the process (Code Listing 9.5). ⌈Ctrl⌉⌈Z⌉ doesn't actually terminate the process; it pauses the job in much the same way that pressing the Pause button on your CD player pauses the CD.

✔ Tips

■ After you've suspended a job, you can restart it in the background using bg, restart it in the foreground using fg, check on its status using jobs, or delete it completely using kill. Refer to the appropriate sections in this chapter for details on using these commands.

■ You can suspend as many jobs at a time as you want. Just use ⌈Ctrl⌉⌈Z⌉ to do so, then use jobs to check the status of each suspended job if you need to.

■ Because it's pretty easy to forget that you've suspended a job, most shells will remind you that "there are stopped jobs" when you try to log out of the system. You should either resume the job or kill it before you can log out. Yes, the Unix system uses the terms "stopped jobs" and "suspended jobs" more or less interchangeably.

```
[ejr@hobbes ejr]$ ftp calvin.raycomm.com
Connected to calvin.raycomm.com.
220 calvin Microsoft FTP Service
 → (Version 2.0).
Name (calvin.raycomm.com:ejr): anonymous
331 Anonymous access allowed, send identity
 → (e-mail name) as password.
Password:
230 Anonymous user logged in.
Remote system type is Windows_NT.
ftp>
[1]+  Stopped      ftp calvin.raycomm.com
[ejr@hobbes ejr]$
```

Code Listing 9.5 Suspending jobs is just like pushing the Pause button on your CD player.

```
[ejr@hobbes ejr]$ jobs
[1]-  Running    ftp calvin.raycomm.com &
[2]+  Stopped    (tty input)    telnet
[3]   Stopped    (signal)       lynx
 → http://www.raycomm.com/
[ejr@hobbes ejr]$
```

Code Listing 9.6 Viewing jobs lets you know which jobs you have suspended and their status.

Checking Job Status with jobs

Occasionally, you may have multiple jobs running or suspended and need a quick update about the jobs' status. Using jobs, you can find out whether a job is running, stopped, or waiting for input, as shown in **Code Listing 9.6**.

To check job status with jobs:

◆ jobs

At the shell prompt, type jobs. You'll see a list of the current jobs (that is, processes that you've suspended or otherwise controlled) either running or stopped, as shown in Code Listing 9.6. Using the job numbers on the left, you can choose to run the jobs in the background or foreground, to resume them, or to kill the jobs, as described in the next few sections in this chapter.

✔ Tip

■ Depending on your shell, you can often kill jobs with kill followed by a % and the job number or command name—for example, you could kill the ftp job in Code Listing 9.6 with kill %ftp or kill %1. See *Deleting Processes with kill* later in this chapter for more on killing jobs.

Running Jobs in the Background with bg

If you're running a job that doesn't require input from you, consider running it in the background using bg (**Code Listing 9.7**). In doing so, you can keep the program running while working on other Unix activities at the same time.

To run jobs in the background with bg:

1. jobs

At the shell prompt, type jobs to see the list of all jobs, running or stopped. Note the job numbers on the left.

2. bg %3

Type bg followed by % and the number of the job you want to run in the background (Code Listing 9.7).

✔ Tips

- If you want to put the most recently suspended job into the background, just type bg (without the number) at the prompt.

- You can also put jobs directly into the background without first suspending them. Just type the name of the job to run, a space, and & (as in bigdog &). The & moves the job directly into the background.

```
[ejr@hobbes ejr]$ jobs
[3]- lynx http://www.raycomm.com/ &
 ↪ calvin.raycomm.com
[2]   Stopped   (tty input)   telnet
[3]   Stopped   (signal)      lynx
 ↪ http://www.raycomm.com/
[4]+  Stopped   man telnet
[ejr@hobbes ejr]$ bg %3
[3]- lynx http://www.raycomm.com/ &
[ejr@hobbes ejr]$
```

Code Listing 9.7 Restarting suspended jobs in the background lets you do two things—or more—at once. To move a job to the background, just type bg followed by % and the job number.

```
[ejr@hobbes ejr]$ jobs
[1]+  Stopped    ftp ftp.cdrom.com
[ejr@hobbes ejr]$ fg %1
ftp ftp.cdrom.com
```

Code Listing 9.8 Typing fg plus the job number brings that job into the foreground. When you bring suspended jobs into the foreground, you'll sometimes see the job activities onscreen. At other times, you'll see only a prompt and will need to summon help to see anything of the program.

Running Jobs in the Foreground with fg

When you're ready to resume a suspended or backgrounded job, you can do so using fg. Remember, when you suspend a job, what you're doing is moving the job into limbo. fg just moves the job into the foreground again (**Code Listing 9.8**), so you can see, for example, what it's doing or provide input.

To run jobs in the foreground with fg:

1. jobs

   At the shell prompt, type jobs to list all stopped or running jobs. Note the job numbers at the left.

2. fg %1

   Enter fg followed by the number of the job that you want to bring back into the foreground (Code Listing 9.8).

   Depending on the job you're bringing back into the foreground, you may or may not get to see the job running onscreen. Sometimes you'll be plunked back into the job and be able to enter information as prompted. Other times, you'll just see the prompt for the program you returned to the foreground. If this is the case, try typing ? (for help), which often forces the program to display something onscreen and refresh the display.

✔ Tip

■ You can bring the last suspended job into the foreground by typing fg (with no job number) at the shell prompt.

Controlling Job Priority with nice

Suppose you need an enormous file from the Internet that would take practically all afternoon to download. By downloading it, you would hog system resources and make the system response time much slower for other users. OK, bad example. Suppose your co-worker needs to download an enormous file and would hog system resources all afternoon. You'd hope that she'd have the courtesy to not tie up system resources that you need to use.

Fortunately, she can, using nice, which lets her control job priority. As **Code Listing 9.9** shows, you rank your job's priority using numbers from 1 to 19, with 1 being somewhat nice (higher priority) and 19 being fabulously nice (lower priority). The Unix system uses the number you provide to determine how much attention to devote to the job.

To control job order with nice:

◆ nice -n 19 slowscript

At the shell prompt, type nice, followed by the appropriate adjustment (19, here), and the name of the program or script to run (Code Listing 9.9). In this example, slowscript is run with the lowest priority possible.

✔ Tips

■ To find out how nice you need to be, you might check out how many processes (and which kinds) are currently running on the Unix system. You can do this using ps, as described later in this chapter.

■ You could use nice and run a job in the background—for example, use nice -n 12 funscript & to run funscript in the background with a niceness level of 12.

```
[ejr@hobbes ejr]$ nice -n 19 slowscript
```

Code Listing 9.9 By using nice plus an adjustment, you can let Unix determine how hard to work on your job.

■ You can just type nice plus the job name (as in nice sortaslow). Doing so will automatically specify 10 as the niceness level (the default setting).

■ If you are the system administrator and logged in as root, you can use negative numbers (down to –20) with nice to increase the priority (nice -n -16 priorityjob).

■ Use renice to change the niceness of a running job. For example, use renice -n 18 2958 (the job number). If you're the system administrator, you can increase or decrease the niceness of any job; if you're a peon—whoops, we mean a regular computer user at your company—you can only decrease the priority of your own jobs, not increase it. In a pinch, you could ask your system administrator to increase the priority of your job.

```
[ejr@hobbes running]$ time slowscript
0.05user 0.06system 0:50.12elapsed 0%CPU
[ejr@hobbes running]$ time ls
bigdog.tar.gz    slowscript testing.gif
0.03user 0.00system 0:00.03elapsed 78%CPU
[ejr@hobbes running]$ time nice -19 ls
bigdog.tar.gz    slowscript testing.gif
0.03user 0.03system 0:00.06elapsed 93%CPU
[ejr@hobbes running]$ time -p nice -n 19 ls
foo
real 0.00
user 0.00
sys 0.00
[ejr@hobbes running]$
```

Code Listing 9.10 Enter time plus the full job command to find out the job time.

Timing Jobs with `time`

Sometimes, you might want to know how long a job takes to complete. You can do so using the `time` command, which times jobs according to the built-in Unix timer. As **Code Listing 9.10** shows, all you have to do is enter `time` followed by the command you want to time.

To time a job using `time`:

◆ `time slowscript`

At the shell prompt, type `time` followed by the complete command. After the command finishes, the system will tell you how long it took, as shown in Code Listing 9.10.

To compare job times with `time`:

1. `time ls /usr`

   At the shell prompt, type `time` followed by a job (here, `ls`).

2. `time nice -n 19 ls /usr`

   Then, type `time` followed by another job. In this example, we're comparing a regular `ls` command to a `nice ls` command. As Code Listing 9.10 shows, the elapsed time for the `nice ls` command was considerably longer than the regular `ls` command.

continues on next page

TIMING JOBS WITH `time`

205

✔ Tips

- Keep in mind that the time a job takes to run may vary according to the system's current load or capacity. For example, a job might take less time to run at 2 a.m., when few people are using the Unix system, compared with 2 p.m., when many more people are using the system.

- Different systems produce slightly different `time` outputs. On some systems, you'll get real (clock) time, user time, and system time. *Real time* is how many seconds on the clock elapsed while the program was running, while *user and system time* both refer to different measures of how long it took the system to run the job. On other systems, you might get a ton of garbage, as shown in **Code Listing 9.11**, but the gist of the information is the same.

- In the case of the `ls` example, you're really not concerned with either the output or the errors—just the time—so you can creatively dispense with all of it. Try `time ls /usr > /dev/null 2>&1` to send standard output to `/dev/null` (the bitbucket) and send error messages to standard output (and thence to the bitbucket). See Chapter 17 for details.

- Try `time -p` to get a more human-readable output.

```
$ time slowscript
0.07user 0.05system 0:50.13elapsed 0%CPU
(0avgtext+0avgdata 0maxresident)k
0inputs+0outputs
 → (219major+59minor)pagefaults 0swaps
$
```

Code Listing 9.11 time output varies from system to system. Here, we get a bunch of garbage to decipher in addition to the time information.

```
[jdoe@frazz jdoe]$ ps
  PID TTY        TIME CMD
21016 pts/22    00:00:00 bash
21707 pts/22    00:00:00 ps
[jdoe@frazz jdoe]$ ps -a
  PID TTY        TIME CMD
21407 pts/3     00:00:00 su
21411 pts/3     00:00:00 bash
21441 pts/3     00:00:00 su
21444 pts/3     00:00:00 bash
19274 pts/11    00:00:05 xterm
23357 pts/12    00:00:04 xterm
13369 pts/5     00:00:00 zsh
23815 pts/9     00:00:00 su
23818 pts/9     00:00:00 bash
23878 pts/9     00:00:00 csh
23942 pts/9     00:00:01 ssh
23972 pts/18    00:00:00 su
23975 pts/18    00:00:00 bash
24103 pts/5     00:00:00 ssh
 4658 pts/15    00:00:11 ssh
24318 pts/8     00:00:01 xterm
29188 pts/4     00:00:00 rxvt-2.7.9
29368 pts/4     00:00:00 rxvt
29440 pts/8     00:00:00 vi
23883 pts/20    00:00:02 xterm
27257 pts/16    00:00:01 ssh
 6004 pts/20    00:00:00 xterm
20531 pts/20    00:00:02 xterm
21013 pts/22    00:00:00 su
21016 pts/22    00:00:00 bash
21708 pts/22    00:00:00 ps
[jdoe@frazz jdoe]$
```

Code Listing 9.12 Using ps, you can find out what processes are currently running.

Finding Out What Processes Are Running with ps

The jobs that we've been talking about so far are actually types of processes. *Processes* are programs, scripts, or commands—including anything you do in the Unix system. All jobs are processes, but not all processes are jobs.

Occasionally, you may want to find out what processes are running on the Unix system. You can do this using ps, as shown in **Code Listing 9.12**.

To find out what processes are running with ps:

◆ ps

At the shell prompt, type ps to see the list of the current processes that you're running in your current shell, including processes for your current shell, as well as any other jobs (Code Listing 9.12).

The exact information you see will vary from system to system. In general, though, you'll find the *PID* (process identification) number at the far left and the process name at the right.

✔ Tips

- You can find out what processes other people are running by typing ps -a at the shell prompt and what processes the system is running (also called *daemons*) with ps -ax. The ps −ef variant is usually pretty useful for us.

- You can sometimes, depending on the system, get a broader look at currently running processes by typing ps −a f. The f flag indicates "forest" view, which lets you see not only the processes, but also how they relate to each other, as shown in **Code Listing 9.13**.

- The results ps offers vary greatly depending on the Unix flavor you're using. Type man ps at the shell prompt to find out more about your specific ps capabilities.

```
$ ps −a f
  PID TTY STAT TIME COMMAND
15043  p0 S  0:00 /bin/login -h calvin raycomm.com -p
15044  p0 S  0:01  \_ -bash
16344  p0 T N   0:00      \_ sh ./slowscript
16345  p0 T N   0:00      |  \_ sleep 50
16449  p0 R 0:00          \_ ps f
15911  p1 S  0:00 /bin/login -h calvin raycomm.com -p
15914  p1 S  0:01  \_ -bash
16216  p1 T  0:00      \_ telnet
16217  p1 T  0:00      \_ lynx http://www.raycomm.com/
16267  p1 T  0:00      \_ man telnet
16268  p1 T  0:00          \_ sh -c (cd /usr/man ; (echo -e ".pl 1100i"; cat /
16269  p1 T  0:00              \_ sh -c (cd /usr/man ; (echo -e ".pl 1100i"; c
16270  p1 T  0:00                  \_ sh -c (cd /usr/man ; (echo -e ".pl 1100i
16272  p1 T  0:00                  |  \_ cat /usr/man/man1/telnet.1
16271  p1 T  0:00                  \_ /usr/bin/gtbl
16273  p1 T  0:00                  \_ sh -c (cd /usr/man ; (echo -e ".pl 1100i
$
```

Code Listing 9.13 The forest view gives you a broader look at running processes.

```
$ ps -a f
  PID TTY STAT TIME COMMAND
15911  p1 S  0:00 /bin/login -h calvin
  → raycomm.com -p
15914  p1 S  0:01  \_ -bash
16216  p1 T  0:00     \_ telnet
16217  p1 T  0:00     \_ lynx
http://www.raycomm.com/
$ kill -9 16217
$ ps -a f
  PID TTY STAT TIME COMMAND
15911  p1 S  0:00 /bin/login -h calvin
  → raycomm.com -p
15914  p1 S  0:01  \_ -bash
16216  p1 T  0:00     \_ telnet
$
```

Code Listing 9.14 Using `kill` plus the PID number, you can delete practically any process running or suspended on the system.

Deleting Processes with `kill`

In addition to suspending jobs and running them in the foreground and background, you can also choose to just delete them completely. For example, you might realize midway through a job that you goofed and need to redo it. Or perhaps you've accessed and suspended a man page and no longer need to reference it.

Using `kill`, you can delete essentially any process running or suspended on the Unix system. As **Code Listing 9.14** shows, you delete a process by first listing the processes, then using the `kill` command.

To kill a job with `kill`:

1. `jobs`

   At the shell prompt, type `jobs`, then note the number or name of the job you want to kill.

2. `kill %ftp`

   In most shells, you can kill jobs with `kill` followed by `%` and the job number or command name—for example, you could kill an `ftp` job with a job number of 1 using `kill %ftp` or `kill %1`. If your shell doesn't cooperate, read on.

To delete a process with `kill`:

1. `ps`

   At the shell prompt, type `ps` to see the list of all your current jobs (Code Listing 9.14). Note the PID (process identification) number of the process you want to delete.

2. `kill 16217`

   Type `kill` followed by the PID number of the job you're deleting.

continues on next page

✔ Tips

- Occasionally, you'll use `kill` and find that the process just keeps going. Try `kill -9` followed by the PID number to delete the process.

- Be careful not to kill your current shell process, or you'll abruptly find your connection broken. Doing so would be like sawing off the branch you're sitting on.

- Many newer Unix systems allow you to use `pkill` to kill processes by name, not number. For example, you might use `pkill ftp` to kill a suspended ftp session.

DELETING PROCESSES WITH kill

Writing Basic Scripts

So far in this book, you've been typing in commands (or perhaps combining commands), pressing Enter, then waiting for Unix to execute the command(s) you specified...and typing in commands, pressing Enter, and waiting for Unix... and typing in commands.... You get the idea, and you probably have tired fingers by now.

Using shell scripts, you can create a series of commands, save them as a single file, and then execute them any time you want—without having to re-create the commands or do all that tedious typing over and over again. For example, suppose you want to do a complex search-and-replace on all the .htm files in your home directory. With a shell script, you can take the time to structure the commands just one time, save the commands as a single file, and then apply it to any directory at any time. You do the hard work one time, and then reuse the script any time you need to.

In this book we'll discuss creating scripts using the sh (Bourne) shell. Scripts can be written with any shell—and zsh and bash in particular are quite good for scripting.

In this chapter, we'll show you how to get started creating and using shell scripts. We won't go into the gory details about scripting (thank goodness, right?!), but we will give you enough information to create your own scripts and apply them to your particular uses.

Chapter Contents

- Creating shell scripts
- Running shell scripts
- Making scripts executable
- Getting a head start on creating scripts
- Embedding commands in scripts
- Looping scripts
- Creating if-then statements
- Accepting command-line input
- Accepting command-line input while a script is running
- Debugging scripts

Creating a Shell Script

A *shell script* is nothing more than a list of commands for Unix to execute. To write a shell script, you'll

1. Open your favorite editor and start a script file.

2. Start the shell script with #!/bin/sh.

3. Add the shell script code one line at a time. This code will look strangely familiar—it's similar to code you've already used in this book.

4. Save and close the file.

In the following steps, we'll show you how to try out this process by writing a script that prints three lines onscreen (**Figure 10.1**). Yeah, we know—whoopee!—but you have to start somewhere, and you can apply the same principles to other shell scripts you create.

To create a shell script:

1. `pico myscript`

    For starters, access the editor of your choice and start a new file. In this case, we call it `myscript`.

2. `#!/bin/sh`

    On the first line of the script, enter `#!/bin/sh`, which specifies the complete path to the shell that should run the script.

3. `# this is my first shell script`

    On the next line, type a # (to indicate a comment), and then add any other notes you want to make. It's always a good idea to use extensive comments in your scripts to help you see what's going on. Remember, comments are for your reference only and won't show up onscreen or do anything.

Figure 10.1 You create shell scripts in an editor one line at a time.

```
[ejr@hobbes scripting]$ sh myscript
friendsjustfriends

    standing
    good
```

Code Listing 10.1 Using echo options, you can get good under standing. Or, perhaps, a good understanding just between friends.

Getting Fancy with echo

In addition to the basic print-to-screen function that echo offers, you can also use these formatting flags with echo -e (the -e enables these special formatting characteristics):

◆ \b moves the cursor back one space.

◆ \c forces the following text to appear on the same line as the current text.

◆ \f forces the following text to appear on the next line at a specified horizontal location.

◆ \n forces the following text to appear on a new line.

◆ \t indents the following text output by one tab.

For example, echo -e "\tGreetings! \c" would move "Greetings!" one tab space to the right (as specified by the \t) and not insert a new line for any text following it (as specified by the \c).

4. echo friendsjustfriends

   On the next line of the script, type echo followed by the text you want to see onscreen. Here, echo tells Unix to display friendsjustfriends onscreen—a message just between friends.

5. echo

   Add another line with echo and nothing else to display a blank line.

6. echo " standing"

   Add another echo command. Note that if you use leading spaces or tabs, as we've done here, you must use quotes, as Figure 10.1 shows.

7. echo -e "\tgood"

   Using the -e flag plus \t, you can insert a tab character. See *Getting Fancy with echo* for more echo options.

8. Save and close your script.

   Check Chapter 4 if you need help saving a file and closing your editor.

9. sh myscript

   Use sh myscript to run your new script. In doing so, you get good under standing (literally), as shown in **Code Listing 10.1**. Ta-daaaaa! You just wrote your first shell script! (See the following section for more information and details on running scripts.)

✔ Tip

■ Unless you have some compelling need to use a different shell (for example, if you're taking advantage of functions that exist only in zsh), just stick with sh for your scripts for now.

Running a Shell Script

After you've created a script in your editor and saved the script file, your next step is to run it, which means to execute every command in the script in the order provided. (Yes, you did this in the previous section, but we'll expand on it here.) As **Figure 10.2** shows, you do this using the sh command (or the name of the shell you're using) followed by the name of the shell script you want to run.

To run a script:

◆ sh myscript

At the shell prompt, type sh (or the name of the shell, like ksh or csh, you want to run the script) followed by the name of the script. In this case, you're really just telling sh to run and to use the list of commands in the myscript file. You'll see the results of the script—in this case, words appear onscreen, as shown in Figure 10.2.

✔ Tip

■ Note that in this example, you're explicitly telling Unix the name of the script to run (myscript). When you do so, the #!/bin/sh line at the top of the script in the previous section is technically superfluous. It's essential only when the script is executable, as in the following section.

Figure 10.2 Running a script is as easy as typing sh plus the filename of the script.

```
[ejr@hobbes scripting]$ head -2 myscript
#!/bin/sh
# This is my first shell script
[ejr@hobbes scripting]$ chmod u+x myscript
[ejr@hobbes scripting]$ pwd ; echo $PATH
/home/ejr/scripting
/usr/local/bin:/bin:/usr/bin:/usr/X11R6/
→ bin:/usr/local/games:/home/ejr/bin:/
→ home/ejr/scripting
[ejr@hobbes scripting]$ myscript
friendsjustfriends

        standing
        good

[ejr@hobbes scripting]$
```

Code Listing 10.2 After a little one-time preparation, you can run executable scripts by typing the script name at the shell prompt.

Making a Script Executable

In the previous section, we showed you that you can run a shell script by typing sh followed by the name of the shell script file. You can also make a script *executable*, which means that you can run it simply by typing the script name at the shell prompt (omitting the name of the shell). Doing so is handy because it allows you to use the script as conveniently as you'd use any other command. As **Code Listing 10.2** shows, you must set up a little before you can just execute the script.

1. head -2 myscript

At the shell prompt, check to verify that your script does have the #!/bin/sh line at the top to specify the shell that runs it. Remember from Chapter 6 that head -2 will list the top two lines of the file specified.

2. chmod u+x myscript

Here, use the chmod command to give the user (that's you) execute permission. See the section in Chapter 5 called *Changing Permissions with chmod* for details on setting permissions.

3. pwd ; echo $PATH

Display the name of your current directory and the full path, and verify that the current directory is in the path. The current directory (the one in which you just granted yourself execute permission) must be contained in the path; otherwise, the script will not be as easily executable from the shell prompt.

4. myscript

At the shell prompt, type the name of the script. Assuming that your current directory is in the path, the script will run.

continues on next page

✔ Tips

- Every time you open up a new script, check to verify that the first line is #!/bin/sh so the file will run correctly. Also, check the permissions and your path to make sure you can run the script from the shell prompt. (You'll almost always find it more convenient to use executable scripts than to specify the shell or path each time you want to run a script.)

- If the current directory isn't in the path (either explicitly or through a . notation, as in PATH=/usr/bin:.:), you'll have to take an additional step to execute the script. You could

  - ▲ Add the current directory to the path with something like PATH=$PATH:/home/yourid/tempdir. Read more about this option in Chapter 8.

  - ▲ Execute the script with ./myscript instead of just myscript.

  - ▲ Move the script to a directory in the path.

```
 jdoe@frazz.raycomm.com: /home/jdoe/scripts
 994    date +"Today is %A"
 995    man test
 996    mail jdoe
 997    mutt
 998    which mutt
 999    ssh sulley
1000    clear
1001    at 12:01 1 Jan 2004
1002    crontab -e
1003    pwd
1004    ls
1005    cd scripts/
1006    ls
1007    which pico
1008    pico myscript
1009    sh myscript
1010    clear
1011    sh myscript
1012    history
1013    history | tail -20 > history-jumpstart
~
~
~
"standyou" 20L, 367C
```

Figure 10.3 You can enter a series of commands, and then use the code provided with history to help create a shell script.

✔ Tip

■ If you use vi, do a global search-and-replace to get rid of the line numbering (that history introduced) at the left—just use :%s/^ *[0-9]* *// (one space after the ^), and you're in business. See Chapter 4 for more about clever vi tricks.

Getting a Head Start on Scripts with history

If you find yourself performing a particular process over and over again, consider making that process into a script. An easy way to create a script is to work from the session history, as shown in **Figure 10.3**. Basically, all you have to do is complete the procedure one time, and then use the session history to help build the script for you.

To get a head start on your script with history:

1. Go through the process that you want to include in the script.

   We'll wait.

2. Keep a rough count of the commands you issue.

   Don't worry about the exact number of commands you use, but have an idea as to whether it's 3, 30, or 300 commands.

3. history 20 > standyou

   When you've finished the process, type history followed by the approximate number of commands for your script. When estimating the number of commands, err on the high side, as it's easier to delete extra commands than to add in missing ones. Then, redirect the output to the desired filename, and see your in-the-making script stand before you.

4. vi standyou

   Use the editor of your choice to edit your script file, deleting the initial line numbers and spaces and generally whipping that script into shape. See the section *Creating a Shell Script* earlier in this chapter for more details.

Embedding Commands

Suppose you create a script that will automatically run when you log in each day. The script might, for example, print "Greetings!" onscreen and possibly deliver a cle(a)ver message: "Say, you're looking sharp today!" You could easily do this with the information you've learned so far in this chapter.

What would be handy here would be to add a line to the script that tells Unix to do all those things plus name the most recently used file—for those of you who need a reminder about what you were last working on. You could just use an `ls` command, but that would only list the filenames and not integrate the information with the rest of your morning greeting. Instead, a better (and more attractive) idea would be to bundle a couple of commands and use them with echo (**Figure 10.4**) to embed the information right into the greeting.

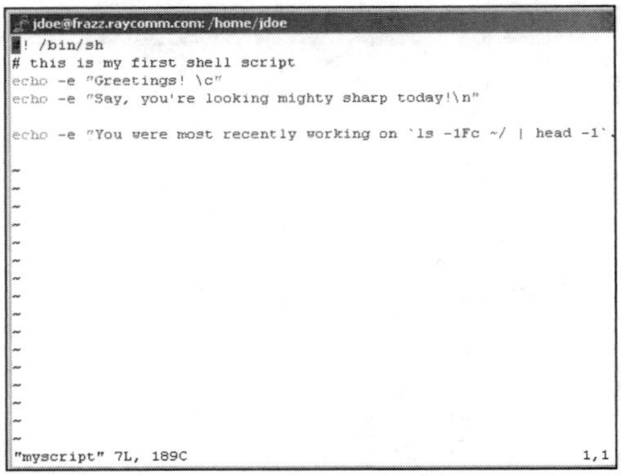

To embed a command:

1. `vi myscript`

   To begin, open `myscript` or another script in your favorite editor. Your script might look like Figure 10.4, with the greeting onscreen.

Figure 10.4 Embedding commands just requires an additional couple of lines in the script.

Using Clever Dates

You can use the `date` command to deliver any date with any format. In general, use `date +"Today is %A"`, but you can use any or all of the following bits:

- %d includes the two-digit day of month.
- %y includes the two-digit year.
- %Y includes the four-digit year.
- %m includes the numeric month.
- %b includes an abbreviated month.
- %B includes the full month name.
- %a includes the abbreviated day of the week.
- %A includes the full day of the week.
- %R includes the time in hours and minutes.
- %D includes the date in month/date/year format.

Check the `man` pages for the remaining several dozen options.

```
[ejr@hobbes scripting]$ myscript
Greetings!  Say, you're looking mighty
sharp today!

You were most recently working on figlet.
[ejr@hobbes scripting]$
```

Code Listing 10.3 The results of embedded commands can be impressive.

2. `echo "You were most recently working`
→ `on `ls -1Fc ~/ | head -1`."`

Type echo followed by the descriptive text you want to see. Then embed the ls command (`ls -1Fc ~/ | head -1`) within the descriptive text. Note that the embedded code begins and ends with ` before . (dot).

The embedded command here lists just the most recently changed file or directory in the home directory. 1 provides for one entry per line, F formats the directory names with a / so we can tell whether we're working in a subdirectory or on a file, and c sorts by the modification date. We then pipe the output to head -1, which displays the top line of the file.

3. Save your script and exit the editor, and then try it out, as in **Code Listing 10.3**.

✔ Tips

- You can embed dates into scripts, too. Try echo -e "Today is `date +%A`" if you work so much that you forget what the day of the week is. See the sidebar *Using Clever Dates* for more date details.

- When you embed commands that are directory-dependent—such as ls or find— be sure to specify the complete path. If you don't, you'll get paths relative to where the script is rather than relative to where you're running the script from.

- Embedded commands are useful in many ways. You can use them anytime that you want to have one program act based on the output of another program, just as echo displays something based on the output of a program.

EMBEDDING COMMANDS

Looping Your Scripts

Suppose you've created a script that you'd like to apply to several files. For example, say that at the end of each day you need to make backup copies of all .html files in your www directory. You could make a backup of each individual .html file, but that's a lot of work. An easier way would be to create a short script to copy an .html file, and then *loop* (repeat) the script to apply to all .html files in your www directory (**Figure 10.5**). You create one short script; Unix does the tedious work for you.

To make a loop:

1. vi head_ache

At the shell prompt, start your editor and open the script you want to loop. In this case, we're using vi and the head_ache file. (Of course, you could name the script html -backup or something mundane like that.)

2. #!/bin/sh

Tell your Unix system which shell to use to run the shell script. In this example, we're telling it (with #!) to run the shell script with /bin/sh.

3. cd ~/www

Make sure that you're in the directory in which the loop will take place. In this example, our shell script resides in our home directory, but the files to which the loop will apply reside in the www directory.

4. for i in `ls -1 *.html`

OK, don't panic. Read this as: "Look for items in the list of .html files." In this code, we're providing the output of the embedded command (`ls -1 *.html`) to the for loop (the .html files), as shown in Figure 10.5. The -1 flag on the ls command, by the way, forces a single list of output, which is ideal for script use, rather than several columns, which is easy to read onscreen but doesn't work well for scripts.

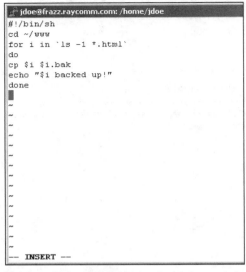

```
jdoe@frazz.raycomm.com: /home/jdoe
#!/bin/sh
cd ~/www
for i in `ls -1 *.html`
do
cp $i $i.bak
echo "$i backed up!"
done

~
~
~
~
~
~
~
~
~
~
~
-- INSERT --
```

Figure 10.5 Using a loop with an embedded command, you can automatically apply a script to several files.

LOOPING YOUR SCRIPTS

```
[ejr@hobbes scripting]$ more head_ache
#! /bin/sh
cd ~/www
for i in `ls -1 *.html`
do
cp $i $i.bak
echo "$i backed up!"
done

[ejr@hobbes scripting]$ ./head_ache
above.html backed up!
file1.html backed up!
html.html backed up!
reference.html backed up!
temp.html backed up!
[ejr@hobbes scripting]$
```

Code Listing 10.4 This loop reports progress as it backs up each file.

- Loops are particularly handy for searching and replacing throughout multiple documents. For example, if you're the new Webmaster and want to replace the old Webmaster's name at the bottom of all .html files with your name, you can do so using a loop with sed. Check out Chapter 6 for more information about sed, which introduces sed to loops.

5. do

On the line immediately after the for statement, type do. This tells the Unix system that the following information will be the loop to apply.

6. cp $i $i.bak

Here, we copy (cp) the specified items ($i) to a backup file ($i.bak)—that is, one backup file per file copied. So, if you have 72 .html files to begin with, you'll end up with those original 72, plus 72 new backup files.

7. echo "$i backed up!"

Add echo "$i backed up!" so that the system displays onscreen what it has done.

8. done

On the next line, announce that you're done with the loop.

9. Save it, make it executable, and try it out. This example script will make backup copies of all .html files in the www directory, as in **Code Listing 10.4**.

✔ Tips

- Loop instructions can be much more complex. For example, you could make a loop to spell-check each of the chapter files in the directory and report how many misspelled words there are in each file. To do that, use this line in the loop: echo -e "$i has \t `cat $i | spell | wc -l` misspelled words". Here again just build the loop one step at a time.

Creating If-Then Statements

The basic principle of *if-then statements* is that if a certain condition is met, then one thing happens; if the condition is not met, then another thing happens. That is, if you walk into your office in the morning and you see your daily to-do list, then you sit down and work. If you walk into your office in the morning and you don't see your to-do list, then you get to lounge all day. Or something like that.

As **Figure 10.6** shows, you can create if-then statements using `if`, `then`, and `else` commands. When you set up these conditional statements, the computer then has to test the condition to determine whether it's true or false, and act accordingly. In the next example, we set up a fairly simple if-then conditional statement requiring the computer to test whether or not a file exists and tell us what it finds. Use the following steps to get started with if-then statements, and see the *More on If-Then* sidebar in this section to learn how to expand your if-then statements.

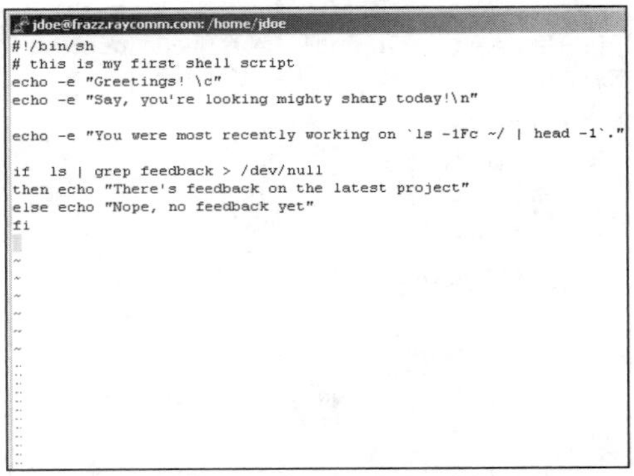

To write an if-then conditional statement:

1. `vi deef`

To begin, access your editor and the script file. Here we're adapting an existing script (for feedback) in `vi`.

```
jdoe@frazz.raycomm.com: /home/jdoe
#!/bin/sh
# this is my first shell script
echo -e "Greetings! \c"
echo -e "Say, you're looking mighty sharp today!\n"

echo -e "You were most recently working on `ls -1Fc ~/ | head -1`."

if   ls | grep feedback > /dev/null
then echo "There's feedback on the latest project"
else echo "Nope, no feedback yet"
fi
```

Figure 10.6 Using if-then conditional statements, you can let the computer determine if something is true or not, and then act accordingly.

2. `if [ -f feedback ]`

Start the loop with if, and then follow it with a conditional statement, in this case if [-f feedback], which checks for the existence of a file named feedback in the current directory. If that file exists, then the expression is true. See the whole script in Figure 10.6.

continues on next page

More on If-Then

Using the steps provided in this section, try some of these other if-then possibilities:

◆ `[ -f filename ]` checks to see whether a file exists.

◆ `[ ! -a filename ]` checks to see whether a file does not exist. The ! symbol (not) makes this test report "true" when the previous example would be "false."

◆ `[ -d name ]` checks to see whether name exists and is a directory.

◆ `[ first -nt second ]` checks to see whether the modification date of the first file or directory is newer than the second.

◆ `[ first -ot second ]` checks to see whether the modification date of the first file or directory is older than the second.

◆ `[ -n string ]` checks to see whether the string has a length greater than 0.

◆ `[ -z string ]` checks to see whether the string is null or 0 length.

◆ `[ string1 = string2]` checks to see whether the first string is equal to the second.

◆ `[ string1 != string2]` checks to see whether the first string is not equal to the second.

◆ `[ \( condition1 \) -a \( condition2 \) ]` checks to see whether both conditions are true (conditions can include other conditions).

◆ `[ \( condition1 \) -o \( condition2 \) ]` checks to see if either condition1 or condition2 is true.

Type `man test` for more information about creating conditional statements.

CREATING IF-THEN STATEMENTS

3. `then echo "There's feedback on the`
`→ latest project"`

On the line immediately after the `if` statement, enter the command to be carried out or message to be displayed if the `if` statement is true. In this example, a true `if` statement would result in "There's feedback on the latest project" being printed onscreen.

4. `else echo "Nope, no feedback yet"`

On the next line, use `else` followed by a statement specifying what should happen if the `if` statement is false. Here, we specify that "Nope, no feedback yet" would be printed onscreen if the `feedback` file was not found or had nothing in it.

5. `fi`

Immediately after the `else` statement, announce that you're finished with `fi`.

6. Save the script and try it out.

In this example, the script will check to see if `feedback` exists and print a different message depending on what it finds (**Code Listing 10.5**).

```
[ejr@hobbes scripting]$ ./deef
Greetings!  Say, you're looking mighty
sharp today!

You were most recently working on
scripting/.
Nope, no feedback yet
[ejr@hobbes scripting]$ touch feedback
[ejr@hobbes scripting]$ ./deef
Greetings!  Say, you're looking mighty
sharp today!

You were most recently working on
scripting/.
There's feedback on the latest project
[ejr@hobbes scripting]$
```

Code Listing 10.5 The last line produced by the feedback script differs, depending on the files found.

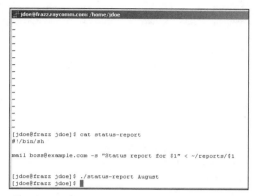

Figure 10.7 Using command-line input, you can add flexibility to a script and still have the script do the grunt work for you.

```
[ejr@hobbes scripting]$ more status-
report
#! /bin/sh

mail boss@whereever.com -s "Status report
→ for $1" < ~/reports/$1

[ejr@hobbes scripting]$ ./status-report
→ August
[ejr@hobbes scripting]$
```

Code Listing 10.6 By providing command-line input, you can control what the script does.

✔ Tips

- To see the information provided at the command line, echo it back out with echo $*. The $* variable provides all of the command-line input, with $1, $2, and $3 containing the individual items.

- You can also accept input at specified points while a script is running. See the next section for more details.

Accepting Command-Line Arguments in Your Scripts

Suppose that at the end of every month you need to send a progress report to your boss. You might set up a script to address an email message to your boss, provide an appropriate subject line, and send the file containing the progress report. You'd likely have this script automatically address a message to your boss and put in the subject line, but you'd want to use command-line input to tell the script which file you want to send. By using command-line input, you can give your scripts a bit more flexibility and still have much of a process automated for you. You run the script and specify the input at the shell prompt, as shown in **Figure 10.7**.

To accept command-line arguments in a script:

1. `vi status-report`

   Use your favorite editor to edit your script.

2. `mail -s "Status report for $1"`
   `→ boss@example.com < ~/reports/$1`

   Enter a command, with $1 appearing in each place you want to use the first item of input from the command line. In this example, the script starts a message to the boss, fills in the subject line (adding the month automatically), and sends the appropriate monthly report (the one specified on the command line) from the reports directory under your home directory.

3. Save and exit, and then run the script (**Code Listing 10.6**), though you might first have to find a boss to take your status report and provide the content for the status report.

Accepting Input While a Script Is Running

Figure 10.8 You can also input information while a script is running.

In the previous section, we showed you that you can require that information be provided along with the script in order for the script to run, but it's easy to forget to input the information and thus not get the results you expected. You can also require input while a script is running. The script runs, you input some information, and then the script continues (probably) using the information that you input (**Figure 10.8**). In this case, the script counts misspelled words, but you can apply it to anything you want.

To accept input while a script is running:

1. `pico retentive`

Use your favorite editor to edit your script.

2. `echo -e "Which file do you want`
`→ to analyze?"`

Specify the text for the prompt that you'll see onscreen. Here, the onscreen text will read, "Which file do you want to analyze?"

3. `read choice`

At whatever point in the script you want the script to accept information, type `read` followed by the name of the variable to accept the input. Here, we name the variable `choice`.

4. `echo "$choice has `cat $choice |`
`→ spell | wc -l` misspelled words"`

Echo a phrase (and embedded command) to check the spelling, count the misspelled words, and report the number for the file specified. At each place where the filename should appear, substitute `$choice`.

```
[ejr@hobbes scripting]$ ./retentive
Which file do you want to analyze?
testfile
testfile has        11 misspelled words
and was last changed at 05:08 on Jan 12
[ejr@hobbes scripting]$
```

Code Listing 10.7 Accepting input while a script runs helps ensure that you don't forget to type it in, and still gives customized results.

5. `echo -e "and was last changed \c"`
Echo another line with text and (because of the \c) no line break at the end of the line.

6. `ls -l $choice | awk '{ print "at " $8 "`
`→ on " $6 " " $7 }'`
This very long and complex line uses awk to pluck the time, month, and day of the month fields out of the ls -l listing for the file given as $i (Figure 10.8). See Chapter 6 for details about awk.

7. Save and exit.
You have the hang of this by now.

8. `./retentive`
Run the script (after making it executable and specifying the current directory, if necessary) and provide a filename when prompted, as shown in **Code Listing 10.7**.

✔ Tips

■ A great example of a use of prompted input is configuration files. See *Using Input to Customize Your Environment* in Chapter 17 for details and a specific example.

■ See Chapter 8 for more information about setting up configuration files and starting scripts upon log in.

■ You can use a set of lines like `echo -e "Please enter the name: \c"` and `read name` to have the input line and the introduction to it both appear on the same line.

ACCEPTING INPUT WHILE A SCRIPT IS RUNNING

227

Debugging Scripts

As you're developing scripts, you'll no doubt encounter a few problems in getting them to run properly. As **Figure 10.9** shows, you can help debug your scripts by printing the script onscreen as it runs. That way, you can follow the script as it runs and see where the problems might be.

To print the script onscreen as it runs:

◆ `sh -x retentive`

At the shell prompt, type `sh` `-x` followed by the script name (and any additional information you need to provide). The `-x` tells the shell to both execute the script (as usual) and print out the individual command lines, as shown in Figure 10.9.

✔ Tip

■ Use the name of any shell, followed by `-x`, followed by the script name for this kind of debugging output. For example, try `bash -x retentive`.

```
  jdoe@frazz.raycomm.com: /home/jdoe
[jdoe@frazz jdoe]$ sh -x retentive
+ echo -e 'Which file do you want to analyze?'
Which file do you want to analyze?
+ read choice
limerick
++ cat limerick
++ wc -l
++ spell
+ echo 'limerick has          1 misspelled words'
limerick has       1 misspelled words
+ echo -e 'and was last changed \c'
and was last changed + ls -l limerick
+ awk '{ print "at "$8 " on " $6 " " $7 )'
at 05:02 on Dec 30
[jdoe@frazz jdoe]$ █
```

Figure 10.9 Printing the script onscreen as it runs is a great way to debug it.

Sending and Reading Email

If you're anything like us, your whole day revolves around getting goodies in your email in-box and sending "highly important" messages (of course, they're important, right?). In any case, sending and receiving email will probably be rather common tasks in your Unix experience.

In this chapter, we'll introduce you to a few Unix email programs and show you how to get started with them. (Of course, just use the instructions that apply to the program you're using!) Then, we'll show you some clever things you can do with email in Unix, such as creating signature files and sending automatic vacation email replies.

Chapter Contents

- Choosing an email program and getting started
- Reading email with pine
- Sending email with pine
- Customizing pine
- Reading email with mutt
- Sending email with mutt
- Reading email with mail
- Sending email with mail
- Creating a signature file
- Automatically forwarding incoming messages
- Announcing an absence
- Configuring procmail
- Responding to email with procmail

Choosing an Email Program and Getting Started

In general, you'll have a choice of two kinds of programs for sending and receiving email on a Unix system:

Figure 11.1 pine's interface and features are intuitive and easy to use.

◆ An email program installed on your local computer or network that interacts with the Unix system for you. You might know these programs as *mail clients* and might have used ones like Thunderbird, Eudora, Outlook Express, or Mozilla's mail program, Messenger. These are handy because they usually have a spiffy interface and can handle attachments without a lot of hassle on your part, but they're not really Unix email programs. These programs also let you store your mail on your desktop system (Windows or Macintosh or even Unix desktops, but those are beyond the scope of this book).

◆ An email program that you access and use directly on the Unix system. These programs, such as pine, mutt, and mail, let you send and receive email easily. Additionally, pine and mutt let you send attachments with not a lot of hubbub. Because the mail remains on the Unix system, you can access your mail from anyplace you can access the Internet.

In this chapter, we'll focus on the email programs that you access directly from the Unix system, as these are the true Unix email programs. Although there are a bazillion different ones available, you'll likely have access to one (or more) of these:

◆ pine: This program is intuitive to use and lets you send and receive email and attachments very easily. pine is our recommendation if you have it available. **Figure 11.1** shows its relatively simple interface. Just use the menu commands listed at the bottom of the screen.

Figure 11.2 mutt's interface and features are fairly easy to use but not as easy as pine's.

Figure 11.3 mail's interface and features are, well, kind of a pain to use.

```
login: ejr
Password:
Last login: Sun Aug  2 07:41:00 on tty4
You have mail.
[ejr@hobbes ejr]$
```

Code Listing 11.1 Read with great interest the line that says "You have mail" when you log in.

◆ mutt: This program is a bit less user-friendly, but it lets you send and receive email and can deal with attachments nicely. mutt is our second choice, if pine is not available, but mutt is quite friendly if you put a bit of time into customizing it for your needs. **Figure 11.2** shows its interface, which provides ample features for most purposes.

◆ mail: This program is available on practically every Unix system; however, it's fairly difficult to use and does not provide intuitive options or commands, as **Figure 11.3** shows. We recommend choosing another email program if at all possible. Use this program for emergencies only.

✔ Tips

■ How do you know whether someone has sent you something? The shell will often announce (but not usually audibly) "You have mail" or "You have new mail" when you log in, as shown in **Code Listing 11.1**. That is, if you do in fact have email waiting for you.

■ You're not limited to using just a regular Unix email program or a POP mail program; you can use either or both, depending on your specific preferences and needs. You're also not limited to using just one Unix email program if you have more than one available, although reading mail from two different Unix programs can sometimes make it a little hard to keep track of what's where. Try them out and see which program or combination of programs meets your needs.

■ We recommend using character-based email programs like these to read mail. After you get used to the interface, you can whiz through your email much faster than you can with a GUI mailer (like Outlook or Mozilla mail), and you don't have spam graphics opened in your face either.

Reading Email with `pine`

It's likely that your first step in using `pine` will be to read email. As Figures 11.4 through 11.7 show, you start by entering the `pine` command, and then work screen by screen, depending on what you want to do.

To read email with `pine`:

1. `pine`

At the shell prompt, type `pine` to start the program. The first time you use `pine`, it will ask you if you want to be counted as a `pine` user (see **Figure 11.4**) before you get started. Thereafter, you'll see the normal main screen, as shown in **Figure 11.5**.

If you get an error message about the `pine` command not being found, look around on the system to try to find the program. See Chapter 1 for details on where to look.

2. L

Press L to view the folder list, which includes an in-box folder as well as (eventually) other folders that you set up.

3. Use the arrow keys to navigate the folder list (if you have other folders).

4. V

Press V to view the selected folder. Note that the default selection in the bottom menu is shown with [brackets] (see **Figure 11.6**). Rather than use arrow keys to select the default, you can, instead, press Enter.

5. Use the ↑ and ↓ keys to move up and down in the message list.

Your unread messages will appear at the bottom of the list by default.

6. Enter

Press Enter to read the selected message.

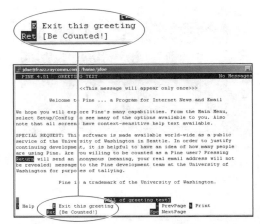

Figure 11.4 When you start `pine` for the first time, it will ask whether you want to be counted as a user before you begin.

Figure 11.5 You'll become well acquainted with `pine`'s main screen.

Figure 11.6 All you have to do is press e to select the default selection, which is shown at the bottom in [brackets].

Figure 11.7 Do you really want to quit pine? Just checking.

7. Hmmm. Uh-huh. Wow. Marvy.

Read your messages. Press ⟨<⟩ to get out of the current message and back to the message index for the current folder.

8. ⟨Q⟩

Press ⟨Q⟩ when you're ready to quit pine. You'll be prompted to verify that you want to quit, as shown in **Figure 11.7**. Just press ⟨Y⟩ to quit, or ⟨N⟩ if you really didn't want to quit.

✔ Tips

■ Notice the menu commands listed at the bottom of the pine screen. You can choose any of these options by pressing the appropriate key. pine is conveniently case-insensitive, so either lowercase or upper-case commands will work.

■ Start with pine -i to start in your in-box, rather than at the main menu.

■ As you're perusing your email, you can use ⟨Tab⟩ to jump to the next unread message in the folder.

■ Delete messages by pressing ⟨D⟩, either when the message is highlighted in the message list or when the message is open onscreen. When you quit the program, pine will verify that you want to discard the deleted messages. Just press ⟨Y⟩ to confirm the deletion, or ⟨N⟩ if you really didn't want to get rid of the messages. (Note that deleting in pine does not send them to the Recycle Bin, as the ⟨Delete⟩ key does when using a Windows email program. In Unix, pressing ⟨D⟩ really deletes messages ... they're gone!)

■ You can reply to messages by pressing ⟨R⟩ with a message selected or while reading a message.

■ When using pine, keep your eyes open for an O in the menu at the bottom of the screen indicating that there are other options.

Printing with pine

Although many Unix email programs don't let you print to your local printer, pine does. All you have to do is choose %, take the default printout on "attached to ansi," as pine suggests, and your printout will most likely appear on your regular printer. Printing to a local printer this way doesn't work with some communications programs (notably Windows telnet), but it does work with many. If you're sitting in front of a Linux or Mac OS X system, you could also use other printing utilities on your system—the "attached to ansi" option is really for people who are connected to the Unix system with ssh or telnet.

Sending Email with pine

Our next favorite thing to do with pine is to send new messages. Commonly, you'll send messages after you've already started pine (**Figure 11.8**), but you can also start a new message directly from the shell prompt (see the tips).

To compose and send a message using pine:

1. pine

Type pine at the shell prompt to start pine, if it isn't already running.

2. [C]

Press [C] to compose a new message.

3. [Tab]

Press [Tab] to move through the message header fields. Fill in carbon copy recipients (cc:) and the Subject: line. See the sidebar called *Our Two Cents on the Subject of Subjects* for details about including subject lines.

If you're sending an attachment, type in the Unix filename (and path, if appropriate) on the Attchmnt: line. For example, type ~/myfile, which includes the full path name and the filename.

4. Hi, John, when should we schedule
→ that golf game -- er, um --
→ business meeting?

In the message window, type in your message. Figure 11.8 shows our message, complete with the header information and the message body.

5. [Ctrl][X]

When you're ready to send, press [Ctrl][X]. pine will ask you to confirm that you really want to send the message. Press [Y] (or press [Enter]) to send it, or [N] if you don't want to send it.

Figure 11.8 Preparing a message in pine is as easy as filling in the blanks.

✔ Tips

- Rather than type in someone's lengthy email address (such as joeblow@ acmefancompany.com), set up an *alias*— a shortened name that replaces the long-winded address. Yeah, you'd be able to just type in Joe or whatever, and Unix will know which long-winded address goes with that name. To set up aliases, use the address book (press Ⓐ from the main menu) and follow the instructions given.

- If you're at the shell prompt and want to send email without bothering with the main pine interface, type pine followed by the email address you want to send mail to (for example, pine bigputz@raycomm. com). If you want to send email to multiple addresses, just separate them with commas or spaces, as in pine unixvqs3@ raycomm.com,info@raycomm.com.

Our Two Cents on the Subject of Subjects

- ◆ Always include a descriptive subject line that succinctly summarizes the message's contents. For example, rather than say "Here you go," say "Comments on the Baskins proposal."

- ◆ Never leave the subject line blank. Many people toss subjectless messages, thinking that they might be spam or otherwise not important enough to read.

- ◆ Never use ALL CAPS in the subject line (or anywhere else, for that matter), as recipients may perceive this as being YELLED AT VERY LOUDLY.

- ◆ Be aware of how spam filters work. Many ISPs use them to reduce the amount of spam (bulk messages, like junk mail, that are sent out to hundreds or thousands of people at one time) that goes through. Some filters are set to toss messages with subject lines typed in ALL CAPS. Others toss ones with a lot of exclamation points in the subject.

Customizing `pine`

Although `pine` is rather intuitive to use, it is also quite powerful, giving you ample options for customizing it. **Figure 11.9** shows `pine`'s customization screen, as well as a few of the options you can choose.

To customize `pine`:

1. `pine`

At the shell prompt, type `pine` to start the program.

2. Ⓜ

Press Ⓜ to visit the main menu.

3. Ⓢ

Press Ⓢ to summon the setup menu.

4. Ⓒ

Press Ⓒ to access the configuration setup menu, which is shown in Figure 11.9.

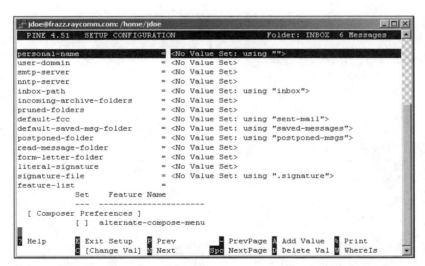

Figure 11.9 By using the configuration setup menu, you can tailor `pine` to your needs.

CUSTOMIZING pine

5. Scroll through the configuration list using the ⬆ and ⬇ keys.

   pine offers you gobs of options to configure. **Table 11.1** describes the ones you might find most useful.

6. Enter

   Press Enter to select the option you want to change.

7. Make your selection or fill in the necessary information.

8. E

   Press E to exit the configuration menu and return to the setup menu. You'll be prompted to save your changes. If you want to do so, press Y; if not, press N. You'll then whiz back to the main menu.

✔ Tip

■ You can customize pine so that it automatically opens up your in-box whenever you start it. In the initial keystroke list, just type l,v, and then press Enter, to specify the initial characters.

CUSTOMIZING pine

Table 11.1

Commonly Used Configuration Options

Option	Description
initial-keystroke-list	Specifies key commands for pine to use when starting, just as if you'd typed them in directly.
nntp-server	Sets the news server name so you can read Usenet news in pine, as mentioned in Chapter 12.
quit-without-confirm	Allows you to exit pine without the "are you sure?" message.
signature-at-bottom	Puts your automatic signature at the end of the message you're replying to, rather than above it.
saved-msg-name-rule	Sets pine to automatically file your saved messages in a specific folder, based on the characteristics (sender, etc.) of the message.
fcc-name-rule	Sets your file copy of outgoing messages to be saved in a particular folder. We like the by-recipient option, which files messages according to whom we sent them to.
use-only-domain-name	Sets pine to send all outgoing messages with just the domain name and not the machine name on the From: line. For example, our messages come from @raycomm.com, not from @frazz.raycomm.com.

Reading Email with mutt

If you're using mutt, you'll probably find that reading email messages is rather straightforward. As **Figure 11.10** shows, you just scroll through your list of messages with the ↑ and ↓ keys and press Enter to open the message you want to read.

To read email with mutt:

1. mutt

   Type mutt at the shell prompt to start the program. The system might ask you if you want it to create folders for you, as shown in **Code Listing 11.2**. We say let it do the work for you and enter [yes]. Enter [no] if you don't want folders created. Figure 11.10 shows the main mutt screen.

2. Use the ↑ and ↓ keys to move up and down in your list of email messages.

   Your unread messages will be at the bottom of the list.

```
[awr@hobbes awr]$ mutt
/home/jdoe/Mail does not exist. Create
→ it? ([yes]/no):
```

Code Listing 11.2 mutt will create a mail directory for you.

Figure 11.10 mutt's main index screen shows many of your options.

3. [Enter]

Press [Enter] to open a message to read.

4. [I]

Press [I] to return to the list of messages (index) or press the [Spacebar] to scroll down through the current message. Figure 11.10 shows the menu of commands, which should help you remember some of the basics of mutt.

5. [Q]

Press [Q] (for quit), then wave goodbye to mutt. You might be prompted with questions to answer (for example, about discarding deleted messages or moving read messages to your read-mail folder). Answer yes only if you'll be using mutt as your primary mailer in the future.

✔ Tips

- You can customize virtually every aspect of mutt but only by editing the ~/.muttrc configuration file. If you think you might like the flexibility of mutt, search the Internet for sample .muttrc files to get an idea of what all you can do with it.

- You can delete a message by pressing [D] when you're viewing it or when it's selected in the message index screen. When you quit mutt, you'll be asked whether mutt should "Move unread messages to /home/yourid/mbox." At that time, press [N] to keep them in your in-box or [Y] to move them.

- You can reply to messages by pressing [R] with the message selected in the message list or while reading the message.

- You can access mutt help, such as it is, from most any screen by pressing [?].

- You can move to a specific message in the message index by typing the message number.

READING EMAIL WITH mutt

Sending Email with mutt

Sending messages with mutt is similar to sending messages with pine. Most commonly, you'll compose a message while you're already futzing around in mutt (**Figure 11.11**).

To compose and send a message using mutt:

1. mutt

   To begin, type mutt at the shell prompt to start mutt.

2. M

   Press M to start a new message.

3. Enter

   Press Enter after entering each bit of information that mutt asks for (see Figure 11.11). Fill in the To: and Subject: lines. (See the sidebar *Our Two Cents on the Subject of Subjects* earlier in this chapter.)

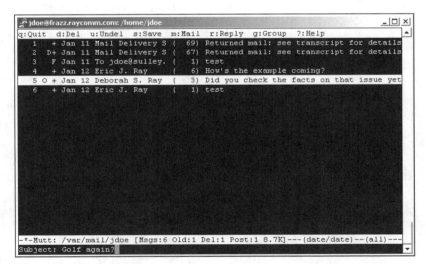

Figure 11.11 You fill in the message header by answering questions or filling in blanks (Subject:, in this case), and then move on using the *e* key.

4. Say hello to vi.

   Huh? After you enter the message header contents (filling in what you want), you'll be plunked right into vi, facing the top of a very blank message. See Chapter 4 for a quick reminder about using vi.

5. John, I was having this dream that
   I had my alarm clock installed in
   my stomach. I remembered this
   because, when my alarm went off,
   I found myself pushing my belly
   button trying to turn off the noise.
   Good grief...I need a vacation!

   Type your message, whatever it may be.

6. [Esc]

   When you're finished, press [Esc] (to get into command mode).

7. :wq

   Then type :wq to save your work and exit the editor.

8. [Y]

   Press [Y] to send the message. If you decide you don't want to share details about your belly button after all, you can press [E] to edit your message or press [Q] to quit and forget the whole thing.

✔ Tips

■ You can change the default editor from vi to something else available on your Unix system. All you have to do is edit your ~/.muttrc file (or create one if it doesn't exist) and add set editor="emacs" (or whatever editor) to the file. See Chapter 8 for more information about changing variables.

■ To send a quick message from the shell prompt, type mutt followed by the recipient's email address, as in mutt winchester@ raycomm.com. If you want to send email to multiple addresses, just separate them with commas or spaces, as in mutt unixvqs@ raycomm.com,info@raycomm.com.

Reading Email with mail

In general, using mail is a bit less intuitive than using either pine or mutt; however, reading email with mail is particularly—um—challenging. Although we'd recommend using another program to read email if at all possible, here are the steps for reading email with mail if you're daring enough or if you have no other options. **Figure 11.12** illustrates this fairly quick task.

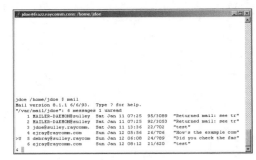

Figure 11.12 The mail screen is anything but intuitive, but you can see the messages you have.

To read email with mail:

1. mail

   Type mail at the shell prompt. You'll get a list of messages and a prompt (Figure 11.12).

2. 3

   Type the number of the message you want to read and press (Enter).

3. Marvelous...he's such a jerk...oh,
   → that's neat....

   Read your messages. Press (N)(Enter) to move to the next message, or more to page through the message a screen at a time.

4. (Q)

   Press (Q) to quit mail when you're ready.

✔ Tips

- If somebody really long-winded sends you a long message, your Unix system might just zip the message on by, leaving you reading only the bottom few lines. To read the message in its entirety, either type more to page through the message, or type s followed by the message number, followed by the file name (s 18 message-in-a-file) to save it to a file, then use the editor of your choice read it.

- Type h followed by a message number to see different message headers. For example, type h 117 to see the messages leading up to number 117.

- Find a different mail program if at all possible—it's useful to be able to cope with mail for times of need, but it's not a good long-term solution.

READING EMAIL WITH mail

```
[ejr@hobbes ejr]$ mail debray
Subject: You're in big trouble now!
So, anyway, Winchester had perched
himself on my stereo turntable (those were
sooooo low-tech, weren't they?!). He was
waiting for me to turn on the stereo so he
could go back to sleep while spinning in
circles. I used to let him sleep that way
at night. Well, that was until one night
when the lid closed on him...
EOT
[ejr@hobbes ejr]$
```

Code Listing 11.3 Using mail, you can dash off a quick note by including the recipient's address and the message text.

Sending Email with mail

Despite mail's unintuitive interface and features, it is a great program to use if you just want to dash off a quick message without fussing with niceties. As **Code Listing 11.3** shows, you can send messages while in mail or from the shell prompt. You can also use mail to send files fairly easily.

To compose and send a message using mail:

1. mail unixvqs@raycomm.com

   At the shell prompt, type mail followed by the recipient's address. If you want to send email to multiple addresses, just separate them with commas but no spaces, as in mail putz@raycomm.com,putz2@raycomm.com.

   If you're already in mail, just type m followed by the address or addresses, like m putz@raycomm.com,deb@raycomm.com.

2. So, anyway, Winchester had perched himself on my stereo turntable (those were sooooo low-tech, weren't they?!). He was waiting for me to turn on the stereo so he could go back to sleep while spinning in circles. I used to let him sleep that way at night. Well, that was until one night the lid closed on him...

   Type in your message text (see Code Listing 11.3).

3. Ctrl D

   Announce that you're done with either a . (dot) by itself on the last line or with Ctrl D, and the message will zip off to the recipient(s).

SENDING EMAIL WITH mail

To send text files with mail:

◆ mail unixvqs@raycomm.com < sendit.txt

  At the shell prompt, type mail followed by the recipient's address. Then use < and the filename to redirect the file (< sendit.txt), which tells Unix to send the file to the address provided (**Code Listing 11.4**).

✔ Tips

■ See *Scheduling Regularly Occurring Jobs with cron* in Chapter 9 for a spiffier way of using mail to send messages directly.

■ See the section in Chapter 1 called *Redirecting Output* for a refresher on redirection.

■ You'll notice that the mail interface on some systems does not provide for a subject line. On some systems, you can add one by including -s plus the subject text, like this: mail -s "An old Winchester story...dumb cat!" unixvqs3@raycomm.com.

■ You can accomplish all of these command-line mail sending options with mutt as well as mail, but you get added benefits with mutt, including being able to send attachments. For example mutt –s "Sending that file" -a bigolefile.tgz suggest @example.com < /dev/null will do the whole nine yards at once, including attaching the big ol' file. Don't try that with mail!

```
[ejr@hobbes ejr]$ mail unixvqs@raycomm.com
→ < sendit.txt
[ejr@hobbes ejr]$
```

Code Listing 11.4 To send a text file through the mail, you just redirect the file to mail.

Figure 11.13 Your signature file can contain any information you want. Be creative, but keep it concise!

Creating a Signature File

If you've been using email for any length of time, you've undoubtedly noticed *signature files*, which appear at the bottom of messages and include contact information, company name, and perhaps a short funny quote or saying. You can add a signature to your outgoing messages by creating a `.signature` file (**Figure 11.13**).

To create a signature file:

1. `pico ~/.signature`

   At the shell prompt, type an editor's name (here we use `pico`, but you can use the editor of your choice), specify the home directory (with ~/), and then specify the `.signature` filename. Note the leading dot in the filename, which makes the file hidden.

2. `Eric J. Ray ejray@raycomm.com My`
   `→ thoughts are my own ... is that`
   `→ OK, honey?`

   Go ahead, type your signature information (Figure 11.13). We recommend that your `.signature` file include, at minimum, your name and email address. You can also add funny sayings ("You know you're a geek when you refer to going to the bathroom as 'downloading.' ") or disclaimers ("My opinions are mine and not my company's."). Whatever you want, really. Keep your signature as short as possible; long signatures are hard to wade through.

3. Save and exit the file.

   If you're using `pico` or `vi`, you can get a quick reminder about this in Chapter 4.

   continues on next page

✔ Tips

- If you want to get really fancy with your signature, use a *figlet*, which is a text representation of letters, as shown in **Code Listing 11.5**. Check out www.yahoo.com or your favorite Internet search engine and search for "figlet" or "figlet generator" for more information about creating your own.

- Many email purists think that four lines is the longest signature anyone should have. If you create one that's longer, expect some people to chew you out for it.

- Both `mutt` and `pine` automatically include a `.signature` file in outgoing mail.

```
[ejr@hobbes ejr]$ more figlet


   _____            _____                              _____
  |  __ \          / ____|                            |_   _|
  | |__) |__ _   _| |       ___  _ __ ___   _ __ ___    | |  _ __   ___
  |  _  // _' | | | |      / _ \| '_ ' _ \ | '_ ' _ \   | | | '_ \ / __|
  | | \ \ (_| | |_| | |___| (_) | | | | | | | | | | | |_  _| |_| | | | (__ _
  |_|  \_\__,_|\__, |_____/|_| |_| |_|_| |_| |_( ) |_____|_| |_|\___(_)
               __/ |                              |/
              |___/
```

Code Listing 11.5 Figlets are fun and fancy.

Figure 11.14 All you have to do is tell Unix where you want your messages forwarded to.

- If you want, you can keep a copy of all incoming messages (in your incoming email box, just where they'd usually be) and forward them to unsuspecting recipients. Just type \yourid, other@address.com (filling in your userid on the current system for yourid and the address to which to forward the mail for the other one).

- Forwarding messages is also handy when you change ISPs. You can forward all messages sent to your old address to your new one, which helps tremendously in ensuring that you receive all your important messages while your friends and co-workers update their address books.

Automatically Forwarding Incoming Messages

Suppose you're the boss of a big project, and everyone sends you all the important related email messages. You can tell Unix to automagically forward these incoming messages to the people who will actually do something about them. Hey, you're the boss, right? Or maybe you just got a different email account, and you want to incoming mail sent to your old address forwarded to your new address. As **Figure 11.14** shows, all you have to do is create a .forward file.

To forward incoming email messages:

1. vi ~/.forward

   To begin, type vi at the shell prompt (or the appropriate command for whichever editor you are using), indicate your home directory (with ~/), and then put .forward as the filename.

2. mynewid@raycomm.com

   Add, as the first line of the file, the address to which you want your email forwarded (Figure 11.14). In addition to forwarding to a single address, you can also use a .forward file with multiple addresses on multiple lines to send incoming email to several addresses at once.

3. Save and close the file.

   Check out Chapter 4 for details about saving and closing files using pico or vi.

✔ Tips

- Check with your system administrator to see if a .forward file will really do what you want. Many newer Linux and Unix systems automatically send mail to procmail (and ignore the .forward file), so you might need to use a procmail recipe to forward your mail. It's equally effective, but just different. See the section on procmail later in this chapter for details.

Announcing an Absence with vacation

If you're planning a vacation and will be away from your email for a while, let Unix announce your absence for you (**Figure 11.15**). Using the vacation program, you can have Unix send a reply saying that you're out of the office to everyone who sends you email.

Keep in mind that vacation is quite variable among different Unix systems and ISPs. What you have might be different from the "standard" form used here. Be sure to check with your system administrator for specific instructions if you have any problems, and also look at the procmail section of this chapter, as many newer Linux and Unix systems use procmail instead of a .forward file to tell vacation to respond to your messages.

To send "I'm on vacation" messages using vacation:

1. vi ~/.vacation.msg

   At the shell prompt, type vi ~/vacation.msg. You'll need to edit a message (a template, actually) for the response that people should receive when they email you, as shown in Figure 11.15.

2. Subject: away from my mail! Thanks for emailing me about $SUBJECT. Fortunately for me, I'm taking a fabulous vacation mowing my lawn, doing laundry, and catching up on other things I can't do because I usually work so much. If you would like me to stay on vacation, please email my boss (boss@example.com) and let her know. Thanks!

   Create and edit the text to say what you want.

   The $SUBJECT term in the text will be replaced with the actual subject of the email sent to you.

Figure 11.15 Using a template, you can customize the vacation message—even extensively, as we've done.

```
[ejr@hobbes ejr]$ cat ~/.forward
\ejr, "|vacation ejr"
[ejr@hobbes ejr]$
```

Code Listing 11.6 Your .forward file should reference the vacation file.

✔ **Tip**

■ Remember to unsubscribe to all mailing lists before you start vacation. If you don't, you may send a vacation announcement to a whole list of people who likely don't care (not to mention that you'll really irritate the list administrator!). Or, worse, you might cause a *mail loop* (in which your messages to the list are acknowledged by the server, and the acknowledgements are in turn sent vacation announcements), causing hundreds or thousands of messages to accumulate in your account. It shouldn't happen, but it sometimes does.

3. Save your text and exit the editor.
Chapter 4 has the gory details about saving and exiting in pico and vi.

4. vacation -I
Type vacation -I at the shell prompt to start vacation and tell it to respond to all incoming messages. You'll still get the incoming messages in your in-box. In fact, they'll pile up in your in-box and wait for you to return.

5. cat ~/.forward
Look at the .forward file in your home directory to verify that it contains a reference to the vacation program. Your .forward file specifies what should happen to your mail upon receipt. In this example, it should be processed by vacation. The reference to vacation is usually automatically inserted by the vacation program, but if it's not there, you'll need to edit the .forward file and add text like \yourid, "|vacation yourid". Of course, substitute your real userid for the placeholder above, and possibly include the full path to vacation (/usr/bin/vacation on our system). (See **Code Listing 11.6**.)

To stop vacation **emails:**

◆ mv .forward vacation-forward
At the shell prompt, move the .forward file that references the vacation program to a different name (in this case, vacation-forward). You could just delete it or remove the reference to vacation, but it's easier to save it so you can reuse it for your next vacation.

ANNOUNCING AN ABSENCE WITH vacation

Configuring procmail

Let's see...two messages from the boss...17 messages from the string collector's discussion group...oh, hey, a message from mom...and....

One of the handiest things you can do to make your Unix life easier is to use procmail (a mail-filtering program) to automatically handle some of your incoming email.

In this section, we'll show you how to configure procmail so you can manage incoming messages. As **Figures 11.16** and **11.17** show, you need to do two things to set up your system to manage mail with procmail:

◆ Specify settings for procmail (Figure 11.16). For example, incoming mail normally gets plunked directly into your in-box; however, procmail filters mail before it even gets to your in-box, so you need to tell procmail where your mail folders are, among other things.

◆ Tell procmail to do its thing (Figure 11.17). Essentially, you create a .forward file that sends your incoming mail to procmail for processing before you ever see it. This step is not necessary for many systems, particularly newer Linux and Unix systems.

To specify settings for procmail:

1. pico ~/.procmailrc

   To begin, access your editor and create a .procmailrc file in your home directory.

2. LOGFILE=$HOME/.maillog

   Give procmail a place to log all of its activities, so it can tell you what it's done: "I threw away 7 messages from your boss... filed 3 messages from Joe in the GolfBuddies folder...." In this example, we tell procmail to keep a log file called .maillog in our home directory (Figure 11.16). Keep an eye on this file, because it can grow large over time.

Figure 11.16 You specify the procmail settings you need, and then you're off and running.

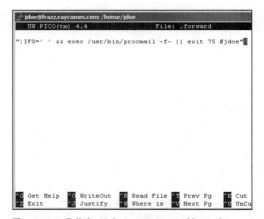

Figure 11.17 Tell the Unix system to send incoming messages to procmail for processing to ease your mail management.

3. `PATH=/usr/bin:/usr/local/bin:/bin`

Specify the path for your executable programs. It's a good idea to do this now, just in case you eventually use `procmail` to more extensively filter or autorespond to messages.

4. `DEFAULT=/var/spool/mail/yourid`

Specify the location for your incoming mail. Remember, the filter gets the mail before it ever reaches the in-box, so you need to tell `procmail` where your in-box is. Check with your system administrator to confirm the `DEFAULT`. (`/var/spool/mail /yourid` is typically, but not always, the location, but obviously with your real `userid`, not `yourid`.)

5. `MAILDIR=$HOME/mail`

Specify where `procmail` should find your mail program and all the folders and information it creates. If you're using `pine`, you will probably type this line exactly as shown. If you're using `mutt`, you might need to use `Mail` instead of `mail`.

To turn on `procmail` filtering:

1. `pico ~/.forward`

Use your favorite editor to create a `.forward` file in your home directory.

2. `"|IFS=' ' && exec /usr/bin/procmail → -f- || exit 75 #yourid"`

Enter the text exactly as shown, but substitute your userid for `yourid` above (Figure 11.17). If `procmail` is not located at `/usr/bin`, type in the actual location. `/usr/local/bin` would be another likely directory.

3. Save and close the file.

That's it! Now all you have to do is wait for incoming messages and see if they get filtered as you intended (as you'll set up in the next section).

Responding to Email with procmail

procmail can help you automatically—or selectively—respond to email. As you'll see, procmail is very similar to forwarding email and using the vacation program, but you'll probably find procmail much more flexible.

To specify how messages should be filtered (to "write a recipe"):

1. vi ~/.procmailrc

   In vi, access your .procmailrc file.

2. Move to the end of the file, below the setup information.

3. :0:

   Start a new recipe with :0:, as shown in **Figure 11.18**. (Don't ask why to use :0:. That's just the way it is.)

4. * ^TOGolfBuddies

   Set the criteria for procmail to filter with. Here,

   ▲ * ^TO tells procmail to examine the TO line (and, actually, the CC line, too) of all incoming messages.

   ▲ GolfBuddies is the text to match in the TO line (as in TO: GolfBuddies@ nowhere.nowhen.com). Of course, you'd put in the actual name of the list to look for (or the alias for your mailing list, or whatever), rather than GolfBuddies.

5. $MAILDIR/FriGolfBuddies

   Specify where the filtered mail should go. In this case, filtered mail would go in the FriGolfBuddies folder, but you might filter messages from mailing lists into a listmail folder.

6. Save and close the file.

Figure 11.18 Add the recipes of your choice to your .procmailrc file.

RESPONDING TO EMAIL WITH procmail

To forward mail with `procmail`:

1. `pico ~/.procmailrc`

   To begin, access your editor and edit the `.procmailrc` file that you previously created in your home directory.

2. `:0:`

   On a new line at the bottom of the file, add `:0:`, which starts a `procmail` recipe. This basically tells `procmail` to "lock" your mail directory while it's processing mail.

3. `! myotheremail@example.com`

   Provide an exclamation point (!) and the address to which to send the mail.

4. Save and close the file.

   Now all email that you receive will be automatically forwarded to `myother-email@ example.com`.

Use `procmail` to Toss Spam Messages

The following recipe,

`:0:`

`* !^TO.*awr@.*raycomm.com`

`$MAILDIR/spam`

uses a regular expression to filter messages that aren't explicitly addressed to a userid with `awr` before the @ and `raycomm. com` at the end and places them into a special folder called `spam`. Put the spam filter at the end of your list of rules so all of the messages originating from your mailing lists and other important messages are filed first. After testing this and making sure that you like it and it doesn't pitch valuable messages, you could change the last line to `/dev/null` to just throw away the garbage.

For more complex and sophisticated spam solutions, check the options with a Google search for `procmail spam filter` at http://www.google.com/.

To invoke vacation with procmail:

1. `pico ~/.procmailrc`

   To begin, access your editor and edit the `.procmailrc` file that you previously created in your home directory.

2. `:0 c`

   `| /usr/bin/vacation jdoe`

   On a new line at the bottom of the file, add the recipe shown to send a copy (the c at the end of the first line) of your email to the vacation program. See Announcing an Absence with vacation in this chapter for more information about the vacation program.

3. Save and close the file.

   Now all email that you receive will be stored and passed along for the vacation program to respond to.

✔ Tips

- Your `.procmailrc` file gets processed in order. As soon as a recipe matches an incoming email message, it's applied. So if your first recipe is the forwarding recipe above, procmail will never even get to any later recipes. If no recipes are matched, mail will be delivered to the DEFAULT location you specified (see *Configuring procmail*, earlier).

- After you set up your procmail processing, be patient. Sometimes procmail processes email on a specific schedule (hourly, for example), so testing it may be a little time-consuming.

RESPONDING TO EMAIL WITH procmail

Sample procmail Recipes

The following recipes, with annotations, should help you get started filtering with procmail.

```
# Filter based on the To:, Cc: and
→ similar headers

:0:

* ^TO.*awr@.*raycomm.com

$MAILDIR/interesting

# Filter based on the subject

:0:

* ^Subject:.*Status Report.*

$MAILDIR/status-reports

# Filter based on sender

:0:

*^From:.*spammer@example.com

$MAILDIR/IN.TO-DELETE

# Filter directly to garbage,
→ irrevocably, based on sender

:0:

*^From:.*spammer@example.com

/dev/null

# Filter based on size (greater than
→ 1000 bytes)

:0:

* > 1000

$MAILDIR/longish
```

ACCESSING
THE INTERNET

So far in this book, you've been working with files and scripts located on the Unix system. In this chapter, we'll show you how to venture beyond your Unix system and take advantage of the information on the Internet.

Chapter Contents

- Getting familiar with Unix Internet lingo
- Logging in to remote systems
- Communicating with other users
- Getting files from the Internet
- Sharing files on the Internet
- Surfing the Web
- Downloading Web Sites
- Checking connections
- Tracing connections
- Matching domain names
- Choosing a news reader
- Reading news

Getting Familiar with Unix Internet Lingo

Before you venture out onto the Internet using the information in this chapter, you should become familiar with some concepts and terminology.

A *server* is a computer that stores files and "serves" them whenever requested. For example, you might think of a Web server as a big storehouse for `.html` files. Its job is to store `.html` files, wait for another computer to request files, and then find the requested files and "serve" them to the requesting computer. And, yes, your Unix system might be a Web server, but it doesn't have to be.

A *client* is a program that runs on your Unix system and is used to access data on a server. For example, your `lynx` Web browser is a client—that is, it runs on your Unix system and is used to access files on a Web server.

An *IP* (*Internet Protocol*) *address* is the address of a specific computer. This address identifies a computer, much the way your street address identifies your home. You use IP addresses, for example, every time you access a Web page. You may type in `www.raycomm.com` (which is called the *host name*), but behind the scenes, that's translated into a specific IP address, such as `192.168.141.12`. You will use host names (such as `www.ibm.com` or `www.sun.com`) more often, because they're easier to remember than a string of numbers. Whether you type in a character address or a number address, all you're doing is accessing a specific address for a specific computer.

Table 12.1

Internet Ports and Protocols	
PORT	PROTOCOL
21	ftp
22	ssh
23	telnet
70	gopher
80	http
119	nntp
8080	http (usually for test servers)

Protocols are the languages that computers use to communicate with one another. For example, *FTP* (*File Transfer Protocol*) is used to transfer files from one computer to another. *HTTP* (*Hypertext Transfer Protocol*) is used to transfer data on the World Wide Web.

Ports are like a computer's ears—they're "places" that computers listen for connections. Most Web servers run at port 80, and if you connect to `http://www.raycomm.com:80/`, you're explicitly saying that you want to talk to the `www.raycomm.com` computer, at port `80`, using HTTP. You could specify a different protocol (FTP, for example) or a different port (`8080`, for example) to communicate with the same computer in a different way, as **Table 12.1** shows.

Logging in to Remote Systems with ssh

You might already be using **ssh** to connect to your Unix system. You can, though, use it to connect to and use practically any other computer system on the Internet (assuming you have rights to log in to it), as **Code Listing 12.1** shows.

To connect to another computer using ssh:

1. **ssh server.example.com**

   At the shell prompt, type **ssh** followed by the name of the system to which you want to connect.

2. Log in using the instructions you have for accessing the system.

   Presumably, if you're accessing a system over the Internet, you have some reason to do so and permission to do so. In some cases, you'll type the name of the application, or you might be using the remote system just as you use the system from which you are connecting.

3. After you've finished using the remote system, log out according to the instructions and policies of the remote system.

✔ Tips

- For help with **ssh**, type **ssh** at the shell prompt and look at the list of options, or do **man ssh** for more help. When you have an active session, use (Enter)(~)(?) to get help with the current session.

- If you have a different login name on the remote system, you can specify that to **ssh** with **ssh server.example.com -l otherusername** to log in more easily. Or, if it's easier to remember, try **ssh otherusername@server.example.com**.

```
[jdoe@frazz jdoe]$ ssh server.example.com
jdoe@server's password:
jdoe /home/jdoe $ whoami
jdoe
jdoe /home/jdoe $ uname -a
Linux server.example.com 2.4.19-ac4 #13 SMP
→ Sat Nov 16 05:30:56 MST 2002 i686
→ unknown unknown GNU/Linux
jdoe /home/jdoe $ logout
[jdoe@frazz jdoe]$
```

Code Listing 12.1 Use **ssh** to connect securely to other systems on the Net.

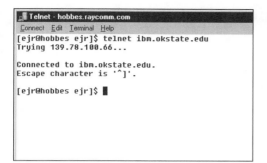

Figure 12.1 Note the Escape character as it flashes by.

Figure 12.2 After you're connected, you can use the remote system just like your own.

Logging in to Remote Systems with `telnet`

You might already be using `telnet` to connect to your Unix system. You can, though, use it to connect to and use practically any other computer system on the Internet (assuming you have rights to log in to it and that the system administrator allows telnet access rather than requiring SSH), as **Figure 12.1** shows.

To connect to another computer using `telnet`:

1. `telnet ibm.okstate.edu`

   At the shell prompt, type `telnet` followed by the name of the system to which you want to connect. In this example, we're connecting to the Oklahoma State University online library catalog.

2. Make note of the Escape character announced when you log in—look quickly, as it'll whirl by onscreen. The *Escape character* is what you'll press should your `telnet` connection stall or the system lock up. In our example, the Escape character is Ctrl [], which will return us to the `telnet` prompt so we can `quit` the connection (Figure 12.1).

3. Log in using the instructions you have for accessing the system.

   Presumably, if you're accessing a system over the Internet, you have some reason to do so and permission to do so. In some cases, you'll type the name of the application. In our example, we type `pete`, which is the name of the card catalog. In most other systems, you'll log in with a userid and password, just as you log in to your Unix system (**Figure 12.2**).

continues on next page

4. After you've finished using the remote system, log out according to the instructions and policies of the remote system.

✔ Tips

■ For help with `telnet`, type `telnet` at the shell prompt, and then enter a ? at the `telnet>` prompt. `open`, `close`, and `exit` will be the most useful tools for you.

■ You'll find that `telnet` connections to libraries and other mainframe computers are often difficult to use because of oddities in keyboard emulations. Your best bet is to contact the site owner and ask for a FAQ list (with answers!). You'll assuredly not be the first to have questions.

■ A program closely related to `telnet`, `tn3270`, is designed specifically for communicating with IBM mainframes, which are commonly used for college library catalogs as well as other professional and academic systems. If you know that you're communicating with an IBM mainframe, `tn3270` will probably be better to use.

■ You can use the `wall` command to send `write`-type messages to everyone logged in to the system. System administrators commonly use `wall` when they need to warn people that the system is being brought down.

■ Use `w` or `who` to find out who else is logged into the system. See the sections called *Learning Who Else Is Logged In with who* and *Learning Who Else Is Logged In with w* in Chapter 7 for more information.

Figure 12.3 You can send quick messages to another user on your system with write.

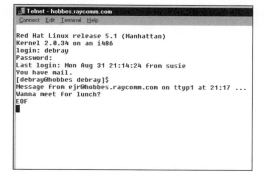

Figure 12.4 The message suddenly appears on the user's screen.

Communicating with Other Users Using write

Most of the time when you connect to a Unix system, you'll be communicating with the computer. You can, though, communicate with other people logged in to the same system. write is ideal for getting a quick message to other users—kind of like putting a yellow sticky note on their computer, as **Figure 12.3** shows.

To communicate with other users using write:

1. write userid

   At the shell prompt, type write followed by the userid of the person to whom you want to send a message. You'll get a blank line with a blinking cursor on it, just waiting for you to type something.

2. Wanna meet for lunch?

   Go ahead and type your message (Figure 12.3).

3. Ctrl D

   When you're finished typing, press Ctrl D to send the message. What you typed will appear on the other user's screen (**Figure 12.4**).

✔ Tips

- Keep in mind that a write message will suddenly appear on the recipient's screen and can be an intrusive surprise!

- If you don't want to receive write messages, type mesg n at the shell prompt. This command will keep other people from sending you write messages for the current session. Type mesg y to enable write again.

COMMUNICATING WITH OTHER USERS USING write

Communicating with Other Users Using talk

You can also have a real-time, two-way conversation (very much like an instant-messaging chat) with another user logged in to the system by using talk. As **Figure 12.5** shows, you type your messages, the other person types his, and you can both see the exchanges onscreen.

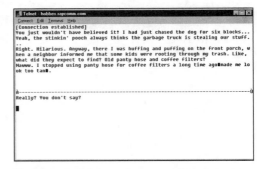

Figure 12.5 talk lets you have a real-time, two-way online conversation.

To communicate with other users using talk:

1. talk deb

   At the shell prompt, type talk and the userid of the person to whom you want to talk. The other user will be prompted to enter talk and your userid. Then, you'll see the talk screen, as shown in Figure 12.5.

2. You just wouldn't have believed it! I had just chased the dog for six blocks...Yeah, the stinkin' pooch always thinks the garbage truck is stealing our stuff... Right. Hilarious. Anyway, there I was huffing and puffing on the front porch, when a neighbor informed me that some kids were rooting through my trash. Like, what did they expect to find? Old panty hose and coffee filters? Nawww. I stopped using panty hose for coffee filters a long time ago. It made me look too tan.

   Type anything you want. Each keystroke will show up on the other person's screen, so they'll see exactly how quickly (and how well) you type.

3. Ctrl C

   When you're finished, break the connection.

✔ Tips

- You can also talk to people logged in to other Unix systems. Just use talk userid@wherever.com. Of course, fill in the other person's actual userid and address, which will often be the same as that person's email address. Firewalls often—but not always—block these chats, though.

- If someone requests a talk with you, just type talk and the person's userid (or userid@wherever.com, if the person's host name isn't the same as yours).

- As with write, you can type mesg n and mesg y at the shell prompt to turn talk off and on for the current session.

- Though talk is not as groovy as some of the GUI-based instant messaging programs, it's still pretty cool, huh? It's also a good way to ask for help from more experienced users on your system.

Getting Files from the Internet with ftp

Some of the Internet's great information resources are FTP sites, which contain hundreds of thousands of files from all over the Internet. FTP sites are similar to Web sites, but are directory-oriented and speak a different protocol. They're less fun than the Web usually is but often more practical.

One of the easiest ways to access information on FTP sites is to use anonymous ftp, which lets you access the sites and download files to your computer (**Code Listing 12.2**, shown on the next page).

Getting a single file through anonymous ftp:

1. ftp calvin.raycomm.com

   At the shell prompt, type ftp followed by the name of the FTP site to which you're connecting. Of course, if the computer has an IP number but no name, type the IP number instead. You'll be prompted to log in, as shown in Code Listing 12.2.

2. anonymous

   For the user name, type anonymous. (Type ftp if you get tired of typing anonymous—it nearly always works.)

3. you@wherever.com

   Use your email address for the password. It's polite to identify yourself to the people who provide the FTP service. Just you@ is usually sufficient.

4. cd /pub/files

   Use standard Unix cd commands to move through the directory tree to the file you want.

continues on next page

```
[ejr@hobbes ejr]$ ftp calvin.raycomm.com
Connected to calvin.raycomm.com.
220 calvin Microsoft FTP Service (Version 2.0).
Name (calvin.raycomm.com:ejr): anonymous
331 Anonymous access allowed, send identity (e-mail name) as password.
Password:
230 Anonymous user logged in.
Remote system type is Windows_NT.
ftp> cd /pub/files
250 CWD command successful.
ftp> binary
200 Type set to I.
ftp> hash
Hash mark printing on (1024 bytes/hash mark).
ftp> get jokearchive.gz
local: jokearchive.gz remote: jokearchive.gz
200 PORT command successful.
150 Opening BINARY mode data connection for jokearchive.gz(1481035 bytes).
##############################################################################
##############################################################################
##############################################################################
##############################################################################
##############################################################################
##############################################################################
##############################################################################
##############################################################################
##############################################################################
##############################################################################
##############################################################################
##############################################################################
##############################################################################
##############################################################################
##############################################################################
##############################################################################
######
226 Transfer complete.
1481035 bytes received in 4.07 secs (3.6e+02 Kbytes/sec)
ftp> quit
221
```

Code Listing 12.2 Use anonymous ftp to get files from archives across the Internet.

5. binary

Specify the file type—in this case, binary, because we're downloading a gzipped archive file. Specify ascii for README files, text, and HTML files.

6. hash

Next, you have the option of typing hash to tell the ftp client to display a hash mark (#) for every 1,024 bytes transferred. If you're transferring a small file or using a fast connection, this might not be necessary; however, for large files and slow connections, the hash marks will let you know that you're making progress.

If you'll be downloading multiple files, check out the sidebar *Getting Multiple Files* in this section before proceeding. The instructions for getting single and multiple files differ at this point in the process.

7. get jokearchive.gz

At the ftp> prompt, type get and the filename to get the file from the remote system and plunk it into your own account.

8. quit

When it's finished, just type quit.

continues on next page

GETTING FILES FROM THE INTERNET WITH ftp

✔ Tips

■ If the FTP connection seems to get stuck as soon as you log in, try `-yourid@wherever.com` as the password. The - character disables system announcements and helps keep your `ftp` client happy.

■ Some firewalls—particularly the ones on home networks—do not deal gracefully with some of the intricacies of the FTP protocol. If you can connect and log in, but not list files or get anything, the firewall might be the problem. As soon as you log in, type `pass` (for passive) and the problem should go away.

■ Another handy use for - is to view text files onscreen. For example, type `get filename -` to have the text just scroll by on the screen.

■ Instead of using `get`, use `newer` (as in `newer goodjokes.gz`) to get a more recent file with the same name as one you have.

■ If you start downloading a file and the FTP connection breaks, type `reget` and the filename to continue the transfer from wherever it left off. (You'll have to reestablish the connection first, of course.)

■ You can tell the `ftp` client to make sure that all the transferred files have unique names by using `runique` instead of `get`. This way, you can ensure that files don't overwrite existing files on your local system.

■ Use regular Unix commands like `ls`, `pwd`, and `cd` to move around in the remote system, and preface them with an `!` to apply to your system. For example, `cd ..` would change to the next higher directory on the remote system, and `!cd ..` (from within the `ftp` client) would change to the next higher directory on the local system. The current local directory is where your files will be saved.

Getting Multiple Files

If you'll be getting multiple files with `ftp`, follow steps 1 through 6 in this section, then

◆ `prompt`

Optionally, type `prompt` to tell the `ftp` client not to prompt you for each individual file that you want to get. You'll be informed that prompt is set to no. If you want to turn it back on, issue `prompt` again.

◆ `mget start*`

At the `ftp>` prompt, type `mget` (for "multiple get") followed by the string or filenames to match. In this example, we use `start*` to get all files with names that begin with "start." You could also use `mget *.gz`, for example, to get files with the `.gz` file extension. See Chapter 1 for more about using wildcards.

◆ `quit`

When you're finished getting files, just type `quit`.

```
[ejr@hobbes ejr]$ ftp ftp.raycomm.com
Connected to www.raycomm.com.
220 ftp.raycomm.com FTP server (NcFTPd
 → 2.1.2, registered copy) ready.
Name (ftp.raycomm.com:ejr): ejray
331 User ejray okay, need password.
Password:
230-You are user #8 of 100 simultaneous
 → users allowed.
230-
230 Logged in.
Remote system type is UNIX.
Using binary mode to transfer files.
ftp> cd incoming
250
"/home/ftp/pub/users/e/ejray/incoming"
 → is new cwd.
ftp> binary
200 Type okay.
ftp> put myjokes.gz
local: myjokes.gz remote: myjokes.gz
200 PORT command successful.
150 Opening BINARY mode data connection.
226 Transfer completed.
128889 bytes sent in 15.5 secs
 → (8.1 Kbytes/sec)
ftp> quit
221 C-ya!
[ejr@hobbes ejr]$
```

Code Listing 12.3 Using put, you can share your files with other people on the Internet.

Sharing Files on the Internet with ftp

Sharing files on the Internet with ftp is similar to getting files; instead of retrieving files, however, you give files to other people (**Code Listing 12.3**).

To share files on the Internet with ftp:

1. ftp ftp.raycomm.com

   Open the FTP connection as shown in the previous section.

2. youruserid

   Log in with your userid.

3. password

   Enter your password.

4. cd incoming

   Use standard Unix directory commands (ls, cd, and so on) to move into the directory into which you want to put the files (**Code Listing 12.3**). incoming is often the right directory name to use, particularly on public FTP servers.

5. binary

   Set the file type. You'll want to use the binary file type for any files other than text or HTML files; use ascii for text or HTML.

6. put myjokes.gz

   Type put followed by the name of the file you're making available.

7. quit

   Type quit when you're done.

continues on next page

SHARING FILES ON THE INTERNET WITH ftp

✔ Tips

■ On public FTP servers that accept incoming files, you might not be able to list the files in the incoming directory or see anything in there. In this case, you essentially just cast your file into a big open room and close the door. This allows FTP administrators to screen the incoming files before making them available for downloading.

■ You can use the mput command to make multiple files available.

■ If you're transferring a lot of files at once—say, for example, you're moving all of your files from your old ISP to your new one—consider using tar and gz to collect and zip up all of your files, and then transferring just a single file. See Chapter 13 for more information about these commands.

Navigate in your local system (for example, to change to a directory containing files to put) with regular Unix commands like ls, pwd, and cd, prefaced with an ! . For example, pwd would display the path and name of the current directory on the other system, and !pwd would display the path and name of the current directory on the local system.

Navigating with links

◆ → (or Enter) follows the currently highlighted link to a new page.

◆ ← returns to the previous page.

◆ ↓ moves the highlight down to the next link in the document.

◆ ↑ moves the highlight up to the previous link in the document.

◆ Spacebar or Page Down scrolls down to the next page.

◆ Page Up or B scrolls up to the previous page.

◆ Q quits links.

Figure 12.6 The links browser provides great surfing capabilities, even without images.

Surfing the Web with links

Using links, a really fancy text-based Web browser, you can surf the Web just as you might with Firefox or Internet Explorer, except with no graphics. That's really not a bad thing; consider that you don't have to deal with pop-up ads, banner ads, or similar junk. Just content, all the time. links even supports tables and complex Web page designs, which is unusual for a text-based browser (**Figure 12.6**). Related advantages of using links are that you won't have to deal with slow download times for graphics, annoying sound files, plug-ins, or other showy Web page features.

To surf the Web with links:

1. links http://www.google.com/

   At the shell prompt, type links followed by the name of an .html file or a Web site address. Here, we're accessing the Google Web site (Figure 12.6).

2. Surf the Web or Google for your favorite subject.

   See the sidebars called *Navigating with links* and *Useful links Keystrokes* in this section for details.

3. Q

   Press Q to quit and return to the shell prompt. That's it!

✔ Tip

■ Press Esc to bring up a handy—and very familiar—menu at the top of the screen. Use arrow keys to navigate through the menu and Esc to get out of it.

Useful links Keystrokes

◆ /findme finds text within the file. (Replace findme with the text you're looking for.) This is also handy to quickly navigate through a page.

◆ ? finds text backward (moving up from the cursor) through the file.

◆ D downloads the current link.

◆ G goes to an address or file. You enter the address at the prompt.

◆ Shift G lets you edit the current address.

◆ Esc usually lets you back out (escape from) the current menu.

◆ S brings up a menu to manage your bookmarks, including bookmarking the current page.

◆ \ lets you toggle back and forth between viewing the formatted page and viewing the HTML source.

◆ Ctrl R reloads the current page and refreshes the screen.

Surfing the Web with lynx

You can also surf the Web using lynx, a text-based Web browser. It's not as spiffy as links and doesn't handle many Web pages as gracefully, but it has its place in your toolbox, too. Generally, you can access the wealth of information available on the Web (**Figure 12.7**), and you can use lynx to easily download and reformat pages.

To surf the Web with lynx:

1. lynx http://www.yahoo.com/

   At the shell prompt, type lynx followed by the name of an .html file or a Web site address. Here, we're accessing the Yahoo Web site (Figure 12.7).

   If you only type in lynx, you'll get the default page for your system, which is likely the lynx home page or the main page for your ISP.

2. Surf, surf, surf!

   See the sidebars Navigating with lynx and Useful lynx Keystrokes in this section for details.

3. Q

   Press Q to quit and return to the shell prompt. That's it!

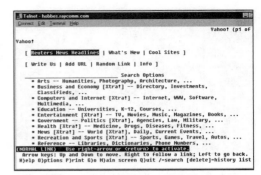

Figure 12.7 You can use lynx to navigate to any site on the Web.

Navigating with lynx

- → (or Enter) follows the currently highlighted link to a new page.

- ← returns to the previous page.

- ↓ moves the highlight down to the next link in the document.

- ↑ moves the highlight up to the previous link in the document.

- M returns you to the first screen you accessed in the session—the one you saw in step 1.

- Spacebar scrolls down to the next page.

- B scrolls up to the previous page.

Figure 12.8 Some sites are considerably less friendly than others if you're not using graphics.

✔ Tips

- If you access a `lynx`-unfriendly page, like the one shown in **Figure 12.8**, press the [Spacebar] to scroll down a few times. Usually you'll be able to find the content.

- `lynx` is a great way to get a spiffy plain text file out of an `.html` document. Try `lynx -dump http://example.com/ goodpage.html > newname.txt` to start `lynx` and direct it to send the display to standard output, and then redirect the output to the file called `newname.txt`. This will give you the text from the page, without HTML code, in a file in your Unix account.

- `lynx` makes it really easy to get a quick view of a local `.html` document, but it isn't as flexible as `links` for Web browsing in general.

Useful `lynx` Keystrokes

- ◆ `/findme` finds text within the file. (Replace `findme` with the text you're looking for.)

- ◆ [?] lets you access help.

- ◆ [D] downloads the current link.

- ◆ [G] goes to an address or file. You enter the address at the prompt.

- ◆ [Shift][G] lets you edit the current address.

- ◆ [A][L] adds the current link to your bookmark list.

- ◆ [V] lets you view the bookmark list.

- ◆ [Backspace] lets you see a list of pages you've visited (your history).

- ◆ \ lets you toggle back and forth between viewing the formatted page and viewing the HTML source.

- ◆ [Ctrl][R] reloads the current page and refreshes the screen.

Downloading Web Sites with wget

The wget utility allows you to download Web pages—and whole Web sites—to use offline. You just specify a URL and how many levels (links away from the starting page) you want to download, and let wget do its thing (as in **Code Listing 12.4**). Then you can use the Web pages when you're not connected to the Internet, like while on an airplane, in a hotel, or in a waiting room, for example.

To download Web Sites with wget:

1. wget http://www.cnn.com/

   At the shell prompt, type wget followed by the URL of a Web site or FTP site. Here, we're accessing the CNN Web site (Code Listing 12.4) and downloading the home page.

2. Slurp!

3. links index.html

   Then use your favorite Web browser to check out your handiwork.

✔ Tips

■ We recommend using a separate directory to contain the contents of different Web sites. Otherwise, wget will either rename files to avoid clobbering existing files (thus breaking links) or clobber existing files (thus making it highly likely that only the last Web site you downloaded will be complete. If you use wget with the –x option (as in, wget –x http://www.example.com/), it'll do this automatically. See Chapter 2 for more on using directories.

```
jdoe /home/jdoe $ wget http://www.cnn.com/
-18:07:51- http://www.cnn.com/
       => `index.html'
Resolving www.cnn.com... don   e.
Connecting to www.cnn.com[64.236.24.4]:
→ 80... connected.
HTTP request sent, awaiting response...
→ 200 OK
Length: unspecified [text/html]

   [ <=>        ] 51,290    53.28K/s

18:07:53 (53.28 KB/s) - `index.html' saved
→ [51290]

jdoe /home/jdoe $
```

Code Listing 12.4 You can use wget to download as much of the Web as you can handle.

■ wget --recursive --level=2 http:// www.example.com/ lets you get several (two, in this case) levels of a Web site. Be careful, because it's easy to bite off more than you can chew. If you use wget -r http://www.example.com/, wget will try to recursively download the whole thing. We ended up with more than 20 MB from the first command on www.cnn.com.

■ wget also works for FTP sites. Just use wget ftp://ftp.example.com or wget jdoe:imAsecret@ftp.example.com if you need to specify a password.

   Check out the man page for wget (man wget) for more on the extensive options available.

```
[ejr@hobbes ejr]$ ping www.raycomm.com
PING www.raycomm.com (204.228.141.12): 56
→ data bytes
64 bytes from 204.228.141.12: icmp_seq=0
→ ttl=251 time=190.3 ms
64 bytes from 204.228.141.12: icmp_seq=1
→ ttl=251 time=197.7 ms
64 bytes from 204.228.141.12: icmp_seq=2
→ ttl=251 time=166.5 ms
64 bytes from 204.228.141.12: icmp_seq=3
→ ttl=251 time=157.5 ms


-- www.raycomm.com ping statistics --
4 packets transmitted, 4 packets received,
→ 0% packet loss
round-trip min/avg/max = 157.5/178.0/
→ 197.7 ms
[ejr@hobbes ejr]$
```

Code Listing 12.5 Using ping, you can find out whether or not you can connect to a specific computer.

Checking Connections with `ping`

Think of using `ping` as saying "Are you there?" to a remote computer. For example, suppose you're trying to connect to a Web page but are getting no response from the computer. Rather than wait and wonder what's going on, type `ping` to find out if the computer is up and functional (**Code Listing 12.5**).

To check a computer with `ping`:

◆ ping www.raycomm.com

At the shell prompt, type `ping` and the host name to test the connection to a specific host, as shown in Code Listing 12.5.

Depending on your Unix system, it may check the connection one time and report the results. Or, it may continue to pester the other computer every second or so until you tell it to stop. If that's the case, just press [Ctrl][C] to stop it.

✔ Tips

■ If you're having problems connecting to a particular computer, you might consider using `traceroute`, which pings all the computers on the path between point A and point B. While `ping` tells you if a host responds or not, `traceroute` will give you an idea of where the problem might lie. See the next section for more details about `traceroute`.

■ The `ping` command doesn't provide a definitive answer to the status of the remote computer. Some systems are configured not to respond to pings for security reasons. If you get a response from `ping`, the system is definitely up and you can communicate with it; however, a lack of response from `ping` may not mean anything about that system's status.

Tracing Connections with `traceroute`

When you're connecting to a remote computer, you're actually connecting through a series of computers (and routers and other expensive Internet stuff). That is, your computer connects to another computer, which connects to another, which connects to yet another, and so on until your computer connects to the one you're trying to reach.

The data that you're sending or receiving actually meanders through the path in *packets* (little chunks of data) that are reassembled into the correct sequence at the other end. But not all packets take precisely the same route from the sending computer to the destination computer. Communication on the Internet is much more like sending a lot of letters than making a telephone call. It's a bunch of little messages being passed along, not a continuous connection.

```
ejray> traceroute www.yahoo.com
traceroute to www10.yahoo.com (204.71.200.75), 30 hops max, 40 byte packets
 1  198.60.22.1 (198.60.22.1)  8 ms  2 ms  3 ms
 2  903.Hssi5-0-0.GW1.SLT1.ALTER.NET (157.130.160.141)  18 ms  13 ms  14 ms
 3  124.ATM4-0-0.CR1.SFO1.Alter.Net (137.39.68.9)  68 ms  65 ms  52 ms
 4  311.atm3-0.gw1.sfo1.alter.net (137.39.13.49)  60 ms  50 ms  39 ms
 5  Hssi1-0.br1.NUQ.globalcenter.net (157.130.193.150)  40 ms  39 ms  28 ms
 6  pos0-1-155M.wr1.NUQ.globalcenter.net (206.132.160.25)  30 ms  48 ms  42 ms
 7  pos1-0-622M.wr1.SNV.globalcenter.net (206.251.0.74)  50 ms  67 ms  61 ms
 8  pos5-0-0-155M.cr1.SNV.globalcenter.net (206.251.0.105)  48 ms  40 ms  41 ms
 9  www10.yahoo.com (204.71.200.75)  43 ms  50 ms  53 ms
ejray>
```

Code Listing 12.6 Using `traceroute`, you can see how data meanders between your computer and a remote computer.

```
jdoe /home/jdoe $ /usr/sbin/traceroute
→ www.google.com

traceroute to www.google.com
→ (216.239.51.101), 30 hops max, 38 byte
→ packets
  1  192.168.1.1 (192.168.1.1)  0.907 ms
→ 0.683 ms  0.632 ms
  2  * * *
  3  * * *
  4  * * *
  5  * * *
  6  * * *
  7  * * *
  8  * * *
  9  * * *
 10  * * *
 11  * * *
 12  * * *
 13  * * *
 14  * * *
 15  * * *
 16  * * *
 17  * * *
 18  * * *
 19  * * *
 20  * * *
 21  * * *
 22  * * *
 23  * * *
 24  * * *
 25  * * *
 26  * * *
 27  * * *
 28  * * *
 29  * * *

jdoe /home/jdoe $
```

Code Listing 12.7 Sometimes, traceroute has problems with firewalls between you and the target system.

- Many firewalls do not pass through the ICMP (ping) packets (there's a techie term for you) that traceroute uses. If you get a lot of lines with * * * in them, as shown in **Code Listing 12.7**, that might be the problem.

Using traceroute, you can satisfy your curiosity or, possibly, identify bottlenecks. How? You find out what route the packets take to arrive at the destination computer, as shown in **Code Listing 12.6**. If, for example, you see that the routes to your three favorite (but currently inaccessible) Web sites all end at a specific computer, that's where the network outage is and who you're waiting for to get things up and running.

To trace a connection with traceroute:

- traceroute www.yahoo.com

  At the shell prompt, type traceroute plus the address of the other computer in the connection. You'll see results similar to those shown in Code Listing 12.6. Each line in the traceroute output represents a computer (or other device) on the Internet that receives your packets and passes them on to the next computer.

✔ Tips

- If you're experiencing connectivity problems, try using traceroute to several different, geographically dispersed hosts to isolate the problem. For example, if you're in the Midwest and can traceroute all the way to www.stanford.edu (physically located in Palo Alto, California) but not to www.mit.edu (in Boston, Massachusetts), there's likely trouble on the Internet between you and the East Coast.

- You can speed the traceroute process by using the -n flag; for example, traceroute -n hostname. This checks the path using only IP numbers and does not translate the IP numbers into the DNS (Domain Name Server) addresses with which you're familiar.

Matching Domain Names with IP Numbers

When accessing a computer on the Internet, you generally type in a domain name (such as www.raycomm.com) and your system translates it into an IP number (such as 204.228.141.12). As a rule, the translation from domain name to IP number proceeds without a problem. Heck, most of the time, you won't even notice that it happened. Occasionally, though, you'll come across an error message that says something like "failed DNS lookups." All that this message means is that the domain name server (probably on your Unix system) cannot match the domain name you provided to an IP number.

So, what do you do?

◆ Just be patient for a day or two until the problem is resolved. (In the meantime, make sure the problem isn't a typo on your part.)

◆ Use nslookup or dig, which manually convert a domain name to the matching IP number (**Code Listing 12.8**). Then you can connect directly to the IP number, rather than use the domain name.

To match a domain name with an IP number using nslookup:

◆ nslookup www.raycomm.com
  → ns1.netrack.net

At the shell prompt, type nslookup followed by the domain name you want to look up and the server you want to do the looking for you (Code Listing 12.8). Remember, if you get one of those pesky "failed DNS lookup" messages, the problem likely resides with your name server; therefore, you'll need to specify a different name server to match the domain name and IP number for you.

```
jdoe /home/jdoe $ nslookup www.raycomm.com
→ ns1.netrack.net
Note:  nslookup is deprecated and may be
→ removed from future releases.
Consider using the `dig' or `host' programs
→ instead.  Run nslookup with
the `-sil[ent]' option to prevent this
→ message from appearing.
Server:          ns1.netrack.net
Address:         206.168.112.16#53


Non-authoritative answer:
Name:   www.raycomm.com
Address: 206.168.112.83
```

Code Listing 12.8 You can manually translate a domain name into an IP address using nslookup.

MATCHING DOMAIN NAMES WITH IP NUMBERS

```
jdoe /home/jdoe $ dig @ns1.netrack.net
→ www.raycomm.com

; <<>> DiG 9.2.1 <<>> @ns1.netrack.net
→ www.raycomm.com
;; global options:  printcmd
;; Got answer:
;; ->>HEADER<<- opcode: QUERY, status:
→ NOERROR, id: 32957
;; flags: qr rd ra; QUERY: 1, ANSWER: 1,
→ AUTHORITY: 2, ADDITIONAL: 0

;; QUESTION SECTION:
;www.raycomm.com.              IN      A

;; ANSWER SECTION:
www.raycomm.com.        3585    IN      A
→ 206.168.112.83

;; AUTHORITY SECTION:
raycomm.com.            3585    IN      NS
→ ns2.raycomm.com.
raycomm.com.            3585    IN      NS
→ ns1.raycomm.com.

;; Query time: 60 msec
;; SERVER:
→ 206.168.112.16#53(ns1.netrack.net)
;; WHEN: Sun Jan 26 18:20:47 2003
;; MSG SIZE  rcvd: 85

jdoe /home/jdoe $
```

Code Listing 12.9 You can use dig to look up domain names and IP numbers.

To match a domain name with an IP number using dig:

◆ dig @ns1.netrack.net www.raycomm.com
   At the shell prompt, type dig followed by @server-you-want-to-query and the domain name you want to look up (**Code Listing 12.9**).

✔ Tips

■ You can also do reverse lookups (matching number to name). This can be handy for identifying the origins of unknown email (from the IP addresses in the email headers), among many other tasks. Use nslookup 192.168.1.23 (substituting the appropriate IP address) or dig -x 192.168.1.82 to match a number to a name. Note that many servers have a single IP number that supports many domain names, so the answer from this may not be as definitive as it looks.

■ For most purposes, nslookup provides more quickly comprehensible output (Code Listing 12.8) than dig does. However, dig (with appropriate options) can help provide extra information that can be useful in some cases. See man dig for information about available options.

■ You can find alternate domain name servers by using the whois query server at http://www.internic.net/whois.html and looking up the domain name you want. All domain names have to be listed with two different domain name servers that are responsible for the domain names. Either of those listed servers should be able to provide the IP number for the domain name you enter.

MATCHING DOMAIN NAMES WITH IP NUMBERS

Choosing a News Reader

Usenet news (often called *Netnews* or just *news*) is a collection of more than 20,000 different discussion groups on a variety of topics. Several main categories of Usenet newsgroups exist, as well as dozens of local, regional, and esoteric categories. Our ISP carries about 25,000 newsgroups, which is fairly typical. The *Common Usenet Categories* sidebar lists some of the main Usenet categories. The newsgroups you'll have available through your Unix system depend on which ones your ISP or company subscribes to.

You can read news using a variety of news readers, including `pine` and `tin`, which we'll cover in this section. Both of these are fairly easy to use and available on many Unix systems.

Common Usenet Categories

The main Usenet categories include

- `comp.` computer-related topics
- `news.` Usenet administration topics, including answers to questions frequently asked by new users
- `rec.` recreational topics
- `sci.` science-related topics
- `soc.` social/sociology topics
- `talk.` discussion for its own sake
- `misc.` anything that's left over

Other common categories include

- `alt.` practically any topic imaginable
- `bit.` mirrors of discussions from Listserv lists (that were originally on the BITnet network)
- `k12.` education topics, from K–12

Dozens of other categories exist for universities, states, companies, and other purposes. Ask your system administrator about what's available to you, or just take a look for yourself.

Figure 12.9 You often have to manually set pine so it knows where your news server is.

Figure 12.10 You have to subscribe to newsgroups before you can read them in pine.

Figure 12.11 From here, you can choose messages to read.

Reading News with pine

pine is great for reading news, particularly if you use pine to read and send email. pine has an easy-to-use interface and a slew of features. To use pine to read news, you'll need to

◆ Configure pine to read news (**Figure 12.9**).

◆ Subscribe to one or more newsgroups (**Figure 12.10**).

◆ Read your newsgroup messages (**Figure 12.11**).

To configure pine to read news:

1. pine

   At the shell prompt, type pine.

2. Ⓜ

   Press Ⓜ to get to pine's main menu.

3. Ⓢ

   Press Ⓢ to enter pine's setup menu.

4. Ⓒ

   As shown in the setup menu, press Ⓒ to access the configuration screen (Figure 12.9).

5. Scroll down to nntp-server and press [Enter].

   nntp stands for Network News Transport Protocol, and the server is where you'll find the news.

6. news.yourisp.com

   Type in the news server name—something like news.yourisp.com or news.yourserver.com (with your specific information in there, of course). Check with your system administrator for the specifics.

7. Ⓔ

   Press Ⓔ to exit the configuration screen.

   continues on next page

8. $\boxed{Y}$

Confirm that you really want to exit and save your changes by pressing $\boxed{Y}$.

9. $\boxed{Q}$

Quit pine.

10. $\boxed{Y}$

Confirm that you really want to quit.

To subscribe to newsgroups with pine:

1. pine

For starters, type pine at the shell prompt.

2. $\boxed{L}$

Press $\boxed{L}$ to see the folder list. You'll notice that you now have a news section at the bottom of the folder list.

3. $\boxed{\downarrow}$

Scroll down to the News on section.

4. $\boxed{A}$

Press $\boxed{A}$ to subscribe to a newsgroup. You have to subscribe for groups to show up in your list.

5. $\boxed{Ctrl}\boxed{T}$

Press $\boxed{Ctrl}\boxed{T}$ to get a list of all newsgroups, and then scroll through the list with the arrow keys until you find one you want to try out, as Figure 12.10 shows. Note that this can be pretty time-consuming on a slow connection.

6. $\boxed{S}$

Press $\boxed{S}$ to subscribe to the newsgroup you highlighted in the previous step.

7. Continue subscribing to any groups that look interesting by following the same process.

8. $\boxed{Q}$

Press $\boxed{Q}$ (and confirm with $\boxed{Y}$) when you're finished and ready to exit pine, or just move to the next section to read your new newsgroups.

To read newsgroup messages with pine:

1. pine

At the shell prompt, type pine (unless you're still in pine from the previous section).

2. L

Press L to view the list of folders.

3. Tab Tab Tab. Ah-ha!

Tab down to the news collection (Figure 12.11).

4. V

Press V to view the folder you choose.

5. Read messages just like you'd read mail.

Check back with Chapter 11 for a quick reminder about reading, sending, and replying with pine.

✔ Tips

- When subscribing to newsgroups, you can just enter the name of a newsgroup (or part of the name) after you press A to add a new subscription, rather than search through the entire list of newsgroups.

- Use $h from the message index in pine to first specify that you want to sort (the $), and then that you want to sort by message threads (the h). Using $h makes news reading much more enjoyable and less frustrating.

- After you subscribe to a newsgroup, you might have a few initial messages that show up as "No Message Text Available." Just scroll down to other messages.

READING NEWS WITH pine

Reading News with `tin`

Another program you can use to read news is `tin`, which is very similar to the `mutt` email program. You'll find that it's fairly intuitive to use (as news readers go) and that the menu options and interface are similar to those of `mutt`. However, `tin` is just a news reader (unlike `pine`, which is also an email program), so your only tasks here are subscribing to newsgroups (**Figure 12.12**) and reading newsgroup messages (**Figure 12.13**).

Figure 12.12 The main `tin` screen is very similar to mutt's main screen.

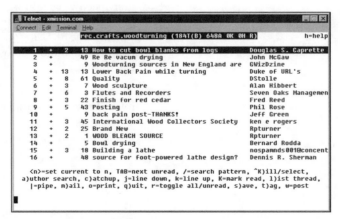

Figure 12.13 Choose a thread from the listing `tin` provides.

To subscribe to newsgroups with `tin`:

1. `tin`

At the shell prompt, type `tin`. You'll see a list (quite possibly empty) of all of the groups to which you've subscribed and a menu at the bottom (Figure 12.12). You might need to type `tin -r`, depending on the news configuration on your system.

2. Ⓨ

Optionally, press Ⓨ to "yank" the whole list of newsgroups into the reader if you want to see your choices.

3. `s rec.woodworking`

Type `s` followed by the newsgroup name to subscribe to a newsgroup.

4. Ⓠ

Keep subscribing to other newsgroups if you want, and then press Ⓠ to quit `tin` when you're done.

To read newsgroup messages with `tin`:

1. `tin`

At the shell prompt, type `tin`.

2. 2

Enter the number of the newsgroup you want to read (the number is in the list of newsgroups that `tin` displays). You can use your ⬆ and ⬇ keys to navigate and the [Spacebar] to move to the next screen.

3. 1

Choose the thread you want to read by number as well (Figure 12.13). You can use your ⬆ and ⬇ keys to navigate and the [Spacebar] to move to the next screen.

4. [Enter]

Press [Enter] an extra time to open a newsgroup message.

continues on next page

5. N

Use N (for next) and P (for previous) to read the messages and Q to return to the list of threads.

6. Q

Press Q to quit tin.

✔ Tips

■ You can reply to any newsgroup message by pressing R, which will send your reply only to the person who posted the message. Type your message in the resulting editor screen and use S to send the message, I to spell-check it, Q to quit (cancel), or E to return to the editor and keep revising.

■ If you'd rather reply to the entire newsgroup, press F (to follow up) instead of R.

■ Many "binary" groups post encoded pictures, programs, and sound files. Save the newsgroup posting, then use uudecode (discussed in Chapter 13) to restore the file to its original state.

■ Press W from any tin screen to start a new posting to that newsgroup. Fill in the subject and type your message in the resulting editor screen.

■ If a newsgroup thread wanders onto a topic you don't want to read about, just press K to kill it. All of the articles with that subject will be marked as already read, so you won't see them again.

■ If your server doesn't provide tin, slrn is another news reader that might be appropriate.

■ You can press H from any tin page to get help.

WORKING WITH ENCODED & COMPRESSED FILES

13

As you use Unix, you will likely encounter encoded or compressed files and need to extract, unencode, encode, or otherwise manipulate the files to be able to view or use them. This chapter discusses different ways of encoding and compressing files.

Chapter Contents

- Encoding files
- Decoding files
- Archiving files
- Unarchiving files
- Compressing files
- Uncompressing files
- Zipping single files
- Unzipping single files
- Zipping multiple files and directories
- Unzipping multiple files and directories
- Combining commands

Encoding Files
with uuencode

You'll use *encoding* whenever you're sending
a *binary* file (a nontext file) through email or
posting one to a newsgroup. Although many
email programs and news readers will take
care of encoding for you (and, therefore,
you won't need to mess with the information here), you may occasionally need to
do it yourself.

Files must be encoded so that they can pass
through Internet email and news gateways
unscathed. If you don't encode a file and
your program doesn't do it for you, the file
will arrive as a bunch of unusable gibberish
(because the gateways assume that all text
passing through uses 7-bit words (bytes),
while binary files use 8-bit words, thus binary
files are garbled). To prevent gibberish, just
uuencode your files before you send them
along, as shown in **Code Listing 13.1**.

```
[ejr@hobbes compression]$ ls
Folder    bigfile.uuefolderzip.zip home.gz.uue
Zipadeedoodah    file1.htm  fortunes1.txt  newzip.zip
bigfile.gz   file2.html fortunes1.zip  ournewhouse.jpg
bigfile.new.gz  folder.tar gzip    temp
[ejr@hobbes compression]$ uuencode ournewhouse.jpg ourhouse.jpg > house.uue
[ejr@hobbes compression]$ head house.uue
begin 664 ourhouse.jpg
M"<@>H@C("'@C"'@C"'@C"'@C"'@C"'@C"'@C"'@C"'@C"'@C"'@C"'@C"'@C
M("'@4F%N9&]M(%(=%5.5.25@@1F]R='H*'9B!Y;W4@F]-97=I;F<
M<G@@;V8@&AE('5U96YC;V1E('1O;VPL(&]R('1O(')E9&ER96-T('1H92
M71A:&PN(D)N.E:&A0Y;VX
M;'5M96YC;V1E('1O;VQ0;2!;F]-97=I;F<
M96%D>2!B965N(&EU:&%Y.E%971H92!G971H92!G=8)O(')E<@90
M<FT@&AE(%5.25@@1F]R='H;V8@&A
M97N."'@C"'@C"'@C"'M+2)*79E($A)A<G+"N+"B;A
M9R!09B!T:&%4Y-R<B@H@@HB!(%4Y V-,6@'@7,6:,6=VAA="!@VAA
[ejr@hobbes compression]$
```

Code Listing 13.1 Use uuencode to encode files and, optionally, to redirect the output to disk.

To encode a file using uuencode:

◆ uuencode ournewhouse.jpg ourhouse.jpg
  → house.uue

At the shell prompt, type uuencode followed by

▲ The name of the unencoded file (ournewhouse.jpg, in this case).

▲ The name you want the (eventually) unencoded file to have (ourhouse.jpg).

▲ A command to redirect the output to a new filename (> house.uue). You add this bit so the file will be saved on disk and not displayed on the screen instead. We've used the .uue extension so we'll more easily remember that the file is uuencoded.

Code Listing 13.1 lists the files in a directory (to verify the name) and then uuencodes the file. Also, notice that it shows what the top of a uuencoded file looks like.

To encode with uuencode and email at once:

◆ uuencode ournewhouse.jpg house.jpg |
  → mail -s "Here's the new picture"
  → debray@raycomm.com

At the shell prompt, use uuencode followed by

▲ The name of the unencoded file (ournewhouse.jpg in this case).

▲ The name you want the (eventually) unencoded file to have (house.jpg).

▲ A command to pipe the output (| 'mail -s "Here's the new picture" debray@raycomm.com). This mails the file to a specific email address with specific text in the subject line, which the -s flag sets. See Chapter 11 for more about mailing files and mailing from the shell prompt.

continues on next page

ENCODING FILES WITH uuencode

Code Listing 13.2 shows this command and gives a glimpse into a uuencoded file.

✔ Tips

- If you're sending a file to someone with a MIME-compliant email program, you might try base64 encoding, using uuencode -m. See Chapter 11 for more about email.

- A relatively new development on Usenet is to use yEnc (yencoding/ydecoding). Look for yencode and ydecode on your system, or consider installing them if needed. See Chapter 14 for more information about installing software.

- Also check out Chapter 11 for information about email programs that will automatically handle attachments, including encoding files for you.

- You must (either manually or automatically) encode all binary files (graphics, programs, compressed files, etc.) before emailing them. Plain text (text files, scripts, or HTML documents) don't need to be encoded.

```
[ejr@hobbes compression]$ uuencode
→ ournewhouse.jpg house.jpg | mail -s
→ "Here's the new picture"
→ debray@raycomm.com
```

Code Listing 13.2 You can uuencode and mail all in one step to work more efficiently.

```
[ejr@hobbes compression]$ uudecode
→ rowboat.uue
[ejr@hobbes compression]$ ls -l row*
-rw-rw-r-1 ejr    users   128886 Jul 27
→ 09:52 rowboat.jpg
-rw-r-r- 1 ejr    users   177606 Jul 27
→ 09:51 rowboat.uue
[ejr@hobbes compression]$
```

Code Listing 13.4 Uudecoding files is straightforward.

- If you have a file that you suspect is uuencoded, use **head** plus the filename to view the top ten lines of the file. If it's really uuencoded, you'll see a line saying so at the top, as shown in Code Listing 13.3. The **644** in the list is the file's permissions, and **rowboat.jpg** is the filename that the extracted file will have. See Chapter 5 for highly interesting details about file permissions.

Decoding Files with uudecode

You'll decode files whenever you receive binary files through email—it's the only way you can use encoded files. Although most email programs and news readers will take care of decoding files for you (and, therefore, you won't need the information here), you may need to do it manually on occasion. (Hint: If you open up a file or an email message and see something like **Code Listing 13.3**, you've got a little decoding to do. To avoid the gibberish, decode your files, as shown in **Code Listing 13.4**.

To decode files with uudecode:

- ◆ **uudecode rowboat.uue**

  At the shell prompt, type **uudecode** followed by the name of the file to decode (Code Listing 13.4).

✔ Tips

- When you receive an encoded file, you might have to uncompress or unzip it in addition to decoding it. See the appropriate sections later in this chapter for details.

```
[ejr@hobbes compression]$ head rowboat.uue
begin 664 rowboat.jpg
M"<@>H@("'@("'@("'@("'@("'@("'@("'@("'@("'@("'@("'@("'@("'@("'@("
M(''@4F%9N9&]M(%%5.25@@1F]R=':'5N97,A9G!8;(;'H-":'5B;'H'6=S:8";OV9P
M<G8;@;;4;R8+A35R[6]G;(B)R8<(5E79G2B6((!2H';$>];D;)F>="I';$
M:71A=&N"'@I4:&$<&GVYL>2!R96%L;;";'@D;@9V]']"!3C;9I!T';R!B=7D@
M;;'5M8F5;3;(&$S8&%$(&$$<W1$<W10;<&&@=&G2@$M("$6@@@AH87@4,@@$6QO
M96%]CD>2B$B;965(@&$+$U;&F%;@F06$$&$]]G971H97(#:@6X=&$(&&90
M<;&@;&]Q;@8;@8]G;5R;;;@@F;)7+9I;&$&@$$Y'$&G-I9&$8E]X
M97N,N"'@("'@("'@("'@("'@("$M;"!$879`E($$!A<&G+@$6$&@&$;@6EN
M9R"O8;B$;>.'@86)T97$<&F;64@B$!E;8;=;)@:7,7;,@6@=8;66@="$!%
[ejr@hobbes compression]$
```

Code Listing 13.3 Use the **head** command to view the top of a file. The "begin" line is the tipoff that it's a uuencoded file, with 644 permissions and the name of **rowboat.jpg**.

Archiving with `tar`

Occasionally, you'll want to take a bunch of files and make them into one file, such as when you're archiving information, for example. You might think of it as tossing a bunch of toys into a toy box—that is, taking a bunch of related things and storing them all in one place.

Using `tar` (which came from "tape archive"), you can take a bunch of files and store them as a single, uncompressed file (see **Code Listing 13.5**). You'll use `tar` files not only to store information, but also to create a single source for compressing and gzipping files, which are discussed later in this chapter.

```
[ejr@hobbes compression]$ ls -l
total 2290
drwxrwxr-x     2 ejr      users        1024 Jul 23 10:56 Feather
drwxrwxr-x     2 ejr      users        1024 Jul 23 10:49 Zipadeedoodah
-rw-rw-r–      1 ejr      users       53678 Jul 23 06:42 bigfile.gz
-rw-rw-r–      1 ejr      users       53678 Jul 23 10:16 bigfile.new.gz
-rw-rw-r–      1 ejr      users       73989 Jul 23 10:16 bigfile.uue
-rw-rw-r–      1 ejr      users      128886 Jul 23 11:45 file1.htm
-rw-rw-r–      1 ejr      users      128886 Jul 23 11:45 file2.html
-rw-rw-r–      1 ejr      users      686080 Jul 23 10:41 folder.tar
-rw-rw-r–      1 ejr      users      268156 Jul 23 06:53 folderzip.zip
-rw-rw-r–      1 ejr      users      128886 Jul 23 06:37 fortunes1.txt
-rw-rw-r–      1 ejr      users       55124 Jul 23 06:38 fortunes1.zip
-rw-rw-r–      1 ejr      users           0 Jul 23 11:21 gzip
-rw-rw-r–      1 ejr      users       73978 Jul 23 11:15 home.gz.uue
-rw-r–r–       1 ejr      users      177607 Jul 27 09:34 house.uue
-rw-rw-r–      1 ejr      users       53792 Jul 23 06:52 newzip.zip
-rw-rw-r–      1 ejr      users      128886 Jul 23 08:19 ournewhouse.jpg
-rw-rw-r–      1 ejr      users      128886 Jul 27 09:52 rowboat.jpg
-rw-r–r–       1 ejr      users      177606 Jul 27 09:51 rowboat.uue
drwxrwxr-x     3 ejr      users        1024 Jul 23 12:56 temp
[ejr@hobbes compression]$ tar -cf tarredfilename.tar Feather
[ejr@hobbes compression]$
```

Code Listing 13.5 Tarring files binds them all together into a single file.

To archive a directory with `tar`:

1. `ls -l`

For starters, type `ls -l` at the shell prompt to verify the name of the directory you're going to `tar`.

2. `tar -cf tarredfilename.tar Feather`

Type `tar` followed by

- ▲ The `-cf` flags (to create a file)

- ▲ The name you want the tarred (archived) file to have (`tarredfilename.tar` in this example)

- ▲ The name (or names) of the directory or files to tar (`Feather`, here)

✔ Tips

- ■ See the section called *Combining Commands* later in this chapter for time-saving ideas for combining and compressing files all in one fell swoop.

- ■ Some versions of `tar` also support `gzip`, so you can use `tar -czf tarredfilename.tgz Feather` to `tar` and `gzip` all at once.

- ■ You can add the `v` flag to the `tar` command flags (`-vcf`) to get a verbose description of what's being tarred.

- ■ If you want to sound like a real Unix geek, refer to tarred files as "tarballs."

ARCHIVING WITH tar

Unarchiving Files
with `tar`

You'll also use `tar` to unarchive files, where you take all of the individual files out of the single tarred file—like dumping the bunch of toys out of the toy box—as shown in **Code Listing 13.6**.

To unarchive files with `tar`:

◆ `tar -xf labrea.tar`

At the shell prompt, type `tar -xf` (here, x means extract) followed by the name of the tarred file you want to unarchive. The bunch of once-tarred files will be separated into the original files or directories, as shown in Code Listing 13.6.

To unarchive selected files with `tar`:

◆ `tar -xf labrea.tar "*mammoth*"`

You can also extract only specified files from a `tar` file. You might do this to restore just a couple of files from a backup archive, for example. This command extracts all files that have `mammoth` in their names from the `labrea.tar` file and places them back where they belong (**Code Listing 13.7**).

✔ Tips

■ Consider moving tarred files into a temporary directory before you unarchive them. When you unarchive, `tar` overwrites any files with the same names as files that are extracted. Using a temporary directory will prevent this.

■ Use `tar -tf filename` to list the files (to check your work, perhaps, or find a backup file) without actually unarchiving the files.

```
[ejr@hobbes compression]$ tar -xf
→ labrea.tar
[ejr@hobbes compression]$ ls -l Labrea/
total 483
-rw-r-r- 1 ejr   users    53678 Jul 27
→ 10:05 bigfile.gz
-rw-r-r- 1 ejr   users   128886 Jul 27
→ 10:06 mammoth.jpg
-rw-r-r- 1 ejr   users   177607 Jul 27
→ 10:05 house.uue
-rw-r-r- 1 ejr   users   128886 Jul 27
→ 10:06 rowboat.jpg
 [ejr@hobbes compression]$
```

Code Listing 13.6 Untarring files reconstructs the original directory structure.

```
[ejr@hobbes compression]$ tar -xf
→ labrea.tar "*mammoth*"
[ejr@hobbes compression]$ ls -l Labrea/m*
-rw-r-r- 1 ejr   users   128886 Jul 27
→ 10:06 Labrea/mammoth.jpg
[ejr@hobbes compression]$
```

Code Listing 13.7 Unarchive just a single file to replace a missing or corrupt file.

```
[ejr@hobbes compression]$ ls -l l*
-rw-r-r- 1 ejr   users   501760 Jul 27
→ 10:06 labrea.tar
[ejr@hobbes compression]$ compress
→ labrea.tar
[ejr@hobbes compression]$ ls -l l*
-rw-r-r- 1 ejr   users   297027 Jul 27
→ 10:06 labrea.tar.Z
[ejr@hobbes compression]$
```

Code Listing 13.8 Listing files before and after compressing them lets you see how much smaller the new file is.

Compressing Files
with compress

Compressing a file just means making it smaller so that it takes up less hard-disk space. It's like filling a toy box, closing the lid, then sitting on it to moosh the contents so that they fit into a smaller space. Any time you create a file that you'll be sending via FTP or that people will access through the Web, you'll want to compress the file so that it takes less time to send and download. As **Code Listing 13.8** shows, you compress files using the compress command.

To compress a file with compress:

◆ compress labrea.tar

At the shell prompt, type compress followed by the filename. Here, we're compressing a tarred file, which contains multiple files. As you can see in Code Listing 13.8, the compressed file has a new extension (.Z) that shows that it's compressed, and it replaces the original, uncompressed file.

✔ Tips

■ You can compress only one file at a time. If you have multiple files you want to compress, consider archiving them first using tar, and then compressing the single archived file. See the section called *Archiving with tar* earlier in this chapter.

■ You can add the -c flag to compress to leave the original file untouched and send the compressed version to standard output (where you'll probably specify a name and save it to a file). For example, you might use compress -c labrea.tar > labrea.tar.Z. See Chapter 1 for some mighty interesting information on redirecting output, as is shown here.

COMPRESSING FILES WITH compress

Uncompressing Files
with uncompress

Compressing a file is handy for reducing the amount of disk space it uses, but you can't do much with a compressed file—directly, at least. You'll need to uncompress it first. As **Code Listing 13.9** shows, you do so using the uncompress command.

To uncompress a file with uncompress:

◆ uncompress labrea.tar.Z

At the shell prompt, type uncompress followed by the full filename of the file to uncompress. The compressed file is replaced by the uncompressed file, which is named like the original, but without the .Z (see Code Listing 13.9).

✔ Tips

■ Remember that uncompressed files take up more space—sometimes a lot more space—than compressed files. You might want to check your storage quota with your ISP before you uncompress a file to make sure that you don't exceed your limit. As Chapter 7 explains, you can often check your quota by typing quota -v at the shell prompt.

■ You can add the -c flag to uncompress to leave the original file untouched and send the uncompressed version to standard output. For example, you might use uncompress -c tarred.tar.Z > tarred.tar. See Chapter 1 for more information on redirecting output, as is shown here.

■ You can also use gunzip to uncompress compressed files. Check out *Unzipping a gzip File with gunzip* later in this chapter.

```
[ejr@hobbes compression]$ ls -l l*
-rw-r-r- 1 ejr   users   297027 Jul 27
→ 10:06 labrea.tar.Z
[ejr@hobbes compression]$ uncompress
→ labrea.tar.Z
[ejr@hobbes compression]$ ls -l l*
-rw-r-r- 1 ejr   users   501760 Jul 27
→ 10:06 labrea.tar
[ejr@hobbes compression]$
```

Code Listing 13.9 You can uncompress files with a single swift command and possibly double your disk usage at the same time, as shown here.

Zipping a File or Directory with gzip

If you want to compress only a single file or directory, you might choose gzip, rather than compress. gzip is more efficient, so you wind up with smaller files than you do with compress. As **Code Listing 13.10** shows, you use gzip much the same way that you use compress.

To zip a file or directory with gzip:

1. ls -l z*

   At the shell prompt, use ls -l to confirm the name of the file or directory you want to zip. In this example, we're looking for z (as in zipadeedoodah) files.

2. gzip zipadeedoodah.tar

   Type gzip followed by the name of the file or directory to gzip. The zipped file will replace the unzipped version and will have a new .gz extension.

✔ Tips

■ If the compressed files will be accessed by someone using Windows, you should consider using zip, which is discussed later in this chapter. Although gzip is more convenient in the Unix world, gzip is not the same as good old Pkzip or .zip files used in DOS and Windows.

■ Another utility used for compressing files is bzip (bzip2, actually). You can find more information about it at http://www.bzip.org/. It's quite powerful and quickly gaining popularity.

■ You can tar a group of files and then compress the single file using gzip.

■ If you want to keep a copy of the original, unzipped file, try gzip -c filetogzip > compressed.gz.

```
[ejr@hobbes compression]$ ls -l z*
-rw-r--r--    1 ejr     users      501760 Jul 27 10:22 zipadeedoodah.tar
[ejr@hobbes compression]$ gzip zipadeedoodah.tar
[ejr@hobbes compression]$ ls -l z*
-rw-r--r--    1 ejr     users      239815 Jul 27 10:22 zipadeedoodah.tar.gz
[ejr@hobbes compression]$
```

Code Listing 13.10 Use gzip to zip up those bulky tar files.

Unzipping a gzip File with gunzip

To access gzipped files, you'll need to unzip them. You do so using gunzip, as **Code Listing 13.11** shows.

To unzip a gzip file with gunzip:

1. `ls –l *.gz`

   At the shell prompt, verify the name of the gzipped file with `ls *.gz` (Code Listing 13.11).

2. `gunzip zipadeedoodah.gz`

   Enter gunzip and the name of the file to unzip. gunzip will uncompress the file(s) and return you to the shell prompt.

✔ Tips

- When you're unzipping files with gunzip, you're not required to enter the file extension. gunzip zipadeedoodah would work just as well as gunzip zipadeedoodah.gz.

- You might encounter gzipped files with a .tgz (tarred, gzipped), tar.gz, or just .gz extension. It'll handle any of those gracefully.

- Some systems don't recognize the gunzip command, so you might need to use gzip -d to uncompress the files.

- If you have a compressed file that you know is text—oldfunnysayingsfromthenet.gz, for example—you can uncompress it (without deleting the original file) and view it with a single command: gzcat oldfunnysayingsfromthenet | more.

- gunzip understands how to uncompress most (compressed) files, including those compressed with compress or .zip files from DOS/Windows systems.

```
[ejr@hobbes compression]$ ls -l *.gz
-rw-rw-r–    1 ejr      users      53678 Jul 23 06:42 bigfile.gz
-rw-rw-r–    1 ejr      users      53678 Jul 23 10:16 bigfile.new.gz
-rw-r–r–     1 ejr      users     239819 Jul 27 10:22 zipadeedoodah.tar.gz
[ejr@hobbes compression]$ gunzip zipadeedoodah.tar
[ejr@hobbes compression]$ ls -l z*
-rw-r–r–     1 ejr      users     501760 Jul 27 10:22 zipadeedoodah.tar
[ejr@hobbes compression]$ ls -l *.gz
-rw-rw-r–    1 ejr      users      53678 Jul 23 06:42 bigfile.gz
-rw-rw-r–    1 ejr      users      53678 Jul 23 10:16 bigfile.new.gz
[ejr@hobbes compression]$
```

Code Listing 13.11 Use gunzip to uncompress zipped files.

Zipping Files and Directories with zip

If you're working with files and directories that will be accessed on the Windows platform, you might need to use zip (rather than gzip). This zip is like DOS or Windows zip, so it's a safer option than gzip, which can work, but it depends on the software available on the Windows system. zip files are compressed to save disk space and sometimes contain multiple files (see **Code Listing 13.12**).

To zip files or directories with zip:

1. ls -l z*

   At the shell prompt, use ls -l to confirm the names of the files or directories you want to zip.

2. zip -r zipped zipadeedoodah

   Type zip -r followed by the name of the zip file you're creating (without an extension), followed by the name of the file or directory to zip. Then just twiddle your thumbs while waiting for Unix to zip your files (Code Listing 13.12).

✔ Tips

- Some Unix systems don't offer the zip command. In this case, if you need to share files with Windows users, use either gzip or compress, send the file, and tell your colleagues that they can use WinZip, among other programs, to extract the files.

- If you zip a directory (remember to include the -r for recursive argument), you zip all the files within it.

- If you can't get the tune "Zip-A-Dee-Doo-Dah" out of your head after these examples, try humming "The Candy Man" or "I'd Like to Teach the World to Sing," or whistling the "Colonel Bogey March" (theme from *The Bridge on the River Kwai*).

```
[ejr@hobbes compression]$ ls -l z*
-rw-r-r-   1 ejr    users    501760 Jul 27 10:22 zipadeedoodah
[ejr@hobbes compression]$ zip -r zipped zipadeedoodah
  adding: zipadeedoodah (deflated 52%)
[ejr@hobbes compression]$ ls -l z*
-rw-r-r-   1 ejr    users    501760 Jul 27 10:22 zipadeedoodah
-rw-r-r-   1 ejr    users    239943 Jul 27 10:41 zipped.zip
[ejr@hobbes compression]$
```

Code Listing 13.12 Use zip to compress files, particularly those you'll share with Windows users.

Unzipping Zipped Files
with unzip

You can unzip zipped files using unzip, which is logical because you certainly wouldn't unzip zipped files with unVelcro or unsnap (**Code Listing 13.13**).

To unzip a zip file using unzip:

1. `ls -l *.zip`

   At the shell prompt, verify the name of the zip file with `ls *.zip`.

2. `unzip zipped.zip`

   Enter unzip and the name of the file to unzip (with or without the .zip extension). unzip will uncompress the file(s) and return you to the shell prompt.

✔ Tips

■ If you attempt to unzip a file and the file or files to be unzipped already exist, unzip will prompt you for each one to determine if you want to overwrite (destroy) the existing file, cancel the unzipping process, or rename the file you're unzipping to a safe name. Alternatively, use the -n (never overwrite) or -o (always overwrite) flags to avoid this prompt entirely.

■ gunzip also understands how to uncompress some .zip files, so you can use gunzip instead of unzip, if you'd like. On the Unix side of things, use whatever seems easiest to you, or gunzip if you really don't care. If you're providing files to Windows users, zip is somewhat more reliable because the format it creates is more standard.

```
[ejr@hobbes compression]$ ls -l *.zip
-rw-rw-r–     1 ejr     users      268156 Jul 23 06:53 folderzip.zip
-rw-rw-r–     1 ejr     users       55124 Jul 23 06:38 fortunes1.zip
-rw-rw-r–     1 ejr     users       53792 Jul 23 06:52 newzip.zip
-rw-r–r–      1 ejr     users      239943 Jul 27 10:41 zipped.zip
[ejr@hobbes compression]$ unzip zipped.zip
Archive:  zipped.zip
replace zipadeedoodah.tar? [y]es, [n]o, [A]ll, [N]one, [r]ename: y
  inflating: zipadeedoodah.tar
[ejr@hobbes compression]$
```

Code Listing 13.13 unzip lets you uncompress files without accidentally obliterating them.

Combining Commands

As we've shown you in this chapter, you use separate commands to encode/unencode, tar/untar, compress/uncompress, and zip/unzip files and directories. A lot of times, however, you can pipe commands together and run them in sequence, saving you time and hassle. For example, as **Code Listing 13.14** shows, you can uudecode and gunzip files at the same time by piping the commands together. You can also uncompress and untar at one time, and you can tar and gzip at one time.

To uudecode **and** gunzip **at one time:**

1. ls -l h*

Use ls -l to verify the existence of your uuencoded and zipped file.

2. uudecode -o /dev/stdout home.gz.uue
→ | gunzip > home

Here, we use -o /dev/stdout to send the uudecode output to the standard output, then pipe the output of the uudecode command to gunzip, then redirect the output of gunzip to the home file. Whew! See Code Listing 13.14 for the details.

```
[ejr@hobbes compression]$ ls -l h*
-rw-rw-r–     1 ejr     users     73978 Jul 23 11:15 home.gz.uue
-rw-r–r–      1 ejr     users    177607 Jul 27 09:34 house.uue
[ejr@hobbes compression]$ uudecode -o /dev/stdout home.gz.uue | gunzip > home
[ejr@hobbes compression]$ ls -l h*
-rw-r–r–      1 ejr     users    128886 Jul 27 10:48 home
-rw-rw-r–     1 ejr     users     73978 Jul 23 11:15 home.gz.uue
-rw-r–r–      1 ejr     users    177607 Jul 27 09:34 house.uue
[ejr@hobbes compression]$
```

Code Listing 13.14 Decoding and unzipping at once is a little cryptic but saves your typity typity fingers.

To uncompress and untar at one time:

◆ zcat filename.tar.Z | tar -xf -

At the shell prompt, type zcat followed by the filename (as usual) and pipe that output to tar. Follow the tar command and flags with a - so that tar will be able to save the file to the intended name (**Code Listing 13.15**).

To tar and gzip at one time:

◆ tar -cf - Feather | gzip >
→ feather.tar.gz

At the shell prompt, enter your tar command as usual but add a – (and a space) before the filename so the output can be piped. Then, pipe the output to gzip and redirect the output of that to a filename with the .tar and .gz extensions to show that the file has been tarred and gzipped (**Code Listing 13.16**).

```
[ejr@hobbes compression]$ ls -l *.Z
-rw-r-r- 1 ejr  users  297027 Jul 27
→ 10:06 labrea.tar.Z
[ejr@hobbes compression]$ zcat
→ labrea.tar.Z | tar -xf -
[ejr@hobbes compression]$ ls -l l*
-rw-r-r- 1 ejr  users  501760 Jul 27
→ 10:06 labrea.tar
[ejr@hobbes compression]$ ls -ld L*
drwxr-xr-x  2 ejr  users  1024 Jul 27
→ 10:16 Labrea
[ejr@hobbes compression]$
```

Code Listing 13.15 After you find the compressed files, you can uncompress and untar them at once, and then use ls -ld (long and directory flags) to check your work.

COMBINING COMMANDS

```
[ejr@hobbes compression]$ ls -ld F*
drwxrwxr-x  2 ejr  users  1024 Jul 23 10:56 Feather
[ejr@hobbes compression]$ tar -cf - Feather | gzip > feather.tar.gz
[ejr@hobbes compression]$ ls -l f*
-rw-r-r- 1 ejr  users  106752 Jul 27 10:54 feather.tar.gz
-rw-rw-r-      1 ejr    users    128886 Jul 23 11:45 file1.htm
-rw-rw-r-      1 ejr    users    128886 Jul 23 11:45 file2.html
-rw-rw-r-      1 ejr    users    686080 Jul 23 10:41 folder.tar
-rw-rw-r-      1 ejr    users    268156 Jul 23 06:53 folderzip.zip
-rw-rw-r-      1 ejr    users    128886 Jul 23 06:37 fortunes1.txt
-rw-rw-r-      1 ejr    users    55124 Jul 23 06:38 fortunes1.zip
[ejr@hobbes compression]
```

Code Listing 13.16 You can efficiently tar and gzip all at once as well.

INSTALLING YOUR OWN SOFTWARE

If you use Unix long enough, you'll eventually want or need to install new software. Installing software could mean just installing a shell script that you get from a friend, or it could mean compiling and installing a full-fledged program that you download from the Internet.

In this chapter, we'll explore the process for installing software on Unix systems. Work through each section in the order provided, and keep in mind that

◆ The process for installing Unix software is a bit more complicated than doing the same on Windows or Macintosh systems.

◆ The example we use here will probably differ slightly from the exact process you'll need to use for the programs or scripts you choose for your system.

◆ You should probably check with your system administrator for specifics on what you can and cannot install on the system. Many ISPs will let you install what you want, but others may have specific restrictions or even make it impossible to compile software in your account.

◆ Installing software if you do not have system administrator (root) access on your system is much more difficult.

Chapter Contents

◆ Understanding Unix software installation

◆ Finding Unix software

◆ Downloading, placing, and uncompressing software

◆ Configuring software

◆ Compiling and installing software

Understanding Unix Software Installation

When installing software on your Unix system, keep in mind two things. First, most software, including a script, relies on other programs or scripts being available at specific places within the system. For example, a script might require that the bash shell be available and located at /bin/bash. Or, a program might expect that it will be in /usr/local/bin and that all user home directories will be under /home. So, you should pay special attention during the installation process to make sure that all other required scripts or programs are available.

Second, programs (but not scripts) are *compiled*, which means that they're taken from one probably-mostly-readable-to-you language (generically called *source code*) and translated into computer-readable files (often called *binaries*). As software is compiled, hardware and operating system-specific characteristics (or dependencies) are built in. So, a program that's compiled to run on a specific platform and operating system cannot run on other ones—that is, a program compiled on Linux on a Pentium cannot run on Linux on a SPARC, Solaris on a Pentium, or Digital Unix on an Alpha.

In fact, most Unix programs are distributed as source code, not as binaries, so you can compile them for your particular system when installing.

✔ Tip

■ Before you get started with the next section, you might cruise back to Chapters 1 and 2 for information about exploring your Unix system and to Chapter 7 for a reminder of how to find out what operating system and hardware you're using.

Figure 14.1 You'll find all the software you could ever want on many software archives on the Web, such as HotScripts.

Finding Unix Software

Before you can install software on your Unix system, you have to find the software and locate the correct version of the software. We recommend the following places to look:

◆ Search the Web using Yahoo (`www.yahoo.com`) or Google (`www.google.com`) to find downloadable software.

◆ Visit specific software sites, such as HotScripts at `www.hotscripts.com` (**Figure 14.1**) or SourceForge at `http://sourceforge.net` or FreshMeat at `http://freshmeat.net`.

In using these resources, you'll come upon the following:

◆ Code for Perl, shell, or other scripts: You'll generally have to download, uncompress, and unarchive these, and then edit some of the files to insert system-specific settings.

◆ Source code for programs: With these, you'll have to download, uncompress, and unarchive, and then set some system-specific settings. Then, you'll have to "make" them, which tells the make program on your system to compile and install the programs.

◆ Precompiled binaries: You'll have to scout through the names available and find the name (and operating system and platform) that corresponds to the system on which you want to run the software to run. Then, you'll have to download it, uncompress it, and put it where you want it. This is the easiest solution—when it works; however, keep in mind that you might download it, uncompress it, and find that it still won't work, leaving you with no choice but to download and compile the source code.

✔ Tips

■ If you'll be downloading and installing a lot of software, and if you have no significant quota limitations, look into using or even downloading and installing **rpm**. It's a neat compression/installation/configuration program that makes installing Unix software in this special format as easy as installing a program in Windows or on a Macintosh. It's standard on RedHat, SuSE, and Mandrake Linux but has been used on many different Unix systems. The **apt** package system, used by Debian Linux, is similar in intent and is also extremely popular.

■ Unless you're **root** on your system, your options for installing software will be rather limited. Consider using a home Linux system to experiment with if you want to be able to install whatever and whenever you want.

Downloading, Placing, and Uncompressing Software

Once you've found software you want to install, your next step is to download it, put it in the proper place, and then uncompress it (**Code Listing 14.1**). This process includes several tasks that you've already learned in other parts of this book, so we won't go over them in detail here. For this section, we assume that you already know what you want to download and where it can be found. In the example, we're downloading the latest version of yencode, using links, from the www.yencode.org Web site.

To download, place, and uncompress software:

1. `links www.yencode.org`

   Use links to connect to the software archive, Web site, or whatever you're downloading from.

2. Browse to the correct location.

   Go ahead. We'll wait.

3. Choose the file to download by pressing (Enter) when the link to the file is highlighted.

   Confirm that you want to download the file.

4. Q

   Quit the links program after the transfer is complete.

```
jdoe /home/jdoe $ mv yencode-0.46.tar.gz
→  ~/src/
jdoe /home/jdoe $ cd ~/src
jdoe /home/jdoe/src $ tar -xzf
→ yencode-0.46.tar.gz
jdoe /home/jdoe/src $ cd yencode-0.46
jdoe /home/jdoe/src/yencode-0.46 $
```

Code Listing 14.1 The process of downloading software and getting ready to install it is rather straightforward.

5. `mv yencode-0.46.tar.gz ~/src/`

Move the archive file into the `src` subdirectory under your home directory. (Create the directory first, if necessary.) You could use any directory, but it's standard to use an `src` directory.

6. `cd ~/src`

Change into the `src` directory.

7. `tar -xzf rpm-2.5.1.tar.gz`

Unzip and untar the source code archive with `tar`.

8. `cd yencode-0.46`

Change into your new directory, and get ready to compile and install. Whew! See Code Listing 14.1 for much of the process.

✔ Tip

- You can also use `wget` or `ftp` to download your software, which might be easier if you know exactly the URL of the software you want to download.

Configuring Software

After you've downloaded and uncompressed your new software, you'll have to configure and tweak it to conform to your system. In general, the changes you'll make will be things like

◆ Adjusting path names (e.g., to install it into /home/yourid/bin rather than into /usr/local/bin, where you likely cannot install software).

◆ Specifying what kind of Unix system you're working on.

◆ Inserting your email address and similar data.

◆ Choosing one of two or three system-specific settings. What to choose for each system is clearly marked in the files you'll be using.

If you're installing a program that will be compiled, your steps will closely resemble these. If you're installing a script, the steps will likely differ somewhat, but go ahead and read through these steps because the principles of what to change are the same for scripts and programs.

Precisely what changes you'll have to make (in programs or scripts) are almost always documented in the INSTALL (or README, if there isn't an INSTALL) file that comes with the software—in the Makefile (in the case of programs) or in the actual .pl or .sh files that you'll run (in the case of scripts). (See **Code Listing 14.2.**) So be sure to read these files! The steps in this section assume that you're starting in the main directory of uncompressed and untarred files that you downloaded.

```
jdoe /home/jdoe/src/yencode-0.46 $ more README
This is yencode, an encoder/decoder package for the Usenet "yEnc" format, licensed under the
GNU General Public License.


FEATURES
____

    * Portable program for all Unix operating systems.


    * The encoder can output single part or multipart yencoded archives of any size.


    * Smart decoder can handle multiple files, including files specified out of order or with
      nonsense file names.


    * Easy to use Usenet posting software enables one-liner posting of individual files or
      groups of files, including creation of SFV/CRC checksum files if desired.


    * Optional scan mode: automatically locate and decode single or multipart yencoded
      archives in specified directories or recursively.


    * Fully compliant with all versions of the yEnc specification (currently v1, v2, v3).


    * Properly implements CRC values, including the pcrc32 on each part of multipart
      archives, and a crc32 for the last part of a multipart archive.


    * Full internationalization (multilingual) support provided by GNU gettext.



For more information on yEnc, visit http://www.yenc.org/.

The yencode homepage is located at http://www.yencode.org/.

I do not have access to very many system types.  If you have trouble compiling or installing
this program, please email me (or send patches!) and I will try to add support for your
operating system.  This version has been tested on FreeBSD and Linux.

Internationalization support is currently only supported for English, because I'm an ignorant
American.  Translations are welcomed.


This program should be considered "alpha quality" software.  It has not been extensively
tested in real-world applications.  Please email me with bug reports, comments, and
suggestions.


--
Mail suggestions and bug reports to <bboy@bboy.net>.
jdoe /home/jdoe/src/yencode-0.46 $ ls configure
configure*
```

Code Listing 14.2 Checking out the instructions is essential.

CONFIGURING SOFTWARE

To configure software:

1. `more README`

   To begin, type `more README` at the shell prompt to see the `README` file one screen at a time. This file should give you installation instructions as well as information about what details you need to provide. **Code Listing 14.2** shows part of yencode's `README` file.

2. `ls configure`

   Type `ls configure` to see if there's a file named `configure` in the current directory.

   ▲ If you have a `configure` file, just continue to step 3.

   ▲ If you don't have a `configure` file, skip ahead to step 4.

3. `./configure --prefix=/home/jdoe`

   Usually you can just enter `./configure` to run `configure` and let the configuration happen by itself (**Code Listing 14.3**), though you may have a little more to do. We opted to add `--prefix=/home/jdoe` to set everything up to be installed into jdoe's home directory. `configure` makes a special `Makefile`, just for you, which makes the next steps much easier. Run `"./configure --help | more"` to see what flags are available (it differs greatly between packages).

```
jdoe /home/jdoe/src/yencode-0.46 $ ./configure –prefix=/home/jdoe
checking for a BSD compatible install... /usr/bin/install -c
checking whether build environment is sane... yes
checking for mawk... mawk
checking whether make sets ${MAKE}... yes
checking for mawk... (cached) mawk
checking for gcc... gcc
checking for C compiler default output... a.out
checking whether the C compiler works... yes
checking whether we are cross compiling... no
checking for executable suffix...
checking for object suffix... o
checking whether we are using the GNU C compiler... yes
checking whether gcc accepts -g... yes
checking for style of include used by make... GNU
checking dependency style of gcc... gcc3
checking for a BSD compatible install... /usr/bin/install -c
checking whether ln -s works... yes
checking for ranlib... ranlib
checking how to run the C preprocessor... gcc -E
checking for ANSI C header files... yes
checking for errno.h... yes
checking for getopt.h... yes
checking for libintl.h... yes
checking for memory.h... yes
checking for stdarg.h... yes
checking for stddef.h... yes
checking for stdlib.h... yes
checking for string.h... yes
checking for strings.h... yes
checking for termios.h... yes
checking for time.h... yes
checking for sys/time.h... yes
checking for unistd.h... yes
checking for arpa/inet.h... yes
checking for netdb.h... yes
checking for netinet/in.h... yes
 ...
Type `make' to build the package.
Type `make install' to install the package.

jdoe /home/jdoe/src/yencode-0.46 $
```

Code Listing 14.3 The ./configure program goes on and on.

4. `vi Makefile`

Use the text editor of your choice to review the Makefile, reading the instructions in it and checking the accuracy of things like directory and path names, program names, and similar settings. If you don't know what something is or does, ignore it for now. Even if `configure` automatically sets up the Makefile for you, you should still glance through it to make sure that it's putting stuff into the correct directories and that it doesn't expect any additional information from you.

If you find errors in the Makefile, review the INSTALL or README files and rerun `configure` with the appropriate options to get the Makefile in order.

Figure 14.2 shows the Makefile for yencode. All we did was verify the prefix (base directory).

5. Save the file and close out of the editor. There! You've configured your software installation!

✔ Tips

■ Exactly what steps you'll have to take will depend on the software. Scripts will come as plain text files and you might not have to do anything besides download them. Most of the time, however, you'll have to tweak scripts as well as programs (although the scripts won't need to be compiled).

■ A good rule of thumb is to make minimal changes to the Makefile. Doing more than is required often causes the program not to compile or gives you a bazillion error messages. If this happens, just go to your backup Makefile, make a new copy, and try again, making only the necessary modifications. Better to make too few changes than to take the time and effort to make too many.

```
jdoe@frazz.raycomm.com: /home/jdoe/src/yencode-0.46
top_srcdir = .

#prefix = /usr/local
prefix = /home/jdoe
exec_prefix = $(prefix)

bindir = $(exec_prefix)/bin
sbindir = $(exec_prefix)/sbin
libexecdir = $(exec_prefix)/libexec
datadir = $(prefix)/share
sysconfdir = $(prefix)/etc
sharedstatedir = $(prefix)/com
localstatedir = $(prefix)/var
libdir = $(exec_prefix)/lib
infodir = $(prefix)/info
mandir = $(prefix)/man
includedir = $(prefix)/include
oldincludedir = /usr/include
pkgdatadir = $(datadir)/yencode
pkglibdir = $(libdir)/yencode
pkgincludedir = $(includedir)/yencode
top_builddir = .

-- INSERT --
```

Figure 14.2 Fortunately, many programs require minimal changes.

Compiling and Installing with `make install`

Your final step is to get the software installed on the Unix system. With some programs, all you'll have to do is put the files in the directory where you want them to live (often ~/bin for programs or scripts or sometimes cgi-bin for scripts or programs for Web use). With others, though, you'll have to compile first and then install.

You can compile and install using make install, which reads the Makefile (to see how to set everything up) and takes care of compiling and installing for you (**Code Listing 14.4**). Again, be sure to read the instructions carefully before you start and follow them exactly.

```
jdoe /home/jdoe/src/yencode-0.46 $ make
cd . \
  && CONFIG_FILES= CONFIG_HEADERS=config.h \
     /bin/sh ./config.status
config.status: creating config.h
config.status: config.h is unchanged
make  all-recursive
make[1]: Entering directory `/home/jdoe/src/yencode-0.46'
Making all in intl
make[2]: Entering directory `/home/jdoe/src/yencode-0.46/intl'
make[2]: Nothing to be done for `all'.
make[2]: Leaving directory `/home/jdoe/src/yencode-0.46/intl'
Making all in po
make[2]: Entering directory `/home/jdoe/src/yencode-0.46/po'

 ...

gcc -DLOCALEDIR=\"/home/jdoe/share/locale\" -DSYSTYPE=\"i686-pc-linux-gnu\" -I. -I. -I..
→ -I../lib -I../intl   -Wall -Wno-unused -g -O2 -c `test -f ydecode.c || echo './'`ydecode.c
gcc -Wall -Wno-unused -g -O2   -o ydecode  ydecode.o crc.o file.o output.o ../lib/libmisc.a
make[3]: Leaving directory `/home/jdoe/src/yencode-0.46/src'
make[2]: Leaving directory `/home/jdoe/src/yencode-0.46/src'
make[2]: Entering directory `/home/jdoe/src/yencode-0.46'
make[2]: Leaving directory `/home/jdoe/src/yencode-0.46'
make[1]: Leaving directory `/home/jdoe/src/yencode-0.46'
```

Code Listing 14.4 make delivers incredible quantities of junk (but hopefully no error message) to your screen.

311

To compile and install using
`make install`:

1. `make`

   For starters, type `make` at the shell prompt (in the main directory containing your program setup files) to set up all of the variables you specified in the previous section. Code Listing 14.4 shows what `make` displays on the screen.

   If you see error messages that aren't accompanied by a reassuring "Will continue to use something else" message, you may need to return to editing the `Makefile`. When you `make` successfully, without nasty error messages, you're ready to move ahead to step 2.

```
jdoe /home/jdoe/src/yencode-0.46 $ make install
Making install in intl
make[1]: Entering directory `/home/jdoe/src/yencode-0.46/intl'
if test "yencode" = "gettext" \
   && test '' = 'intl-compat.o'; then \
  /bin/sh `case "./mkinstalldirs" in /*) echo "./mkinstalldirs" ;; *) echo
→ "../.mkinstalldirs" ;; esac` /home/jdoe/lib /home/jdoe/include; \
  /usr/bin/install -c -m 644 libintl.h /home/jdoe/include/libintl.h; \
  @LIBTOOL@ –mode=install \
    /usr/bin/install -c -m 644 libintl.a /home/jdoe/lib/libintl.a; \
else \
  : ; \
fi
if test 'no' = yes; then \
  /bin/sh `case "./mkinstalldirs" in /*) echo "./mkinstalldirs" ;; *) echo
→ "../.mkinstalldirs" ;; esac` /home/jdoe/lib; \
  temp=/home/jdoe/lib/t-charset.alias; \
 /home/jdoe/man/ypostrc.5
    Manual page describing the `~/.ypostrc' format.
 ...


make[2]: Leaving directory `/home/jdoe/src/yencode-0.46'
make[1]: Leaving directory `/home/jdoe/src/yencode-0.46'
jdoe /home/jdoe/src/yencode-0.46 $
```

Code Listing 14.5 Type make install to finish the installation process.

2. `make install`

Type `make install` to finish the process (see **Code Listing 14.5**).

3. `~/bin/yencode`

Try out the new software! (Of course, replace `yencode` with the name of the software you installed.) (See **Code Listing 14.6**.)

Zowie! It works!

4. `cd ; rm -Rf ~/src/yencode*`

After you're sure that everything works right, tar and gzip the complete source tree (in case you need to reinstall). Or, if space is tight, save the `Makefile` and any other files you edited, and remove the rest. (If space is tight and you didn't make any substantive changes to get everything to compile, just `rm` it all.)

continues on next page

```
jdoe /home/jdoe/bin $ ~/bin/yencode
no input files
Try `~/bin/yencode -help' for more information.
jdoe /home/jdoe/bin $ ~/bin/yencode -help
Usage: ~/bin/yencode [OPTION]... FILE...
Usenet file encoder.

  -d, --debug            output extra debugging information while running
  -e, --extension=EXT    use EXT for file extension instead of the default
  -f, --force            overwrite existing files, never prompt
  -l, --line=LEN         output lines that are LEN bytes in length
  -m, --multipart=SIZE   create multipart output each containing SIZE bytes (defaults to
                         620k if SIZE is not specified)
  -o, --output=DIR       create output in DIR instead of the current dir
  -p, --paths            maintain paths in input filenames
  -q, --quiet            inhibit all messages written to the standard output
      --sfv=NAME         create SFV checksum file for all input files
      --crc=NAME         create CRC checksum file for all input files
      --help             display this help and exit
      --version          output version information and exit

Report bugs to bugs@yencode.org.
jdoe /home/jdoe/bin $
```

Code Listing 14.6 It works! We didn't do anything with it, but it works.

COMPILING AND INSTALLING WITH makeinstall

✔ **Tips**

- Be patient, and puzzle your way through if you encounter unexpected errors or if something just doesn't go right. Reading the Makefile and source code is your best bet for solving problems.

- After a failed attempt, type make clean or make distclean to clear out the garbage before you try again.

- Sometimes stuff just isn't worth the trouble. Compiling and installing new software can be fairly difficult, and sometimes the problems you encounter aren't easily resolved. In writing this chapter, for example, we had a great program to install but had to spend about four hours tweaking and fixing it to get it to compile. (That's about three hours and 15 minutes longer than we'd planned on.) This can happen to anyone, so don't get discouraged, but feel free to seek out help or simply find another program that does essentially the same thing; There's enough software out there that technical difficulties in one place shouldn't be any kind of serious obstacle.

- Pay particular attention to the paths to programs and files as you're editing scripts and other setup files—a little error in a path can be hard to spot and completely prevent the new software from working.

USING HANDY UTILITIES

Just when you thought Unix was great...it gets better! Unix gives you a plethora of handy-dandy *utilities*—small programs—that can make your life a bit easier. For example, you might want to use the calendar, calculator, or interactive spell-checker. None of these utilities is likely to be essential to your day-to-day Unix doings; however, they are handy to have and use. Ask your system administrator about which utilities you have available or venture to Chapter 1 to explore your system and find out what's there. In this chapter, we'll look at a few of the most useful ones.

Chapter Contents

- Using the calendar utility
- Using the calculator utility
- Evaluating expressions
- Converting units
- Checking spelling interactively
- Looking up definitions
- Printing your work
- Keeping session records

Calendaring with `cal`

One of the handiest Unix utilities is `cal`, which—logically—is a calendar. Find out what today's date is, what day of the week December 31 is, or what the calendar year looks like. As **Code Listing 15.1** shows, all you have to do is type `cal` and any specific options you want.

To use the `cal` utility:

1. `cal`

Type `cal` at the shell prompt to see the current month's calendar, as shown in **Code Listing 15.1**. Then, start playing with options, as shown in the next few steps.

2. `cal -j`

Use `cal -j` to see the Julian calendar, which shows each day numbered from the beginning of the year. (This argument doesn't work on all systems.)

3. `cal 2004 | more`

Pipe `cal 2004` to `more` to see the whole year's calendar.

4. `cal 12 1941`

Type `cal` plus specific dates to view dates for a particular year.

✔ Tips

■ Note that `cal` is Y2K compliant. If you ask for `cal 98`, you'll get the calendar for the year 98. That is, 1,900 and a few years ago.

■ Put `cal` into your startup configuration files to get a reminder of the date whenever you log in. Check out Chapter 8 for details.

```
[jdoe@frazz jdoe]$ cal
      January 2003
Su Mo Tu We Th Fr Sa
          1  2  3  4
 5  6  7  8  9 10 11
12 13 14 15 16 17 18
19 20 21 22 23 24 25
26 27 28 29 30 31

[jdoe@frazz jdoe]$ cal -j 3 2004
       March 2004
Sun Mon Tue Wed Thu Fri Sat
       61   62   63   64   65   66
67   68   69   70   71   72   73
74   75   76   77   78   79   80
81   82   83   84   85   86   87
88   89   90   91

[jdoe@frazz jdoe]$ cal 2004 |  more
                    2004

      January               February               March
Su Mo Tu We Th Fr Sa   Su Mo Tu We Th Fr Sa   Su Mo Tu We Th Fr Sa
             1  2  3     1  2  3  4  5  6  7        1  2  3  4  5  6
 4  5  6  7  8  9 10     8  9 10 11 12 13 14     7  8  9 10 11 12 13
11 12 13 14 15 16 17    15 16 17 18 19 20 21    14 15 16 17 18 19 20
18 19 20 21 22 23 24    22 23 24 25 26 27 28    21 22 23 24 25 26 27
25 26 27 28 29 30 31    29                      28 29 30 31


       April                  May                   June
Su Mo Tu We Th Fr Sa   Su Mo Tu We Th Fr Sa   Su Mo Tu We Th Fr Sa
             1  2  3                    1        1  2  3  4  5
 4  5  6  7  8  9 10     2  3  4  5  6  7  8     6  7  8  9 10 11 12
11 12 13 14 15 16 17     9 10 11 12 13 14 15    13 14 15 16 17 18 19
18 19 20 21 22 23 24    16 17 18 19 20 21 22    20 21 22 23 24 25 26
25 26 27 28 29 30       23 24 25 26 27 28 29    27 28 29 30
                        30 31
       July                 August               September
Su Mo Tu We Th Fr Sa   Su Mo Tu We Th Fr Sa   Su Mo Tu We Th Fr Sa
             1  2  3     1  2  3  4  5  6  7           1  2  3  4
 4  5  6  7  8  9 10     8  9 10 11 12 13 14     5  6  7  8  9 10 11
11 12 13 14 15 16 17    15 16 17 18 19 20 21    12 13 14 15 16 17 18
18 19 20 21 22 23 24    22 23 24 25 26 27 28    19 20 21 22 23 24 25
25 26 27 28 29 30 3129 30 31                    26 27 28 29 30
```

continues on next page

Code Listing 15.1 Just type cal to see the current month's calendar, or check out other calendar options with flags.

CALENDARING WITH cal

```
       October              November              December
Su Mo Tu We Th Fr Sa   Su Mo Tu We Th Fr Sa   Su Mo Tu We Th Fr Sa
             1  2        1  2  3  4  5  6                 1  2  3  4
 3  4  5  6  7  8  9     7  8  9 10 11 12 13    5  6  7  8  9 10 11
10 11 12 13 14 15 16    14 15 16 17 18 19 20   12 13 14 15 16 17 18
17 18 19 20 21 22 23    21 22 23 24 25 26 27   19 20 21 22 23 24 25
24 25 26 27 28 29 30    28 29 30               26 27 28 29 30 31
31
[jdoe@frazz jdoe]$ cal 12 1941
    December 1941
Su Mo Tu We Th Fr Sa
    1  2  3  4  5  6
 7  8  9 10 11 12 13
14 15 16 17 18 19 20
21 22 23 24 25 26 27
28 29 30 31

[jdoe@frazz jdoe]$
```

Code Listing 15.1 *continued*

```
xmission> bc
6*5
30
xmission>
```

Code Listing 15.2 Using the bc utility, you can calculate and calculate and calculate....

Calculating with bc

Unix even offers a handy calculator utility that lets you...er, um...calculate things. Just use bc, as shown in **Code Listing 15.2**.

To calculate with bc:

1. bc

At the shell prompt, type bc. You'll find yourself at a blank line, waiting for math to do.

2. 6*5

Enter the numbers, operators, expressions, or whatever you want to calculate. Use + to add, - to subtract, * to multiply, and / to divide. The answer appears on the next line (Code Listing 15.2).

3. Ctrl D

Quit bc when you're done.

✔ Tips

■ You can tell bc to calculate expressions within a file with bc filename. (Of course, replace filename with the real filename.) Then, bc waits for more to do from the command line.

■ Type man bc for more details about bc's capabilities.

Evaluating Expressions with expr

Unix also provides expr, which you can use for evaluating expressions. (In this use, the term expressions refers to the mathematical, logical, scientific meaning of the word.) In addition to evaluating mathematical expressions, you can evaluate darn near anything else. The expr utility is often used in shell scripts—and you'll probably find the most value in expr in that context—but it works just fine at the command line, too, as shown in **Code Listing 15.3**.

To evaluate with expr:

◆ expr 3 * 4

At the shell prompt, enter expr followed by the expression it should evaluate. In this example, we're multiplying 3 times 4. (We have to use a \ to escape (protect) the * from being interpreted as a wildcard by the shell.)

◆ expr 5 % 3

Determine the modulo (remainder) of 5 divided by 3. The answer appears on the next line (**Code Listing 15.3**).

◆ a=$PWD; b=$HOME; expr $a = $b

This cryptic expression sets a equal to the current directory, b equal to the home directory, and compares the two. If it returns 1 (true), you're in your home directory. If it returns 0 (false), you're not.

✔ Tips

■ Comparisons within shell scripts allow you to check to see whether something is true or not, and then act accordingly. See Chapter 10 for more information.

■ The expr man page isn't particularly helpful; search the Internet to get help with expr.

```
[jdoe@frazz jdoe]$ expr 3 \* 4
12
[jdoe@frazz jdoe]$ expr 5 % 3
2
[jdoe@frazz jdoe]$ a=$PWD; b=$HOME; expr
→ $a = $b
1
[jdoe@frazz jdoe]$ cd bin
[jdoe@frazz bin]$ a=$PWD; b=$HOME; expr
→ $a = $b
0
[jdoe@frazz bin]$
```

Code Listing 15.3 Using the expr utility, evaluating the value or the truth (or lack thereof) of expressions is straightforward.

EVALUATING EXPRESSIONS WITH expr

```
[jdoe@frazz bin]$ units
1948 units, 71 prefixes, 28 functions

You have: inch
You want: feet
        * 0.083333333
        / 12
You have:
[jdoe@frazz bin]$
```

Code Listing 15.4 Use the units utility to find out how to convert from anything to anything else—really!

Converting with units

Do you always forget how many drams there are in an ounce? Never fear. The units utility makes converting measurements a snap. See **Code Listing 15.4** to learn how to convert with units.

To convert with units:

1. units

   At the shell prompt, type units. The Unix system will prompt you with "You have:" as shown in Code Listing 15.4.

2. inch

   Enter the units you're starting with. You'll then be prompted with "You want:"

3. feet

   Enter the kind of units you want, and watch with amazement as Unix counts on its fingers and toes to figure out the answer.

4. Ctrl D

   Quit units when you're done.

✔ Tips

- You can create your own units file, if you want, defining relationships between units and values of constants. This way, if the value of pi changes, you can create your own file with the new value. Do man units for more information.

- Mess around with units much, and you'll be astounded at the many units it can convert.

CONVERTING WITH units

Checking Spelling with `ispell`

Back in Chapter 4, we showed you how to spell-check your files. Unix also offers you `ispell`, which gives you an interactive way of spell-checking files, similar to the spell-checking capabilities of many word processing programs (**Figure 15.1**).

To check spelling with `ispell`:

1. `ispell gudspeler`

   At the shell prompt, type `ispell` followed by the name of the file you want to spell-check. You'll be greeted with your first (allegedly) misspelled word, the sentence the misspelling appears in, suggested words to replace the misspelled word with, and (probably) a menu at the bottom of the screen, as shown in Figure 15.1. The key menu items are listed in **Table 15.1**.

2. Complete your spell-check using `ispell`'s menu items.

3. Ⓠ

   Press Ⓠ to exit `ispell`, saving all of your changes.

✔ Tip

- Try one (or more) of these flags with the `ispell` command:

  -b creates a backup file.

  -S sorts guesses by likely correctness.

  -B reports run-together words as spelling errors.

  -M makes sure the menu appears at the bottom of the screen, assuming it doesn't appear automatically.

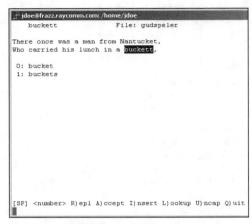

Figure 15.1 `ispell` lets you interactively spell-check your files.

Table 15.1

ispell Menu Items	
ITEM	**DESCRIPTION**
Spacebar	Accept the word this time only.
R	Replace with a word that you'll specify (after you type R).
A	Accept the word for the rest of the current session.
I	Insert the word into your dictionary.
U	Insert the word (as all lowercase) into your dictionary.
Q	Quit `ispell`, without saving any changes.
X	Exit `ispell` saving all changes.
n	Replace highlighted word with a suggested word by typing the appropriate number

```
[jdoe@frazz jdoe]$ look unfo
unfold
unfolded
unfolding
unfolds
unforeseen
unforgeable
unforgiving
unformatted
unfortunate
unfortunately
unfortunates
unfounded
[jdoe@frazz jdoe]$
```

Code Listing 15.5 Look up words with look.

Figure 15.2 Use look to find words, even within vi.

Looking It up with look

Speaking of spelling, you can also have Unix just look up a word for you in the system dictionary. It's just like saying, "Hey, honey, how do I spell 'unforgivably,' as in 'unforgivably lazy'?" Just type look and the beginning of the word you want to look up (**Code Listing 15.5**).

To look up a definition with look:

◆ look unfo

At the shell prompt, type look followed by the first letters—all you know—of the word you want to look up. You'll see a listing of all the words that start with those letters, as shown in Code Listing 15.5.

✔ Tip

■ You can use look from within vi, with Esc :!look unfo, as shown in **Figure 15.2**.

Printing with lp

If your Unix system is hooked up to a printer that you can access, you can print easily using the lp utility (**Code Listing 15.6**). (lp stands for line printer...you know, from the dark ages, practically.) If printing with lp is not a cinch, you likely have a system issue that you should address with the system administrator.

To print with lp:

◆ `lp filename`

At the shell prompt, type lp followed by the name of the file to print. Usually, you'll see confirmation that the file went to the printer, as shown in Code Listing 15.6.

◆ `lp -d otherprintername filename`

You might, depending on your environment, want to specify a printer name. You do that by adding a –d (for destination) flag, as shown here.

✔ Tips

■ Refer back to Chapter 6 for some text-formatting information. You can pipe data to lp, as in `fmt ugly | pr | lp` to format your document, add headers and footers, and print all at once.

■ Use lpq to get information about the printer queue. lpq will usually just respond that it's ready, but if you catch it at the right moment (or a lot of people are printing), it'll tell you which jobs are queued for printing.

```
[jdoe@frazz jdoe]$ lp limerick
request id is lp-46 (1 file(s))
[jdoe@frazz jdoe]$ lp -d hplaser
→ limerick.rot13
request id is hplaser-85 (1 file(s))
[jdoe@frazz jdoe]$
```

Code Listing 15.6 Use the lp utility to print your files, rhymes, and more.

PRINTING WITH lp

```
[ejr@hobbes ch15]$ more covermybutt
Script started on Fri Aug 28 14:30:16
2005
[ejr@hobbes ch15]$ pwd
/home/ejr/ch15
[ejr@hobbes ch15]$ who
root      tty1     Aug 28 14:18
ejr       ttyp0    Aug 28 14:20
→ (calvin.raycomm.com)
ejr       ttyp1    Aug 28 14:28
→ (calvin.raycomm.com)
[ejr@hobbes ch15]$ ps ax
  PID TTY STAT TIME COMMAND
    1 ?    S    0:02 init [3]
    2 ?    SW   0:00 (kflushd)
    3 ?    SW<  0:00 (kswapd)
   48 ?    S    0:00 /sbin/kerneld
  229 ?    S    0:00 syslogd
  238 ?    S    0:00 klogd
  260 ?    S    0:00 crond
  272 ?    S    0:00 inetd
  283 ?    S    0:00 lpd
  298 ?    S    0:00 sendmail: accepting
connections on port 25

  310 ?    S    0:00 gpm -t ms
  321 ?    S    0:00 httpd

  355 ?    S    0:00 nmbd -D
  368 1    S    0:00 /bin/login - root
  369 2    S    0:00 /sbin/mingetty tty2
  370 3    S    0:00 /sbin/mingetty tty3
  371 4    S    0:00 /sbin/mingetty tty4
  372 5    S    0:00 /sbin/mingetty tty5
  373 6    S    0:00 /sbin/mingetty tty6
  375 ?    S    0:00 update (bdflush)
  381 1    S    0:00 -bash
  402 ?    S    0:00 in.telnetd
  436 ?    S    0:00 in.telnetd
  249 ?    S    0:00 /usr/sbin/atd
  327 ?    S    0:00 httpd
  328 ?    S    0:00 httpd
  329 ?    S    0:00 httpd
  330 ?    S    0:00 httpd
  331 ?    S    0:00 httpd            continued
```

Code Listing 15.7 Using script is a great way to keep records.

Keeping a Record of Your Session with `script`

Occasionally, you may need to keep a record of a Unix session—for example, if you're using Unix as part of a class assignment or need a session record to submit to your untrusting boss. You can do this using `script`, which keeps a record of every command you type from the shell prompt (**Code Listing 15.7**). You might think of typing `script` as pressing a Record button on a tape recorder.

```
continued

  332 ?    S    0:00 httpd
  333 ?    S    0:00 httpd
  334 ?    S    0:00 httpd
  335 ?    S    0:00 httpd

  403 p0   S    0:00 /bin/login -h calvin
→ raycomm.com -p
  404 p0   S    0:00 -bash
  437 p1   S    0:00 /bin/login -h calvin
→ raycomm.com -p
  438 p1   S    0:00 -bash
  449 p1   S    0:00 ispell gudspeler
  450 p0   S    0:00 script covermybutt
  451 p0   S    0:00 script covermybutt
  452 p3   S    0:00 bash -i
  455 p3   R    0:00 ps ax
[ejr@hobbes ch15]$ exit

Script done on Fri Aug 28 14:30:44 2005
[ejr@hobbes ch15]$
```

To record your session with `script`:

1. `script covermybutt`

At the shell prompt, type `script` to start recording your actions. You can save the transcript to a specified filename, as in `script covermybutt`. If you don't specify a file, Unix will save the transcript in the current directory as `typescript`.

2. Do your thing. See you in a couple of hours.

3. `Ctrl` `D`

When you're done, press `Ctrl` `D` to stop recording the session.

4. `more covermybutt`

Use `more` or the editor of your choice to view the script. Code Listing 15.7 shows a sample transcript.

✔ Tips

■ Screen-based programs, such as `vi`, `pico`, `pine`, `mutt`, or `links`, tend to wreak havoc with the output of `script`. You can still read the content, but the formatting is often badly out of whack, as shown in **Figure 15.3**.

■ You would use `script` if you want to record both what you did and what happened ("geez, I typed `rm unbackedupdata`, then `ls`, and sure enough, the `ls` listing showed that I was in big trouble"). On the other hand, if you just want the list of commands you typed with no indication of what happened, check out `history` from Chapter 3 ("geez, I typed `rm unbackedupdata`, then I typed `ls`, then I logged out and cried").

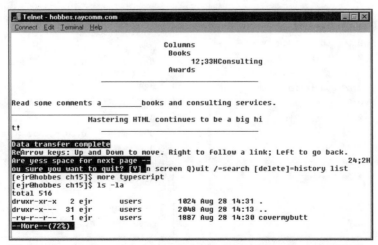

Figure 15.3 Some programs give you oddly formatted script output and strange beeps when you view the script.

BEING ROOT

Up to now, we've been addressing Unix tools and tips that you, as a normal user of the system, can take advantage of. And, as a normal user, you can't hurt the system as a whole—you can mess up your own files, certainly, but that's as far as it goes. As we've mentioned, though, there's also a different class of user, called "superuser" or root. The root user has complete power within the system and can (must) handle configuration issues, software installation for everyone using the system, and troubleshooting. The root user can also easily wreck the system with a single tpyo. Thorough coverage of system administration and being root is out of the scope of this book (look for the sequel, *Unix Advanced: Visual QuickPro Guide*), but it's important to have some tools in your arsenal. In this chapter, we'll give you some very basic tools to use as root.

Chapter Contents

- Acting with root authority
- Becoming root
- Starting, stopping, and restarting daemons
- Changing the system configuration
- Monitoring the system
- Setting the date and time

Acting Like root
with sudo

As you know by now, logging in as root gives you the power to make changes across the entire Unix system, not just within the directories and files that you individually have permissions to access, read, or modify. Of course, having all this power also comes with responsibilities—not to screw up the entire system, among other possibilities. Especially as you're learning about system administration, you may want to experiment with these skills by logging in as sudo instead. Using the sudo utility, you can run some commands as if you were root, but it's not as risky as being root. The real root user has to give permission to use sudo, and sometimes the permission is limited to using specific utilities—you'll have to experiment.

```
[jdoe@frazz jdoe]$ cd /var/log
[jdoe@frazz log]$ tail messages
tail: messages: Permission denied
[jdoe@frazz log]$ sudo tail messages

We trust you have received the usual lecture from the local System Administrator. It usually
boils down to these two things:

    #1) Respect the privacy of others.
    #2) Think before you type.

Password:
Jan 25 06:01:01 frazz CROND[22809]: (root) CMD (nice -n 19 run-parts /etc/cron.hourly)
Jan 25 06:01:01 frazz CROND[22810]: (mail) CMD (/usr/bin/python -S /var/lib/mailman/cron/qrunner)
Jan 25 06:01:01 frazz su(pam_unix)[22814]: session opened for user news by (uid=0)
Jan 25 06:01:01 frazz su(pam_unix)[22814]: session closed for user news
Jan 25 06:01:02 frazz msec: unable to run chage: chage: unknown user: ejray
Jan 25 06:01:03 frazz msec: changed mode of /var/log/news/nntpsend.log from 660 to 640
Jan 25 06:02:00 frazz CROND[22865]: (mail) CMD (/usr/bin/python -S /var/lib/mailman/cron/qrunner)
Jan 25 06:03:00 frazz CROND[22867]: (mail) CMD (/usr/bin/python -S /var/lib/mailman/cron/qrunner)
Jan 25 06:04:00 frazz CROND[22872]: (mail) CMD (/usr/bin/python -S /var/lib/mailman/cron/qrunner)
Jan 25 06:04:17 frazz sudo: jdoe : TTY=pts/1 ; PWD=/var/log ; USER=root ;
COMMAND=/usr/bin/tail messages
[jdoe@frazz log]$.
```

Code Listing 16.1 The sudo command lets you do things that you can't do as a normal user, but that isn't as risky as being root.

```
1001 jdoe@foo $ sudo ls
Password:
My mind is going. I can feel it.
Password:
Take a stress pill and think things over.
Password:
He has fallen in the water!
sudo: 3 incorrect password attempts
 1002 jdoe@foo $
```

Code Listing 16.2 More surprisingly, sudo has a sense of humor.

Note that all uses of sudo are logged. If your system administrator won't be happy with your experimenting with being root, don't use sudo on any system other than your own. In **Code Listing 16.1**, we show the difference between being a normal user and acting with authority with sudo.

To act like root with sudo:

1. `cd /var/log; tail messages`

   As plain-old you, try to look at the system log files in /var/log. On a Linux system, it's usually /var/log/messages; on a Solaris system, it's usually /var/adm/messages. Other Unix flavors will have other, but similar, locations.

   Note that some of these files will require root access to view them, while others won't. If you can view a file as you, then choose a different file to see how sudo helps.

2. `sudo tail messages`

   After permission was denied on the previous attempt, use sudo before the command to try to issue the same command with root authority.

3. `*******`

   Enter your password after the interesting warning, and then note that the command succeeded this time (see Code Listing 16.1).

✔ Tips

- If you haven't been given permission (not just technical permission, but actual, "you may do this" permission) to use sudo, don't. Everything that happens with sudo is logged, and you'll probably have to answer for your actions.

- Whenever possible, it's better to use sudo only when you need it, than to become root. Any typo can be problematic, and it's a good thing to have to consciously add sudo when you want to act with root authority.

- After you've used sudo once, you can use it again within a specific amount of time (usually five minutes) without entering your password again.

- Some versions of sudo have pretty entertaining prompts if you mess up your password (**Code Listing 16.2**). You're likely to irritate your system administrator tremendously if you try to look at these on purpose, though.

ACTING LIIKE root WITH sudo

329

Becoming root with su

Becoming root, assuming that you know the root password, is really quite easy. To do so, you just apply the su command (introduced in the *Changing Your Identity with su* section of Chapter 3), where you change to the root identity (**Code Listing 16.3**).

Once again, we'll say: Being root on a Unix system carries with it a lot of responsibility. First, you must be extraordinarily careful about what you type and where you type it. Every system administrator out there has a horror story about wrecking (to a greater or lesser degree) a system through careless use of the root shell. We've done it, too. Second, you must be very responsible about what you do. You can read anything, see anything, watch anything, and change anything. You can, therefore, easily infringe upon the privacy of your users. Don't.

To become root:

1. su

Enter su to become root.

2. *******

Enter the root password when prompted. Note that, after you succeed, you'll see a different prompt (#). This is your confirmation that you succeeded and are now root (Code Listing 16.3).

3. exit

Use exit or Ctrl D to exit the root shell and become yourself again.

```
jdoe /home/jdoe $ su
Password:
[root@sulley jdoe]# exit
jdoe /home/jdoe $ su -
Password:
[root@sulley root]#
```

Code Listing 16.3 Becoming root is remarkably easy.

✔ Tips

■ As with using su to become yourself (or another user), you can use su – to ensure that all of the root environment variables are set correctly. If you just use su without the hyphen, environment variables and the like will not be set for you, only the root identity. Which is more appropriate depends completely on your situation. If you get unexpected error messages (file not found, for example) with one approach, try the other.

■ If you're connecting to a system with telnet (as opposed to ssh), do not become root. The root password could be "sniffed" by malicious users, and if a hacker gains your root password, you're potentially in big trouble. Your best choice is just to use ssh or to use sudo if ssh is simply impossible.

■ Usually, you'll have to log in to a system as you, and then become root. It's a rare system that will allow you to log directly in remotely as root. Again, this is a security measure to help minimize the possibility of break-ins. Even if someone gets the root password on a system, they can't act as root if they can't also log in as a normal user.

■ There are no real secrets on a Unix system. If you have something that must be a secret, you must encrypt it, or the root user (as well as other users) could know it.

BECOMING root WITH su

Starting, Stopping, and Restarting Daemons

As root, you can do anything on the system, but you shouldn't have much to do at all. Generally, Unix (or Linux) systems are configured so that the programs that should be running all the time (like the Web server software, mail server software, or similar programs) are automatically started in the background when the system is booted. Then you, as root, need only handle crises and problems. (Ha! Easier said than done.)

That said, sometimes you'll need to start or stop these *daemons* (programs running in the background—see Chapter 9 for details). Say, for example, that you get an email from one of the system users complaining that the Web server (or, technically, the httpd daemon) isn't running. As the system administrator, you'll have to start it.

To start a daemon:

1. `ps -ef | grep httpd`

   Verify that the Web server really isn't running. Sometimes users are wrong. If you see lines that list httpd (other than the one that reports the command you're running), httpd is active and doesn't need to be started. The problem may lie elsewhere.

2. `cd /etc/init.d`

   Change to the directory containing the generic init (for initialization) scripts. This directory is likely /etc/init.d or /etc/rc.d/init.d/, as **Code Listing 16.4** shows.

3. `sudo ./httpd start`

Use `sudo ./httpd` (to be absolutely sure that you're running `httpd` from the current directory and not a program of the same name from elsewhere on the system) and `start`. The `httpd` in the `/etc/init.d` directory is a script to start the daemon with the appropriate options.

4. `ps -ef | grep httpd`

Verify that the Web server now is running.

✔ Tips

- To stop a daemon, use the same process, but use `stop` (as in, `sudo ./httpd stop`) to stop a daemon cleanly.

- Sometimes you might need to restart a daemon. You could stop it, and then start it, but in many cases you could also use `restart` or `reload` (as in, `sudo ./httpd restart`).

- Be careful about stopping or restarting daemons with which you are not familiar. Unix has a lot of interdependencies that are often not clear, and stopping something you think you don't need might have unexpected consequences.

```
[jdoe@frazz jdoe]$ ps -ef | grep httpd
jdoe   656 21562 0 04:51 pts/5  00:00:00 grep httpd
[jdoe@frazz jdoe]$ cd /etc/init.d
[jdoe@frazz init.d]$ sudo ./httpd start
Password:
Starting httpd-perl:[ OK ]
Starting httpd: [ OK ]
[jdoe@frazz init.d]$ ps -ef | grep httpd
root       793   1 0 04:52 ?        00:00:00 httpd-perl -f /etc/httpd/conf/ht
apache     794 793 0 04:52 ?        00:00:00 httpd-perl -f /etc/httpd/conf/ht
apache     795 793 0 04:52 ?        00:00:00 httpd-perl -f /etc/httpd/conf/ht
apache     796 793 0 04:52 ?        00:00:00 httpd-perl -f /etc/httpd/conf/ht
apache     800 793 0 04:52 ?        00:00:00 httpd-perl -f /etc/httpd/conf/ht
root       808   1 0 04:52 ?        00:00:00 httpd -DPERLPROXIED -DHAVE_PHP4
apache     816 808 0 04:52 ?        00:00:00 httpd -DPERLPROXIED -DHAVE_PHP4
apache     817 808 0 04:52 ?        00:00:00 httpd -DPERLPROXIED -DHAVE_PHP4
apache     818 808 0 04:52 ?        00:00:00 httpd -DPERLPROXIED -DHAVE_PHP4
apache     819 808 0 04:52 ?        00:00:00 httpd -DPERLPROXIED -DHAVE_PHP4
jdoe       822 21562 0 04:52 pts/5   00:00:00 grep httpd
[jdoe@frazz init.d]$
```

Code Listing 16.4 Sometimes you have to manually start system daemons.

Changing the System Configuration

Most (nearly all) of the system configuration files for Unix systems are contained in the /etc directory. If it's a configuration setting that's specific to a user, the setting will be located in the user's home directory; otherwise, configuration settings for the whole system are located in the /etc directory.

We're not going to get into changing much here—you really should know what you're doing before you start futzing with the system configuration. However, if you're root, you should have some fun with it, so here's something fun to play with. In the following example, you'll see how to change the Message of the Day (aka, the motd), which users are greeted with when they log into the system (**Figures 16.1** and **16.2**).

To change the motd:

1. sudo vi /etc/motd

   Use sudo to gain root access and edit the /etc/motd file.

2. Hey, you have wrinkles in your stockings! Oh…sorry, you're not wearing stockings!

   Uhhh, yikes! Add your favorite slogan, saying, or comment to the file. Keep in mind that everyone who logs into the system will see this message, so keep it clean…and be nice! (Figure 16.2)

3. logout

   Log out, so you can log back in and see your handiwork.

4. ssh yoursystem.example.com

   Log back in to see the new message.

Figure 16.1 Any user will see the motd when logging in.

```
jdoe@frazz.raycomm.com: /home/jdoe
login as: jdoe
Sent username "jdoe"
jdoe@frazz.raycomm.com's password:

If you're not authorized to use this system, please disconnect
now. Failure to do so subjects you to prosecution.

Welcome to Frazz!

Hey, you have wrinkles in your stockings!
Oh... sorry, you're not wearing stockings!
```

Figure 16.2 After a user with root privilege edits it, it's…er…different.

CHANGING THE SYSTEM CONFIGURATION

✔ Tips

- The /etc/motd file is really handy for providing warnings, notes, and comments to system users. Particularly if you're planning on having system downtime or maintenance, it's nice to warn users with a message in /etc/motd.

- Virtually every other change you might make in /etc will also affect everyone on the system. Be careful.

- Depending on what you choose to change or edit in /etc, you might need to restart the appropriate daemon (as described in the previous section) for your changes to take effect. If it looks like your change didn't work, restart the daemon.

- Unix man pages also usually describe the configuration files found in /etc. Use man filename (as in, man exports) to find out what the configuration does.

Monitoring the System

Monitoring the system is one of the key responsibilities of a system administrator. You need to make sure that everything is as it should be on the system, or yell at people, call the cops, order a new hard drive, or whatever else is required. On a single-user system, there's really not much to do, but on a larger system with many users, monitoring is a significant part of a system administrator's job.

Among other things, you can monitor the system logs (located in /var/log), the users logged in, and the overall system load.

To monitor logs:

◆ sudo tail –1000 /var/log/messages
→ | more

Use sudo to gain root access and look at the end (last 1,000 lines) of the messages log file. The output of tail is piped to more so you can actually read it.

Or

◆ sudo tail –f /var/log/httpd/error_log

If you're looking for a specific occurrence of an event as it happens, you can use tail –f to keep displaying the log as new errors, in the case of this log, are added to it. In this example, we're looking at the very end of the Web server's error log, as shown in **Figure 16.3**.

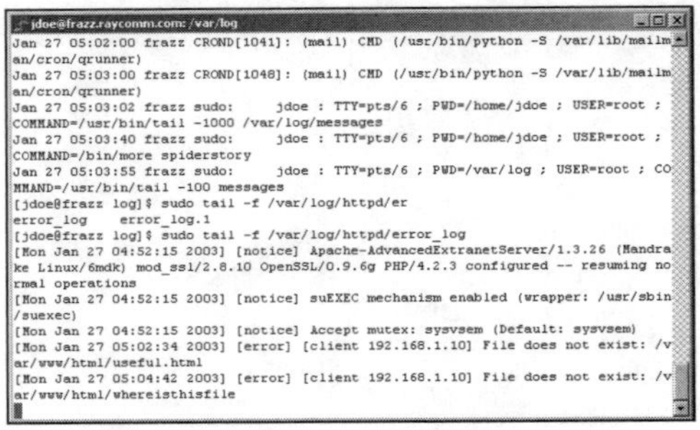

Figure 16.3 Monitoring logs is an important responsibility of the root user.

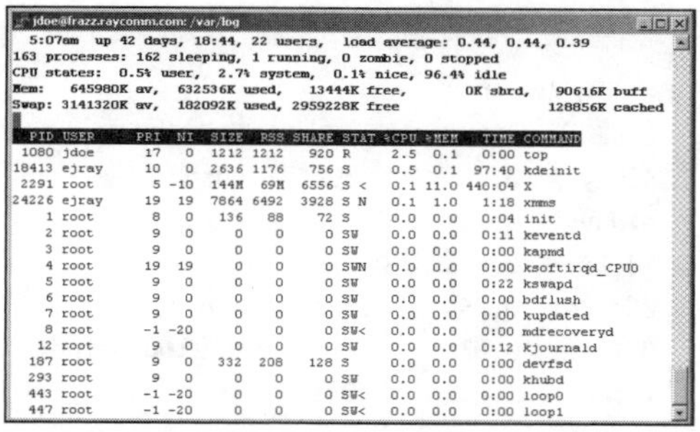

Figure 16.4 The top utility helps monitor the system status.

- Develop shell scripts that automatically run when you log in and go through the "normal" system checks. By doing so, you don't have to do routine checks manually, and you can come up to speed quickly on what's going on.

- Use top −d 2 | grep Mem for a running status check on your available memory. grep for other characteristics from top output, as appropriate.

- Anything that's different from usual is worth being concerned about. Check man pages or search the Web to find out for sure.

To monitor users:

◆ w; who

You don't even need sudo for this one, but you do want to keep an eye on the users logged in, and where they're coming from. After a while, you'll get to recognize patterns and react to them. If jdoe usually logs in by 9 a.m. and logs out by 4 p.m., and always logs in from the same system, then you see jdoe suddenly logging in from a different address at 1 a.m., you should wonder if jdoe's secret password isn't quite so secret anymore.

Or

◆ last

The last utility tells you who logged in (and out) and when, and from where, as shown in **Code Listing 16.5** (on the next page). Good stuff to know, particularly if you're not online and actively monitoring w and who all of the time.

To monitor system load:

◆ top

Use top to monitor your system loads, as shown in **Figure 16.4**. Different systems will show distinctly different patterns, but if you get accustomed to checking top when everything seems normal on your system, you'll be able to better tell if something is abnormal or even what's wrong when the time comes. Press Q to quit top.

✔ Tips

- There's a lot to monitor and a lot to keep up with. Take time to read man pages, search the Web, and ask around for tips and tricks. A wide variety of additional utilities exist to make these processes easier for you.

MONITORING THE SYSTEM

```
[jdoe@frazz init.d]$ w; who
 5:05am up 42 days, 18:42, 22 users, load average: 0.44, 0.40, 0.38
USER     TTY    FROM              LOGIN@    IDLE    JCPU    PCPU    WHAT
root     vc/1   -                 15Dec02   42days  0.06s   0.06s   -bash
ejray    pts/0  -                 16Dec02   41days  0.00s   ?       -
ejray    pts/1  -                 Sat 6am   12:28m  0.88s   0.77s   ssh mike
ejray    pts/2  -                 28Dec02   28days  0.25s   0.25s   /bin/zsh
jdoe     pts/6  192.168.1.104     4:58am 1:12 0.11s 0.02s   tail -f /var/log/httpd/
ejray    pts/19 mike.raycomm.c    Sat12pm   12:28m  1.05s   0.94s   ssh sulley
root     vc/1                     Dec 15 10:25
ejray    :0                       Dec 16 16:10
ejray    pts/0                    Dec 16 16:11
jdoe     pts/6                    Jan 27 04:58 (192.168.1.104)
ejray    pts/8                    Dec 23 19:49
ejray    pts/17                   Jan 7 18:29
ejray    pts/20                   Jan 4 08:31
jdoe     pts/16                   Jan 13 19:39 (192.168.1.104)
ejray    pts/19                   Jan 25 12:03 (mike.raycomm.com)
ejray    pts/22                   Jan 25 12:03
[jdoe@frazz init.d]$ last
jdoe     pts/6   192.168.1.104    Mon Jan 27 04:58   still logged in
jdoe     pts/6   192.168.1.104    Mon Jan 27 04:57 - 04:58 (00:01)
jdoe     pts/6   192.168.1.104    Mon Jan 27 04:55 - 04:57 (00:01)
jdoe     pts/6   192.168.1.104    Sun Jan 26 18:05 - 20:16 (02:11)
jdoe     pts/6   mike.raycomm.c   Sat Jan 25 12:12 - 06:52 (18:40)
ejray    pts/19  mike.raycomm.c   Sat Jan 25 12:03   still logged in
ejray    pts/19  mike.raycomm.c   Sat Jan 25 12:02 - 12:02 (00:00)
jdoe     pts/6   mike.raycomm.c   Sat Jan 25 10:35 - 12:11 (01:36)
jdoe     pts/19  192.168.1.104    Tue Jan 21 20:59 - 00:11 (03:12)
jdoe     pts/19  192.168.1.104    Mon Jan 13 20:59 - 23:56 (02:57)
jdoe     pts/16  192.168.1.104    Mon Jan 13 19:39 - 23:34 (03:54)
jdoe     pts/23  192.168.1.104    Sun Jan 12 06:02 - 08:14 (02:12)
jdoe     pts/14  192.168.1.104    Mon Jan 6 20:54 - 23:42 (02:47)
ejray    pts/17  frazz.raycomm.co Thu Jan 2 20:50 - 06:27 (1+09:36)
ejray    pts/4                    Wed Jan 1 04:55    gone - no logout

wtmp begins Wed Jan 1 04:55:40 2003
[jdoe@frazz init.d]$
```

Code Listing 16.5 You can keep an eye on the users logged in and where they're coming from using w; who and last.

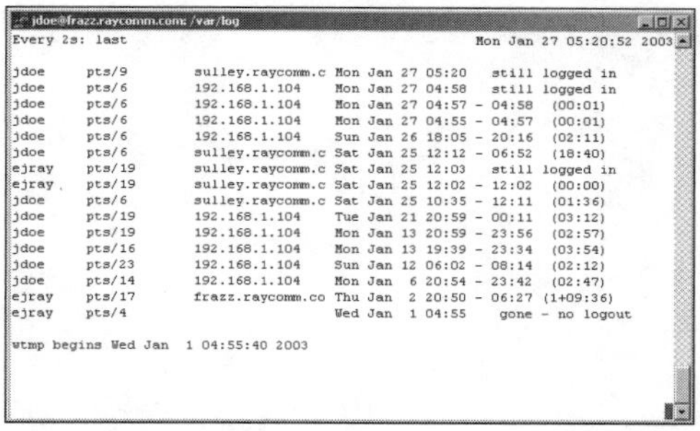

Figure 16.5 Use watch to keep an eye on the system.

Keeping up with watch

As a system administrator, you practically have to have eyes in the back of your head and be aware of all kinds of activities that might be going on. The watch command is your friend. It keeps an eye on pretty much anything (users, system, or files) you want to monitor.

To watch:

◆ watch last

Use watch to monitor the output of a specific command. When something changes, you'll see it in the watch output (**Figure 16.5**). In this case, we're monitoring who logged in and when.

Or

◆ watch --differences=cumulative
→ ls -l /var/spool/mail

You can watch to see if mail's getting delivered by monitoring an ls -l output from the /var/spool/mail directory. The extra flags show cumulative differences since you started watch.

✔ Tips

■ The watch utility can be really handy, but sometimes it'd be easier to just do something like tail -f /var/log/httpd/access_log to keep track of the Web server access log or to write a shell script to periodically run last. Basically, watch is useful, but it's not the only way to monitor what's going on.

■ On the lighter side, you can also use watch to periodically run other programs. For example, watch -n 5 fortune will display a new fortune every five seconds.

Checking Boot Messages with dmesg

Sometimes you might need extra information, beyond what is available on the running system, about the configuration or the hardware. The system automatically probes the hardware and generates all kinds of potentially useful information at that time but keeps it socked away in the bowels of the system. Use dmesg to get at what you need...in appalling detail.

To check status with dmesg:

◆ dmesg | more

Use dmesg (with the help of sudo and more) to gain some insight into the system (**Code Listing 16.6**).

Or

◆ dmesg | mail goodfriend@example.com
→ -s "Help me understand"

Send the output of dmesg to a friend for advice, if you're really stuck.

✔ Tip

■ See Chapter 11 for more information about mailing files and data from the command line.

```
[jdoe@frazz jdoe]$ dmesg | more
x98 ptys configured
Serial driver version 5.05c (2001-07-08) with HUB-6 MANY_PORTS MULTIPORT SHARE_IRQ SERIA
L_PCI ISAPNP enabled
ttyS00 at 0x03f8 (irq = 4) is a 16550A
Uniform Multi-Platform E-IDE driver Revision: 7.00alpha2
ide: Assuming 33MHz system bus speed for PIO modes; override with idebus=xx
PIIX4: IDE controller on PCI bus 00 dev 39
PIIX4: chipset revision 1
PIIX4: not 100% native mode: will probe irqs later
    ide0: BM-DMA at 0x1440-0x1447, BIOS settings: hda:pio, hdb:DMA
    ide1: BM-DMA at 0x1448-0x144f, BIOS settings: hdc:DMA, hdd:pio
hda: QUANTUM FIREBALLP LM30.0, ATA DISK drive
hdb: Maxtor 32049H2, ATA DISK drive
hdc: SAMSUNG DVD-ROM SD-612, ATAPI CD/DVD-ROM drive
ide0 at 0x1f0-0x1f7,0x3f6 on irq 14
ide1 at 0x170-0x177,0x376 on irq 15
hda: 58633344 sectors (30020 MB) w/1900KiB Cache, CHS=3649/255/63, UDMA(33)
hdb: 40021632 sectors (20491 MB) w/2048KiB Cache, CHS=2491/255/63, UDMA(33)
Partition check:
 /dev/ide/host0/bus0/target0/lun0: p1 p4 < p5 p6 >
 /dev/ide/host0/bus0/target1/lun0:<6> [EZD] [remap 0->1] [2491/255/63] p1
 p1: <solaris: [s0] p5 [s1] p6 [s2] p7 [s3] p8 [s4] p9 [s5] p10 [s6] p11 [s7] p12 >
RAMDISK driver initialized: 16 RAM disks of 32000K size 1024 blocksize
md: md driver 0.90.0 MAX_MD_DEVS=256, MD_SB_DISKS=27
md: Autodetecting RAID arrays.
md: autorun ...

  ...


Mounted devfs on /dev
Freeing unused kernel memory: 136k freed
Real Time Clock Driver v1.10e
usb.c: registered new driver usbdevfs
usb.c: registered new driver hub
usb-uhci.c: $Revision: 1.275 $ time 18:49:04 Sep 20 2002
usb-uhci.c: High bandwidth mode enabled
PCI: Found IRQ 9 for device 00:07.2
PCI: Sharing IRQ 9 with 00:10.0
usb-uhci.c: USB UHCI at I/O 0x1400, IRQ 9
usb-uhci.c: Detected 2 ports
usb.c: new USB bus registered, assigned bus number 1
hub.c: USB hub found
hub.c: 2 ports detected
—More—
```

Code Listing 16.6 The dmesg utility helps you see what happens at boot, including the processes started and hardware found.

Setting the Date and Time

Setting the date and time is very important for a system administrator. Why? Because if you find something inappropriate or possibly problematic in your log files (e.g., repeated unsuccessful login attempts from a specific location), you want to be able to accurately cross-reference your log files with the log files of your colleagues at the other location. That can happen only if the time on both hosts is pretty close to accurate.

To set the time with ntpdate:

◆ sudo /usr/sbin/ntpdate 192.168.96.3

Use ntpdate with the name of a time server (currently available servers are listed at www.ntp.org) to update your system clock to the current, accurate time (**Code Listing 16.7**). If you get an error message about the socket being in use, use ps –ef | grep ntp to find the ntp daemon that's running to keep your time synchronized. (If this happens, your time is probably OK and doesn't need to be set.) Or

◆ sudo date –s "Tues Jan 27 5:30:23
→ 2003"

If your system doesn't have ntpdate, you'll have to set the time manually. Use sudo, date, and all the rest of the needed information. (If you need to change, say, only the time, you can just provide the time, as in sudo date –s 5:45).

✔ Tip

■ It's much better to use ntpdate or have the nptd daemon run to keep your time up-to-date at all times. Using date manually is a poor second choice.

```
[jdoe@frazz jdoe]$ sudo /usr/sbin/ntpdate
→ 192.168.96.3
27 Jan 05:26:50 ntpdate[1470]: adjust time
→ server 192.168.96.3 offset -0.004140 sec
[jdoe@frazz jdoe]$ sudo date -s 5:30
Mon Jan 27 05:30:00 MST 2003
[jdoe@frazz jdoe]$ sudo date -s "Tues
→ Jan 28 5:30:21"
Tue Jan 28 05:30:21 MST 2003
[jdoe@frazz jdoe]$ sudo date -s "Tues
→ Jan 28 5:30:21 2004"
Password:
Wed Jan 28 05:30:21 MST 2004
[jdoe@frazz jdoe]$ sudo date -s "Mon Jan
→ 27 5:30:21 2003"
Mon Jan 27 05:30:21 MST 2003
[jdoe@frazz jdoe]$ date
Mon Jan 27 05:30:35 MST 2003
[jdoe@frazz jdoe]$ sudo /usr/sbin/
→ ntpdate 192.168.96.3
27 Jan 05:30:38 ntpdate[1616]: step time
server 192.168.96.3 offset -7.329083 sec
[jdoe@frazz jdoe]$ sudo /usr/sbin/
→ ntpdate 192.168.96.3
27 Jan 05:30:44 ntpdate[1622]: adjust time
server 192.168.96.3 offset 0.000479 sec
[jdoe@frazz jdoe]$
```

Code Listing 16.7 Setting the date (and making sure it stays up-to-date) is an important root user responsibility.

SENSATIONAL UNIX TRICKS

Throughout this book, we've given you Unix building blocks—individual Unix commands, scripting techniques, and other insights that you can use individually or combine with each other. In this chapter, we'll show you some clever things to do with Unix. You might consider this an "advanced" chapter, but most of the things we'll show you here are simply combinations of things you've already learned about in earlier chapters.

Chapter Contents

- Cleaning up HTML documents
- Searching and replacing throughout multiple documents
- Generating reports
- Using input to customize your environment
- Using ROT13 encoding
- Embedding ROT13 encoding in shell scripts
- Making backups
- Using advanced redirection

Cleaning up HTML Documents with tidy

If you ever have to develop HTML documents—when developing personal Web sites, completing a class project, or creating Web pages on the job—the tidy utility can be a handy resource for you. If you're creating HTML pages by hand, you'll likely make occasional errors. These errors probably won't cause significant problems with using the pages, but they might make the pages harder to read, harder to maintain, and harder to subject to the scrutiny of your peers. Not to worry; tidy can help!

tidy is not usually included with Linux or Unix distributions, but you can download (and install, using the instructions in Chapter 14) from http://tidy.sourceforge.net.

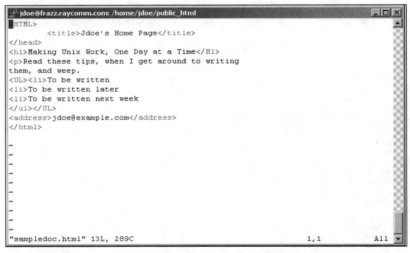

Figure 17.1 Even a flawed HTML document, like this one, can be fixed by tidy.

```
[jdoe@frazz public_html]$ tidy
→ sampledoc.html

Tidy (vers 4th August 2000) Parsing
→ "sampledoc.html" line 10 column 6 -
→ Warning: discarding unexpected </ul>

sampledoc.html: Document content looks
→ like HTML 2.0
1 warnings/errors were found!

<!DOCTYPE html PUBLIC "-//IETF//DTD
→ HTML 2.0//EN">
<html>
<head>
<meta name="generator" content="HTML
→ Tidy, see www.w3.org">
<title>Jdoe's Home Page</title>
</head>
<body>
<h1>Making Unix Work, One Day at a
→ Time</h1>

<p>Read these tips, when I get around to
→ writing them, and weep.</p>

<ul>
<li>To be written</li>

<li>To be written later</li>

<li>To be written next week</li>
</ul>

<address>jdoe@example.com</address>
</body>
</html>

HTML & CSS specifications are available
→ from http://www.w3.org/
To learn more about Tidy see
→ http://www.w3.org/People/Raggett/tidy/
Please send bug reports to Dave Raggett
→ care of <html-tidy@w3.org>
Lobby your company to join W3C, see
→ http://www.w3.org/Consortium
[jdoe@frazz public_html]$
```

Code Listing 17.1 The tidy command is handy for cleaning up HTML documents.

To clean up HTML documents with tidy:

1. vi sampledoc.html

   Use the editor of your choice to create an HTML document. Our sample document is called, well, sampledoc.html (**Figure 17.1**). Don't worry about getting the tagging or syntax exactly right; tidy will take care of the details. Save and close your document.

2. tidy sampledoc.html

   The tidy utility will apply HTML formatting rules and then output a massaged version of your document that is technically correct (**Code Listing 17.1**). Cool, huh?

3. tidy sampledoc.html > fixedupdoc.html

   If you like the results, redirect the document to a new filename, as shown here, or use tidy -m sampledoc.html to replace the original document.

   continues on next page

✔ Tips

- For even spiffier results, we like using tidy -indent -quiet --doctype loose -modify sampledoc.html, which suppresses the informative messages from tidy, makes the output an HTML 4 document, tidily indents the output, and replaces the original with the modified file (**Code Listing 17.2**). All that, and only one command.

- Consider using tidy with the sed script (described in the next section) to do a lot of cleanup at once.

CLEANING UP HTML DOCUMENTS WITH tidy

```
[jdoe@frazz public_html]$ tidy -indent
→ -quiet --doctype loose  sampledoc.html
line 10 column 6 -- Warning: discarding
→ unexpected </ul>
<!DOCTYPE html PUBLIC "-//W3C//DTD HTML
→ 4.01 Transitional//EN">
<html>
  <head>
    <meta name="generator" content="HTML
    → Tidy, see www.w3.org">
    <title>
      Jdoe's Home Page
    </title>
  </head>
  <body>
    <h1>
      Making Unix Work, One Day at a Time
    </h1>
    <p>
      Read these tips, when I get around
      → to writing them, and weep.
    </p>
    <ul>
      <li>
        To be written
      </li>
      <li>
        To be written later
      </li>
      <li>
        To be written next week
      </li>
    </ul>
    <address>
      jdoe@example.com
    </address>
  </body>
</html>


HTML & CSS specifications are available
→ from http://www.w3.org/
To learn more about Tidy see
→ http://www.w3.org/People/Raggett/tidy/
Please send bug reports to Dave Raggett
→ care of <html-tidy@w3.org>
Lobby your company to join W3C, see
→ http://www.w3.org/Consortium
[jdoe@frazz public_html]$
```

Code Listing 17.2 The tidy command, with the appropriate flags, performs miracles—almost.

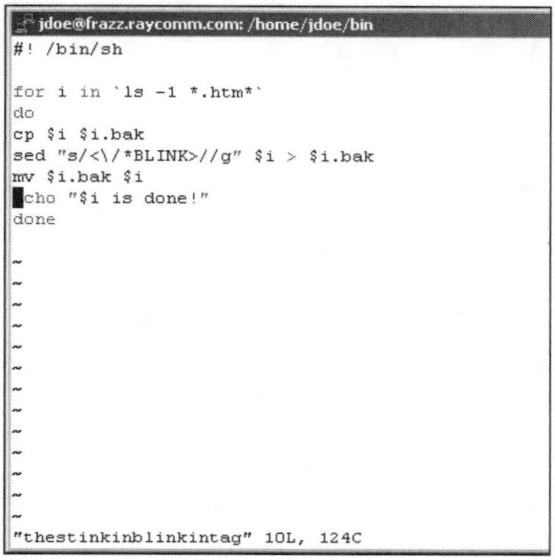

```
jdoe@frazz.raycomm.com: /home/jdoe/bin
#! /bin/sh

for i in `ls -1 *.htm*`
do
cp $i $i.bak
sed "s/<\/*BLINK>//g" $i > $i.bak
mv $i.bak $i
echo "$i is done!"
done
~
~
~
~
~
~
~
~
~
~
~
"thestinkinblinkintag" 10L, 124C
```

Figure 17.2 Create a script to search and replace in multiple documents.

Searching and Replacing Throughout Multiple Documents with sed

Back in Chapter 6, we talked about sed and how to use it to search and replace throughout files, one file at a time. Although we're sure you're still coming down off of the power rush from doing that, we'll now show you how to combine sed with shell scripts and loops. In doing this, you can take your search-and-replace criteria and apply them to multiple documents. For example, you can search through all of the .html documents in a directory and make the same change to all of them. In this example (**Figure 17.2**), we strip out all of the <BLINK> tags, which are offensive to some HTML purists.

Before you get started, you might have a look at Chapter 6 for a review of sed basics and Chapter 10 for a review of scripts and loops.

To search and replace throughout multiple documents:

1. `vi thestinkinblinkintag`

   Use the editor of your choice to create a new script. Name the file whatever you want.

2. `#! /bin/sh`

   Start the shell script with the name of the program that should run the script.

3. ``for i in `ls -1 *.htm*` ``

   Start a loop. In this case, the loop will process all of the .htm or .html documents in the current directory.

4. `do`

   Indicate the beginning of the loop content.

   continues on next page

SEARCHING AND REPLACING MULTIPLE DOCUMENTS

347

5. `cp $i $i.bak`

Make a backup copy of each file before you change it. Remember, Murphy is watching you.

6. `sed "s/<\/*BLINK>//g" $i > $i.new`

Specify your search criteria and replacement text. A lot is happening in this line, but don't panic. From the left, this command contains `sed` followed by

- ▲ **"**,which starts the command.
- ▲ **s/**, which tells `sed` to search for something.
- ▲ **<**, which is the first character to be searched for.
- ▲ **\ /**, which allows you to search for the /. (The \ escapes the / so the / can be used in the search.)
- ▲ *****, which specifies zero or more of the previous characters (/), which takes care of both the opening and closing tags (with and without a / at the beginning).
- ▲ **BLINK>**, which indicates the rest of the text to search for. Note that this searches only for capital letters. You'll want to add a line if your HTML document might use lowercase tags.
- ▲ **//**, which ends the search section and the replace section (there's nothing in the replace section because the tag will be replaced with nothing).
- ▲ **g**, which tells `sed` to make the change in all occurrences (globally), not just in the first occurrence on each line.
- ▲ **"**, which closes the command.
- ▲ **$i** is replaced with each filename in turn as the loop runs.
- ▲ **> $i.new** indicates that the output is redirected to a new filename.

  (See **Code Listing 17.3**.)

```
[ejr@hobbes scripting]$ more
→ >thestinkinblinkintag
#! /bin/sh

for i in `ls -1 *.htm*`
do
cp $i $i.bak
sed "s/<\/*BLINK>//g" $i > $i.new
mv $i.new $i
echo "$i is done!"
done

[ejr@hobbes scripting]$ chmod u+x
→ thestinkinblinkintag
[ejr@hobbes scripting]$
→ ./thestinkinblinkintag
above.htm is done!
file1.htm is done!
file2.htm is done!
html.htm is done!
temp.htm is done!
[ejr@hobbes scripting]$
```

Code Listing 17.3 You can even use sed to strip out bad HTML tags, as shown here.

7. mv $i.new $i

Move the new file back over the old file.

8. echo "$i is done."

Optionally, print a status message onscreen, which can be reassuring if there are a lot of files to process.

9. done

Indicate the end of the loop.

10. Save and close out of your script.

11. Try it out.

Remember to make your script executable with chmod u+x and the filename, and then run it with ./thestinkingblinkintag. In our example, we'll see the "success reports" for each of the HTML documents processed (Code Listing 17.3).

✔ Tip

■ You could perform any number of other operations on the files within the loop, if you wanted. For example, you could strip out other codes, use tidy as shown in the previous section, replace a former Webmaster's address with your own, or automatically insert comments and last-update dates.

SEARCHING AND REPLACING MULTIPLE DOCUMENTS

Generating Reports with awk

Back in Chapter 6, we showed you how to edit delimited files with awk, which is cool because it lets you extract specific pieces of information, such as names and phone numbers, from delimited files. As shown in **Code Listing 17.4**, you can also use awk to generate reports. We start with the information from an ls -la command, and then use awk to generate a report about who owns what.

To generate reports with awk:

◆ ls -la | awk '{print $9 " owned by "
→ $3 } END { print NR " Total
→ Files" }'

Whew! In general, pipe ls -la to the long-winded awk command. (Yes, this is the origin of awkward.) awk then prints the ninth field ($9), the words "owned by," then the third field ($3), and at the end of the output, the total number of records processed (print NR " Total Files"). Code Listing 17.4 shows the printed report.

✔ Tip

■ Remember that you could embed awk scripts in a shell script, as with the previous sed example, if it's something you'll use frequently.

```
[ejr@hobbes /home]$ ls -la | awk '{print
→ $9 " owned by " $3 } END { print NR "
→ Total Files" }'
 owned by
. owned by root
.. owned by root
admin owned by admin
anyone owned by anyone
asr owned by asr
awr owned by awr
bash owned by bash
csh owned by csh
deb owned by deb
debray owned by debray
ejr owned by ejr
ejray owned by ejray
ftp owned by root
httpd owned by httpd
lost+found owned by root
merrilee owned by merrilee
oldstuff owned by 1000
pcguest owned by pcguest
raycomm owned by pcguest
samba owned by root
shared owned by root
22 Total Files
[ejr@hobbes /home]$
```

Code Listing 17.4 Use awk to generate quick reports.

GENERATING REPORTS WITH AWK

```
[ejr@hobbes ejr]$ su - ejr
Password:
Which editor do you want as the default?
(vi or pico)?
vi
You chose vi!
[ejr@hobbes ejr]$
```

Code Listing 17.5 When the system asks your preferences, you know you're on top.

Using Input to Customize Your Environment

Way back in Chapter 8, we talked about setting up your environment variables by customizing the configuration files that run upon log in. You can further customize your environment variables by requiring input whenever a startup script runs. For example, you can set your configuration files (which are actually scripts) so that they request that you specify the default editor for the session (**Code Listing 17.5**).

To use input to customize your environment:

1. vi .bash_profile

   Use your favorite editor to edit your script, and move to the end of the file.

2. echo -e "Which editor do you want as
   → the default? (vi or pico)"

   Using echo -e, specify the text that will prompt you to input information (**Figure 17.3**).

   continues on next page

```
 Telnet - hobbes.raycomm.com                      _ □ ×
 Connect  Edit  Terminal  Help
fi

# User specific environment and startup programs

PATH=$PATH:/usr/local/games
PATH=$PATH:$HOME/bin
ENV=$HOME/.bashrc
USERNAME=""

export USERNAME ENV PATH

# Set default editor

echo -e "Which editor do you want as the default? (vi or pico)"
read choice
if [ $choice = "vi" ]
then EDITOR=/usr/bin/vi ; export EDITOR ; echo "You chose vi!"
elif [ $choice = "pico" ]
   then EDITOR=/usr/bin/pico ; export EDITOR ; echo "You chose pico!"
else echo "Editor unchanged"
fi

~
".bash_profile" 27 lines, 568 characters written
```

Figure 17.3 Add this mini-script to your .zprofile, .bash_profile, or .profile configuration file, right at the end.

3. `read choice`

On the next line, add `read` followed by the name of the variable to read in. We chose `choice` because we're using this input to set the preferred `EDITOR` environment variable.

4. `if [ $choice = "vi" ]`

Start an `if` statement—in this case, one that tests for the `vi` option.

5. `then EDITOR=/usr/bin/vi ; export`
`→ EDITOR ; echo "You chose vi!"`

Here, the `then` clause sets the `EDITOR` environment variable to `vi`, exports the environment variable, and announces your choice.

6. `elif [ $choice = "pico" ]`

Check for your other option with `elif` (else if). This statement covers the `pico` option.

7. `then EDITOR=/usr/bin/pico ; export`
`→ EDITOR ; echo "You chose pico!"`

This `then` clause sets the `EDITOR` environment variable to `pico`, exports the environment variable, and announces your choice.

8. `else echo "Editor unchanged"`

Set up an `else` statement, which will be used if neither option was entered at the `read` prompt. In this example, if neither `vi` nor `pico` was entered, it'll just say that the editor was unchanged.

9. `fi`

End the `if` statement.

10. Save and exit.

11. `su - yourid`

At the shell prompt, type `su -` followed by your userid to log in again and test the revised login script (Code Listing 17.5).

✔ Tip

- This technique is very useful for setting the `TERM`(inal) environment variable if you access the system from different remote locations with different capabilities.

Using ROT13 Encoding with sed

In Usenet newsgroups (among other places), text is often encoded with something called ROT13, which is an abbreviation for "rotate (the alphabet by) 13." That is, A becomes N, B becomes O, and so forth. If text is encoded, people have to take extra steps to decode the message. For example, if a message includes an offensive joke, people who don't want to see the joke won't have to. Similarly, if the message is a movie review, people who don't want to know the ending won't have the surprise spoiled. Instead, the message encoded with ROT13 might look like this:

Tbbq sbe lbh--lbh svtherq vg bhg! Naq ab,

gurer'f ab chapuyvar. Ubcr lbh rawblrq

gur obbx! Qrobenu naq Revp

A great way to use ROT13 encoding (and decoding) is with sed, which will let you easily manipulate text.

To use ROT13 encoding with sed:

1. `vi script.sed`

   Use the editor of your choice to create a file called `script.sed`. Because the command we're using will be reused, we'll use a sed script instead of just typing in everything at the shell prompt.

2. `y/abcdefghijklmnopqrstuvwxyzABCDEFGH`
   `→ IJKLMNOPQRSTUVWXYZ/`

   Start with a y at the beginning of the command. y is the sed command to translate characters (capital to lowercase or whatever you specify).

   After y, type a slash (/), the original characters to look for (all lowercase and uppercase characters), and another slash.

continues on next page

USING ROT13 ENCODING WITH sed

3. y/abcdefghijklmnopqrstuvwxyzABCDEFGH

→ IJKLMNOPQRSTUVWXYZ/nopqrstuvwxyz

→ abcdefghijklmNOPQRSTUVWXYZABCDEFG

→ HIJKLM/

After the second slash, add the translation characters (the lowercase alphabet, starting with n and continuing around to m, then uppercase from N to M), followed by a slash to conclude the replace string.

4. Save the script and exit the editor.

5. `sed -f script.sed limerick | more`

Test the ROT13 encoding by applying it to a file. Here we apply it to the limerick file, and then pipe the output to more for your inspection. You'll see that all you get is gibberish. To test it more thoroughly, use `sed -f script.sed limerick | sed -f script.sed | more` to run it through the processor twice. You should end up with normal text at the end of this pipeline (**Code Listing 17.6**).

✔ Tips

- Text is rotated by 13 simply because there are 26 letters in the alphabet, so you can use the same program to encode or decode. If you rotate by a different number, you'll need to have separate programs to encode and decode.

- Check out the next section to see how to make this lengthy process into a shell script and make it even easier to reuse over and over.

```
[ejr@hobbes creative]$ sed -f script.sed
→ limerick
Bhe snibevgr yvzrevpx
1.
Gurer bapr jnf n zna sebz Anaghpxrg,
Jub pneevrq uvf yhapu va n ohpxrg,
Fnvq ur jvgu n fvtu,
Nf ur ngr n jubyr cvr,
Vs V whfg unq n qbahg V'q qhax vg.
[ejr@hobbes creative]$ sed -f script.sed
→ limerick | sed -f script.sed
Our favorite limerick
1.
There once was a man from Nantucket,
Who carried his lunch in a bucket,
Said he with a sigh,
As he ate a whole pie,
If I just had a donut I'd dunk it.
[ejr@hobbes creative]$
```

Code Listing 17.6 A spiffy sed command can ROT13 encode and decode messages.

Embedding ROT13 Encoding in a Shell Script

If you completed the steps in the previous section, you might have noticed that you did a lot of typing. And, goodness, if you made it through steps 3 and 5, your fingers are probably on strike right about now. If you plan to encode or decode with ROT13 frequently, consider embedding the **sed** commands in a shell script to avoid retyping them each time you encode or decode text, as shown in **Figure 17.4**. You might refer back to Chapter 10 for details on shell scripts before you get started here.

To create a ROT13 shell script:

1. `vi rot13`

   Start a new shell script to process your commands.

2. `#! /bin/sh`

   Add the obligatory shell specification, as shown in Figure 17.4.

continues on next page

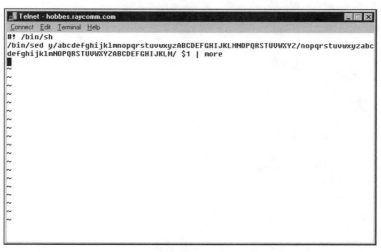

Figure 17.4 A brief shell script makes ROT13 as easy as, well, EBG13.

3. `/bin/sed y/abcdefghijklmnopqrstuvwxy`
→ `zABCDEFGHIJKLMNOPQRSTUVWXYZ/nopqr`
→ `stuvwxyzabcdefghijklmNOPQRSTUVWXY`
→ `ZABCDEFGHIJKLM/`

Specify the sed program (using the full path to make the program a little more flexible) and the command that encodes and decodes ROT13 text. It's better to make the shell script self-contained, so instead of referencing an external file with the sed script, we'll just put it in the command line here.

4. `/bin/sed y/abcdefghijklmnopqrstuvwxy`
→ `zABCDEFGHIJKLMNOPQRSTUVWXYZ/nopqr`
→ `stuvwxyzabcdefghijklmNOPQRSTUVWXY`
→ `ZABCDEFGHIJKLM/ "$1"`

Here, we added $1 to pass the filename from the command line (as in rot13 thisfile) to sed.

5. `/bin/sed y/abcdefghijklmnopqrstuvwxy`
→ `zABCDEFGHIJKLMNOPQRSTUVWXYZ/nopqr`
→ `stuvwxyzabcdefghijklmNOPQRSTUVWXY`
→ `ZABCDEFGHIJKLM/ "$1" | more`

Next, pipe the output to more so you see the file one screen at a time.

6. Save and exit out of the file.

7. `chmod u+x rot13`

Make the shell script executable, so you can just enter the name rot13 rather than sh rot13.

8. `./rot13 limerick`

Test the script. Because we developed this script in a directory that's not in the path, we have to execute the script with ./rot13. If you develop the script in a directory in your path, you should just be able to type rot13.

✔ Tip

- You can also build in an option to redirect the output of the script to a file and save it for later. Basically, all you do is create an if-then statement and give yourself the option of automatically redirecting the output to a filename, as **Code Listing 17.7** shows. Check out Chapter 10 for more information about scripts and if-then statements.

EMBEDDING ROT13 ENCODING IN A SHELL SCRIPT

```
[ejr@hobbes creative]$ more rot13
#! /bin/sh

#    If the first item (after the script name) on the command
#    line is save or s, and the second item is a readable file
#    then do the first case.
if [ \( "$1" = "save" -o "$1" = "s" \) -a \( -r "$2" \)  ]
then

#    This case saves the ROT13 output under the same filename with
#    a rot13 extension.
/bin/sed
y/abcdefghijklmnopqrstuvwxyzABCDEFGHIJKLMNOPQRSTUVWXYZ/nopqrstuvwxyzabcdefghijklmNOPQRST
→ UVWXYZABCDEFGHIJKLM/ "$2" > "$2.rot13"
else

#    This case pipes the ROT13 output to more, because a save
#    wasn't specified.
/bin/sed
y/abcdefghijklmnopqrstuvwxyzABCDEFGHIJKLMNOPQRSTUVWXYZ/nopqrstuvwxyzabcdefghijklmNOPQRST
→ UVWXYZABCDEFGHIJKLM/ "$1" | more

fi

[ejr@hobbes creative]$
```

Code Listing 17.7 If you want to get really fancy with the script, you can bring together some of the handiest bits of other chapters to make a masterpiece.

Making Backups
with rsync

The rsync utility is a fancy way to synchronize files and directories, either locally or across a network. We like to use it to make backups so we don't have to worry when we mess something up. Yes, we could use cp or something equally boring, but we like the speed and flexibility of rsync. In this example, we're copying files locally, but we could as easily be making remote backups to another server somewhere else.

To make backups with rsync:

1. mkdir ~/.BACKUPDIR

   Create a directory to house your backups. Ideally, you'll create the directory on a different physical disk from the stuff you're backing up, but do what you can. We're creating a backup directory that's a subdirectory of the home directory, which will help protect us against self-inflicted damages but not against a disk failure. (We trust the system administrator for protecting against disk failures...er, Eric, you are up-to-date on our backups, aren't you?!)

2. rsync –v –a /home/jdoe/data ~/
   → .BACKUPDIR

   Specify the rsync command, the –v (for verbose) and –a (for archive) options, and the source and destination directories (**Code Listing 17.8**).

   Wait while it does the initial backup (showing you each file as it gets copied). The first backup takes awhile but no longer than using cp would.

```
[jdoe@frazz bin]$ rsync -v -a
→ /home/jdoe/data ~/.BACKUPDIR
building file list ... done
data/
data/#*scratch*#
data/#all.programs#
data/#local.programs.txt#
data/*scratch*
data/1
data/2
data/Mail/
data/News/
data/Project/
data/Project/keep
data/Project/keeper.jpg
data/Project/kept
data/Project/kidder.txt
data/Project/kiddo
data/Project/kidnews
data/Project/kidneypie
data/Project/kids
data/Project/kidupdate
data/address.book
data/address.book~
data/all.programs
data/b
data/backup-files/
data/backup-files/.Xauthority
data/backup-files/.bash_history
data/backup-files/.bash_logout
data/backup-files/.bash_profile
data/backup-files/.bashrc
data/backup-files/.mailcap
data/backup-files/.screenrc
data/backup-files/.ssh/

 ...
wrote 24841142 bytes  read 14708 bytes
→ 741965.67 bytes/sec
total size is 24779055  speedup is 1.00
[jdoe@frazz bin]$
[jdoe@frazz jdoe]$ rsync -v -a
→ /home/jdoe/data ~/.BACKUPDIR
building file list ... done
data/newer.programs.txt
wrote 30149 bytes  read 36 bytes
→ 20123.33 bytes/sec
total size is 24765461  speedup is 820.46
[jdoe@frazz jdoe]$
```

Code Listing 17.8 The rsync utility is a handy tool for making backups. Note that it takes much less time for all updates after the first one.

MAKING BACKUPS WITH rsync

✔ Tips

■ If rsync isn't available on your system, revisit Chapter 14 to learn how to install it.

■ When you subsequently run rsync, you'll discover that it's far faster because it copies only the files that have changed. Handy, huh?

■ You can gain benefits from rsync if you start making backups across a network. For example, you can synchronize your Web server content with your friend's content located on a different server. Check the rsync man page (man rsync) for the specifics.

MAKING BACKUPS WITH rsync

Using Advanced Redirection with stderr

Throughout this book, we've been redirecting input to output, piping the output of one command to the input of another, and generally getting fairly fancy. Can you believe that there's even more you can do with redirection?

Unix provides three channels (technically known as file descriptors) for communication between the user and the system:

- Standard input (stdin), which refers to providing information at the shell prompt or accepting information from a different program.

- Standard output (stdout), which refers to the output you see whirring by on your screen after you issue a command—for example, if you issue the command find / -name test.

- Standard error (stderr), which includes error messages you might see whir by on your screen after you issue a command. You might think of this channel as the "second" output channel.

Until now, you've been redirecting stdin and stdout with <, >, |, >>, and sometimes tee. Everything on stderr has just accompanied stdout. Adding separate redirection of stderr to your arsenal can make your Unix experience even more flexible.

To redirect `stderr` in zsh, bash, ksh, and similar shells:

1. `time -p ls`

   Use the `time` utility, covered in Chapter 9, and note that you get both the output of `ls` and the output of `time`. As it happens, the output of `time` is on the `stderr` channel, although you can't see that (the output all just shows up on the screen).

2. `time -p ls 2> time-results.txt`

   Where you'd usually put a > to redirect everything to a file, use 2> to redirect the second output channel to a file. Now you'll get the output of `ls` on `stdout` on your screen, and the output of `time`, sent to `stderr`, in `time-results.txt` (**Code Listing 17.9**).

continues on next page

USING ADVANCED REDIRECTION WITH stderr

```
[jdoe@sulley Project]$ ls
keep  keeper.jpg  kept  kidder.txt  kiddo  kidnews  kidneypie  kids  kidupdate
[jdoe@sulley Project]$ time -p ls
keep  keeper.jpg  kept  kidder.txt  kiddo  kidnews  kidneypie  kids  kidupdate
real 0.00
user 0.00
sys 0.01
[jdoe@sulley Project]$ time -p ls 2> time-results.txt
keep kept    kiddo  kidneypie  kidupdate
keeper.jpg   kidder.txt kidnews kids    time-results.txt
[jdoe@sulley Project]$ time -p ls 1> /dev/null
real 0.00
user 0.00
sys 0.00
[jdoe@sulley Project]$ time -p ls >/dev/null 2>&1
[jdoe@sulley Project]$
```

Code Listing 17.9 Redirecting standard output and standard error separately can be handy.

3. `time -p ls 1> /dev/null`

Or you can send the **stdout** to oblivion (/dev/null, which just throws it away) and get **stderr** on your screen.

4. `time -p ls >/dev/null 2>&1`

Or you can send the **stderr** to **stdout**, and **stdout** to oblivion. It's apparently pointless but useful in shell scripts if you care only to know whether something succeeded or failed.

✔ Tips

■ If you're using **zsh**, you'll need to specify the full path to **time** (/usr/bin/time). **time** is a special **zsh** built-in command, so it works a bit differently from the other shells.

■ Redirecting **stdout** and **stderr** separately in **csh** is more challenging, but you can accomplish the same thing with `time -p ls >& /dev/null`. This works in **csh**, **bash**, and **zsh**.

■ If you send both **stderr** and **stdout** to /dev/null, you can `echo $?` to find out whether your command succeeded. You'll get bonus points for being the first person who emails a valid original example of the value of this operation to *unixvqs@raycomm.com*.

UNIX
REFERENCE

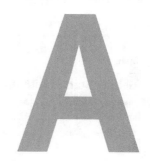

Table A.a

Summary of Appendix Tables

TABLE NUMBER	DESCRIPTION
Table A.1	Getting Started with Unix
Table A.2	Using Directories and Files
Table A.3	Working with Your Shell
Table A.4	Creating and Editing Files
Table A.5	Controlling File Ownership and Permissions
Table A.6	Manipulating Files
Table A.7	Getting Information About Your System
Table A.8	Configuring Your Unix Environment
Table A.9	Running Scripts and Programs
Table A.10	Writing Basic Scripts
Table A.11	Sending and Reading Email
Table A.12	Accessing the Internet
Table A.13	Working with Encoded and Compressed Files
Table A.14	Installing Software
Table A.15	Using Handy Utilities

In this appendix, you'll find a fairly thorough reference on Unix commands and flags as well as examples and descriptions of each. We organized this appendix to generally parallel the book, so that you can easily reference key commands and related flags without being overwhelmed with long lists of commands.

Table A.a summarizes what you'll find in this appendix.

Tables A.1–A.15 contain commands and flags that relate to the topics covered by the similarly numbered chapter (Chapters 16 and 17 do not introduce many new commands, so the commands from those chapters are included with similar commands in the other appendixes). In addition to the commands and flags discussed in the chapters, you'll also find related commands and options that you might find useful in your Unix adventures, reference information that will jog your memory, and ideas to help you get off and running on additional projects. If you're looking for a thorough command flag reference, check out Appendix C.

UNIX REFERENCE

Table A.1

Getting Started with Unix: Survival Skills

COMMAND	DESCRIPTION
apropos keyword	Find appropriate man pages for keyword.
cat *file*	Display file contents onscreen or provide *file* contents to standard output.
cat *file1 file2*	Display *file1* and *file2*.
cd	Return to your home directory from anywhere in the Unix system.
cd ..	Move up one level in the directory tree.
cd /etc	Change to the /etc directory relative to the system root.
cd ~/subdir	Use a tilde (~) as a handy shortcut for your home directory.
cd Projects	Move to the Projects directory relative to the current directory.
col -b	Filter backspaces and reverse line feeds out of input. Use to make man pages editable without odd formatting.
Ctrl D	Close your current process (often a shell) and your Unix session if you close the login shell.
exit	Close your current shell and your Unix session if you're in the login shell.
less *file*	Use to view *file* screen by screen.
logout	Close your Unix session.
ls	List files and directories.
ls /	List the files and directories in the root directory.
ls *directory*	List the files and directories in *directory*.
ls -a	List all files and directories, including hidden ones.
ls -c	List files and directories by modification date.
ls -l	List files and directories in long format, with extra information.
ls -lh	List files and directories in long format, with extra information and human readable sizes.
man 5 *command*	View the specified section (5) of the man pages for *command*. Sometimes used as man -s 5 *command*.
man *command*	View the manual (help) pages for *command*.
man -k *keyword*	Find appropriate man pages for *keyword*.
more *filetoview*	View *filetoview* screen by screen.
passwd	Change your password.
pwd	Display the path and name of the directory you are currently in.
reset	Reset the shell to fix display problems.
stty sane	Try to fix unexpected, sudden, and strange display problems.
su - *yourid*	Relog in without having to log out.
su	Become the root user.
sudo *command*	Run *command* with the authority of the root user.

Table A.2

Using Directories and Files

COMMAND	DESCRIPTION
cp *existingfile* *newfile*	Copy *existingfile* to a file named *newfile*.
cp -i *existingfile* oldfile	Copy *existingfile* to a file named *newfile*, prompting you before overwriting existing files.
cp -r /Projects /shared/Projects	Copy the directory /Projects to the new name /shared/Projects, specifying recursive copy.
find . -name lostfile -print	Find a file or directory in the current directory or subdirectories named lostfile.
find /home -name "pending*" -print	Find all files or directories with names starting with "pending" in the home directory or subdirectories.
find /home/shared -mtime -3 -print	Find all files or directories in the shared directory that were modified within the past three days.
find ~ -name '*.backup' -exec compress {} \;	Compress all files in the home directory with names containing ".backup," without confirmation.
find ~ -name '*.backup' -ok rm {} \;	Find and remove, with confirmation, all files in the home directory whose names end with ".backup".
ln /home/a /home/b	Hard link all of the files in the *a* directory to the files in the *b* directory.
ln *afile* *alink*	Link *afile* and *alink*, making the same file essentially exist in two different directories.
ln -s /home/deb/Projects /home/helper/Project	Create a soft link from /home/deb/Projects to /home/helper/Project.
locate *string*	Locate files with *string* in their names.
mkdir *Newdirectory*	Make a new directory named *Newdirectory*.
mv *existingfile* *newfile*	Rename *existingfile* to *newfile*.
mv -i *oldfile* *newfile*	Rename *oldfile* to *newfile*, requiring the system to prompt you before overwriting (destroying) existing files.
rm *badfile*	Remove *badfile*.
rm -i *	Delete interactively, with prompting before deletion. Good for files with problematic names that Unix thinks are command flags.
rm -i *badfile*	Remove *badfile* interactively.
rm -ir dan*	Interactively remove all the directories or files that start with "dan" in the current directory and all of the files and subdirectories in the subdirectories starting with "dan".
rmdir *Yourdirectory*	Remove the empty directory *Yourdirectory*.
touch *newfile*	Create a file named *newfile* with no content.
touch -t *200112312359 oldfile*	Update file date for *oldfile* to December 31, 23 hours, and 59 minutes in 2001.
which *command*	Find out the full path to *command*. This is valuable for seeing which of multiple commands with the same name would be executed.
whereis *file*	Find out the full path to *file* and related files.

UNIX REFERENCE

Table A.3

Working with Your Shell	
COMMAND	DESCRIPTION
!10	Rerun command 10 from the history list in csh or zsh.
bash	Start a bash subshell or run a bash script.
chsh	Change your shell.
csh	Start a csh (C) subshell or run a csh shell script.
echo $SHELL	Display the value of the $SHELL environment variable.
exit	Leave the current shell and return to the previous one, or log out of the login shell.
history	View a numbered list of previous commands.
ksh	Start a ksh (Korn) subshell or run a ksh shell script.
r 2	Repeat a specific command in ksh from the history output (in this case command 2).
set -o emacs	Enable command completion with emacs commands in the ksh shell.
set -o vi	Enable command completion with vi commands in the ksh shell.
sh	Start a sh (Bourne) subshell or run a sh shell script.
stty erase '^?'	Make ⟨Delete⟩ erase characters to the left of the cursor.
stty erase '^H'	Make ⟨Ctrl⟩⟨H⟩ erase characters to the left of the cursor. Type stty erase then press ⟨Ctrl⟩⟨V⟩ ⟨Ctrl⟩⟨H⟩.
su - *yourid*	Start a new login shell as *yourid*.
su user	Switch user to *user*.
tcsh	Start a tcsh subshell or run a tcsh shell script.
zsh	Start a zsh subshell or run a zsh shell script.

Table A.4

Creating and Editing Files	
COMMAND	DESCRIPTION
ed	Choose a line-oriented text editor.
emacs	Choose a tremendously powerful, somewhat easy to use text editor.
emacs -n	Open emacs and force a terminal-window- (not graphical window-) oriented session.
emacs *filename*	Open emacs and edit *filename*.
joe	Choose a fairly friendly editor.
pico	Choose for menu-oriented, user-friendly text editing.
pico *filename*	Open and edit *filename* in pico.
pico -w *filename*	Disable word wrapping for *filename* in pico. This is particularly useful for configuration files.
vi	Choose a powerful editor with lots of power but little ease of use.
vi *filename*	Open and edit *filename* in vi.

Table A.5

Controlling File Ownership and Permissions	
COMMAND	DESCRIPTION
chgrp	Change the group association of files or directories.
chgrp *groupname* *filename*	Change the group association of *filename* to *groupname*.
chgrp -R *group directory*	Recursively change the group association of *directory* and all subdirectories and files within it to *group*.
chmod	Change the permissions for a file or directory.
chmod *a-w* *file*	Remove write permission for *file* for all (everyone).
chmod *g+w* *file*	Add write permission for *file* for the owning group.
chmod -R *go-rwx* *	Revoke all permissions from everyone except the user for all files in the current directory and all subdirectories and their contents.
chmod *u=rwx,g=rx,o=r* *file*	Set the permissions on *file* to user read, write, and execute, group read and write, and others read.
chmod *ugo=* *	Revoke all permissions for everything in the current directory from everyone.
chown	Change the ownership of files or directories.
chown -R *user Directory*	Recursively change the ownership of *Directory* and all contents to *user*.
chown *user* *file*	Change the ownership of *file* to *user*.
umask *022*	Specify the default permissions for all created files.

Table A.6

Manipulating Files	
COMMAND	DESCRIPTION
awk	Manipulate a file as a database.
awk /CA/'{ print $2 $1 $7 }' file	Select (and display) three fields in each record in file on lines that contain "CA".
awk '{ print $1 }' file	Select (and display) the first field in each record in file.
awk -f script.awk file	Run an awk command from a script called script.awk on file.
awk -F, '{ print $1 }' file > newfile	Select the first field in each record in file, specifying that a "," separates fields, and redirect the output to newfile.
awk -F: '{ print $2 " " $1 " in " $7 }' file	Select (and display) several fields and some text for each record in file, using a colon (:) as a field delimiter.
basename	Remove the path from a filename, leaving only the name proper. Good to use in scripts to display just a filename.
cmp newfile oldfile	Compare newfile to oldfile.
crypt	Encrypt or decrypt a password-protected file.
csplit	Divide files based on line number or other characteristics.
diff -b newfile oldfile	Find differences (ignoring white space) between newfile and oldfile.
diff Directory Newdirectory	Find differences between Directory and Newdirectory.
diff -i newfile oldfile	Find differences (except in case) between newfile and oldfile.
diff -iBw file1 file2	Find all differences between file1 and file2 except those involving blank lines, spaces, tabs, or lowercase/uppercase letters.
diff newfile oldfile	Find the differences between newfile and oldfile.
diff -w newfile oldfile	Find differences (ignoring spaces) between newfile and oldfile.
fmt file	Reformat file so it has even lines and a nicer appearance.
fold -w 60 file	Reformat file so no lines exceed a specified length (60 characters here).
grep expression file	Find expression in file and view the lines containing expression.
grep -c expression file	Count how many times expression appears in file.
grep -i expression file	Find all lines containing expression in file, using any capitalization (case-insensitive).
grep -n expression file	Display each found line and a line number.
grep 'Nantucket$' limerick*	Find the lines in the limerick files that end with "Nantucket".
grep -v expression file	Find all lines in file that do not contain expression.
grep '^[A-Z,a-z]' limerick	Find all the lines in limerick that start with any letter, but not with a number or symbol.
grep '^[A-Z]' limerick	Find all the lines in limerick that start with a capital letter.
grep '^There' limerick*	Find all the lines in the limerick files that start with "There".
grep -5 'word[1234]' file	Find word1, word2, word3, or word4 in file and view the surrounding five lines as well as the lines containing the words.
head -20 file	View the first 20 lines of file.
head file	View the first 10 lines of file.
pr file	Reformat file for printing, complete with headers and footers.
pr --columns=2 file	Reformat file for printing, complete with headers and footers and two columns.

Table A.6

Manipulating Files *(continued)*	
COMMAND	DESCRIPTION
sdiff *newfile oldfile*	View the differences between *newfile* and *oldfile*.
sdiff -s *newfile oldfile*	View the differences between *newfile* and *oldfile*, without showing identical lines.
sed	Make changes throughout a file according to command-line input or a sed script.
sed '/old/new/g' *file.htm* > *file.htm*	Search through *file.htm* and replace every occurrence of "old" with "new".
sed -f script.sed *file* > *file.new*; → mv *file.new file*	Run the commands in script.sed, apply them to *file*, and replace *file* with the manipulated content.
split —b 500k *file*	Split *file* into 500 KB chunks.
sort *file* | uniq	Sort *file* and send it to *uniq* to eliminate duplicates.
sort *file* > *sortedfile*	Sort the lines in *file* alphabetically and present the sorted results in *sortedfile*.
sort *file1* | tee *sorted* | mail *boss@raycomm.com*	Sort *file1* and, with tee, send it both to the file *sorted* and to standard output, where it gets mailed to the boss.
sort *file1 file2* | uniq -d	Sort *file1* and *file2* together and find all the lines that are duplicated.
sort *file1 file2 file3* > *bigfile*	Sort and combine the contents of *file1*, *file2*, and *file3* and put the sorted output in *bigfile*.
sort -n *file*	Sort *file* numerically.
sort -t, +2 *file*	Sort on the third (really) field in the comma-delimited *file*.
sort -t, *file*	Sort fields in the comma-delimited *file*; the character following -t (,) indicates the delimiter.
spell *file*	Check the spelling of all words in *file*. Returns a list of possibly misspelled words.
tail -15 *file*	View the last 15 lines of *file*.
tail *file*	View the last 10 lines of *file*.
tidy *file.html*	Clean *file.html* to make it "good" HTML, and optionally also easier to read and maintain.
tr A-Za-z a-zA-Z < file	Change uppercase to lowercase and lowercase to uppercase.
uniq	Use with sorted files to eliminate duplicate lines.
wc -b *file*	Count the bytes in *file*.
wc *file*	Count the lines, words, and bytes in *file*.
wc -l *file*	Count the lines in *file*.
wc -w *file*	Count the words in *file*.

UNIX REFERENCE

Table A.7

Getting Information About the System	
COMMAND	DESCRIPTION
df	See what file systems are mounted where, and how much space is used and available.
df /usr/local/src	Find out where /usr/local/src is mounted and how much space is available on it.
df -k /home	View the file system for /home with the usage reported in 1 KB, not 512-byte, blocks.
df -h /home	View the file system for /home with the usage reported in human-readable terms.
du	Get information about disk usage in the current directory as well as in all subdirectories.
du /home	Get information about disk usage in the /home directory.
du -k	Get information about disk usage, measured in 1 KB blocks.
du -h	Get information about disk usage, displayed in human-readable terms.
file /usr/bin/pico	Find out the file type of /usr/bin/pico.
finger	See who else is logged into the system and get a little information about them.
finger @stc.org	Find out who is logged into the stc.org system.
finger ejr	Get information about user ejr on your system.
finger ejray@xmission.com	Get information about user ejray@xmission.com.
id	Find out the numeric value of your userid and what groups (by name and numeric userid value) you belong to.
id otheruser	Check someone else's status to find out what groups they're in.
quota	Find out if you're over quota.
quota -v	View your current quota settings and space usage.
uname	Use to find out what kind of Unix system you're using.
uname -a	Print all system information, including the Unix system type, host name, version, and hardware.
uname -sr	Find both the system type and release level.
watch	Monitor a file or other data for changes.
w	Get information about other users on the system and what they're doing.
who	Get information about the other users on the system.
whoami	Find out what userid you're currently logged in as.

UNIX REFERENCE

Table A.8

Configuring Your Unix Environment	
COMMAND	DESCRIPTION
alias ourterm="longhonking →· command -w -many –flags →· arguments"	Create the alias *ourterm* to substitute for the command longhonking command -w -many -flags arguments.
set	Find out what environment variables are set and their current values in zsh, bash, and ksh.
set *VARIABLE*="long value"	Use in csh to set the value of VARIABLE with spaces or special characters in it.
set *VARIABLE=value*	Use in csh to set VARIABLE to *value*.
setenv	Use in csh to find out what environment variables are set and their current values.
setenv *VARIABLE value*	Use in csh to make the VARIABLE available to other scripts in the current shell.
VARIABLE="long value"	Use in zsh, bash, and ksh to set the value of VARIABLE with spaces or special characters in it.
VARIABLE=value	Use in zsh, bash, and ksh to set the *VARIABLE* to *value*.
export *VARIABLE*	Use in zsh, bash, and ksh to make the value of VARIABLE available to other scripts.

Table A.9

Running Scripts and Programs	
COMMAND	DESCRIPTION
at 01:01 1 Jan 2004	Schedule a job or jobs to run at 01:01 on January 1, 2004.
at 01/01/04	Schedule a job to run on 1/1/04.
at 3:42am	Schedule a job to run at 3:42 a.m.
at noon tomorrow	Schedule a job to run at noon tomorrow.
at now + 3 weeks	Schedule a job to run in three weeks.
at teatime	Schedule a job to run at 4 p.m.
atq	Review jobs in the at queue.
atrm 3	Remove the specified queued job (3, in this case).
batch	Schedule jobs to run when system load permits.
bg	Run the most recently suspended or controlled job in the background.
bg %2	Run job 2 in the background.
crontab -e	Edit your crontab in the default editor to schedule regular processes or jobs.
Ctrl Z	Suspend a running job, program, or process.
fg	Run the most recently suspended or controlled job in the foreground.
fg 1	Run job 1 in the foreground.
jobs	See a list of the currently controlled jobs.
kill %ftp	Kill a job by name or job number.
kill 16217	Kill process number 16217.
kill -9 16217	Kill process 16217; the -9 flag lets you kill processes that a regular kill won't affect.
nice	Run a job "nicely"—slower and with less of an impact on the system and other users. Bigger numbers are nicer, up to 19. 10 is the default.
nice -n 19 *slowscript*	Run *slowscript* nicely with a priority of 19.
pkill *badjob*	Kill the process called *badjob*.
ps	View the list of current processes that you're running.
ps -e	View all processes, including those from other users.
ps -f	View processes and their interrelationships (the forest view).
ps -x	View the processes that the system itself is running (also called daemons).
renice 19 *processid-of* → *-slowscript*	Run *slowscript* more nicely (change the niceness) with a priority of 19.
time *script*	Time how long it takes (in real time and system time) to run *script*.
top	Monitor system load and processes in real time.

Table A.10

Writing Basic Scripts

COMMAND	DESCRIPTION
break	Use in a shell script to skip the rest of the commands in the loop and restart at the beginning of the loop.
case ... in ... esac	Use in a shell script to perform separate actions for a variety of cases.
clear	Clear the screen.
continue	
echo	Display a statement or the value of an environment variable onscreen.
echo "Your shell is $SHELL"	Display "Your shell is" and the name of your shell onscreen.
echo -e "\tA Tab Stop"	Move one tab stop to the right and print "A Tab Stop" on the screen.
for ... do ... done	Use in a shell script with conditions and commands to specify a loop to occur repeatedly.
getopts	Use in a shell script to read flags from the command line.
if ... then ... else ... fi	Use in a script (with conditions and commands) to set a conditional process.
read variable	Use in a script to get input (the variable) from the terminal.
sh -x script	Execute *script* and require the script to display each command line as it is executed.
sleep 4h5m25s	Pause for 4 hours, 5 minutes, and 25 seconds here.
sleep 5s	Pause for 5 seconds.
test	Use in a script to check to see if a given statement is true.
test expression	See if *expression* is true or false—usually used with conditional statements.
while ... do ... done	Use in a shell script to perform a loop only while the condition is true.

UNIX REFERENCE

Table A.11

Sending and Reading Email	
COMMAND	DESCRIPTION
elm	Start the elm mail program and read, respond to, or send email.
elm unixvqs2@raycomm.com	Start a new elm mail message to unixvqs2@raycomm.com.
elm unixvqs2@raycomm.com,info@raycomm.com	Start a new elm mail message to unixvqs2@raycomm.com and info@raycomm.com.
mail	Start the mail program. (Use pine or mutt rather than mail if possible.)
mail unixvqs2@raycomm.com < file	Send file to unixvqs2@raycomm.com.
mail unixvqs2@raycomm.com -s "For you!" < file	Send file to unixvqs2@raycomm.com with the subject "For you!".
mail unixvqs2@raycomm.com	Start a simple mail message to unixvqs2@raycomm.com.
mail unixvqs2@raycomm.com,info@raycomm.com	Start a simple mail message to unixvqs2@raycomm.com and info@raycomm.com.
mutt	Start the mutt mail program and read, respond to, or send email.
mutt unixvqs2@raycomm.com	Start a new mutt mail message to unixvqs2@raycomm.com.
mutt unixvqs2@raycomm.com -a file.tgz	Start a new mutt mail message to unixvqs2@raycomm.com and attach file.tgz.
mutt unixvqs2@raycomm.com,info@raycomm.com	Start a new mutt mail message to unixvqs2@raycomm.com and info@raycomm.com.
pine	Start the pine mail program and read, respond to, or send email, or to read Usenet newsgroups.
pine unixvqs2@raycomm.com,info@raycomm.com	Start a pine mail message to unixvqs2@raycomm.com and info@raycomm.com.
pine user@raycomm.com	Start a pine mail message to user@raycomm.com.
procmail	Filter and sort mail according to a "recipe." Run from the .forward file or automatically by the system.
vacation	Initialize vacation and edit the message template.
vacation -I	Start vacation and tell it to respond to incoming messages.
vacation -j	Start vacation and automatically respond to all messages.

UNIX REFERENCE

Table A.12

Accessing the Internet	
COMMAND	DESCRIPTION
dig @nameserver.some.net www.raycomm.com	Look up the name *www.raycomm.com* from the name server *nameserver.some.net*.
dig -x 192.168.12.52	Look up the name corresponding to the IP number *192.168.12.52*.
ftp ftp.raycomm.com	Transfer files to or from *ftp.raycomm.com* using the FTP protocol.
irc wazoo irc.netcom.com	Connect to the irc server at *irc.netcom.com* and use the nickname *wazoo*.
links	Start the links Web browser.
links http://www.google.com/	Start the links Web browser at *http://www.google.com/*.
lynx -dump http://url.com > newname.txt	Get a spiffy plain text file named *newname.txt* out of an HTML document from *http://url.com*.
lynx	Start the lynx Web browser.
lynx http://www.yahoo.com/	Start the lynx Web browser on *http://www.yahoo.com/*.
mesg n	Refuse talk and write messages.
mesg y	Accept talk and write messages.
nn	Read Usenet news.
nslookup www.raycomm.com → nameserver.some.net	Look up the name *www.raycomm.com* from the name server *nameserver.some.net*.
nslookup www.raycomm.com	Look up the IP number for the host *www.raycomm.com*.
ping www.raycomm.com	Test the connection to the host *www.raycomm.com*.
rn	Read Usenet news.
ssh somewhere.com	Securely connect to and use a computer on the Internet named *somewhere.com*.
slrn	Read Usenet news.
talk deb	Talk interactively with the owner of the ID *deb*.
talk id@wherever.com	Talk interactively with a user *id* the system *wherever.com*.
telnet somewhere.com	Connect to and use a computer on the Internet named *somewhere.com*.
tin	Read Usenet news.
tin comp.unix.userfriendly	Read Usenet news from the *comp.unix.userfriendly* group.
tn3270 library.wherever.edu	Connect to a host computer named *library.wherever.edu* that uses an IBM-mainframe-type operating system, like many library card catalogs.
traceroute www.yahoo.com	Identify the computers and other devices between you and the host *www.yahoo.com*.
traceroute -n hostname	Check the path to *hostname* without resolving the intervening host names for faster results.
trn	Read Usenet news.
trn comp.unix.shell	Read Usenet news from the *comp.unix.shell* group.
wall	Send a write-type message to all users on the system.
wget http://www.example.com/	Download the file found at *http://www.example.com/*.
wget -r -l 2 http://www.example.com/	Download the files found at *http://www.example.com/* for two levels down in the Web structure.
write otherid	Send a message to the user *otherid* on the same system.

Table A.13

Working with Encoded and Compressed Files	
COMMAND	DESCRIPTION
compress -c file.tar > file.tar.Z	Compress *file.tar* under the same name with a .Z ending while retaining the original file.
compress file.tar	Compress *file.tar*. The named file will be replaced with a file of same name ending with .Z.
gunzip archive.tar.gz	Uncompress (un-gzip) *archive.tar.gz*. Including .gz on the end of the filename is optional.
gzip archive.tar	Gzip (compress) *archive.tar*. The zipped file will replace the unzipped version and will have a new .gz extension
gzip -c filetogzip > compressed.gz	Gzip *filetogzip* and keep a copy of the original, unzipped file.
gzip -d	Uncompress (un-gzip) a file. Including .gz on the end of the filename is optional.
tar -cf newfile.tar Directory	Create a new tar archive containing all of the files and directories in *Directory*.
tar -czf newfile.tgz Directory	Create a new gzipped tar archive containing all of the files and directories in *Directory*.
tar -v	Add the -v flag to tar for a verbose description of what is happening.
tar -xf archive.tar "*file*"	Extract the files with names containing "file" from the tar archive.
tar -xf archive.tar	Extract the contents of *archive.tar*.
tar -xzf archive.tgz	Uncompress and extract the contents of *archive.tgz*.
uncompress archive.tar.Z	Uncompress *archive.tar.Z*, resulting in a file of the same name but without the .Z ending.
uncompress -c archive.tar.Z > archive.tar	Uncompress *archive.tar.Z* and retain the original file.
unzip zipped	Unzip *zipped* without specifying the extension.
uudecode file.uue	Uudecode *file.uue*.
uuencode afile.jpg a.jpg > tosend.uue	Uuencode *afile.jpg* and *a.jpg* and save the encoded output as *tosent.uue*.
uuencode -m	Use uuencode with the -m flag to specify base64 encoding, if your version of uuencode supports it.
gzcat archive.gz	more	Uncompress (on the fly without deleting the original) *archive.gz* to read the contents.
zip zipped file	Create a new zip file named *zipped* from *file*.
yencode file	Create a new yencoded file from *file*.

UNIX REFERENCE

Table A.14

Installing Software

COMMAND	DESCRIPTION
make	Set up, link, and compile new programs.
make clean	Clear out the garbage from a messed-up installation before you try again.
make install	Complete installation of new programs.

Table A.15

Using Handy Utilities

COMMAND	DESCRIPTION
bc	Use a calculator to add, subtract, multiply, divide, and more.
bc *bcfile*	Do the calculations specified in *bcfile*, then more calculations from the command line.
expr	Evaluate mathematical or logical expressions.
cal	View the current month's calendar.
cal 12 1941	View the calendar for December 1941.
cal 1999	View the calendar for 1999.
cal -j	View the Julian calendar.
calendar	View reminders for the current date, read from the file ~/calendar.
fortune	Display a fortune, saying, quotation, or whatever happens to come up.
ispell *gudspeler*	Interactively spell-check the *gudspeler* file.
look	Look up a word in the system dictionary.
lp	Print a file.
rsync *file backupfile*	Remotely synchronize (copy) *file* to *backupfile*.
script	Record your actions in a file called *typescript* in the current directory.
script *covermybutt*	Record your actions in the file *covermybutt*.
units	Convert from one kind of unit to another.

WHAT'S WHAT AND WHAT'S WHERE

As you're using Unix, you'll undoubtedly encounter files that look important or directories that look interesting, but it's often hard to know what files belong to which programs, and even harder to figure out what some directories are for. Therefore, we're trying to help out a little with the information in this appendix.

Table B.1 lists important Unix files and directories.

Table B.2 lists the contents of common Unix directories. In practice, the contents of these directories (and their existence) vary greatly by system, but the configuration described here is fairly standard.

Table B.1

Key Files in Your Unix Environment	
FILE NAME	DESCRIPTION
~/.forward	Includes address(es) to forward mail to or redirects mail to a vacation program or to procmail.
~/.newsrc	Includes records of read, unread, and subscribed newsgroups for use by news readers.
~/.procmailrc	Includes configuration information for procmail.
~/.pinerc	Includes configuration information for pine.
~/.muttrc	Includes configuration information for mutt.
~/.signature	Contains your signature, which is appended to your messages by email programs and news readers.
/etc/bashrc	Systemwide bash resource file shared by all bash users.
/etc/csh.cshrc	Systemwide csh resource file.
/etc/group	System group records.
/etc/ksh.kshrc	Systemwide configuration files for ksh users.
/etc/passwd	System passwords and user records.
/etc/profile	Systemwide configuration file used by bash and ksh.
/etc/skel	Original configuration files placed into the home directory of new users.
~/.bash_profile	Primary personal configuration file for bash users.
~/.cshrc	Resource file for csh users.
~/.kshrc	Configuration file for ksh users.
~/.login	Configuration file for csh users in a login shell.
~/.profile	Primary configuration file for ksh users; used by bash if .bash_profile isn't available.
~/.zlogin	Configuration file for zsh users in a login shell.
~/.zshrc	Resource file for zsh users.
~/.zprofile	Configuration file for zsh users.
~/.zshenv	Environment file for zsh users.
~/mail	Mail directory customarily used by pine.
~/Mail	Mail directory customarily used by system mailer and mutt.
Makefile	Includes configuration information used by make to compile and install new software.
README	Includes important information, usually distributed with a new program or script, about installation or usage.

Table B.2

Common Unix Directories and Their Contents	
DIRECTORY	CONTENTS
/bin	Essential programs and commands for use by all users.
/boot	Files that the system boot loader uses.
/dev	Devices (CD-ROM, serial ports, etc.) and special files.
/etc	System configuration files and global settings.
/etc/skel	Template configuration files for individual users.
/etc/X11	Configuration files and information for the X Window System.
/home	Home directories for users.
/lib	Essential shared libraries and kernel modules.
/mnt	Mount point for temporarily mounted file systems.
/opt	Directory for add-on application software packages.
/proc	Location of kernel and process information (virtual file system).
/root	Home directory for the root user/system administrator.
/sbin	Essential programs and commands for system boot.
/tmp	Temporary files.
/usr/bin	Commands and programs that are less essential for basic Unix system functionality than those in /bin but were installed with the system.
/usr/include	Standard include files and header files for C programs.
/usr/lib	Libraries for programming and for installed packages.
/usr/local	Most files and data that were developed or customized on the system.
/usr/local/bin	Locally developed or installed programs.
/usr/local/man	Manual (help) pages for local programs.
/usr/local/src	Source code for locally developed or installed programs.
/usr/sbin	Additional nonessential standard system binaries.
/usr/share	Shared (system-independent) data files.
/usr/share/dict	Word lists.
/usr/share/man	Manual (help) pages for standard programs.
/usr/share/misc	Miscellaneous shared system-independent data.
/usr/src	Source code for standard programs.
/usr/X11R6	X Window System, Version 11 Release 6.
/usr/X386	X Window System, Version 11 Release 5, on x86 platforms.
/var	Changeable data, including system logs, temporary data from programs, and user mail storage.
/var/account	Accounting logs, if applicable.
/var/adm	Administrative log files and directories.
/var/cache	Application-specific cache data.
/var/cache/fonts	Locally generated fonts.
/var/cache/man	Formatted versions of manual pages.
/var/crash	Information stored from system crashes, if applicable.
/var/games	Variable game data.
/var/lock	Lock files created by various programs.
/var/log	Log files and directories.
/var/mail	User mailbox files.

continues on next page

WHAT'S WHAT AND WHAT'S WHERE

Table B.2

Common Unix Directories and Their Contents *(continued)*	
DIRECTORY	CONTENTS
/var/run	Run-time variable files.
/var/spool	General application spool data.
/var/spool/cron	Contains cron and at job schedules.
/var/spool/lpd	Line-printer daemon print queues.
/var/spool/mail	Contains incoming mail for users.
/var/state	Variable state information for the system.
/var/state/editorname	Editor backup files and state information.
/var/state/misc	Miscellaneous variable data.
/var/tmp	Temporary files that the system keeps through reboots.
/var/yp	Database files that the Network Information Service (NIS) uses.

COMMANDS AND FLAGS

This appendix provides a list of many (but certainly not all) Unix commands and programs as well as many of the related command-line flags.

In general, flags offer a thorough selection of options for programs that operate exclusively from command-line input, as well as an overview of the functionality for many other programs. Please keep in mind, however, that command flags only touch the surface of the capabilities of interactive programs (like pico, vi, links, or pine) or particularly complex programs that rely on special expressions (such as grep or tr) or that use multiple files or sources for information (such as procmail).

Table C.1 should provide you with a brief reminder and starting point for learning more about these Unix commands. While the flags we've included here work on our systems, they will likely vary somewhat on different systems, different Unix versions or with different shells. Check your local man pages for specifics.

Note that multiple equivalent commands or flags all appear on the same line, separated by commas. Additionally, multiple flags (unless contradictory) can be used with all commands. The [] brackets indicate that one of the options enclosed may be used.

A

Table C.1

Commands and Flags	
COMMAND/FLAG	DESCRIPTION
alias	Use to create command aliases.
at	Use to schedule, examine, or delete jobs for queued execution.
-V	Displays version information.
-q queue	Specifies queue to use (as a letter). Higher letters are nicer.
-m	Specifies mail notification to user when job has completed.
-f file	Reads job from file.
-l	Lists queues, just like atq.
-d	Deletes scheduled jobs, just like atrm.
atq	Use to show queues of scheduled jobs.
-q queue	Specifies queue to use (as a letter).
atrm	Use to remove a job from the queue.
-q queue	Specifies queue to use (as a letter).
awk	Use to manipulate files as databases.
-Ffieldseparator	Specifies field separator.
-v variable=value	Sets variable to value.
-f program -file	Specifies file or files containing awk program source.
--help	Prints help information.
--version	Prints version information.
--	Specifies end of option list.
bash	Use the efficient, user-friendly shell bash.
-c string	Reads commands from string.
-i	Makes the shell interactive, as opposed to noninteractive, as in a shell script.
-s	Specifies that additional options, beyond those given, should be read from standard input.
-, --	Indicates the end of options and stops further option processing.
--norc	Specifies not to read ~/.bashrc.
--noprofile	Specifies not to read systemwide or individual configuration files.
--rcfile file	Specifies alternative configuration file.
--version	Displays bash version number.
--login	Specifies to start bash as a login shell.
--posix	Specifies Posix compliance, which helps make anything more portable from system to system.
batch	Use to schedule jobs for low system loads.
bg	Use to move a job to the background.
cal	Use to display a calendar.
-j	Displays Julian dates with days numbered through the year from January 1.
-y	Displays the current year's calendar.
month year	Specifies month (1 to 12) and year (1 to 9999).
cat	Use to send text to standard output, usually the screen.
-b, --number-nonblank	Specifies to number all nonblank output lines.

Table C.1

Commands and Flags *(continued)*	
COMMAND/FLAG	DESCRIPTION
`-n, --number`	Specifies to number all output lines.
`-s, --squeeze-blank`	Specifies to replace adjacent blank lines with a single blank line.
`-v, --show-nonprinting`	Specifies to display control characters with "^" preceding them.
`-A, --show-all`	Specifies to show all control characters.
`-E, --show-ends`	Specifies to display a "$" at the end of each line.
`-T, --show-tabs`	Specifies to display tab characters as "^I".
`--help`	Displays a help message.
`--version`	Displays the version number.
`cd`	Use to change the working directory.
`chgrp`	Use to change the group ownership of files.
`-c, --changes`	Specifies to list files whose ownership actually changes.
`-f, --silent, --quiet`	Suppresses error messages for files that cannot be changed.
`-v, --verbose`	Specifies to describe changed ownership.
`-R, --recursive`	Specifies to recursively change ownership of directories and contents.
`--help`	Displays help message.
`--version`	Displays version information.
`chmod`	Use to change the access permissions of files.
`-c, --changes`	Specifies to list files whose permissions actually change.
`-f, --silent, --quiet`	Suppresses error messages.
`-v, --verbose`	Specifies to describe changed permissions.
`-R, --recursive`	Specifies to recursively change permissions of directories and contents.
`--help`	Displays help message.
`--version`	Displays version information.
`chown`	Use to change the user and group ownership of files.
`-c, --changes`	Specifies to list files whose ownership actually changes.
`-f, --silent, --quiet`	Suppresses error messages for files that cannot be changed.
`-v, --verbose`	Specifies to describe changed ownership.
`-R, --recursive`	Specifies to recursively change ownership of directories and contents.
`--help`	Displays help message.
`--version`	Displays version information.
`chsh`	Use to change your login shell.
`-s, --shell`	Specifies the new login shell.
`-l, --list-shells`	Displays the shells in `/etc/shells`.
`-u, --help`	Prints a help message.
`--version`	Prints version information.
`cmp`	Use to compare two files.
`-l`	Displays the byte number (which starting byte in the file) in decimal and the differing bytes in octal for each difference.

continues on next page

C

Table C.1

Commands and Flags *(continued)*	
COMMAND/FLAG	**DESCRIPTION**
-s	Displays nothing for differing files except exit status.
compress	Use to compress and expand archives.
-c	Specifies that compress/uncompress write to standard output (usually your screen) and leave files unchanged.
-r	Specifies to recursively process directories.
-V	Displays version information.
cp	Use to copy files or directories.
-a, --archive	Specifies to preserve file structure and attributes.
-b, --backup	Specifies to make backups of files before overwriting.
-d, --no-dereference	Specifies to copy symbolic links as symbolic links rather than the files that they point to.
-f, --force	Specifies to overwrite all existing destination files.
-i, --interactive	Requires prompting before overwriting.
-l, --link	Specifies to make hard links instead of copies of files.
-P, --parents	Completes destination filenames by appending the source filename to the target directory name.
-p, --preserve	Specifies to preserve the original file characteristics, including permissions and ownership.
-r	Specifies to copy directories recursively.
-s, --symbolic-link	Specifies to make symbolic links instead of copies of files.
-u, --update	Specifies not to overwrite newer files.
-v, --verbose	Displays filenames before copying.
-x, --one-file-system	Restricts action to a single file system.
-R, --recursive	Specifies to copy directories recursively.
--help	Prints a help message.
--version	Prints version information.
-S, --suffix *backup-suffix*	Specifies a suffix for backup files.
crontab	Use to maintain crontab files.
-l	Displays current crontab.
-r	Removes current crontab.
-e	Opens crontab in default editor.
df	Use to display information about free disk space.
-a, --all	Specifies that all file systems, including special ones (e.g. CDROM, MSDOS), should be processed.
-i, --inodes	Displays inode (disk element) usage information.
-k, --kilobytes	Displays sizes in 1 KB blocks instead of 512-byte blocks.
-h	Provides file sizes in human-readable format.
-P, --portability	Uses Posix standard output format.
-T, --print-type	Displays type of each file system.
-t, --type=*fstype*	Displays only named file system types.
-x, --exclude-type=*fstype*	Displays only non-named file system types.
--help	Prints help information.

COMMAND FLAGS

Table C.1

Commands and Flags *(continued)*	
COMMAND/FLAG	DESCRIPTION
--version	Prints version information.
diff	Use to display differences between text files.
-b	Specifies to ignore trailing blanks (spaces and tabs) and consider other blanks equivalent.
-i	Specifies case-insensitive comparisons.
-t	Specifies to expand tab characters to spaces in output.
-w	Specifies to ignore all blanks.
-c	Specifies a listing of differences with three lines of context.
-C *number*	Specifies a listing of differences with *number* lines of context.
-e	Specifies output of a script for the ed editor to re-create the second file from the first.
-f	Specifies output of a script to create the first file from the second. This does not work with ed.
-h	Specifies fast and not necessarily complete comparison.
-n	Specifies output of a script to create the first file from the second along with a total of changed lines for each command.
-D *string*	Outputs combined version of first and second files with C preprocessor controls to compile as the first or the second file.
-r	Specifies that diff should recursively process subdirectories common to both given directories
-s	Outputs names of identical (not different) files.
-S *name*	Begins comparison within a directory with the specified filename.
dig	Use to look up IP numbers or domain names.
-b *ip-address*	Specifies to set the source IP address of the query.
-f *filename*	Specifies to read lookup requests from a file (*filename*).
-p *portnumber*	Specifies a port number to use instead of the standard 53.
-t *type*	Specifies the query type.
-x	Specifies reverse lookups (addresses to names).
du	Use to display disk usage information.
-a, --all	Displays information for all files.
-b, --bytes	Displays sizes in bytes.
-c, --total	Displays totals for all arguments.
-k, --kilobytes	Displays sizes in kilobytes.
-h, --human-readable	Provides file sizes in human-readable format.
-l, --count-links	Displays sizes of all files, including linked files counted elsewhere.
-s, --summarize	Displays only totals for each argument.
-x, --one-file-system	Specifies not to process directories on other file systems.
-L, --dereference	Displays space used by linked file or directory, not just space used by link.
-S, --separate-dirs	Counts directories separately.
--help	Prints help information.
--version	Prints version information.
elm	Use to send and receive mail.
-a	Specifies arrow cursor.

echo p 213

continues on next page

COMMAND FLAGS

COMMAND FLAGS

Table C.1

Commands and Flags *(continued)*	
COMMAND/FLAG	DESCRIPTION
-c	Expands specified aliases and exits.
-d *level*	Specifies debugging output.
-f *folder*	Specifies folder to read instead of incoming mail folder.
-h, -?	Displays help message.
-i *file*	Read named file into message editor.
-m	Disables menu.
-s *subj*	Specifies subject for mail messages.
-v	Displays version information.
-z	Specifies not to start elm if no mail is present.
emacs	Use to edit files.
file	Specifies name of file to edit.
+*number*	Specifies to go to the specified line number.
-q	Specifies not to load an initialization file.
-u user	Specifies to load *users*'s initialization file.
-t file	Specifies to use *file* as the terminal.
expr	Use to evaluate expressions.
--help	Specifies to display help information.
--version	Specifies to display version information.
fg	Use to move a job to the foreground.
file	Use to determine file type.
-m *list*	Specifies alternative list of files with magic numbers (helping to indicate file type).
-z	Attempts to look into compressed files.
-b	Specifies brief output mode.
-c	Checks magic file.
-f *file*	Specifies to read names of the files to be examined from *file*.
-L	Specifies to follow symbolic links.
find	Use to find files in the Unix system.
-daystart	Specifies to measure all times starting today, not 24 hours ago.
-depth	Specifies to process directory contents before the directory.
-follow	Specifies to follow symbolic links.
-help, --help	Prints a help message.
-maxdepth *levels*	Specifies how many *levels* below starting directory level to descend.
-mindepth *levels*	Specifies how many *levels* below starting directory level to start processing.
-mount, -xdev	Specifies not to descend directories on other file systems.
-noleaf	Specifies not to optimize for Unix systems, which is needed for CD-ROM directories, for example.
--version	Prints version information.
-amin *n*	Finds files accessed *n* minutes ago.
-anewer *file*	Finds files accessed more recently than they were modified.
-atime *n*	Finds files accessed *n* days ago.
-cmin *n*	Finds files whose status was changed *n* minutes ago.

Table C.1

Commands and Flags *(continued)*	
COMMAND/FLAG	DESCRIPTION
-cnewer *file*	Finds files whose status was changed more recently than the *file* was modified.
-ctime *n*	Finds files whose status was changed *n* days ago.
-empty	Finds files that are empty.
-fstype *type*	Finds files on file systems of specified *type*.
-gid *n*	Finds files with numeric group ID of *n*.
-group *gname*	Finds files with group name of *gname* or corresponding group ID.
-ilname *pattern*	Finds files that are symbolic links with *pattern* text in the name, case-insensitive.
-iname *pattern*	Finds files with *pattern* in the name, case-insensitive.
-inum *n*	Finds files with inode number *n*.
-ipath *pattern*	Finds files with *pattern* in the path, case-insensitive.
-iregex *pattern*	Finds files with regular expression *pattern* in name, case-insensitive.
-links *n*	Finds files with *n* links.
-lname *pattern*	Finds files that are symbolic links with *pattern* in the name.
-mmin *n*	Finds files last modified *n* minutes ago.
-mtime *n*	Finds files last modified *n* days ago.
-name *pattern*	Finds files with name of *pattern*.
-newer *file*	Finds files modified more recently than *file*.
-nouser	Finds files with no user name corresponding to the numeric userid.
-nogroup	Finds files with no group name corresponding to the numeric group ID.
-path *pattern*	Finds files with paths matching *pattern*.
-regex *pattern*	Finds files with regular expression *pattern* in name, case-sensitive.
-size *n[bckw]*	Finds files using *n* blocks, bytes, kilobytes, or words, respectively, of space.
-type *type*	Finds files of type type, where b is block (buffered) special, c is character (unbuffered) special, d is directory, p is named pipe (FIFO), f is regular file, l is symbolic link, or s is socket.
-uid *n*	Finds files with numeric userid of *n*.
-used *n*	Finds files last accessed *n* days after status changed.
-user *uname*	Finds files owned by userid or numeric id user ID.
-exec *command* \;	Executes *command* for each found file.
-fprint *file*	Prints full filename into *file*.
-ok *command* \;	Executes *command* with confirmation for each found file.
-print	Prints results to standard output.
finger	Use to display information about users.
-s	Displays the login name, real name, terminal name and write status, idle time, login time, office location, and office phone number.
-l	Specifies multiple-line format with information from -s option plus user's home directory, home phone number, login shell, mail status, and the contents of the .plan, .project, and .forward files.
-p	Prevents -l from displaying contents of .plan and .project files.
-m	Disables matching user names.
fmt	Use to format files.
-c, --crown-margin	Specifies to preserve indent of first two lines.

continues on next page

COMMAND FLAGS

Table C.1

Commands and Flags *(continued)*	
COMMAND/FLAG	DESCRIPTION
-p, --prefix=chars	Specifies to combine lines with chars at the beginning.
-s, --split-only	Specifies to split long lines, but not to combine short ones.
-t, --tagged-paragraph	Specifies that the indent of the first line differs from the next.
-u, --uniform-spacing	Specifies to ensure one space between words, two after sentences.
-w, --width=n	Specifies a maximum line width (default of 75 chars).
--help	Specifies to display a usage message.
--version	Specifies to display version information.
ftp	Use to put files in or get files from FTP (File Transfer Protocol) archives.
-v	Specifies verbose output of responses and statistics.
-n	Restricts automatic log in.
-i	Turns off interactive prompting during multiple file transfers.
-d	Enables debugging output.
-g	Disables wildcards ("globbing").
grep	Use to display lines matching a given pattern.
-n	Displays matches with *n* lines before and after matching lines.
-A *n*, --after-context=*n*	Displays matches with *n* lines after matching lines.
-B *n*, --before-context=*n*	Displays matches with *n* lines before matching lines.
-C, --context	Displays matches with two lines of surrounding context.
--version	Displays version information.
-c, --count	Displays count of matches for each file.
-e pattern, → --regexp=*pattern*	Specifies pattern explicitly.
-f file, --file=file	Reads patterns from *file*.
-h, --no-filename	Specifies not to display filenames in output.
-i, --ignore-case	Searches without regard to case.
-L, --files-without-match	Prints name of first nonmatching file.
-l, --files-with-matches	Prints name of first matching file.
-n, --line-number	Displays output line numbers.
-q, --quiet	Suppresses output and stops scanning on first match.
-s, --no messages	Suppresses error messages.
-v, --invert-match	Inverts matching to select opposite files.
-w, --word-regexp	Finds only matches for whole words.
-x, --line-regexp	Finds only matches for the whole line.
gzip	Use to compress (gzip) or expand files.
-a –ascii	Specifies to convert ends of lines in ASCII text mode to conform to Unix conventions.
-c --stdout --to-stdout	Sends output to standard output while maintaining original files unchanged.
-d --decompress → –uncompress	Uncompresses files.
-f –force	Forces compression or decompression.
-h –help	Displays help message.
-l –list	Lists information about compressed files.

Table C.1

Commands and Flags *(continued)*	
COMMAND/FLAG	**DESCRIPTION**
--verbose	Displays additional information about archive files.
-L –license	Displays the gzip license.
-n --no-name	Specifies not to save the original filename and time.
-N –name	Specifies to always save the original filename and time-stamp information when compressing.
-q –quiet	Suppresses all warnings.
-r –recursive	Specifies to descend subdirectories.
-S *.suf* --suffix *.suf*	Specifies alternative suffixes.
-t –test	Tests compressed-file integrity.
-v –verbose	Displays name and percentage reductions for each file processed.
-V –version	Displays version information.
head	Use to output the first part of files.
-c, --bytes *n[b,k,m]*	Displays first *n* bytes of file, in b (512-byte blocks), k (1 KB blocks), or m (1 MB blocks).
-*n* N, --lines *n*	Displays first *n* lines of a file.
-q, --quiet, --silent	Specifies not to display filenames.
-v, --verbose	Displays filename.
--help	Displays help message.
--version	Displays version information.
id	Use to display real and effective userids and group IDs.
-g, --group	Displays only group ID.
-G, --groups	Displays only supplementary groups.
--help	Displays help message.
-n, --name	Displays user or group name, not number.
-r, --real	Displays real, not effective, userid or group ID.
-u, --user	Displays only userid.
--version	Displays version information.
jobs	Use to display list of jobs under control.
-l	Displays additional information (long listing) for jobs.
-p	Displays job process IDs.
-n	Displays jobs that have stopped or exited since notification. Only in ksh.
kill	Use to terminate a process.
-s	Specifies kill signal to send.
-l	Displays a list of signal names.
less	Use to page through files; similar to more.
-?, --help	Displays a command summary.
-*a*	Specifies to start searches below visible display.
-b*n*	Specifies number of buffers for each file.
-B	Specifies automatic buffer allocation.
-c	Specifies not to scroll, but rather to paint each screen from the top.
-C	Specifies not to scroll, but rather to clear and display new text.
-d	Suppresses error messages for dumb terminals.
-e	Specifies to automatically exit if you move down after hitting the end of the file.

continues on next page

COMMAND FLAGS

Table C.1

Commands and Flags *(continued)*	
COMMAND/FLAG	**DESCRIPTION**
-E	Specifies to automatically exit when you hit the end of the file.
-f	Forces all files to be opened.
-g	Specifies to highlight only last found string.
-G	Specifies no highlighting of found strings.
-h*n*	Specifies maximum number (*n*) of lines to scroll backward.
-i	Specifies case-insensitive searches except when search string contains capital letters.
-I	Specifies case-insensitive searches always.
-j*n*	Specifies a line on the screen where a target line should be located.
-k *filename*	Specifies to open and interpret *filename* as a lesskey file.
-m	Specifies verbose prompting, displaying percentage into the file viewed.
-M	Specifies even more verbose prompting.
-n	Suppresses line numbers.
-N	Specifies line number for each displayed line.
-o*filename*	Tells less to copy input to *filename* as it is viewed.
-O*filename*	Tells less to copy input to *filename* as it is viewed and overwrite without confirmation.
-p*pattern*	Specifies to start display at first occurrence of *pattern*.
-q	Specifies quiet operation and only rings bell on certain errors.
-Q	Specifies totally quiet operation and never rings bell.
-r	Specifies to display control characters directly, even if display problems result.
-s	Compresses consecutive blank lines into a single blank line.
-S	Specifies that long lines should be chopped off, not wrapped.
-u	Specifies that backspaces and carriage returns should be sent to the terminal.
-U	Specifies that backspaces, tabs, and carriage returns should be treated as control characters.
-V, --version	Displays the version number.
-w	Specifies that blank lines, not tilde (~) represent lines after the end of the file.
-x*n*	Sets tab stops every *n* columns.
-X	Disables termcap initialization strings.
-y*n*	Specifies maximum number of lines to scroll.
-*n*	Specifies the scrolling window size as *n*.
-"	Specifies filename quoting character.
--	Indicates end of options.
links	Use to browse the Web in character-only mode, but with tables and frames.
-g	Specifies to run in graphics mode, on an appropriate terminal.
-async-dns *n*	Specifies to look up domain names as needed (0) or preemptively (1).
-max-connections *n*	Specifies the maximum number of concurrent Web connections.
-max-connections-to-host *n*	Specifies the maximum number of concurrent connections to a specific host.
-retries *n*	Specifies the number of retries to retrieve a Web page.
-receive-timeout *n*	Specifies the length (in seconds) of the timeout when retrieving a Web page.
-unrestartable-receive → -timeout *n*	Specifies the timeout on nonrestartable connections.
-format-cache-size *n*	Specifies the number of Web pages to cache for quicker retrieval.

Table C.1

Commands and Flags *(continued)*	
COMMAND/FLAG	DESCRIPTION
`-memory-cache-size` *n*	Specifies the amount of cache memory in kilobytes.
`-http-proxy` *name:n*	Specifies the name and port number of the HTTP proxy, if needed.
`-ftp-proxy` *name:n*	Specifies the name and port number of the FTP proxy, if needed.
`-download-dir` *path*	Specifies the default download directory.
`-anonymous`	Specifies to restrict capabilities to run in an anonymous account.
`-no-connect`	Specifies to run links as a separate process instead of within an existing process.
`-version`	Specifies to display the version number.
`-help`	Specifies to print help information.
`ln`	Use to make links between files.
`-b, --backup`	Backs up files before removing them.
`-f, --force`	Overwrites destination files.
`-i, --interactive`	Prompts before overwriting files.
`-n, --no-dereference`	Attempts to replace symbolic links.
`-s, --symbolic`	Specifies to make symbolic links when possible.
`-v, --verbose`	Specifies to display filenames before linking.
`--help`	Prints a help message.
`--version`	Prints version information.
`-S, --suffix backup-suffix`	Specifies suffix for backup files.
`-V, --version-control` → *{numbered,existing,simple}*	Specifies version control as numbered, existing, or simple, as with `cp`.
`locate`	Use to find files with a specific string in their names or paths.
`-u`	Specifies to create `locate` database starting at the root directory.
`-U` *path*	Specifies to create `locate` database starting at *path*.
`-e` *dir,dir,...*	Specifies to exclude directories from the `locate` database.
`-f` *fstype*	Specifies to exclude files on named file system types from the database.
`-c`	Specifies to process `/etc/updatedb.conf` file when updating the database.
`-l` *n*	Specifies the security level as 0 (no checking, faster), or 1 (checking, slower).
`-i`	Specifies to do a case-insensitive search.
`-q`	Specifies to use quiet mode and suppress all error messages.
`-n` *n*	Specifies to limit the amount of results shown to *n*.
`-r` *regex*, `--regexp=`*regex*	Specifies to search the database using a regular expression.
`-o` *name*, `--output=`*name*	Specifies the database to create.
`-d` *path*, `--database=`*path*	Specifies the *path* of databases to search in.
`-h, --help`	Specifies to print help information.
`-v, --verbose`	Specifies to use verbose mode when creating database.
`-V,--version`	Specifies to display the version number.
`look`	Use to look up words in the system dictionary.
`-d`	Specifies to use dictionary (alphanumeric) character set and order.
`-f`	Specifies to use case-insensitive search.
`-a`	Specifies to use the alternate dictionary `/usr/share/dict/web2`.
`-t`	Specifies the end of the string to compare.

continues on next page

Table C.1

Commands and Flags *(continued)*	
COMMAND/FLAG	**DESCRIPTION**
lp	Use to print files.
-c	Specifies to copy file to spool directory before printing.
-d name	Specifies to print files to the printer *name*.
-i n	Specifies an existing job number *n* to modify.
-m	Specifies to send email when the job is completed.
-n copies	Specifies the number of copies to print.
-q priority	Specifies the job priority from 1 to 50 (highest).
-s	Specifies not to report the resulting job IDs.
-t name	Specifies the *name* for the job being submitted.
-H handling	Specifies immediate, hold, resume, or hh:mm to determine when the job will be printed.
-P page-list	Specifies which pages to print.
ls	Use to list directory contents.
-a, --all	Lists all files.
-b, --escape	Prints octal codes for nongraphic characters using backslash sequences.
-c, --time=ctime, → --time=status	Sorts according to status change time, not modification time.
-d, --directory	Lists directory names, not contents.
-f	Does not sort directory contents.
--full-time	Provides full, not abbreviated time listings.
-g	Displays filename, file permissions, number of hard links, group, size, and time.
-h	Provides file sizes in human-readable format.
-i, --inode	Displays index number of each file.
-k, --kilobytes	Displays file sizes in kilobytes.
-l, --format=long, → --format=verbose	Displays filename, file permissions, number of hard links, owner, group, size in bytes, and time.
-m, --format=commas	Displays names separated by commas.
-n, --numeric-uid-gid	Displays numeric userid and group ID.
-p, -F	Displays extra character for each filename to show the file type.
-q, --hide-control-chars	Displays question marks rather than nongraphic characters.
-r, --reverse	Sorts names in reverse order.
-s, --size	Displays file sizes in 1 KB blocks.
-t, --sort=time	Sorts directory contents by modification time, newest first.
-u, --time=atime, → --time=access, --time=use	Sorts names by last access time instead of the modification time.
-x, --format=across, → --format=horizontal	Displays names in columns, sorted horizontally.
-A, --almost-all	Lists all names except for "." and "..".
-B, --ignore-backups	Does not display names that end with "~".

L 2

Table C.1

Commands and Flags *(continued)*	
COMMAND/FLAG	DESCRIPTION
`-C, --format=vertical`	Displays names in columns, sorted vertically.
`-G, --no-group`	Does not display group information.
`-L, --dereference`	Lists names of symbolic links instead of the link contents.
`-N, --literal`	Does not quote names.
`-Q, --quote-name`	Quotes names in double quotes and nongraphic characters in C syntax.
`-R, --recursive`	Displays the contents of all directories recursively.
`-S, --sort=size`	Sorts names by file size, largest first.
`-U, --sort=none`	Does not sort names.
`-X, --sort=extension`	Sorts names alphabetically by file extension.
`-1, --format=single-column`	Lists one file per line.
`-w, --width` *n*	Sets display to *n* columns wide.
`-T, --tabsize` *n*	Sets tabs to *n* columns wide.
`-I, --ignore pattern`	Does not display names matching *pattern*.
`--color, --colour,` `↪ --color=yes, --colour=yes`	Displays the names in color depending on the type of file and terminal characteristics.
`--color=tty, --colour=tty`	Displays names in color only if standard output is a terminal.
`--color=no, --colour=no`	Disables color display of names.
`--help`	Displays help message.
`--version`	Displays version information.
`lynx`	Use to browse the Web.
`-`	Specifies to take arguments from standard input.
`-anonymous`	Specifes anonymous account.
`-assume_charset=MIMEname`	Specifies default character set.
`-assume_local_charset=` `↪ MIMEname`	Specifies character set for local files.
`-assume_unrec_charset=` `↪ MIMEname`	Specifies character set to use if remote character set is not recognizable.
`-auth=ID:PASSWD`	Specifies authorization ID and password for protected documents.
`-base`	Specifies HTML BASE tag to use when dumping source code.
`-blink`	Specifies high-intensity background colors for color mode if possible.
`-book`	Specifies bookmark page as initial file.
`-buried_news`	Specifies automatic conversion of embedded URLs to links in Netnews.
`-cache=`*n*	Specifies to cache *n* documents in memory.
`-case`	Specifies case-sensitive searching within pages.
`-cfg=`*file*	Specifies alternative `lynx` configuration file.
`-child`	Specifies no save to disk and quick exit with Ⓓ in first document.
`-color`	Specifies color mode, if possible.
`-cookies`	Toggles handling of cookies.
`-core`	Toggles core dumps on crashes.
`-crawl -traversal`	Specifies to output each browsed page to a file.
`-dump`	Specifies to dump formatted output of specified page to standard output.

continues on next page

COMMAND FLAGS

Table C.1

Commands and Flags *(continued)*	
COMMAND/FLAG	DESCRIPTION
-editor=*editor*	Enables editing with specified *editor*.
-emacskeys	Enables emacs-style key movement.
-enable_scrollback	Toggles scrollback when supported by communications programs.
-error_file=*FILE*	Specifies where to save error code.
-force_html	Specifies that the start document be considered HTML.
-force_secure	Toggles security flag for SSL cookies.
-from	Toggles use of From headers.
-ftp	Specifies no FTP access.
-get_data	Retrieves form data from standard input and dumps results.
-head	Requests MIME headers.
-help	Displays help message.
-hiddenlinks= → [*merge,listonly,ignore*]	Specifies handling of hidden links.
-historical	Toggles use of > or --> as comment terminator.
-homepage=*URL*	Sets home page URL for session.
-image_links	Toggles display of links for all images.
-index=*URL*	Sets the default index file to the specified URL.
-ismap	Toggles presentation of links for client-side image maps.
-link=*NUMBER*	Specifies starting number for files crawled.
-localhost	Specifies only browsing on local host.
-locexec	Enables local program execution from local files.
-mime_header	Displays MIME header with document source.
-minimal	Toggles minimal or valid comment parsing.
-newschunksize=*n*	Specifies *n* articles in chunked news listings.
-newsmaxchunk=*n*	Specifies maximum number of news articles before chunking.
-nobrowse	Disables directory browsing.
-nocc	Disables prompts for user copies of sent mail.
-nocolor	Disables color mode.
-noexec	Disables local program execution.
-nofilereferer	Disables Referrer headers for file URLs.
-nolist	Disables link listings in formatted text output (dumps).
-nolog	Disables mailing error messages to document owners.
-nopause	Disables pauses on status messages.
-noprint	Disables printing.
-noredir	Disables automatic redirection.
-noreferer	Disables Referrer headers for all URLs.
-nosocks	Disables SOCKS proxy use.
-nostatus	Disables retrieval status messages.
-number_links	Numbers links.
-pauth=*ID:PASSWD*	Sets ID and password for a protected proxy server.
-popup	Toggles handling of single-choice SELECT options as pop-up windows or as lists of radio buttons.

Table C.1

COMMAND/FLAG	DESCRIPTION
Commands and Flags *(continued)*	
-post_data	Sends form data from standard input with POST dump results.
-preparsed	Specifies that HTML source be preparsed and reformatted when viewed.
-print	Enables printing.
-pseudo_inlines	Toggles pseudo-ALT text for inline images with no ALT string.
-raw	Toggles default setting of 8-bit character translations or CJK mode for the initial character set.
-realm	Specifies access only to URLs in initial domain.
-reload	Specifies to empty proxy server cache and reload document.
-resubmit_posts	Toggles forced resubmissions of forms when the documents they returned are revisited.
-rlogin	Disables rlogin commands.
-selective	Restricts directory browsing to those specified with .www_browsable.
-show_cursor	Specifies cursor to be shown at start of current link.
-source	Sends output as HTML source to standard output.
-telnet	Disables Telnet commands.
-term=TERM	Specifies terminal type for lynx.
-tlog	Toggles lynx tracing log.
-trace	Enables WWW trace mode.
-traversal	Follows links from start file.
-underscore	Toggles use of underline in dumps.
-useragent=Name	Specifies alternative lynx User-Agent header name.
-validate	Accepts only HTTP URLs for validation.
-version	Displays version information.
-vikeys	Enables vi-like key movement.
-width=n	Specifies number of columns for dump formatting.
man	Use to display online manual pages.
-M path	Specifies the directories to search for man pages.
-P pager	Specifies which pager (more or less) to use.
-S section_list	Specifies list of manual sections to search.
-a	Specifies to display all matching man pages, not just the default first one.
-d	Specifies not to display man page; rather, display debugging information.
-f	Provides whatis information.
-h	Prints help message.
-k	Searches for string in all man pages.
-m system	Specifies alternate man pages for *system*.
section, -s section	Specifies to display man page from the given section.
-w	Specifies not to display man pages; rather, print the path of the files.
-W	Specifies not to display man mages; rather, print the filenames without additional information.
mail	Use to send and receive mail.
-v	Specifies verbose mode and displays delivery details.
-i	Specifies to ignore interrupt signals.
-I	Specifies interactive mode even if input is not from a terminal.

continues on next page

COMMAND FLAGS

Table C.1

Commands and Flags *(continued)*	
COMMAND/FLAG	DESCRIPTION
-n	Disables `mail.rc` reading when starting.
-N	Disables initial display of message headers when reading mail.
-s *subject*	Specifies subject on command line.
-c *addresses*	Specifies addresses for carbon copies.
-b *addresses*	Specifies addresses for blind carbon copies.
-f *file*	Reads contents of file for processing and returns undeleted messages to this file.
mkdir	Use to make directories.
-m, --mode *mode*	Sets the mode of created directories as with `chmod`.
-p, --parents	Makes directories and any necessary parent directories.
--help	Displays help message.
--version	Displays version information.
more	Use to view files a screen at a time.
-*num*	Specifies number of lines onscreen.
-d	Specifies prompting and no bell on errors.
-l	Specifies not to pause after a Ctrl L in the file.
-f	Specifies to count logical lines rather than screen lines.
-p	Specifies not to scroll, but rather to clear and display new text.
-c	Specifies not to scroll, but rather to paint each screen from the top.
-s	Specifies to squeeze multiple blank lines together.
-u	Specifies to suppress underlining.
+/*string*	Specifies a string to find and start at for displaying the file.
+*num*	Specifies to start at line number *num*.
mutt	Use a small but very powerful text-based program for email.
-a *file*	Specifies to attach a file to your message.
-b *address*	Specifies a blind-carbon-copy (BCC) recipient.
-c *address*	Specifies a carbon-copy (CC) recipient.
-e *command*	Specifies a configuration command to be run after initialization files.
-f *mailbox*	Specifies which mailbox to load.
-F *muttrc*	Specifies an initialization file to read instead of ~/.muttrc.
-h	Specifies to display help information.
-H *draft*	Specifies a draft file to use for creating a message.
-i *include*	Specifies a file to include in a message.
-m *type*	Specifies a default mailbox type.
-n	Specifies to ignore the system configuration file.
-p	Specifies to resume a postponed message.
-R	Specifies to open a mailbox in read-only mode.
-s *subject*	Specifies the subject of the message.
-v	Specifies to display version information.
-x	Specifies to emulate mailx compose mode.
-y	Specifies to start with a listing of all mailboxes specified.
-z	Specifies not to start if there are no messages, when used with -f.

COMMAND FLAGS

Table C.1

Commands and Flags *(continued)*	
COMMAND/FLAG	DESCRIPTION
-Z	Specifies to open the first mailbox specified that contains new mail.
mv	Use to rename or move files.
-b, --backup	Specifies to make backups of files before removal.
-f, --force	Specifies to overwrite all existing destination files.
-i, --interactive	Requires prompting before overwriting.
-v, --verbose	Displays filenames before moving.
--help	Prints a help message.
--version	Prints version information.
-S, --suffix *backup-suffix*	Specifies suffix for backup files.
nice	Use to run a program with a different priority.
-n *adjustment*, -*adjustment*, --adjustment=*adjustment*	Adds *adjustment* number to initial priority.
--help	Displays help message.
--version	Displays version information.
passwd	Use to set a password for the system.
pico	Use for user-friendly text editing.
+*n*	Starts pico with the cursor located *n* lines into the file.
-d	Specifies that the Delete key rubs out the character the cursor is on rather than the character to its left.
-e	Enables filename completion.
-f	Specifies to use function keys for commands.
-j	Specifies that goto commands to indicate directories are allowed.
-k	Specifies that "Cut Text" removes characters from the cursor position to the end of the line.
-n*n*	Enables mail notification every *n* seconds.
-o *dir*	Specifies operating directory.
-r*n*	Specifies column *n* for right margin of justify command.
-t	Sets tool mode for when pico is the default editor in other programs.
-v	Specifies view-only.
-w	Disables word wrap.
-x	Disables menu.
-z	Allows Ctrl Z suspension of pico.
pine	Use to read news and email.
-d *debug-level*	Displays diagnostic information at levels from 0 (none) to 9 (complete).
-f *folder*	Specifies to open *folder* instead of in-box.
-F *file*	Opens specified file with pine.
-h	Displays brief help message.
-i	Specifies to start in folder index.
-I *keystrokes*	Specifies initial set of keystrokes to execute on startup.
-k	Specifies to use function keys for commands.
-n *number*	Specifies to start with given message number.
-o	Opens first folder as read-only.

continues on next page

COMMAND FLAGS

Table C.1

P

Commands and Flags *(continued)*	
COMMAND/FLAG	DESCRIPTION
-p *config-file*	Specifies configuration file to use instead of default personal configuration file.
-P *config-file*	Specifies configuration file to use instead of systemwide configuration file.
-r	Requires demo mode.
-z	Allows eventual suspension of pine process.
-conf	Outputs a new copy of systemwide configuration file.
-pinerc *file*	Outputs new pinerc configuration file.
-sort *order*	Specifies sort order in folders as arrival, subject, from, date, size, orderedsubj, thread, score, to, cc, or reverse.
ping	Use to see if a specific host is reachable.
-c *count*	Specifies number of responses to receive before stopping.
-d	Specifies SO_DEBUG option.
-f	Specifies flood ping (for system administrators only).
-i *wait*	Specifies how many seconds to wait between packets.
-l *preload*	Specifies initial flurry of packets before reverting to normal behavior; for system administrators only.
-n	Specifies not to look up domain names.
-p *pattern*	Specifies content for packets to diagnose data-dependent problems.
-q	Specifies quiet output with only initial and ending summary information displayed.
-r	Specifies to ignore routing and send directly to host on attached network.
-s *packetsize*	Specifies size of packet to send in bytes.
-v	Specifies verbose output and lists all received packets.
pgrep	Use to look up processes based on name or other characteristics.
-d *string*	Specifies the string used to delimit each process ID output.
-f	Specifies to match against full path.
-g *pgrp,...*	Specifies to match only processes under the specified process group IDs.
-G *gid,...*	Specifies to match only processes whose real group ID is listed.
-l	Specifies to list the process name as well as the process ID.
-n	Specifies to list only the newest matching process.
-P *ppid,...*	Specifies to match only processes whose parent process ID is listed.
-s *sid,...*	Specifies to match only processes whose process session ID is listed.
-t *term,...*	Specifies to match only processes whose controlling terminal is listed.
-u *euid,...*	Specifies to match only processes whose effective user ID is listed.
-U *uid,...*	Specifies to match only processes whose real user ID is listed.
-v	Specifies to match the opposite of the characteristics given.
-x	Specifies to match only exactly.
pkill	Use to send a kill signal to processes based on name or other characteristics.
-f	Specifies to match against full path.
-g *pgrp,...*	Specifies to match only processes under the specified process group IDs.
-G *gid,...*	Specifies to match only processes whose real group ID is listed.
-n	Specifies to list only the newest matching process.

COMMAND FLAGS

Table C.1

Commands and Flags *(continued)*	
COMMAND/FLAG	DESCRIPTION
-P ppid,...	Specifies to match only processes whose parent process ID is listed.
-s sid,...	Specifies to match only processes whose process session ID is listed.
-t term,...	Specifies to match only processes whose controlling terminal is listed.
-u euid,...	Specifies to match only processes whose effective user ID is listed.
-U uid,...	Specifies to match only processes whose real user ID is listed.
-v	Specifies to match the opposite of the characteristics given.
-x	Specifies to match only exactly.
-signal	Specifies the signal (numeric or by name) to send to each matched process.
procmail	Use to process incoming email.
-v	Specifies to display version information.
-p	Specifies to preserve existing environment.
-t	Specifies to retry failed deliveries later.
-f name	Specifies to regenerate the From line that separates messages with name.
-o	Specifies to override fake From lines.
-Y	Specifies to ignore any Content-Length: fields.
-a argument	Specifies arguments to pass to procmail.
-d recipient ...	Specifies delivery mode.
-m	Specifies that procmail should act as a general-purpose mail filter.
ps	Use to report process status (note that ps arguments work with or without a -, and warn you not to use - in the future).
-l	Specifies long format.
-j	Specifies jobs format.
-s	Specifies signal format.
-v	Specifies vm (virtual memory) format.
-m	Displays thread information.
-H	Specifies "forest" tree format.
-f	Show full listing.
-a	Displays processes of other users on the same terminal.
-x	Displays processes without controlling terminal (daemons).
-S	Displays add child CPU time and page faults.
-w	Specifies wide output and does not truncate command lines.
-h	Disables header display.
-r	Shows running processes only.
-n	Specifies numeric output for user and wchan fields.
-txx	Specifies only processes with controlling tty *xx*.
-pids	Lists only specified processes.
--help	Displays help message.
--version	Displays version information.
pr	Use to convert and reformat files for printing or display.
-n, --columns=n	Specifies to create *n* columns across the page.
-c, --show-control-chars	Specifies to use hat notation (^G) and octal backslash notation.

continues on next page

COMMAND FLAGS

P₂

Table C.1

Commands and Flags *(continued)*	
COMMAND/FLAG	DESCRIPTION
-d, --double-space	Specifies to double space the output.
-D, --date-format=*FORMAT*	Specifies to use FORMAT for the header date.
-F, -f, --form-feed	Specifies to use form feeds instead of newlines to separate pages.
-h header, --header=*header*	Specifies to use a centered header instead of filename in page header.
-t, --omit-header	Specifies to omit page headers and footers.
-T, --omit-pagination	Specifies to omit page headers, footers, and all pagination.
-v, --show-nonprinting	Specifies to use octal backslash notation to display nonprinting characters.
-W *w*, --page-width=*w*	Specifies that page width be *w* (72 default) characters.
--help	Specifies to display help message.
--version	Specifies to display version information.
pwd	Use to display name of current working directory.
--help	Displays help message.
--version	Displays version information.
quota	Use to display disk usage and limits.
-g	Displays group quotas for the executing user's group.
-v	Displays quotas on file systems where no storage is allocated.
-q	Displays only information for file systems over quota.
renice	Use to change the priority (niceness) of jobs.
-g	Specifies to force parameters to be interpreted as process group IDs.
-u	Specifies to force parameters to be interpreted as user names.
-p	Specifies to require parameters to be process IDs.
rm	Use to remove files.
-f, --force	Specifies to overwrite all existing destination files.
-i, --interactive	Requires prompting before overwriting.
-R, --recursive	Specifies to copy directories recursively.
-v, --verbose	Displays filenames before moving.
--help	Displays a help message.
--version	Displays version information.
reset	Use to reset a terminal session to normal behavior.
-q	Specifies to display the terminal type only.
-e *a*	Specifies to set the erase character to the given character.
-I	Specifies not to send initialization strings to the terminal.
-Q	Specifies not to display values for erase, interrupt, and line kill characters.
-V	Specifies to display the version number.
-i *a*	Specifies to set the interrupt character to the given character.
-k *a*	Specifies to set the line kill character to the given character.
-m	Specifies to map a port type to a terminal type.
-r	Specifies to display the terminal type to standard error.
-s	Specifies to display the initialization commands.
rmdir	Use to remove empty directories.

COMMAND FLAGS

Table C.1

Commands and Flags *(continued)*	
COMMAND/FLAG	DESCRIPTION
-p, --parents	Specifies to remove any parent directories listed, if they are empty after the specified files are removed.
--help	Displays a help message.
--version	Displays version information.
rsync	Use to copy files and synchronize directories.
-v, --verbose	Specifies to increase verbosity.
-q, --quiet	Specifies to decrease verbosity.
-c, --checksum	Specifies to calculate a checksum for files, not just check dates.
-a, --archive	Specifies to use archive mode.
-r, --recursive	Specifies to recursively copy.
-R, --relative	Specifies to use relative path names.
-b, --backup	Specifies to make backups with the default ~ suffix.
--backup-dir	Specifies to use this backup directory.
--suffix=*string*	Specifies to change backup suffix to string.
-u, --update	Specifies to update only and not overwrite newer files.
-l, --links	Specifies to copy symlinks as symlinks.
-L, --copy-links	Specifies to copy the associated file for symlinks.
--copy-unsafe-links	Specifies to copy links outside the source directory tree.
--safe-links	Specifies to ignore links outside the destination directory tree.
-H, --hard-links	Specifies to preserve hard links.
-p, --perms	Specifies to preserve permissions.
-o, --owner	Specifies to preserve owner, for use by root only.
-g, --group	Specifies to preserve group.
-D, --devices	Specifies to preserve devices, for use by root only.
-t, --times	Specifies to preserve times.
-S, --sparse	Specifies to handle sparse files efficiently.
-n, --dry-run	Specifies to show what would have been transferred, but not actually transfer.
-W, --whole-file	Specifies to copy whole files without making incremental checks.
--no-whole-file	Specifies not to copy whole files without checking.
-x, --one-file-system	Specifies not to cross file system boundaries.
-B, --block-size=*SIZE*	Specifies the checksum block size (default 700).
-e, --rsh=*COMMAND*	Specifies the rsh replacement command (probably ssh).
--rsync-path=*PATH*	Specifies the path to rsync on the remote machine.
-C, --cvs-exclude	Specifies to autoignore files in the same way CVS does.
--existing	Specifies to update only files that already exist.
--ignore-existing	Specifies to ignore files that already exist on the receiving side.
--delete	Specifies to delete files that don't exist on the sending side.
--delete-excluded	Specifies to also delete excluded files on the receiving side.
--delete-after	Specifies to delete after transferring, not before.
--ignore-errors	Specifies to delete even if there are I/O errors.
--max-delete=*NUM*	Specifies not to delete more than *NUM* files.

continues on next page

COMMAND FLAGS

Table C.1

Commands and Flags *(continued)*

COMMAND/FLAG	DESCRIPTION
`--partial`	Specifies to keep partially transferred files.
`--force`	Specifies to force deletion of directories even if not empty.
`--numeric-ids`	Specifies to set permissions with numeric ids on target.
`--timeout=`*n*	Specifies to set I/O timeout in seconds.
`-I, --ignore-times`	Specifies to copy even files that match in length and time.
`--size-only`	Specifies to copy files only if file sizes differ.
`--modify-window=`*n*	Specifies range of time (*n* seconds) to consider equivalent.
`-T --temp-dir=path`	Specifies to create temporary files in directory path.
`--compare-dest=`*DIR*	Specifies to compare destination files relative to path.
`-z, --compress`	Specifies to compress files when transferring.
`--exclude=`*string*	Specifies to exclude files matching *string*.
`--exclude-from=`*file*	Specifies to exclude patterns listed in *file*.
`--include=`*string*	Specifies to include files matching *string*.
`--include-from=`*file*	Specifies to include patterns listed in *file*.
`--version`	Specifies to display version number.
`--daemon`	Specifies to run as an rsync daemon.
`--no-detach`	Specifies not to detach from the parent.
`--address=`*ADDRESS*	Specifies to bind to the specified address.
`--config=`*file*	Specifies an alternate rsyncd.conf file.
`--port=`*PORT*	Specifies an alternate rsyncd port number.
`--blocking-io`	Specifies to use blocking I/O for the remote shell.
`--no-blocking-io`	Specifies to turn off `--blocking-io`.
`--stats`	Specifies to show some file transfer statistics.
`--progress`	Specifies to show progress during transfer.
`--log-format=`*format*	Specifies to log file transfers using specified format.
`--password-file=`*file*	Specifies to get password from file.
`--bwlimit=`*n*	Specifies to limit I/O bandwidth to *n* KBps.
`--read-batch=`*string*	Specifies to read batch fileset starting with *string*.
`--write-batch=`*string*	Specifies to write batch fileset starting with *string*.
`-h, --help`	Specifies to display help information.
sed	Use for processing and editing files in batch mode.
-e	Specifies edit commands to follow as the next argument.
-f	Specifies edit commands to be taken from named file or files.
-n	Suppresses default output.
set	Use to set or view the values of variables.
setenv	Use to change or view the value of an environment variable (csh).
screen	Use to manage multiple virtual screens in a physical window.
-*a*	Specifies to include all capabilities in each window.
-A	Specifies to adapt the sizes of all windows to the size of the current terminal.
-c *file*	Specifies to override the default configuration file (`~/.screenrc`) with *file*.
-d,-D	Specifies to detach another running screen from the controlling terminal.

Table C.1

Commands and Flags (*continued*)	
COMMAND/FLAG	DESCRIPTION
-d -r	Specifies to reattach a session, after detaching it if necessary.
-d -R	Specifies to reattach a session, after detaching or creating it first if necessary.
-d -RR	Specifies to reattach a session, after detaching or creating it if necessary, and to use the first session if multiple sessions are available.
-D -r	Specifies to reattach a session, after detaching and logging out remotely if necessary.
-D -R	Specifies to attach immediately, after notifying other users.
-D -RR	Specifies to attach immediately, after doing anything necessary to other sessions.
-e *xy*	Specifies the command character (default is Ctrl Aa), specified as ^Aa.
-f, -fn, -fa	Specifies flow-control settings to off, on, or automatic.
-h *n*	Specifies the size of the history as *n* lines.
-l, -ln	Specifies to turn login mode on or off.
-ls, -list	Specifies to display list of existing screen sessions.
-m	Specifies to force creation of a new session.
-d -m	Specifies to start screen in detached mode.
-D -m	Specifies to start screen in detached mode, in existing process.
-q	Specifies to suppress display error messages and exit codes.
-r	Specifies to resume a detached screen session.
-R	Specifies to attempt to resume the first available detached screen session it finds.
-s *string*	Specifies the default shell as *string*.
-S *name*	Specifies to use *name* as the name for the new session.
-t *name*	Specifies the title for the default shell or specified program.
-v	Specifies to display the version number.
-wipe	Specifies to remove destroyed sessions.
-x	Specifies to attach to a session in multidisplay mode.
-X	Specifies to send the specified command to a running screen session.
ssh	Use to securely log in to and run commands on a remote system.
-a	Specifies not to forward the authentication agent connection.
-A	Specifies to forward the authentication agent connection.
-b *bind_address*	Specifies the interface to transmit from if multiple interfaces are available.
-c *blowfish*I*3des*I*des*	Specifies the encrpytion method to use.
-e *ch*I^*ch*I*none*	Specifies the escape character for sessions with a pty (default: ~).
-f	Specifies for ssh to go to the background before the command runs.
-g	Specifies that remote hosts can connect to local forwarded ports.
-i *identity_file*	Specifies the file from which to read the identify key.
-l *login_name*	Specifies the user name to log in as on the remote machine.
-n	Specifies to ignore standard input.
-N	Specifies not to execute a remote command.
-o *option*	Specifies to give options as presented in configuration file.
-p *port*	Specifies the port to connect to on the remote host.
-P	Specifies a nonprivileged port (>1024) for outgoing connections.
-q	Specifies that warning and diagnostic messages should be suppressed.

continues on next page

COMMAND FLAGS

Table C.1

S

Commands and Flags *(continued)*	
COMMAND/FLAG	DESCRIPTION
-s	Specifies to request invocation of a subsystem on the remote system.
-t	Specifies to allocate a pseudo-tty.
-T	Specifies not to allocate a pseudo-tty.
-v	Specifies to provide verbose output.
-x	Specifies to disable X11 forwarding.
-X	Specifies to enable X11 forwarding.
-C	Specifies to compress all data for transmission.
-F *configfile*	Specifies an alternative configuration file.
-L *port:host:hostport*	Specifies port forwarding from local to remote sides.
-R *port:host:hostport*	Specifies port forwarding from remote to local sides.
-D *port*	Specifies dynamic port forwarding from local to remote sides.
-1	Specifies to use only protocol version 1.
-2	Specifies to use only protocol version 2.
-4	Specifies to use only IPv4 addresses.
-6	Specifies to use only IPv6 addresses.
split	Use to split files into smaller parts.
-b, --bytes=*n*	Specifies to put *n* bytes in each output file (use k for kilobytes, m for megabytes).
-C, --line-bytes=*n*	Specifies to put no more than *n* bytes of lines in each output file.
-l, --lines=*n*	Specifies to put *n* lines into each output file.
--verbose	Specifies to provide verbose output.
--help	Specifies to display help information.
--version	Specifies to display version information.
sort	Use to sort text files by line.
-c	Checks to see if file is already sorted.
-m	Merges sorted files together.
-b	Ignores extra spaces at the beginning of each line.
-d	Sorts by ignoring everything but letters, digits, and blanks.
-f	Sorts without case sensitivity.
-M	Sorts by month, recognizing three-character month abbreviations.
-n	Sorts numerically.
-r	Reverses result order.
-o output-file	Sends output to specified file instead of standard output.
-t *separator*	Uses indicated character as field separator.
-u	Displays only one of the matching lines.
--help	Displays help information.
--version	Displays version information.
su *otherid*	Use to substitute *otherid* for current userid.
-c *command*, --command=*command*	Runs specified command as other user.
--help	Displays help information.
-, -l, --login	Specifies to start as login shell.
-m, -p, --preserve-environment	Specifies not to change environment variables from current settings.

COMMAND FLAGS

Table C.1

Commands and Flags *(continued)*	
COMMAND/FLAG	DESCRIPTION
-s, --shell *shell*	Uses the specified shell instead of the default.
--version	Displays program version.
sudo	Use to execute a command as another user.
-V	Specifies to display the version number.
-l	Specifies to list the available and forbidden commands for the issuing user.
-L	Specifies to list configurable default parameters.
-h	Specifies to display a help message.
-v	Specifies to update the timestamp and extend the timeout.
-k	Specifies to set the timeout to a past time, forcing revalidation.
-K	Specifies to remove the timestamp for a current user.
-b	Specifies to run the specified command in the background.
-p	Specifies to replace the default password prompt with a custom prompt.
-u *user*	Specifies user, under whose id the command will run.
-s	Specifies to use the specified (default) shell.
-H	Specifies to change the $HOME environment variable to the target user.
-P	Specifies to preserve the user's group ID when running the command.
-S	Specifies to read password from standard input.
--	Specifies to stop processing command-line options.
-	Specifies to force a login shell.
tail	Use to output the last part of a file.
-c --bytes *n[b,k,m]*	Displays last *n* bytes of file, in b (512-byte), k (1 KB), or m (1 MB) blocks.
-f, --follow	Specifies to keep running and trying to read more from end of file.
-l, -n *N*, --lines *N*	Displays last *N* lines of file.
-q, --quiet, --silent	Specifies not to display filenames.
-v, --verbose	Specifies to always display filenames.
--help	Displays help message.
--version	Displays version information.
talk	Use to talk to another user.
tar	Use to create tar archives.
-A, --catenate, --concatenate	Specifies to append tar files to an archive.
-c, --create	Creates a new archive.
-d, --diff, --compare	Identifies differences between archive and file system.
--delete	Removes files from the archive.
-r, --append	Appends files to the archive.
-t, --list	Lists contents of the archive.
-u, --update	Updates archive with newer files.
-x, --extract, --get	Extracts files from archives.
--atime-preserve	Specifies not to change access times.
-b, --block-size *n*	Specifies block size of *n*x512 bytes.
-C, --directory *DIR*	Changes to specified directory.

continues on next page

COMMAND FLAGS

Table C.1

Commands and Flags *(continued)*	
COMMAND/FLAG	DESCRIPTION
--checkpoint	Displays directory names while processing.
-f, --file	Uses specified file or device.
--force-local	Forces local archive file regardless of filename.
-h, --dereference	Processes linked files, not symbolic links.
-i, --ignore-zeros	Specifies to ignore zeros in archives (and not to interpret as EOF).
-k, --keep-old-files	Specifies that old files should be retained, not overwritten.
-K, --starting-file *file*	Starts at file *file* in the archive.
-l, --one-file-system	Specifies to remain in current file system.
-m, --modification-time	Specifies not to extract the file modification time.
-M, --multi-volume	Specifies to process as multivolume archive.
-N, --after-date *date*, → --newer date	Stores files newer than *date*.
-o, --old-archive, → --portability	Specifies old archive format.
-O, --to-stdout	Specifies to extract files to standard output.
-p, --same-permissions, → --preserve-permissions	Specifies to extract all permissions data.
-P, --absolute-paths	Specifies to maintain absolute paths.
--remove-files	Specifies to remove files that have been added to archive.
-s, --same-order, → --preserve-order	Specifies list of filenames to match archive.
--same-owner	Specifies to extract files with same ownership.
-T, --files-from *file*	Retrieves names of files to extract or create from file *file*.
--totals	Displays total bytes of created files.
-v, --verbose	Displays verbose information about processed files.
-V, --label *name*	Creates archive with volume name of *name*.
--version	Displays version information.
-w, --interactive, → --confirmation	Requires confirmation for actions.
-W, --verify	Verifies information in archive after creating archive.
--exclude *file*	Specifies to exclude *file* from archive.
-X, --exclude-from *file*	Specifies to exclude files listed in *file* from archive.
-Z, --compress, → --uncompress	Specifies to compress or uncompress the archive.
-z, --gzip, --ungzip	Specifies to process the archive with gzip.
--use-compress-program → *program*	Specifies name of compression program as *program*.
tee	Use to read from standard input and write to standard output and files.
-a, --append	Appends to specified files instead of overwriting.
--help	Prints help information.
-i, --ignore-interrupts	Specifies to ignore interrupt signals.
--version	Prints version information.

Table C.1

Commands and Flags *(continued)*	
COMMAND/FLAG	DESCRIPTION
telnet	Use to connect to and use remote computers.
-8	Specifies 8-bit operation, which is not the telnet default.
-E	Disables the escape character.
-L	Specifies 8-bit operation on output.
-a	Attempts automatic log in with the current user name.
-d	Enables debugging output.
-r	Specifies rlogin emulation.
-e *character*	Specifies the escape character to control command-mode access.
-l *user*	Specifies the user for remote log in.
-n *tracefile*	Starts tracing connection to *tracefile*.
tidy	Use to validate, correct, and clean up HTML files.
-config *file*	Specifies to set options from *file*.
-indent, -i	Specifies to indent contents of elements.
-omit, -o	Specifies to omit optional endtags.
-wrap *n*	Specifies to wrap output at column *n*.
-upper, -u	Specifies to output tags in uppercase.
-clean, -c	Specifies to replace formatting tags with CSS-style properties.
-raw	Specifies to output characters with values higher than 127 unchanged.
-ascii	Specifies to use Latin-1 (ISO 8859-1) character set for input, and US ASCII character set for output.
-latin1	Specifies to use Latin-1 (ISO 8859-1) character set for both input and output.
-iso2022	Specifies to use ISO 2022 character set for both input and output.
-utf8	Specifies to use UTF-8 character set for both input and output.
-mac	Specifies to use MacRoman character set for input.
-numeric, -n	Specifies to output numeric rather than named entities.
-modify, -m	Specifies to modify original files in place.
-errors, -e	Specifies to only show errors without modifying the original file.
-quiet, -q	Specifies to suppress extra output.
-f *file*	Specifies to write errors to file.
-xml	Specifies that input is well-formed XML.
-asxml	Specifies to convert HTML to well-formed XML.
-slides	Specifies to break file into slides based on <H2> elements.
-help, -h	Specifies to display a help message.
--configuration-option ⇥ *value*	Specifies to set any configurable option to *value*.
time	Use to time a job.
tin	Use to read Usenet news.
-c	Creates or updates index for listed groups, marking all as read.
-f *file*	Specifies *file* to use for newsrc data.
-h	Displays help information.
-H	Displays introduction to tin.
-I *dir*	Specifies directory to hold newsgroup index files.

continues on next page

COMMAND FLAGS

Table C.1

COMMAND/FLAG	DESCRIPTION
Commands and Flags *(continued)*	
-m *dir*	Specifies mailbox directory to use.
-M *user*	Mails unread articles to *user*.
-n	Specifies to load only active, subscribed groups.
-q	Specifies startup without checking for new newsgroups.
-P	Purges all articles that do not exist. Time-consuming, particularly on a slow connection.
-r	Specifies remote news reading from nntpserver.
-s *dir*	Saves articles to directory specified.
-S	Saves unread articles for later reading with –R option.
-u	Creates and updates index files for all groups.
-U	Starts tin in background to update index files while reading news.
-v	Specifies verbose mode for some commands.
-w	Allows quick posting.
-z	Specifies to start tin only with new or unread news.
-Z	Checks for new or unread news.
touch	Use to change file times and create empty files.
-a, --time=atime, → --time=access, → --time=use	Changes access time only.
-c, --no-create	Specifies not to create files that do not already exist.
-d, --date *time*	Updates files with given (not current) time.
-m, --time=*mtime*, → --time=*modify*	Changes modification time only.
-r, --reference *file*	Updates files with time of *reference file*.
-t [[CC]YY]MMDDhhmm[.ss]	Specifies time argument for setting time.
--help	Displays help message.
--version	Displays version information.
tr	Use to translate or delete characters.
--help	Specifies to display help message.
--version	Specifies to display version information.
traceroute	Use to identify the route packets take to a network host.
-f	Specifies initial time-to-live used in the first probe.
-F	Specifies "don't fragment" setting for probes.
-d	Enables socket-level debugging.
-g	Specifies a source route gateway.
-i	Specifies a network interface to use for probes.
-I	Specifies ICMP ECHO instead of UDP datagrams.
-m	Specifies maximum number of hops to use.
-n	Specifies not to look up domain names for addresses.
-p	Sets base UDP port number for probes.
-r	Specifies to ignore routing and send directly to host on attached network.
-s	Specifies IP address as source for probe.

COMMAND FLAGS

Table C.1

Commands and Flags *(continued)*	
COMMAND/FLAG	DESCRIPTION
-v	Specifies verbose output and lists all received packets.
-w	Specifies the number of seconds to wait for a response to a probe.
umask	Use to set the file creation mask.
unalias	Use to remove aliases from the list.
-a	Removes all alias definitions.
uname	Use to display system information.
-m, --machine	Displays the machine or hardware type.
-n, --nodename	Displays the node or host name.
-r, --release	Displays the operating system release number.
-s, --sysname	Displays the operating system name.
-v	Displays the operating system version.
-a, --all	Displays all the above information.
--help	Displays help information.
--version	Displays version information.
uniq	Use to remove duplicate lines from a sorted list.
-u, --unique	Outputs only unique lines.
-d, --repeated	Outputs only duplicate lines.
-c, --count	Outputs number of occurences of each line followed by the text of each line.
-number, -f, → --skip-fields=*number*	Specifies number of fields to ignore before checking for uniqueness.
+number, -s, → --skip-chars=*number*	Specifies number of characters to skip before checking for uniqueness.
-w, --check-chars=*number*	Specifies number of characters to compare.
--help	Prints help information.
--version	Prints version information.
units	Use to convert from one kind of unit to another.
-c, --check	Specifies to check that the units data file is valid.
--check-verbose	Specifies to check that the units data file is valid, with verbose output.
-o *format*, --output-format → *format*	Specifies the format for numeric output (in printf syntax).
-f *filename*, --file → *filename*	Specifies to use *filename* as the units data file.
-h, --help	Specifies to display a help message.
-q, --quiet, --silent	Specifies quiet output and suppression of prompts.
-s, --strict	Specifies not to convert to reciprocal units.
-v, --verbose	Specifies more verbose output.
-V, --version	Specifies to display version number.
unzip	Use to manipulate and extract compressed files in a zip file.
-f	Specifies to extract only files newer than those on disk.
-l	Lists archive files in short format.
-p	Extracts files to standard output.

continues on next page

COMMAND FLAGS

Table C.1

Commands and Flags *(continued)*	
COMMAND/FLAG	DESCRIPTION
-t	Tests archive files for accuracy and completeness.
-T	Sets the timestamp to the same as the newest file in the archive.
-u	Updates existing files from the archive and creates new files as needed.
-v	Displays verbose or diagnostic version information.
-z	Displays archive comments.
-j	Junks paths and puts all files in the current directory.
-n	Specifies never to overwrite existing files.
-o	Overwrites existing files without prompting.
-P *password*	Requires password to decrypt zip file entries.
-q	Performs operations quietly, without displaying most status information.
-qq	Performs operations even more quietly.
uudecode	Use to decode a file created by uuencode.
-o *file*	Directs output to *file*.
uuencode	Use to encode a binary file.
-m	Specifies MIME (Base 64) encoding.
vacation	Use to reply to mail automatically.
-I	Initializes .vacation.db file and starts vacation.
-a *alias*	Specifies alias for vacation user, so that mail sent to that alias generates a reply.
-j	Specifies to always reply, regardless of To: or CC: addressing.
-t*n*	Specifies the number of days between repeat replies to the same sender.
-r	Specifies to use the "Reply-To:" header if available.
-?	Displays a short help message.
vi	Use for powerful text editing.
-s	Specifies no interactive feedback.
-l	Specifies LISP program editing setup.
-L	Lists names of files saved after crashes.
-R	Forces read-only mode.
-r *filename*	Recovers *filename* edit file saved after a crash.
-t *tag*	Starts editor with cursor at tag position.
-V	Specifies verbose output with input echoed to standard error.
-x	Specifies encryption option like that of ex and prompts for a key.
-w*n*	Specifies default window size.
-x	Specifies encryption option like that of ex and prompts for a key, assuming all text is encrypted.
+command, -c *command*	Starts editor and executes specified command.
w	Use to show who is logged on and what they are doing.
-h	Disables header.
-n	Ignores user name for current process and CPU times.
-s	Specifies short format, omitting log in, JCPU, and PCPU times.
-f	Toggles display of remote host name.
-V	Displays version information.

Table C.1

Commands and Flags *(continued)*	
Command/Flag	**Description**
`watch`	Use to execute a program repeatedly with full-screen output.
`-h, --help`	Specifies to display a help message.
`-v, --version`	Specifies to display version number.
`-n=n, --interval`	Specifies to override the default 2-second interval with n.
`-d, --differences`	Specifies to display differences between successive updates.
`--cumulative`	Specifies to keep all changes highlighted.
`wc`	Use to count the number of bytes, words, and lines in a file.
`-c, --bytes, --chars`	Displays only byte counts.
`-w, --words`	Displays only word counts.
`-l, --lines`	Displays only newline counts.
`--help`	Displays help message.
`--version`	Displays version information.
`wget`	Use to download files or entire Web sites.
`-V, --version`	Specifies to display the version number.
`-h, --help`	Specifies to display a help message.
`-b, --background`	Specifies to start as a background process.
`-e command, --execute → command`	Specifies to execute *command* at end of startup process.
`-o logfile, → --output-file=logfile`	Specifies to log all messages to the specified file.
`-a logfile, → --append-output=logfile`	Specifies to append all messages to the specified file.
`-d, --debug,`	Specifies to display debugging information.
`-q, --quiet`	Specifies to suppress output.
`-v, --verbose`	Specifies to provide verbose output (the default setting).
`-nv, --non-verbose`	Specifies to provide nonverbose, nonquiet output.
`-i file, → --input-file=file`	Specifies to read URLs from the file given.
`-F --force-html`	Specifies to force input to be treated as an HTML file.
`-B URL, --base=URL`	Specifies to prepend URL to relative links in specified file.
`-t n, --tries=n`	Specifies number of retries. Use 0 for infinite.
`-O file, → --output-document=file`	Specifies to concatenate all documents as *file* or - for standard output.
`-nc --no-clobber`	Specifies to not destroy a file of the same name as the file being downloaded.
`-c --continue`	Specifies to continue getting a partially downloaded file.
`--progress=type`	Specifies type of the progress indicator as "dot" and "bar".
`-N --timestamping`	Specifies to enable time stamps.
`-S --server-response`	Specifies to print the headers and responses sent by servers.
`--spider`	Specifies to verify pages but not download them.
`-T seconds --timeout=seconds`	Specifies length of the read timeout in seconds.
`--limit-rate=n`	Specifies to limit the download speed to *n* bytes (or kilobytes with k, or megabytes with m) per second.

continues on next page

COMMAND FLAGS

Table C.1

W

Commands and Flags *(continued)*	
COMMAND/FLAG	DESCRIPTION
-w *n* --wait=*n*	Specifies to wait the specified number (*n*) of seconds between retrievals.
--waitretry=*n*	Specifies interval to wait before retrying failed downloads.
--random-wait	Specifies to wait random intervals between requests.
-Y *on/off*, --proxy=*on/off*	Specifies to turn proxy support on or off.
-Q *quota* --quota=*quota*	Specifies the download quota (in b, k, or m) for automatic retrieval.
-nd --no-directories	Specifies not to create a hierarchy of directories on recursive retrieval.
-x --force-directories	Specifies always to create a hierarchy of directories on recursive retrieval.
-nH --no-host-directories	Specifies not to create host name-prefixed directories.
--cut-dirs=*number*	Specifies to ignore (flatten) specific numbers of directory levels.
-P *prefix* → --directory-prefix=*prefix*	Specifies directory prefix to use.
-E --html-extension	Specifies to append .html to filenames.
--http-user=*user* → --http-passwd=*password*	Specifies the user name *user* and password *password* for an HTTP server.
-C *on/off* --cache=*on/off*	Specifies to avoid or use server-side caching.
--cookies=*on/off*	Specifies to use or disable cookies.
--load-cookies *file*	Specifies to load cookies from *file* before the first retrieval.
--save-cookies *file*	Specifies to save cookies to *file* at the end of the session.
--ignore-length	Specifies to ignore "Content-Length" headers.
--header=additional-header	Specifies to define an additional-header to be passed to the HTTP servers.
--proxy-user=*user* → proxy-passwd=*password*	Specifies the user name *user* and password *password* for authentication on a proxy server.
--referer=*url*	Specifies to include "Referer: url" header in HTTP request.
-s --save-headers	Specifies to save the headers sent by the HTTP server to the file.
-U *agent-string* → --user-agent=*agent-string*	Specifies *agent-string* to send to the HTTP server.
-nr --dont-remove-listing	Specifies not to remove the temporary listing files generated by FTP retrievals.
-g *on/off* --glob=*on/off*	Specifies to turn FTP globbing (wildcard use) on or off.
--passive-ftp	Specifies to use the passive FTP retrieval method for use behind firewalls.
--retr-symlinks	Specifies to retrieve files pointed to by symbolic links.
-r --recursive	Specifies to turn on recursive retrieving.
-l depth --level=*depth*	Specifies the maximum depth for recursive retrieval.
--delete-after	Specifies to delete files downloaded, as soon as they're retrieved.
-k --convert-links	Specifies to convert the links in the document for local viewing.
-K --backup-converted	Specifies to back up the original version with a .orig suffix.
-m --mirror	Specifies to turn on options suitable for mirroring.
-p --page-requisites	Specifies to download all required files to display a page.
-A *acclist* --accept *acclist* → -R *rejlist* --reject *rejlist*	Specifies lists of filename patterns to accept or reject.
-D *domain-list* → --domains=*domain-list*	Specifies domains to be followed.
--exclude-domains *domain-list*	Specifies the domains that are not to be followed.
--follow-ftp	Specifies to follow FTP links from HTML documents.

COMMAND FLAGS

Table C.1

Commands and Flags *(continued)*	
Command/Flag	**Description**
`--follow-tags=list`	Specifies to use *list* for tags that indicate links.
`-G list --ignore-tags=list`	Specifies to ignore listed tags for indication of links.
`-H --span-hosts`	Specifies to recursively retrieve from multiple hosts.
`-L --relative`	Specifies to follow relative links only.
`-I list` → `--include-directories=list`	Specifies a list (with wildcards) of directories to follow when downloading.
`-X list` → `--exclude-directories=list`	Specifies a list (with wildcards) of directories to exclude when downloading.
`-np --no-parent`	Specifies not to download from the parent directory.
`whereis`	Use to find information about the specified file.
`-b`	Specifies to search only for binary files.
`-m`	Specifies to search only for man pages.
`-s`	Specifies to search only for source files.
`-u`	Specifies to search for unusual entries, which are files with fewer than one binary, man, and source entry.
`-B`	Specifies to change or limit where whereis searches for binaries.
`-M`	Specifies to change or limit where whereis searches for man pages.
`-S`	Specifies to change or limit where whereis searches for source files.
`-f`	Specifies to end the directory list and start the filename list for use with the -B, -M, or -S options.
`who`	Use to display information about who is logged onto the system.
`-m`	Specifies "me", as in "who am I?".
`-q, --count`	Displays login names and total number of logged on users.
`-i, -u, --idle`	Displays idle time.
`-H, --heading`	Displays column headings.
`-w, -T, --mesg, --writable`	Displays user message status.
`--help`	Displays a help message.
`--version`	Displays version information.
`write`	Use to send a message to another user.
`ydecode`	Use to decode yencoded files.
`yencode`	Use to encode files with the yEnc algorithm.
`zsh`	Use the flexible, powerful Z shell.
`-c`	Specifies to take the first argument as a command to execute.
`-i`	Specifies to force an interactive shell.
`-s`	Specifies to force shell to read commands on standard input.
`--version`	Specifies to print the version number.
`--help`	Specifies to print help information.
`zip`	Use to create a zip-format file archive.
`-A`	Accommodates a self-extracting executable archive.
`-b path`	Specifies a path for the temporary files.
`-c`	Provides one-line comments for each file in the archive.
`-d`	Deletes entries from an archive.

continues on next page

COMMAND FLAGS

Z

Table C.1

Commands and Flags *(continued)*

Command/Flag	Description
-D	Specifies not to create entries in the zip archive for directories.
-e	Encrypts the contents of the zip archive using a password.
-f	Freshens an existing entry in the archive if the new file has been modified more recently than the version in the zip archive.
-F	Fixes the zip archive.
-g	Appends to the specified archive.
-h	Displays help information.
-i *files*	Includes only specified files.
-j	Junks path name and stores only filename.
-J	Junks prepended data (for self-extracting archives) from the archive.
-l	Translates Unix text files to MS-DOS text files.
-ll	Translates MS-DOS text files to Unix text files.
-L	Displays the zip license.
-m	Moves specified files into the archive and deletes originals.
-n *suffixes*	Specifies not to compress files with the given suffixes.
-o	Sets the modification time of the zip archive to that of oldest of the files in the archive.
-q	Specifies quiet mode to eliminate messages and prompts.
-r	Includes files and directories recursively.
-t *mmddyyyy*	Ignores files modified before the given date.
-T	Tests the new archive and reverts to the old archive if errors are found.
-u	Updates an existing entry in the archive only if the existing file has been changed more recently than the copy in the archive.
-v	Specifies verbose mode to print diagnostic and version information.
-x *files*	Excludes the specified files.
-z	Requires a multiline comment for the entire archive.
-@	Gets a list of input files from standard input.

INDEX

Symbols

\# sign
  comments, 172
  root prompt symbol, 330
\$ (dollar sign)
  function as regular expression, 119
  setting prompt to appear on separate line, 169
' ' (single quotes), 169
/ (root directory), 45
&& (ampersands), 194
* (asterisk)
  function as regular expression, 119
  as placeholder, 19, 21
. (dot)
  function as regular expression, 119
  hiding files starting with, 37
  specifying current directory with find command, 44
\> (greater than symbol), 19
? (question mark), 21
[ ] (square brackets), 119
\ (backslash), 119
^ (caret)
  Ctrl in pico, 77
  function as regular expression, 119
^[^[(Esc sequence), 65
| (pipe symbol), 18
~ (tilde), 16

A

abbreviations for permissions, 99–100
absolute names, 35
accessing
  man pages, 26
  Unix, 3–6
alias command, 190–192, 384, 371
aliases for email, 235
alternative editors, 74
anonymous ftp: command, 263–265
appending output to existing file, 20

apt, 303
archiving files
  about, 290–291, 293
  zipping while, 300
asterisk (*)
  function as regular expression, 119
  as placeholder, 19, 21
at command
  deleting scheduled jobs, 197
  flags for, 384
  scheduling one-time jobs with, 195
  sequential one-time jobs with, 196
awk command
  changing files with, 122–123
  embedding scripts in shell, 350
  flags for, 384

B

backslash (\), 119
backups
  making with cp command, 41
  rsync for, 358–359
  using looping scripts to make, 220–221
bash shell
  adding or changing environment variables, 158–159
  changing path to, 173–174
  command argument completion in, 59
  daisychains in, 172
  defined, 53
  flags for commands, 384
  redirecting stderr in, 361–362
  showing current environment in, 156–157
  viewing
    configuration files, 170–172
    session history, 60–61
.bashrc file, 192
bc utility, 319
bg command, 202, 384
binaries
  defined, 302
  precompiled, 303

binary files
    displaying with cat, 24
    encoding, 288
boot messages, 340–341
Bourne Again Shell. *See* bash shell
Bourne shell. *See* sh shell
breaking lines with tr command, 131
browsers
    links, 268–269, 392–393
    lynx, 270–271, 395–397
buffer, 82
bzip command, 295

C

cal utility, 316–318, 384
calculator utility, 319
calendars, 316–318, 384
caret (^)
    Ctrl in pico, 77
    function as regular expression, 119
cat command
    displaying files with, 23–24
    flags, 384–385
    listing shells available with, 54
cd command
    changing directories with, 15–16
    flags, 385
changing
    directories, 15–16
    passwords, 11–12
    shells, 55–56
characters. *See also Symbols section of index*
    restrictions for directories and filenames, 31
    telnet Escape, 259
    using as delimiter, 122
checking new passwords, 12
chgrp command, 103–104, 385
chmod command, 106–107, 385
choosing editors, 74–76
chown command, 105, 385
chsh command, 55–56, 385
cleaning up HTML documents, 344–346
clients
    choosing mail, 230–231
    defined, 256
cmp command, 35, 124, 385–386
combining commands, 194
command argument completion
    bash shell and, 59
    ksh shell and, 65
    zsh shell and, 62
command mode in vi, 83
command-line arguments in scripts, 225
commands. *See also* flags; utilities; *and
        specific commands*
    cd, 15–16, 385
    about flags, 383
    alias, 190–192, 384
    at, 195–197, 384

awk, 122–123, 350, 384
bash, 384
basic Unix, 364
bg, 202, 384
bzip, 295
cat, 23–24, 54, 384–385
chgrp, 103–104, 385
chmod, 106–107, 385
chown, 105, 385
chsh, 55–56, 385
cmp, 35, 124, 385–386
combining, 194
command argument completion, 59, 62, 65
compress, 293, 386
configuring Unix, 371
cp, 34–35, 41, 386
cron, 198–199
crontab, 198, 386
date, 218
df, 141–143, 386–387
diff, 124, 125, 387
dig, 277, 387
dircmp, 35
du, 144, 387
echo$SHELL, 155
echo, 213
emacs, 92
email, 374
embedding in scripts, 218–219
encoding and compressing files, 376
fg, 203, 388
file, 145, 388
find, 44–45, 388–389
finger, 52, 146–148, 389
fmt, 133–134, 389–390
ftp, 263–268, 390
get, 266
getting system information with, 370
groups, 102
gunzip, 296, 298, 299
gzip, 295, 390–391
head, 115, 391
history, 60–61, 63–64, 66–67, 68, 217
id, 102, 152, 391
Internet, 375
kill, 209–210, 391
links, 392–393
ln, 47–50, 393
locate, 46, 393
make clean, 314
make install, 311–314
man, 25, 26–27, 397
manipulating files, 368–369   Mv -38
mkdir, 30–31, 398
more, 22, 398
nice, 204, 399
nslookup, 276, 277
ntpdate, 342
passwd, 11–12, 399
ping, 273, 400

pipe, 18
pr, 135–136, 401–402
procmail, 250–254, 401
ps, 207–208, 401
put, 267
pwd, 17, 402
reget, 266
renice, 204, 402
rm, 39–41, 43, 48, 402
rmdir, 42–43, 402–403
runique, 266
running, 194
    scripts and programs, 372
sdiff, 126
sed, 121, 221, 347–349, 404
shell, 366
sort, 127–128, 129, 406
split, 137–138, 406
ssh, 7, 11, 258, 405–406
stty, 71
su, 330–331, 406–407
su - yourid, 12
summary table of flags and, 384–416
tac, 24
tail, 116, 407
talk, 262, 407
tar, 268, 290–292, 300, 407
tee, 130, 408
telnet, 7, 259–260, 409
time, 205–206, 362, 409
touch, 32–33, 410
tr, 131–132, 410
traceroute, 273, 274–275, 410–411
umask, 110–111, 411
uname, 140, 411
uncompress, 294, 300
uniq, 129, 411
untar, 300
unzip, 298, 411–412
used for creating and editing files, 367
using directories and files, 365
utility, 377
uudecode, 289, 299, 412
uuencode, 286–288, 412
vacation, 248–249, 254, 412
vi editing, 86
w, 150–151, 412
wall, 260
wc, 114, 413
wget, 272, 413–415
who, 149, 415
whoami, 149
write, 261, 415
writing scripts, 373
ydecode, 288, 415
yencode, 288, 304–305, 415
zip, 295, 297, 415–416
comments (#), 172

comparing
    directories, 35
    files, 35, 124
    job times, 205–206
compiled software programs, 302
compiling and installing software, 311–314
composing and sending email
    configuring procmail, 250–251
    with mail, 243–244
    with mutt, 240–241
    with pine, 234–235
    vacation messages, 248–249
compress command, 293, 386
compressing files
    about, 293
    table of commands and flags for, 376
conditional statements, 222–224
configuration files. See also editing configuration files
    finding with grep, 164, 167, 174
    running order of, 155, 170
    sourcing, 172
configuring. See also editing configuration
        files; prompts
    bash
        changing paths, 173–174
        changing prompts, 175–176
        viewing configuration, 170–172
    commands and flags for, 371
    compatible software, 306–310
    csh
        changing paths, 186–187
        changing prompts, 188–189
        viewing configuration, 183–185
    environment variables
        about, 154–155
        adding or changing, 158–160
        to leave unchanged, 157
    ksh
        changing paths, 180–181
        changing prompts, 182
        viewing configuration, 177–179
    mutt, 239
    pine, 236–237, 279–280
    setting up
        aliases, 190–192
        procmail, 250–251
        prompt on separate line, 169
    showing current environment, 156–157
    zsh
        changing paths, 165–166
        changing prompts, 167–169
        viewing configuration, 161–164
connections. See also SSH connections
    login information for, 9
    pinging Internet, 273
    tracing, 274–275
    troubleshooting ftp, 266
converting measurements, 321

copying directories and files, 34–35
counting files and contents, 114
cp command
    copying directories and files with, 34–35
    flags, 386
    making backups with, 41
CPU information, 151
cron command, 198–199
crontab command, 198, 386
csh shell
    adding or changing environment variables, 160
    advantages of, 68
    defined, 53
    redirecting stdout and stderr in, 362
    setting aliases for users, 192
    showing current environment in, 156–157
    viewing configuration files for, 183–185
    viewing session history, 68
.cshrc file, 188, 192
cutting and pasting text in pico, 79
Cygwin, 6

D

daemons
    defined, 208
    starting and stopping, 332–333
daisychains, 172
date
    formatting options for, 218
    setting with ntpdate, 342
    updating file's time and, 33
debugging scripts, 228
decoding files, 289
    and unzipping, 299–300
default group, 101–102
deleting
    email in mutt, 239
    processes, 209–210
    scheduled jobs, 197
    text in vi, 86
delimited files, 122
delimiters, 122
df command, 141–143, 386–387
diff command, 124, 125, 387
differences in files, 125–126
dig command, 277, 387
dircmp command, 35
directories
    archiving with tar command, 291
    basic commands and flags for using, 365
    changing, 15–16
        group association of, 103–104
        ownership of, 105
    common Unix, 25, 381–382
    comparing, 35
    connecting with soft links, 50
    copying, 34
    creating, 30–31
    determining disk usage for, 144
    displaying name for current, 17

embedding command to list most recent
    changed, 218–219
finding
    files in, 44
    ownership and permissions for, 99–100
getting status of file systems on, 143
hard links for, 48
listing, 13–14, 37
moving, 38
naming, 31
navigating in, 15
removing, 42–43
unzipping, 296, 298
using looping scripts to back up, 220–221
working with remote, 266
zipping, 295, 297
disk usage
    determining, 144
    space required for uncompressed files, 294
    viewing number of blocks on device, 142
dmesg utility, 340–341
documents
    cleaning up HTML, 344–346
    searching and replacing in multiple, 347–349
dollar sign ($)
    function as regular expression, 119
    setting prompt to appear on separate line, 169, 176
domain names, 276–277
DOS aliases, 191
dot (.)
    function as regular expression, 119
    hiding files starting with, 37
downloading
    multiple files, 266
    single files with ftp, 263–266
    tidy, 344
    Web sites, 272
    yencode, 304–305
du command, 144, 387
duplicate files, 129

E

echo$SHELL command, 155
echo command, 213
editing configuration files
    adding or changing environment variables, 158–160
    adding set -o emacs command for ksh
        shells, 65, 67
    changing paths
        bash, 173–174
        csh, 186–187
        ksh, 180–181
        zsh, 165–166
    changing prompts
        bash, 175–176
        csh, 188–189
        ksh, 182
        zsh, 167–169
    in compatible software, 306–310

INDEX

modifying to request editor, 351–352
    as **root** user, 334–335
    running order of configuration files, 155, 170
    setting aliases, 190–192
    sourcing configuration files, 172
    variables to leave unchanged, 157
    viewing files for
        bash shell, 170–172
        csh shell, 183–185
        ksh shell, 177–179
        zsh shell, 161–164
editors
    alternative, 74
    choosing, 74–76
    emacs
        about, 75
        commands in, 92
        exiting, 95
        flags for, 388
        meta key in, 92
        saving files in, 94
        spell check from menus, 93
        spell check with menus, 93
        starting, 91–92
        using commands with **ksh** shell, 65, 67
    pico
        about, 74
        checking spelling in, 80
        cutting and pasting text in, 79
        exiting, 82
        flags for, 399
        getting help, 81
        getting help in, 81
        saving files in, 78, 82
        spell checks in, 80
        starting, 77
        status line in, 81
    setting configuration files to request, 351–352
    switching, 76
    vi
        about, 75
        adding and deleting text in, 86
        exiting, 90
        importing files into, 87
        modes in, 83, 84
        removing line numbering in, 217
        saving files in, 85
        saving in, 85
        searching and replacing in, 88–89
        starting, 83–84
eliminating duplicate files, 129
emacs
    about, 75
    commands in, 92
    exiting, 95
    flags for, 388
    meta key in, 92
    saving files in, 94
    spell check with menus, 93
    starting, 91–92
    using commands with **ksh** shell, 65, 67

email
    announcing vacations in, 248–249
    automatically forwarding incoming, 247
    choosing programs for, 230–231
    commands and flags for, 374
    composing and sending
        with **mail**, 243–244
        with **mutt**, 240–241
        with **pine**, 234–235
    customizing **pine**, 236–237
    encoding files to send via, 287–288
    etiquette for, 235
    figlets, 246
    filtering with **procmail**, 251
    forwarding with **procmail**, 253
    learning to use spam filters, 235
    reading
        with **mail**, 242
        with **mutt**, 238–239
        with **pine**, 232–233
    sending from shell prompt, 235, 241
    signature files for, 245–246
    subject lines in, 235
    writing recipe for **procmail** command, 252
embedding
    commands
        looping with, 220
        using, 218–219
    ROT13 encoding in shell script, 355–357
encoding files
    about, 286–288
    ROT13 in shell script, 355–357
    table of commands and flags for, 376
    using **sed** command with ROT13, 353–354
ENV statements in **ksh** shell, 177
environment variables
    about, 154–155
    adding or changing, 158–160
    list to leave unchanged, 157
    setting **TERM**, 352
    showing current, 156–157
    using input to customize, 351–352
    using **su** - to ensure correct, 331
    viewing, **zsh** configuration files, 161–164
Esc sequence (^[^[), 65
Escape character for **telnet**, 259
etiquette for email, 235
executable scripts, 215–216
execute permission, 98
exit command
    exiting shells, 72
    returning to previous shell with, 70
exiting
    emacs, 95
    pico, 82
    and returning to previous shell, 70
    shells at end of session, 72
    temporary shell, 58
    vi, 90
expr utility, 320, 388

expressions
  evaluating, 320
  regular, 118–120
  table of regular, 119

F

failed login attempts, 10
fg command, 203, 388
fields, sorting comma-delimited, 128
figlets, 246
file command, 145, 388
file systems, 141–143
files. *See also* ownership and permissions
  accessing with ftp, 263–266
  adding or removing permissions, 108
  archiving, 290–291, 293
  basic commands and flags for using, 365
  changing
    with awk, 122–123
    group association of, 103–104
    motd, 334–335
    ownership of, 105
    with tr, 131–132
  checking
    current permissions of, 106
    scripts before running, 216
  cleaning up HTML documents, 344–346
  commands and flags
    for creating and editing, 367
    for encoded and compressed, 376
    for manipulating, 368–369
  comparing, 35, 124
  compressing, 293
  copying, 34, 35
  counting contents of, 114
  creating with touch, 32–33
  decoding, 289
    and unzipping, 299–300
  delimited, 122
  displaying with cat, 23–24
  downloading multiple, 266
  eliminating duplicate, 129
  emailing text, 244
  encoding, 286–288
  finding, 44–45
    differences in, 125–126
    ownership and permissions for, 99–100
    text in, 117
  formatting, 133–134
  .forward, 249, 250
  hiding, 37
  identifying types of, 145
  importing into vi, 87
  key Unix, 380
  linking, 47–50
  listing, 13–14, 36–37
    most recent changed, 218–219
  locating, 46
  looping scripts to back up, 220–221

making global changes in, 121
moving, 38
naming, 31
.plan and .project, 148
printing, 135–136, 324
reading INSTALL and README, 306
redirecting output, 19–20
  to multiple locations, 130
removing, 39–41
running order of configuration, 155, 170
saving
  in emacs, 94
  in pico, 78, 82
  in vi, 85
searching and replacing
  DOS or Windows text in shells, 89
  text with vi, 88–89
setting permissions, 106, 107
sharing with ftp, 267–268
sorting, 127–128
splitting, 137–138
systemwide configuration, 155
unarchiving tar, 292
uncompressing, 294, 296, 300
unzipping, 296, 298, 299–300
viewing
  beginning of, 115
  contents with more, 22
  ending of, 116
zipping, 295, 297
filtering with procmail command, 251
find command, 44–45, 388–389
finding. *See also* searching and replacing
  available shells, 54
  compatible Unix software, 303
  configuration files with grep, 164, 167, 174
  default groups, 101–102
  files, 44–45
  lines with specific characteristics, 120
  out who is logged on, 146–148
  path names, 17
  permissions, 99–100
  text and text strings, 117
  which group you're in, 101–102
finger command, 52, 146–148, 389
firewalls
  ftp connections and, 266
  talk chats and, 262
  traceroute problems with, 275
flags. *See also specific commands*
  about, 383
  listed by command, 383–416
  listed by topic, 363–377
    basic Unix, 364
    configuring Unix, 371
    email, 374
    encoding and compressing files, 376
    Internet, 375
    manipulating files, 368–369
    running scripts and programs, 372

shell command, 366
    using directories and files, 365
    using to get system information, 370
    utility, 377
    writing scripts, 373
fmt command, 133–134, 389–390
formatting
    files, 133–134
    options with date command, 218
fortunes, 10, 46
.forward file, 249, 250
forwarding email with procmail, 247, 253
ftp command
    accessing files with, 263–266
    downloading multiple files, 266
    flags for, 390
    sharing files with, 267–268
    troubleshooting connections, 266
FTP (File Transfer Protocol), 257

G

get command, 266
getting started
    accessing Unix, 3–6
    basic commands and flags for, 364
    changing
        directories, 15–16
        and setting passwords, 11–12
    connecting to Unix system, 7–9
    displaying files with cat, 23–24
    exploring local programs, 25
    finding path names, 17
    getting help with, 25, 26–27
    listing directories and files, 13–14, 36–37
    logging out, 28
    overview, 1–2
    piping input and output, 18
    redirecting output, 19–20
    viewing file contents with more, 22
    wildcards, 21
global changes for files, 121
greater than symbol (>), 19
grep command
    finding
        configuration files with, 164, 167, 174
        lines with specific characteristics, 120
        text strings with, 117
    flags for, 390
    regular expressions with, 118–119
    w command with, 151
groups
    changing file and directory associations
        with, 103–104
    creating special project, 102
    determining which ones userid is in, 152
    file ownership by, 98
    finding out default, 101–102
groups command, 102
gunzip command, 296, 298, 299
gzip command, 295, 300, 390–391

H

hard drives, 141–143
hard links, 47–48
head command, 115, 391
help
    finding for expr utility, 320
    man command for, 25, 26–27
    pico, 81
    software documentation in Makefile, 306
    vi, 84
hidden files
    creating, 37
    viewing, 36
history command
    navigation commands in ksh shell, 67
    recreating scripts with, 217
    viewing session history, 60–61, 63–64, 66–67, 68
home directory
    about, 10
    shortcut to, 16
    system root directory vs., 16
host name, 256
HTML (Hypertext Markup Language)
    document cleanup for, 344–346
    searching and replacing tags in, 347–349
HTTP (Hypertext Transfer Protocol), 257
"human readable" output, 143

I

id command, 102, 152, 391
if-then statements, 222–224, 351, 162
importing files into vi, 87
information about files, 36
input
    accepting command-line arguments in scripts, 225
    accepting while running scripts, 226–227
    piping, 18
    standard, 360
    using to customize environment variables, 351–352
input mode in vi, 83
INSTALL files, 306
installing
    software
        about, 301–302
        configuring compatible software, 306–310
        downloading, placing, and uncompressing, 304–305
        finding compatible Unix versions, 303
    Unix
        on spare computer, 5
        and Windows, 5–6
Internet. See also Usenet news; Web sites
    accessing files with ftp, 263–266
    checking connections with ping, 273
    choosing news readers, 278
    commands and flags for, 375
    communicating to others
        with talk, 262
        with write, 261

connecting to another computer with ssh, 258
downloading Web sites, 272
file sharing with ftp, 267–268
links browser, 268–269
logging in remotely with telnet, 259–260
lynx browser, 270–271
matching domain names with IP numbers, 276–277
navigating Web pages with links, 268
terms used about, 256–257
tracing connections with traceroute, 274–275
Unix terms for, 256
IP (Internet Protocol) addresses
defined, 256
matching domain names with IP numbers, 276–277
ispell utility, 322
ISPs (Internet Service Providers)
forwarding incoming email when changing, 247
interface for changing shells, 56
shell accounts offered by, 4

J
jobs. *See also* scripts
checking
processes running, 207–208
status of, 201
controlling priorities of, 204
deleting scheduled, 197
running
background, 202
sequentially, 196
scheduling one-time, 195
setting up regularly occurring, 198–199
suspending, 200, 203
timing, 205–206

K
keystrokes
for links browser, 269
for lynx browser, 271
kill command, 209–210, 391
killing processes, 209–210
Korn shell. *See* ksh shell
ksh shell
adding or changing environment variables, 158–159
changing prompt for, 182
command argument completion, 65
defined, 53
redirecting stderr in, 361–362
showing current environment in, 156–157
using emacs commands with, 65, 67
viewing
configuration files for, 177–179
session history, 66–67
kshrc file, 177

L
last utility, 337
lines
listing specified number at end of file, 116
viewing specified number at beginning of file, 115

linking files
hard links, 47–48
soft links, 49–50
links browser
commands and flags for, 392–393
keystrokes in, 269
navigating with, 268
surfing Web with, 269
Linux, 6
listing
directories and files, 13–14, 36–37
files by type, 145
jobs by time, 206
specified line at end of file, 116
ln command
flags for, 393
hard links with, 47–48
soft links with, 49–50
locate command, 46, 393
locating files, 46
logging in
checking boot messages, 340–341
connection information for, 9
as different user, 70
finding out who is logged on, 146–148
w, 150–151
who, 149
remotely
with ssh, 258
with telnet, 259–260
as root user, 40
steps for, 10
using cal with, 316
logging out, 28
logs, monitoring, 336
look utility, 323, 393–394
looping scripts, 220–221
lp utility, 324, 394
ls command
flags for, 394–395
listing directories and files, 13–14, 36–37
looking up directory names with, 16
showing permissions with, 99–100
lynx browser
flags for, 395–397
keystrokes in, 271
surfing Web with, 270–271

M
Macintosh
accessing Unix in, 6
viewing contents of drives in, 141
MacSSH, 7
mail
about, 230, 231
composing and sending email with, 243–244
flags for, 397–398
reading email with, 242
sending text files, 244
mail clients, 230–231

INDEX

mail loops, 249
make clean command, 314
make install command, 311–314
Makefile file
  documentation files in, 306
  reading with make install, 311
  reviewing, 310, 314
man command
  editing man pages, 27
  flags, 397
  getting help with, 25, 26–27
manually setting date, 342
memory, 337
Message of the Day (motd) file, 334–335
messaging
  talk command and, 262
  write command for, 261
mkdir command, 30–31, 398
mnemonic permissions, 109
modes in vi, 83, 84
monitoring
  logs, 336
  sudo activities, 329
  system load and memory, 337
  users, 337, 338
  with watch utility, 339
more command, 22, 398
motd file, changing, 334–335
moving
  files and directories, 38
  up/down in directories, 15
multiple files
  downloading, 266
  making global changes for, 121
  showing ending of, 116
  sorting, 128
  viewing beginning of, 115
mutt
  about, 230, 231
  composing and sending email with, 240–241
  flags for, 398–399
  reading email with, 238–239

N

naming
  directories and filenames, 31
  using absolute or relative names, 35
navigating
  in directories, 15
  with links browser, 268
  with lynx browser, 270
  navigation commands in ksh shell, 67
news. See Usenet news
news readers
  about, 278
  pine, 279–281
  tin, 282–284, 409–410
newsgroups
  subscribing via pine, 280
  subscribing via tin, 283

nice command, 204, 399
nslookup command, 276, 277
ntpdate command, 342
numbers
  numeric equivalents for mnemonic permissions, 109
  sorting numerically, 128
  specifying for cron command, 199

O

others permissions, 98
output
  getting readable, 143
  piping, 18
  redirecting
    to files, 19–20
    to multiple locations, 130
    script, 357
    with stderr, 360–362
  standard, 360
overwriting files, 35
ownership and permissions
  about, 98
  changing
    group association of files and directories, 103–104
    ownership of files and directories, 105
    permission defaults, 110–111
  checking current permissions, 106
  commands and flags for, 367
  finding out
    which group you're in, 101–102
    who owns files, 99–100
  setting permissions, 106, 107
  translating mnemonic to numeric permissions, 109

P

packets, 274, 275
passwd command, 11–12, 399
passwords
  changing, 11–12
  checking new, 12
  choosing, 12
  root password security with telnet, 7, 331
paths
  changing
    bash, 173–174
    csh, 186–187
    ksh, 180–181
    zsh, 165–166
  finding name of, 17
  specifying in executable scripts, 216
  spotting errors in installation scripts, 314
pdksh shell, 65
performance
  checking processes running, 207–208
  controlling job priorities, 204
  deleting processes, 209–210
  monitoring system load, 337
  system capacity and time of day, 206
  tracing bottlenecks in, 274–275

permissions
    adding or removing, 108
    changing defaults for, 110–111
    checking current, 106
    commands and flags for, 367
    finding file and directory, 99–100
    interpreting abbreviations for, 99–100
    listing, 99–100
    read, write, and other, 98
    s, 100
    setting, 106, 107
    sticky bits, 100
    translating mnemonic to numeric, 109
pico
    about, 74
    checking spelling in, 80
    cutting and pasting text in, 79
    exiting, 82
    flags for, 399
    getting help, 81
    saving files in, 78
    starting, 77
    status line in, 81
PID (process identification number), 207, 209, 210
pine
    about, 230
    composing and sending email with, 234–235
    configuring to read news, 279–280
    customizing, 236–237
    flags for, 399–400
    reading
        email in, 232–233
        newsgroup messages, 281
    subscribing to newsgroups in, 280, 281
ping command, 273, 275, 400
pipe symbol (|), 18
placing software, 304–305
.plan files, 148
ports, 257
pr command, 135–136, 401–402
Preferences dialog, 11
printing
    email from pine, 233
    files, 135–136
    lp utility for, 324
-print flag, 45
processes
    checking running, 207–208
    displaying system information about, 150–151
    killing, 209–210
    ownership and, 98
procmail command
    about, 250
    flags for, 401
    forwarding email with, 247, 253
    invoking vacation with, 254
    sample recipes for, 254
    setting up, 250–251
    turning on filtering, 251
    writing recipe for, 252

.profile file for kshrc file, 177
programs. See running scripts and programs;
        software; utilities
.project files, 148
prompts
    about default, 167
    about shell, 10, 51
    adding trailing space after, 169, 176
    changing
        bash, 175–176
        ksh, 182
        zsh, 167–169
    sending email from, 235, 241
    sudo, 329
protocols
    defined, 257
    ports used for, 257
ps command, 207–208, 401
put command, 267
PuTTY, 7–8
pwd command, 17, 402

Q

question mark (?) wildcard, 21

R

read permission, 98
reading
    email
        with mail, 242
        with mutt, 238–239
        with pine, 232–233
        INSTALL and README files, 306
    newsgroup messages
        pine, 281
        in tin, 283–284
README files, 306, 308
real time, 206
recipes for procmail command, 252, 253, 254
redirecting output
    to files, 19–20
    to multiple locations, 130
    of scripts and saving, 357
    with stderr, 360–362
reget command, 266
regular expressions (regexp)
    finding lines with specific characteristics, 120
    table of, 119
    using with grep, 118–119
relative names, 35
remote systems
    checking connections to, 273, 275
    connecting
        with ssh, 258
        with telnet, 259–260
    tracing connections with traceroute, 274–275
    working with remote directories, 266
removing
    directories, 42–43
    files, 39–41

line numbering in `vi`, 217
permissions, 108
`renice` command, 204, 402
replacing. *See* searching and replacing
reports, 350
restarting daemons, 333
`rm` command
    deleting directories and files with, 43
    flags for, 402
    removing files, 39–41
    removing hard links, 48
`rmdir` command, 42–43, 402–403
root directory, 16, 45
`root` users. *See also* system administrators
    about, 327
    becoming `root`, 330–331
    changing system configuration, 334–335
    checking boot messages, 340–341
    logging in as, 40
    monitoring system, 336–338
    responsibilities of, 327, 328, 330
    security of `root` password with `telnet`, 7, 331
    setting date and time, 342
    starting and stopping daemons, 332–333
    using `sudo` utility instead of `root`, 328–329
    using `watch` utility, 339
ROT13 encoding
    embedding in shell script, 355–357
    using with `sed`, 353–354
`rpm`, 303
`rsync` utility, 358–359, 403–404
`runique` command, 266
running scripts and programs
    accepting input while running scripts, 226–227
    checking job status, 201
    checking processes running, 207–208
    command-line arguments in scripts, 225
    commands and flags for, 372
    controlling job priorities, 204
    deleting processes, 209–210
    foreground jobs, 203
    making executable scripts, 215–216
    running
        background jobs, 202
        commands, 194
    scheduling one-time jobs, 195–197
    setting up regularly occurring jobs, 198–199
    suspending jobs, 200, 203
    timing jobs, 205–206

S

saving files
    in `emacs`, 94
    in `pico`, 78, 82
    in `vi`, 85
scheduling one-time jobs, 195–197
`script` utility, 325–326
scripts
    accepting input while running, 226–227

checking
    processes running, 207–208
    status of, 201
combining `sed` searches and replaces with, 347–349
command-line arguments in, 225
commands and flags for writing, 373
controlling priorities for, 204
creating shell, 212–213
debugging, 228
deleting
    processes, 209–210
    scheduled, 197
developing monitoring, 337
embedding
    `awk` scripts in shell, 350
    commands, 218–219
    ROT13 encoding in shell, 355–357
if-then statements in, 222–224
looping, 220–221
making executable, 215–216
numbers for `cron` jobs, 199
recording with `script` utility, 325–326
recreating with `history`, 217
redirecting output and saving, 357
running
    in background, 202
    commands, 194
    shell, 214
scheduling one-time, 195
setting up
    regularly occurring, 198–199
    run in foreground, 203
software installation, 302
suspending, 200, 203
timing, 205–206
uses for, 211
using `tidy` with `sed`, 346
`sdiff` command, 126
searching and replacing. *See also* finding
    loops for, 221
    in multiple documents with `sed`, 347–349
    text with `vi`, 88–89
security
    `telnet` vs. SSH connections, 7, 331
    using `su` to change to root access, 70
`sed` command, 121
    flags for, 404
    loops with, 221
    ROT13 encoding with, 353–354
    searching and replacing in multiple documents
        with, 347–349
sequential one-time jobs, 196
servers, 256
sessions
    recording with `script`, 325–326
    viewing history
        for `bash` shell, 60–61
        for `ksh` shell, 66–67
        for `zsh` shell, 63–64

INDEX

sh shell
  creating scripts, 212–213
  defined, 53
  making executable scripts, 215–216
  running scripts, 214
  scripting for, 211, 213
shell prompts. *See* prompts
shell variables, 154
shells. *See also* editing configuration files; prompts;
    and specific shells
  accepting input while running scripts, 226–227
  access via shell accounts, 4
  adding or changing environment variables, 158–160
  basic commands and flags for using, 366
  changing, 55–56
    identity with **su**, 69–70
  command argument completion
    bash, 59
    ksh, 65
    zsh, 62
  command-line arguments in scripts, 225
  creating shell scripts, 212–213
  debugging scripts for, 228
  determining one in use, 155
  embedding
    awk in scripts, 350
    commands in shell scripts, 218–219
    ROT13 encoding in scripts, 355–357
  finding available, 54
  fixing terminal settings, 71
  identifying default system, 52
  killing current process for, 210
  listing daemons running, 208
  mail announcements in, 231
  redirecting **stderr** in, 361–362
  running scripts, 214, 215–216
  searching and replacing DOS or Windows text
      files in, 89
  sending email from prompt
    in **mutt**, 241
    in **pine**, 235
  session history for
    bash, 60–61
    csh, 68
    ksh, 66–67
    zsh, 63–64
  setting aliases, 190–192
  temporary, 57–58
  types of Unix, 53
  viewing configuration files
    bash, 170–172
    csh, 183–185
    ksh, 177–179
    zsh, 161–164
signature files, 245–246
single quotations (' '), 169
soft links, 49–50
software. *See also* utilities
  about installing, 301–302
  compiling and installing, 311–314

configuring, 306–310
  downloading, 304–305
  finding compatible Unix versions, 303
Solaris, 6
sort command, 127–128, 129, 406
sorting
  and eliminating duplicate files, 129
  files, 127–128
  newsgroup messages in **pine**, 281
source code
  downloading programs as, 303
  programs vs., 302
sourcing configuration files, 172
spam
  filters for, 235
  procmail recipe for, 253
special characters. *See* characters
spelling checks
  checking and sorting listed files, 18
  emacs menus, 93
  ispell utility for, 322
  loops for, 221
  pico, 80
split command, 137–138, 406
splitting files, 137–138
square brackets ([ ]), 119
ssh command
  flags for, 405–406
  logging in to remote systems with, 258
SSH (SecureSHell) connections
  configuring options in Preferences dialog, 11
  connecting to Unix, 7
  security and, 7, 331
standard error (**stderr**)
  defined, 360
  redirecting to shell, 361–362
standard input (**stdin**), 360
standard output (**stdout**), 360
starting
  daemons, 332–333
  emacs, 91–92
  pico, 77
  vi, 83–84
status line in **pico**, 81
sticky bits, 100
stopped jobs, 200
stopping
  daemons, 333
  vacation emails, 248–249
strings, 117
stty command, 71
su - yourid command, 12
su command, 69–70, 330–331, 406–407
subject lines
  adding for **mail**, 244
  in email, 235
subscribing to newsgroups
  in **pine**, 280, 281
  in **tin**, 283
subshells, 57

sudo utility, 328–329, 407
suspending jobs, 200, 203
switching editors, 76
system administrators
    asking for alternative shells, 56
    changing system configuration, 334–335
    checking boot messages, 340–341
    diagnosing system problems with df, 143
    monitoring system, 336–338
    security of root password with telnet, 7, 331
    setting date and time, 342
    starting and stopping daemons, 332–333
    sudo utility vs. root, 328–329
    using rm command as, 40
    wall command for communications, 260
    watch utility for, 339
    whoami command used by, 149
system information
    commands and flags for getting, 370
    determining disk usage, 144
    finding out file types, 145
    getting, 140
        userid information, 152
    log on
        finger, 146–148
        w, 150–151
        who, 149
    setting zsh prompt to show, 168
    viewing file systems, 141–143
system load, 337
system root directory, 16
systemwide configuration files, 155

T

tac command, 24
tail command, 116, 407
talk command, 262, 407
tar command
    archiving files with, 290–291, 293
    flags, 407–408
    transferring multiple files with, 268
    unarchiving files with, 292
    using gzip with, 300
tcsh shell
    defined, 53
    using, 68
tee command, 130, 408
telnet command
    connections using, 7
    flags, 409
    logging in with, 259–260
    root password security with, 7, 331
temporary shells, 57–58
TERM environment variable, 352
terminal settings, 71
text. See also spelling checks
    adding and deleting in vi, 86
    cutting and pasting in pico, 79
    finding in files, 117
    looking up words, 323

searching and replacing with vi, 88–89
tidy utility, 344–346, 409
tilde (~), 16
time
    real vs. user and system, 206
    setting with ntpdate, 342
    updating file's date and, 33
time command, 205–206, 362, 409
timing jobs, 205–206
tin, 282–284, 409–410
tn3270, 260
touch command, 32–33, 410
tr command, 131–132, 410
traceroute command, 273, 274–275, 410–411
trailing space after prompts, 169, 176
translating case with tr command, 131
troubleshooting. See also performance
    ftp connections, 266
    removing files and directories, 40
    software installation, 314
    terminal displays, 71
    traceroute problems with firewalls, 275

U

umask command, 110–111, 411
uname command, 140, 411
unarchiving files
    about, 292
    uncompressing while, 300
uncompress command, 294, 300
uncompressing files
    about, 294, 296, 300
    before installing software, 304–305
    unarchiving while, 300
uniq command, 129, 411
units utilities, 321, 411
Unix. See also commands; configuring; utilities
    choosing versions of, 6
    common directories in, 25, 381–382
    connecting to, 7–9
    finding software compatible with, 303
    identifying default system shell, 52
    Internet terminology in, 256–257
    list of key files, 380
    removing files as root user, 40
    responsibilities of root users, 327, 328, 330
    shells in, 53
    summary table of flags and commands, 384–416
    types of access to, 4
untar command, 300
unzip command, 298, 411–412
unzipping files, 296, 298, 299–300
Usenet news
    choosing news reader, 278
    main categories for, 278
    reading news
        with pine, 279–281
        with tin, 282–284
user and system time, 206

users. *See also* **root** users
    changing identity with **su**, 69–70
    checking userid information, 152
    communicating to other, 261–262
    file ownership by, 98
    finding out who is logged on, 146–151
    monitoring, 337, 338
    setting aliases for **csh**, 192
utilities
    bc, 319
    cal, 316–318, 384
    commands and flags for, 377
    defined, 315
    dmesg, 340–341
    expr, 320, 388
    ispell, 322
    last, 337
    look, 323, 393–394
    lp, 324, 394
    rsync, 358–359, 403–404
    script, 325–326
    sudo, 328–329, 407
    tidy, 344–346, 409
    units, 321, 411
    watch, 339, 413
uudecode command, 289, 299, 412
uuencode command, 286–288, 412

V

vacation command, 248–249, 254, 412
vi
    about, 75
    adding and deleting text, 86
    exiting, 90
    importing files into, 87
    modes in, 83, 84
    removing line numbers, 217
    saving in, 85
    searching and replacing text, 88–89
    starting, 83–84
viewing
    bash configuration files, 170–172
    beginning of file, 115
    csh configuration files, 183–185
    file contents with **more**, 22
    file systems, 141–143
    hidden files, 36
    ksh configuration, 177–179
    session history
        in **bash** shell, 60–61
        in **csh**, 68
        in **ksh**, 66–67
        in **zsh** shell, 63–64
    zsh configuration files, 161–164
Vmware, 5–6

W

w command, 150–151, 412
wall command, 260
watch utility, 339, 413
wc command, 114, 413
Web sites
    downloading, 272
    searching for compatible Unix software, 303
    surfing
        with **links**, 268–269
        with **lynx**, 270–271
wget command, 272, 413–415
who command, 149, 415
whoami command, 149
wildcards
    using, 21
    using with **find** command, 44, 45
Windows
    handy DOS aliases, 191
    installing Unix and, 5–6
    using **zip** for files accessed in, 295
    viewing contents of drives in, 141
word lookups, 323
write command, 261, 415
write permission, 98

Y

ydecode command, 288, 415
yencode, 288, 304–305, 415

Z

zip command, 295, 297, 415–416
zipping files
    about, 295, 297
    archiving while, 300
zsh shell
    ability to understand multiple expressions, 164
    changing path, 165–166
    command argument completion for, 62
    defined, 53
    flags for, 415
    modifying environment variables, 158–159
    redirecting **stderr** in, 361–362
    setting prompt for, 167–169
    showing current environment in, 156–157
    viewing
        configuration files, 161–164
        session history in, 63–64

INDEX